LIBRARY

D0359731

WITHDRAWN

HOWLING NEAR HEAVEN

Marcia B. Siegel

HOWLING

NEAR

HEAVEN

Twyla Tharp and the
Reinvention of Modern Dance

ST. MARTIN'S PRESS
NEW YORK

HOWLING NEAR HEAVEN. Copyright © 2006 by Marcia B. Siegel. All rights reserved. Printed in the United States of America. No part of this book may be
used or reproduced in any manner whatsoever without written permission except in the case of brief quotations embodied in critical articles or reviews. For
information, address St. Martin's Press, 175 Fifth Avenue, New York, N.Y.
10010.

www.stmartins.com

Design by Kathryn Parise

LIBRARY OF CONGRESS CATALOGING-IN-PUBLICATION DATA

Siegel, Marcia B.
    Howling near heaven : Twyla Tharp and the reinvention of modern dance /
Marcia B. Siegel.—1st U.S. ed.
      p. cm.
    Includes bibliographical references and index.
    ISBN 0-312-23294-2
    EAN 978-0-312-23294-8
    1. Tharp, Twyla. 2. Choreographers—United States—Biography. 3. Mod-
ern dance—United States—History. I. Title.

GV1785.T43S54 2006
796.8'2092—dc22

                                    2005044685

First Edition: March 2006

10   9   8   7   6   5   4   3   2   1

For Rose and Sara
and all the others who made Tharp dance

CONTENTS

HOWLING NEAR HEAVEN

I

Leotard Days

1965–1966

Judson Memorial Church, in the geographical center of Greenwich Village, stands like an exotic souvenir today on the southern edge of Washington Square Park, among the modern monoliths of New York University. Its Italian Renaissance–style ochre brickwork, ten-story campanile, and tile roofs link it to its neighbor across the park, Washington Square Arch—both were designed by the distinguished American architect Stanford White. The church has seventeen stained-glass windows by John La Farge and a bas relief altarpiece by Augustus St. Gaudens. It was declared a New York City landmark in 1966. The sanctuary has recently been restored to its turn-of-the-century beaux-arts splendor, a high, airy space of imposing beige marble Corinthian pillars; soaring vaults inset with vibrant arched and circular stained-glass windows; a paneled mansard ceiling; and a color scheme of beige, aqua, and cream to complement the marble wall panels.

Revisiting this beautiful house of light, it's hard to recall the way it looked when it was filled with rebellious performance events decades ago. In fact, at the end of the 1990s Judson's Baptist congregation agonized about whether to restore this grand space at all. According to senior minister Peter Laarman, Judson Church has always been more about ephemera than about preservation. Founded in 1890, the church was dedicated to serving the needs of the city. From immigrant job training programs and health centers to teenage sports, civil rights, antiwar protests, and gay-pride marches, the church has taken a leading role in New York's progressive dynamic. The showcasing of avant-garde dance events only extended its mission.

Beaux-arts architecture represented a form of cultural imperialism to the reformers of the 1960s. Over a period of time the walls, ceiling, and columns were painted a political dirt brown, though the altar and stained-glass windows remained. Regular Sunday services never ceased, but by 1966 the pews had been removed from the sanctuary to accommodate art happenings and Judson Dance Theater experiments. Judson Poets Theater held forth in the choir loft, next to the boxy old pipe organ with its pillars, carved wreaths, and trumpeting angels. Protest rallies shook the building and militants gathered outside to begin marches and demonstrations. For dance performances, the audience trudged up a set of creaky wooden stairs to the sanctuary. You came in under the choir loft, through a kind of low cavern, which was usually littered with a random assortment of thrift-shop chairs, props, piano, and equipment. Sometimes this "lobby" area was curtained off from the performance space.

On October 29, 1966, for the first of three concerts by Twyla Tharp and Company, chairs for the audience of about one hundred had been placed on three sides, facing away from the altar. Three pieces were on the program: *Re-Moves* (*in four sections and two introductions*), *Twelve Foot Change*, and a revival of Tharp's first work, *Tank Dive*, given only the year before in a small theater within the Hunter College art department. *Twelve Foot Change* was subsequently called *Yancey Dance*, after the music by jazz pianist Jimmy Yancey. *Re-Moves* was forty-five minutes long and had big ambitions.

Not that there was anything tentative about what Tharp had already done. Just out of college, she had danced for a season with Paul Taylor, then quit to find her own way. To earn money, she'd appeared for a summer at the Alaskan Pavilion of the New York World's Fair, dancing a "sort of furry hootchy-kootchy" in a bearskin rug. Following the approved modern dance practice of throwing out all that preceded one's own discoveries, Tharp's first two serious concerts encapsulated her idea of the basics, nonchalantly disguised in improper elements. After the eight-minute *Tank Dive*, which constituted the entire event at Hunter, she produced a second, slightly longer concert in the same small space. She made a twenty-minute film-dance, *Stride*, which was not intended for a live audience. The same filmmaker, Robert Barry, had also documented *Tank Dive*, just as if it were a dance classic in need of preservation.

With hindsight, one could say she'd laid out all her major credentials in her first year: the talent, ego, and determination to make an individual style, the embrace of popular culture, the fascination with film as a medium for both experimentation and preservation, and the pragmatic exploitation of whatever resources were available in order to create what she deemed worthy. At once a rebel and a puritan, Tharp embraced the avant-garde as an opportunity to experiment with ideas, not as an aesthetic or political statement. She had come from a deeply eccentric family; nonsense was perfectly all right with her. The oldest of four children, she had an ambitious mother who pushed her into improving studies from preschool age: piano, violin, viola, elocution, painting, German and French, baton twirling, and of course, dance lessons. She learned early how to schedule her time so as to get the most out of it, knocking off her school homework in the car as her mother drove her from their home near San Bernardino to classes in Los Angeles. On weekends she worked in the food concession of her mother's drive-in movie. Too busy taking lessons to have a teenage social life, she learned how to be an overachiever, a discriminating workaholic.

Nowadays, Tharp downplays her relationship to Paul Taylor, but her brief presence in his company came at an important time. Taylor in the early '60s was at a crossroads in his career. He'd started out with a dual citizenship in the commonwealth of modern dance, as a member of the Martha Graham Company and a dancer with Merce Cunningham. Taylor began doing his own choreography around 1958. He'd given a few notorious, dadaistic concerts and assembled the core of a company. *Aureole* (1962) scandalized the modern dance community at the American Dance Festival, not for its outrageousness but for its conservatism. A "white ballet" with formal, musical choreography to Handel, it affronted the expressionistic sensibilities that prevailed at the time. The next year he reverted to the bizarre and dissociated. *Scudorama* was just about finished when Tharp came into the company, and as a junior member she was given things to do that she considered beneath her. At one point she executed a slow, deranged somersault across the back of the stage, and at another she made an entrance under a beach towel, perched on the head of Dan Wagoner.

She says Taylor interested her as a dancer but not as a choreographer. After appearing in three other new works, *Party Mix, Junction,* and *Red Room,* she voiced her disapproval so loudly that he gave her what became a permanent leave of absence, advising her to go try doing her own work and see how easy it was. Taylor succeeded in molding his experimental impulses into a repertory and a company that were conventional enough to survive. Tharp faced a similar transition five years after her own initial borderline works.

In staging a concert at Judson Church, Tharp was treading on the turf of the avant-garde dance community, but the concert was anomalous, both in Tharp's career and in the annals of Judson Dance. Tharp was quite aware of the symbolic significance of performing at Judson. After the concert was over, she says, "we had passed through the vale and come out whole . . . we had situated ourselves in the vanguard of the investigation into how dance could relate to and deal with our lives." Tharp was, and always would be, an independent. A tireless inventer of movement, she would try anything, but she wasn't drawn into the waves of communal dissatisfaction that flooded the dance world of the '60s. Her connection to Judson and to the avant-garde was her partner, Robert Huot, a visual artist and filmmaker. Huot had performed at Judson two years earlier in *War*, a collaborative performance piece with his friend, the artist Robert Morris. He designed the costumes and sets for all Tharp's dances from *Tank Dive* until they broke up in 1971.

Tharp's Judson program, on the surface, could have been any one of the avant-garde custard pies that were being pushed into the face of traditional dance at the time. Each of the three works presented a collage of incompatible elements. Unrelated things happened simultaneously. The audience was left to make its own sense of what it saw—or didn't see. The costumes for *Twelve Foot Change/Yancey Dance* consisted of long, hooded sweatshirts over leotards, with dark glasses and bare legs. *Twelve Foot Change* and *Tank Dive* lasted less than ten minutes each.

In *Tank Dive* Tharp, wearing heeled sandals and a leotard cut very low in back, spun a yo-yo out of her fist, bounced it once, and reeled it back. Stepping into a pair of three-foot planklike clogs, she slowly folded her body forward into an upside-down L, then straightened from her flat-back position into a forward lean. She stepped backwards out of the flippers and went up some steps onto a tiny stage. She stood for a long time in relevé, as perfectly posed as a ballerina, her legs turned out and spaced in a wide second position, her arms reaching out and up from her sides. She descended into a plié, rose again and held another relevé, in profile to the audience, absolutely motionless for another forty-four counts, the duration of a recording of Petula Clark's "Downtown."*

---

*In the Hunter performances, after Huot and Christopher Constance had sprinted into a collision, she returned for a series of violent somersaults and a sudden reiteration of her X-relevé pose. She recounts the scenario differently in her autobiography. It's unclear how much she edited the piece for Judson. By then even she had forgotten its original date—the program lists its premiere as 1964, a year before the real date, April 29, 1965.

For *Re-Moves* the leotards had low scoop necks and three-quarter sleeves, a dancerly effect undermined by the one white tennis shoe and one white glove that the dancers wore, and by the stiff white headdresses that curved up from a squared-off back, which framed their necks and dipped into a tri-angle bisecting their foreheads. Sara Rudner walked inside of a large hoop, and Margaret Jenkins imitated the rhythms of a bouncing ball. At some point Tharp reached into a bag and took out eggs, which she dropped, one by one, on the floor. Rudner rigged a rope ladder from the balcony and climbed down it with very precise steps and a concave torso. Descending, she uncoiled smoothly until she achieved a stretched-out shape on the floor. Later on, she tap-danced, unaccompanied, in a strictly laid out rectangular pattern that wove in and out of the audience's sight lines from under the curtained-off balcony.

In an annotated chronology, Tharp describes *Re-Moves* as "a trio in which visibility is determined by the sets: section one, in the open; section two, half-hidden; section three, one-third visible; section four, entirely hidden." An eight-foot-high plywood box was placed in the space for *Re-Moves*, leav-ing about ten feet of working space between the box and the surrounding audience. During part three of the work, the dancers circled the box with precise formations and step patterns. As they disappeared from view, the au-dience could hear their repetitive stepping on the other side of the box. In a revival of the piece a couple of years later, Tharp added a fourth section, where the dancers went inside the box and rehearsed whatever new thing they were working on, heard but unseen by the audience.

Tharp's terse description of *Re-Moves*, probably written at the end of the 1970s, focuses on the formal structure of the piece and eliminates all its sen-sual, visual, and aesthetic effects. In a time when it wasn't fashionable to use music, she kept quiet about Jimmy Yancey. The statement reveals the com-positional preoccupations that never abated during Tharp's multifaceted work of the next decades. Her noncommittal, anti-interpretive '60s prose suited the posture of neutrality demanded by the avant-garde, as well as her personal reticence and her conviction that the audience too had a job to do in discovering what the dance meant. If playing up to the audience was con-sidered manipulative by the downtown dancers, Tharp positively ignored the audience, wrapping herself and her cohorts in a performing style that was taken as disdainful, belligerent, noncommunicative, and indifferent by some critics for years to come.

At the same time, she was cultivating whatever critics she could win over. She invited them to rehearsals, courted their attention. Don McDon-agh and his friend Clive Barnes were early supporters. Barnes, only recently appointed as dance critic of *The New York Times*, found himself sitting in a corner chair at Judson. Tharp admits now that she had deliberately placed him there so that at the beginning of *Re-Moves* he would be in a crucial spot. As Tharp describes the moment, "I came out, pushed a stop watch, paced out around the space, fell onto Clive Barnes's shoulders and fell towards the floor—I turned, probably in passé, rolled down his left arm, extended my arm, brushed his knee, and then brushed by all the ankles in that row."

Tharp understood that at that moment the avant-garde was the only place to align herself. Unknown to the participants, of course, 1966 was a signifi-cant moment in the life of downtown dance and the counterculture, a peak, perhaps, in the long curve of creative dissent that had begun a decade be-fore with the Beats and John Cage and the abstract expressionists. Com-pared to the political and social paroxysms that soon engulfed the artists, 1965–66 seems a moment of idyllic innocence. Experimental theater, dance, art, and music had so thoroughly interacted and dissolved into each other that the term *performance* began to seem more appropriate than any genre-specific label.

After the flamboyant high jinks of the Fluxus group, the Happenings, and a dozen other freewheeling responses to the aesthetic rigidity of the '50s, incongruity had become not only acceptable but desirable. Definitions of who could make art had temporarily expanded. Dances were made by painters and performed by lay persons with no previous dance training. Everyday objects, which weren't supposed to belong on a dance stage ex-cept as props in a narrative, became a creative challenge. If a flower did ap-pear in a performer's hand, the last thing you'd expect was that the performer would smell it. More likely, the flower would be painted blue in the course of the performance, or inserted into some orifice of the body or the building. The everyday was treated like a treasure and treasures were trashed. Events occurred irrationally and out of sequence. The audience was subjected to shocks and tedium in equal doses.

The downtown artists created performance spaces in churches and stu-dios, and also in gymnasiums, parks, anywhere but conventional stages. Dancing didn't belong on a stage anyway, they thought. Proscenium stages automatically coerce the audience into set ways of seeing. They predetermine the dancers' focus, groupings, floor patterns, and they separate the performers from the spectators, to affect both parties' experience of the dance. Dancers wanted to be more human, less remote and awe inspiring than the precious beings found in opera house performances.

Dancing didn't belong in a dance performance either, if the experimenters were to head off the responses and effects that traditional dancing evoked. During the 1960s American modern dance had begun a decline, greatly accelerated by Merce Cunningham and the downtown performers. The founders, Martha Graham, Doris Humphrey, Hanya Holm, and their colleagues, had done their pioneering work in the 1930s and '40s. They had established schools and styles. As the founders aged, their innovative fires cooled. Their work began to look familiar, even formulaic. The passions that had ignited their rebellion against ballet simmered down into a more sensible, rational theater practice. By the end of the '50s, modern dance had become as conventionalized in its own ways as ballet. Bodies were highly trained in specialized individual techniques, and choreographic action was patterned and theatrical. Modern dance's subject matter was often quite contemporary, but it tended to be abstract in a literary sense, asking the audience to see physical activity as a metaphor for psychological interplay.

Leadership was passing to less innovative followers like José Limón, Valerie Bettis, Mary Anthony, Alvin Ailey, and Pearl Lang. They enunciated a credo of humanism with statements like this: "The contemporary artist can do no less than to dedicate the power of his spirit and the flame of his art to bring light to the dark places." (Limón) Young artists in the 1960s didn't aspire to carry flames or light up the dark. Nor were they receptive to the words of authority. The two great theorizers of modern dance composition, Louis Horst and Doris Humphrey, disappeared from college curriculums. Young dancers embarking on choreographic careers sneered at Humphrey's book *The Art of Making Dances*, and didn't see how her advice could inform them. "Dance form is logical," she wrote, "but it is all in the realm of feeling, sensitivity and imagination." Humphrey's point of view, with its underlying idealism, its confidence in the choreographer's right and ability to impose her vision on her dance, struck dissenters as dictatorial. Dance technique and the expressive urges that had given rise to choreography from Isadora Duncan through five decades of modern dance were played out, they thought. Played out and arbitrary and decadent.

According to Ronald Sukenick, one of the chroniclers of the postwar-to-postmodern avant-garde, postmodernism was concerned with dissolving the boundaries between art and life. "If nothing else is clear about Postmodernism, it is glaringly obvious that it is impelled by a passion for reengagement with common experience, including the experience of the citizen in process of helping to create his environment through the imagination." Judson Dance Theater was only one of many loose coalitions of artists that pursued these new directions. The Judson dancers, along with painters, musicians, filmmakers, and writers, wanted to explore what else could be done in the intersection of life and art besides codified theater work. Three years of workshops in dance composition, inspired by John Cage and given by Robert Dunn, had brought together dancers, musicians, and artists for a systematic investigation of alternative artmaking processes. When they decided to show their work to the public, Judson Church opened its doors. Forms and conventions were being shattered; new forms were on the way.

The realignment of life and art was to be effected through a large array of compositional and presentational strategies. Abolishing the proscenium frame and de-emphasizing all established forms of dance training were only the most obvious ones. John Cage's statement that anything can be art was often misinterpreted as a license to throw art itself away. In reality, it simply lifted the power to make art off the exclusive shoulders of the artists. Together with Cage's other Zen-inspired writings, his potent remark became a question about the nature of art and an invitation to find new answers:

Anything can be art if you *think* it's art. This mandated some degree of thought or perceptual activity on the audience's part.

Anything can be art if the processes of art are applied. Countless dances were made by subjecting ordinary activities to structuring in time and space, to ordering, layering, distortion, and triggers outside the dancers' control. Activities were reduced or expanded, elaborated, upended, and juxtaposed with unrelated activities. All these conventional effects could be further removed from an individual artist's conscious control by the systematic use of chance procedures—defining and arranging a given set of elements by random selection, like throwing dice.

Anything can be art if the performer thinks it is. People experimented with the experience of performing, explored whether *any* movement being done before a spectator could be called natural. They induced altered states of consciousness, practiced diffused and inward styles of focusing. They rehearsed material, then intentionally performed it in a different space or with different music, lighting, costumes. They subjected everyday movement to

other classic devices for reconfiguring the familiar so as to give it strange-
ness: exaggeration, interruption, incongruous fit, metacommentary, and un-
derstatement. Even dancing could be art renewed, provided it was thrust
out of its accustomed locations, effects, conventions, and attitudes.

Paradoxically, this work was almost never the simple, spontaneous, and
uncrafted event that it seemed. When movement looked free, it was often
governed by rules or restricted by sets, costumes, or props designed to pre-
vent total spontaneity. When movement was improvised, it had to stay
within a preset range of choices and decisions. The events of the early
dance avant-garde relied on a delicate balance between control and abandon, discipline and anarchy. The successful reform of dance aesthetics
would depend on performers with mind, imagination, and a gift for
collaboration—a sensitivity to the whole event, a responsiveness to their
fellow performers, and a highly developed ability to relinquish their ego demands for the sake of the work.

Only a few months before Tharp's Judson concert, Yvonne Rainer, the
recognized goddess of downtown dance, had stunned the Judson audience
with *Parts of Some Sextets,* a concert of "simple, undistinctive activities made
momentous through their inaccessibility." Rainer published her reflections
on this work in *TDR,* the journal of progressive theater that was still being
published at Tulane University but was soon to move to Greenwich Village
and New York University. *Parts of Some Sextets* was probably the biggest and
best known of the avant-garde dance works of the '60s. Rainer described the
challenge of the piece: ". . . how to move in the spaces between theatrical
bloat with its burden of dramatic psychological 'meaning'—and—the imagery and atmospheric effects of the non-dramatic, non-verbal theatre (i.e.
dancing and some 'happenings')—and—theatre of spectator participation
and/or assault."

Rainer spelled out a whole list of now-unacceptable resources: "NO to
spectacle no to virtuosity no to transformations and magic and make-
believe no to the glamour and transcendency of the star image no to the
heroic no to the antiheroic no to trash imagery no to involvement of performer or spectator no to style no to camp no to seduction of spectator by
the wiles of the performer no to eccentricity no to moving or being moved."
This extraordinary statement became, oddly, both a denial and a revelation.
Seeming to rule out the whole spectrum of dance possibilities, it nevertheless opened up enough new thoughts to inspire the next generation. By the
time it became the manifesto of what was to be called postmodern dance,

Rainer had already violated some of its precepts and moved into filmmaking.

After the last of Robert Dunn's classes, in 1964, the population of Judson Dance held together for a while. Concerts were given at the church by members of the original workshops and by newcomers like Tharp, Meredith Monk, and Kenneth King, all of whom were in college during the workshop years. Rainer gathered her closest Judson associates and formed the improvisational group Grand Union. People gave independent concerts at Judson and elsewhere, digging into the particular aspects of the new liberation that interested them. People returned to their original specialties—painting, plastic arts, dance—with new perspectives. Gradually "postmodernism" emerged from anarchy. Structure and objectivity got more serious. Tharp had these from the beginning. A loner by instinct, she avoided existing centers of the avant-garde, but she shared the utopian impulse toward community, and built a succession of dance communities around her own ideas.

Twyla Tharp went along with the everyday. Uneasily. She wanted to dance and make dances. She continued going to the most exacting classes she could find, mainly at Merce Cunningham's studio, but in her choreography she suppressed the inordinate amount of technical training she had put her body through since childhood. As demanded by the NO imperative, she stipulated walking, hopping, rolling on the floor. But the apparent pedestrianism of the movements was tightened down with rigorous instructions. Everything was meticulously counted, detailed, and spaced. In *Re-Moves*, when Rudner came off the rope ladder, she had to walk backwards on her toes, making a figure eight through the room, avoiding whatever audience members were seated in her path, and eventually fold herself down into the same position on the floor that she'd taken at the end of her descent. She walked around the perimeter of the space, toe to heel, inside the hoop, while Tharp and Jenkins went down to the floor and rose in alternation. They took their timing from Rudner, who years later recalled their anxiety because she performed it much more slowly than in rehearsal.

Sara Rudner had danced most of her life but obliged her family by getting a degree in Russian literature from Barnard before allowing herself to imagine a dancing career. Tharp herself, an art history major, had graduated from the same college only a year before Rudner, having stolen as much time as possible from her academic studies to enroll in the full catalogue of dance classes the New York City studios had to offer. Rudner learned of Tharp's first concerts from her friend Margaret Jenkins.

Jenkins, after intensive training as a conventional modern dancer at the Juilliard School and UCLA, had found her ideal in Cunningham and Cage. When Tharp spotted her in Cunningham's technique class and enlisted her for the second Hunter College concert in 1965, Jenkins was dancing in the independent concerts of Cunningham company member Gus Solomons Jr. Tharp was an unknown in the firmament, but, according to Jenkins, "she was kind of a formidable physical presence in class and I had a lot of respect for how she worked."

She was formidable enough to attract reviewers, and both *The New York Times* and *Dance Magazine* reported on the second Hunter concerts, December 1, 2, and 3, 1965. The two works on the program were a continuation of the concerns outlined in *Tank Dive*. *Cede Blue Lake*, whose title came from a newspaper headline about the government's return of some land to a disfranchised Indian tribe, was called "a silent ritual" by *Dance Magazine*'s Marcia Marks.

In addition to classroom steps repeated and slightly varied, there were props engineered to evoke unlikely movement. Huot had built a slide from the balcony of the little theater to the stage, and Tharp and Jenkins made one of their several entrances that way. Jenkins remembers being wound in elastic or masking tape, and other performers unwinding it to reveal her costume. "I had to walk down backwards on the stairs, with elastic wrapped around my body. Or something that bound me. And I got to the bottom of the stairs and there was a very simple sequence to unwind the bindings. And then I had to go into a kind of deep parallel plié, go down to the floor on my back. I remember doing this backward somersault and I remember it because it was not easy for me." Marcia Marks also noted differences between the two performances. The winding tape, when pulled off Jenkins's body, left a white spiral on the first evening, a black one on the second. Someone dragged a cloth on the floor with her foot—people remembered it later as a paintbrush. At the second concert, the person just dragged a foot.

Bob Huot returned for the second time to his earlier performance piece, *War*. In *Tank Dive*, he had abstracted the gladiatorial duet to a single crouch and shoulder impact with fellow painter Christopher Constance. They looked like football players scrimmaging. For *Cede Blue Lake*, he and Constance, again costumed in heavily padded chest protectors and fencing masks, went at each other so vigorously in rehearsal that Constance was knocked out. Huot remembers performing alone because his partner had several stitches in his forehead. Barnes, reporting in the *Times*, said, "a man . . . indulged in some mock fantasy duel with himself while two girls gravely circled the main dance area."

Unprocessed, another almost-forgotten piece on the same program as *Cede Blue Lake*, had a cellophane or plastic canopy by Huot billowing over it. Marks thought Tharp was suggesting that the ballet, yoga, and athletic movements of the concert, common events in everyday experience, could be looked at in a new way through her "processing" of them.

Margy Jenkins continued dancing in Gus Solomons's performances until about 1967. Dancers, even those attached to major companies, didn't have full-time dance jobs. Choreographers would accumulate regular colleagues around them, who rehearsed when a concert was in prospect and looked for other opportunities. Jenkins says, "There certainly wasn't anything like being paid for what you did and everyone was very respectful of the fact that I would go up to CCNY in the morning from seven to eleven to model for art classes and then I'd rush to take class from Merce and then I'd go to rehearsal with Gus and then I'd work as a waitress and then I'd go work with Twyla. . . . That's what everybody did." Jenkins had taken over a $38.98-a-month apartment on Broome Street vacated by Solomons, and Rudner was her next-door neighbor. During a particularly impoverished period they put ballet barres near their windows and gave each other class across the airshaft between their apartments.

Rudner had been dancing with Paul Sanasardo, a choreographer in the Martha Graham/Anna Sokolow tradition. "It was very dramatic stories," Rudner says of Sanasardo's work. "We would be dressed in slips. We were sisters, and tossing our hair about, and doing things. I didn't have enough background to do that . . . I didn't understand what I was doing." Rudner had a clerical job and had considered giving up dancing more than once. Margy Jenkins suggested Tharp take a look at her in a recital when she needed another dancer for *Re-Moves*, and Tharp made up her mind immediately. She told Rudner to come to rehearsal and they tried out some things. Rudner's longing for dance that represented her own experience *and* challenged her finely developed dance intelligence found an answer in Twyla Tharp. "Thank *God* I'm walking!" she thought, when she got in the studio with Tharp.

Jenkins loved the extremes represented by Tharp's work and that of Solomons. She thought, "I've been trained for fifteen years and I'm walking around with a stopwatch. With Gus it was much more physically rigorous and with Twyla it was much more intellectually, conceptually rigorous." She too was fascinated with Tharp's imposition of paradoxical agendas—exactitude and release: "That I would spend my whole day trying to perfect where my leg was in relationship to my hip and get that kind of clarity that Merce has always demanded, and that I would then spend my evenings bound. I just loved the irony of it . . . being so bound and so restricted and kind of precise in ways that I had never ever had to do in any other kind of dancing. . . . And then the dropping of the egg for me—it was a fuck-you, but it felt like everything that was completely contained in our bodies and wrapped, contained within the egg, was just completely let go. But then the body could never let it go."

Tharp had the services of other friends for *Cede Blue Lake, Stride,* and *Tank Dive,* including Paul Taylor dancers Sharon Kinney and Renée Kimball, Graham dancer Jeanne Nuchtern, and downtown newcomers, Juilliard-trained Marcia Lerner and Art Bauman. But Jenkins and Rudner formed the first Tharp company. After they'd rehearsed for eight months preparing the Judson concert, she gave them each one hundred dollars. They were stunned.

Before all of these dancers, Tharp's first collaborator was Robert Huot, whom she lived with (and later married) at 104 Franklin Street. Huot was deep into the post-Beat art scene by the time he met Tharp. A follower and then denier of abstract expressionism, Huot was one of the artists included in the first important exhibition of minimal art, at the Hudson River Museum in October 1964, curated by his boss, E. C. Goossen, who chaired the Art Department at Hunter College. Besides providing Tharp with an entrée to the art world and its presenters, Huot influenced her thinking at this crucial time. A teenage habitué of Birdland and progressive jazz, Huot took her to clubs in the Village and shared his records of early jazz greats like Jelly Roll Morton. A sports fan, he took her to games and some of his costume designs for her were influenced by sports uniforms. He thought it might be possible to create a new barre exercise that would expand the dancer's movement range, and she incorporated some athletic movement in her first pieces, including a baseball slide in the last part of *Tank Dive.* Tharp was a socially recessive personality, but she quickly absorbed his jockish confidence.

2

Dance Activities
1967–1969

After the Judson concert, Tharp engineered a European tour. Typically, she was thinking big even though her resources were miniscule. She had two fine dancers in addition to herself, and an embryonic repertory—*Re-Moves* and *Tank Dive* seemed solid enough, and she started making new pieces. Jenkins and Rudner were delighted with the opportunity, and all of their parents helped pay their expenses. They hand carried their costumes and props, and, like thousands of young Americans backpacking around the world in those days, they stayed in whatever modest accommodations they encountered.

The infant company didn't have any professional management or office staff, but Tharp leveraged some crucial connections to put together the three-week round of galleries and studio spaces in Cologne, Stuttgart, The Hague, Amsterdam, Paris, and London. Bob Huot had exhibited his work in Germany and Switzerland, and he prepared the ground for Tharp with his dealer in Stuttgart. Robin Howard, the English impresario and patron of Martha Graham, had spotted Tharp's potential at the Judson concert. Despite his more conservative tastes, he thought she should be seen in the U.K. He arranged performances in Queen Alexandra's House at the Royal College of Music, and put up the little troupe in an apartment he owned during their stay in London. The Paris engagement was arranged by Bénédicte Pesle, an important European promoter of Merce Cunningham and a number of other avant-garde dancers. Pesle had also attended Tharp's Judson concert.

On February 15, 1967, tagged onto the end of a longer notice about the plans of Martha Graham's company, came an announcement in *The New York Times* that Tharp was embarking on a tour and would open the next day in Cologne. She may have been a minnow compared to the mighty Graham, but the *Times* headlined them as equals: "2 Dance Companies Will Visit Europe."

Bob Huot's influence pervaded the tour. In Germany and Holland his work as a minimalist was well-known, and his following of avant-garde art-goers probably constituted most of Tharp's audience. Huot had designed the sets and costumes for the repertory, and he had also helped conceptualize the dances. *One Two Three*, the first of two pieces Tharp made for the tour, was accompanied by football signals: "Ready, set! or hut two, hut three!" according to the sports-minded Huot. Tharp later described this as a "classical trio with long repetitive introduction built of fouettés en dehors and en dedans." Rudner remembered endless turns into arabesque, meticulously counted in odd-numbered sets, and a solo where she ran in circles and changed to movement in place without warning.

One Two Three represented Tharp's first overt linkage to Balanchine. When one dancer was doing her solo, one of the others would make "a crossover behind a scrim or curtain that was raised just high enough to see our sneakered feet," according to Rudner. Perhaps only a voracious art historian would have been aware of the startling way George Balanchine had carried out one of his first jobs in the West. He had joined Serge Diaghilev's Ballets Russes at the end of 1924 and two seasons later was assigned to do the entr'acte for Bronislava Nijinska's avant-garde *Romeo and Juliet*, designed by the surrealists Max Ernst and Joan Miró. The classic story was told within a modern-day ballet rehearsal, and the lovers eloped in an airplane at the end. Balanchine's contribution was to raise the act curtain just high enough for the audience to see the dancers' feet moving behind it, preparing for their next appearance. Tharp's 1967 dance antedated the revival of interest in Diaghilev by several years, and she has no recollection of this incident today, but if she wasn't quoting Balanchine deliberately, the coincidence was uncanny.

After two years of acting like a Judson dancer, Tharp was frustrated with denying or disguising what she wanted to do most of all, which was dancing. *Jam*, a "melodramatic trio," was later characterized by Rudner as "a total rage." Highway warning beacons flashed on one side of the space and glared from the other side with a relentless white beam, providing appropriate shock value. During the thirteen-minute piece, the dancers picked the lights up and aimed them around at one another. Merce Cunningham's *Winterbranch*, choreographed three years earlier, might have inspired this dramatic design. For that dance Robert Rauschenberg had created notorious effects with spotlights, alternately aimed into the eyes of the audience and turned off so that the stage went dark, while the dancers kept on doing the choreography.

In *Jam*, Tharp and Rudner performed intense, disjointed moves, while Jenkins had a more lyrical part. They all wore heavy, clear plastic jumpsuits over leotards. Says Rudner: ". . . when you took a step, [the costume] made this awful noise. And so while we were throwing a fit . . . it would be rattling and crunching and cracking." Tharp had choreographed the piece to James Brown's music, but it was danced in a crumpling-plastic silence. Rudner thought the title came from the jam they were in, longing to dance but having to somehow endorse the avant-gardist prohibition against dancing.

Jam had a New York preview on a concert at Columbia's Minor Latham Playhouse, part of the Barnard College Dance Uptown series. Tharp insisted that it be given the opening spot on the program, over the misgivings of the dance department. After an advance viewing, the faculty had tried to put the piece at the end, according to Rudner, "because they felt it would ruin your palate for the rest of the dances. At which point Twyla wanted to be the first on the program. Whatever she wanted. And she got what she wanted."

Tharp was acquiring a reputation for contrariness and ego. She certainly had a big sense of self, and a disconcerting but useful propensity to make last-minute changes. With an imagination unimpeded by the rules, she could improvise brilliant solutions to unanticipated roadblocks. In Paris, she discovered that the performing space at the American Center was smaller than the audience space, so she reversed the locations. She seated the audience on the stage and reserved the rest of the room for the dancers. In London, the audience's chairs were placed in a rectangle and the dancers moved around them. Some spectators, including one critic, refused to swivel around to follow the movement behind them, but John Percival got into the spirit of the event. Percival, who wrote for two important venues, *The Times* (London) and the periodical *Dance and Dancers*, was an early Tharp supporter. Like Robin Howard, he had great confidence in Tharp although he didn't really know why. Something about the London concert grabbed him. "I must say I found the evening rather fun. Which probably proves something rather odd about me, but I can't help it. I tried to be high-minded like other

people, but happiness kept breaking in. Could it be that she really *was* dancing after all?"

At the end of the tour, Margy Jenkins left the company. Jenkins had always been more attuned to Merce Cunningham than to Tharp, and her
silent hopes of getting into his company had received an unexpected boost.
The Cullberg Ballet of Stockholm had requested *Summerspace* for its repertory.
The 1958 work, with its pointillist costumes and backdrop by Rauschenberg,
was one of Cunningham's most harmonious dances. It had been set on the
New York City Ballet in the spring of 1966. This would be a rare occasion,
the first revival of a Cunningham dance in Europe and only the second time
he allowed his choreography to be performed outside of his own company.
He wondered if Jenkins would go to Sweden and teach it. Cunningham
didn't make any further commitment to Jenkins, but she felt the offer established a closer tie between them. In any case, she saw the opportunity as an
honor and an important personal challenge. She accepted the job.

Jenkins also felt, perhaps wrongly, she thinks now, that Tharp was moving away from her, toward developing Rudner's special abilities rather than
her own. After a post-tour vacation in Majorca with Rudner, she went on to
Stockholm. No one remembers now whether Jenkins purposely delayed
telling Tharp she wouldn't return after the Cullberg job or whether she herself didn't decide the break would be final until they parted company in
London. Tharp was hurt. The company had no immediate prospects, but
she had assumed Jenkins would continue working with her indefinitely.
Jenkins's departure was the first the company sustained, and as in many subsequent breakups, the warm relationship between Tharp and the defector
frosted over immediately.

The process of dancer turnover is a painful one for every company director and choreographer. Dancers grow and need to find their own identities; they want diversified experiences; they get injured doing one style and
feel they have to try another, or they need long therapeutic layoffs. They
leave, and especially in small, marginal groups, they leave a hole. Every role
in the repertory, every distinctive body in the studio, is essential. There are
few understudies, and when a dancer is gone, the company feels the loss
deeply. Knowing of the Stockholm possibility, Jenkins tried to ease the
transition by scouting a new dancer before leaving New York.

Theresa Dickinson, another highly intelligent dancer with an eclectic
background, got her B.A. from Radcliffe/Harvard. Her family disapproved of
dancing as a career. She had danced all her life but "I had given it up a few

times because smart people go to college and don't become dancers. The pressure was very intense from my family," who had "a puritanism about the intellect." Like Tharp and Rudner she was small and dark haired and quick. She had studied ballet as a child with Leon Fokine in Washington, but her teenage trajectory toward American Ballet Theater was cut short when her family moved to Philadelphia and she couldn't find any ballet teachers she liked. At Harvard she gravitated to the extracurricular theater group, where exciting new work was being done. There she became devoted to Robert Cohan of the Martha Graham company, who was teaching movement for actors. Having satisfied her family by graduating, she went off on her own for a year in Europe, then landed in New York, where she quickly shifted from Graham classes to Cunningham. She became friends with Margy Jenkins, who urged her to see Tharp's Judson concert.

Dickinson knew Tharp casually from Cunningham classes. The scene after the Judson concert is imprinted on her mind. "Twyla's sitting there smoking furiously and looking very uptight because the show has just finished and I'm the first person backstage afterwards, and she's kind of hunched over with the cigarette going in and out of her mouth real fast. And I said, Oh I loved the show and do you want any other dancers, can I dance with you? And she said, Yes. And that was the end of the conversation." Dickinson started rehearsing soon after that.

Tharp got what she wanted out of the tour: international recognition from critics, and the inevitable cachet conferred by foreign appearances. The audiences were small but influential—artists and patrons who would spread Tharp's name among the culturati. With opportunities to perform out of town as well as an occasional New York concert booking, she settled down to a period of exploration. Two tall women joined the company, blond and beautiful Margery Tupling, a Connecticut College graduate; and Carol Laudenslager (now Carolyn Lord), a ballet dancer and graduate of the University of Chicago. Tharp still relied on Bob Huot's contribution of costume and set designs, but she grew increasingly confident about her dance focus. Serious viewers got past their initial impression of her as an offbeat character, an individualist with promise, and started taking notice of her special gifts for movement and choreography.

Jill Johnston, the dance critic of the *Village Voice*, went to a concert in the gym at Wagner College in Staten Island (9 February, 1968), and devoted a

thoughtful and admiring column to Tharp. In her literary pose of the innocent but receptive dancegoer, Johnston claimed she didn't know anything
much about Tharp, but "this girl is no drooping daisy." She appreciated the
movement most of all, and gave a detailed description of the program. Although she could see Tharp probing various choreographic approaches, "I'm
more impressed by the extraordinary range of movement and her performing
assets: Cool confident commanding aggressive relaxed and a bit of a hostile
'damned what you think, I know that I'm good' sort of thing."

Johnston's interests were already veering away from dance and, after
what she describes as a kind of breakdown, she had committed herself to
personal journalism. The 1968 column is apparently the only time she reviewed Tharp. She left the *Voice* a year later and was succeeded by Deborah
Jowitt. But Johnston wasn't the only follower of downtown dance to skim
over Tharp. When the evolved Judson dance became canonized as "postmodern dance," with Sally Banes's 1980 survey, *Terpsichore in Sneakers*, Tharp
wasn't even included. It might have been her dance emphasis that distanced
her from the post-Judson avant-gardists. Her poorly hidden ambition didn't
endear her to the determinedly dirt-poor avant-garde either.

But she couldn't be ignored. She was asked to appear on several shared
concerts during the late '60s. She was still doing pieces that defied conventional definitions, and she thought of everything as a potential for extending dance. At C. W. Post College on Long Island in 1967 she did *Forevermore*,
which she later described as a "three and a half minute spectacular for
soloist, trio, and two marching snare drummers." In a balcony above the
main performing space, Tupling, wearing a long black dress, walked in a circle, fell to the floor and rose again, rolled and unrolled her long blond hair,
in a calm but somehow glamourous sequence. Meanwhile, Tharp, Rudner,
and Dickinson, wearing leotards with sequins, ran and jumped in increasingly larger circles on the gym floor below. The drummers simply entered,
crossed the space, and left, producing a sound that got louder and then re-
ceded. The dance may have struck the audience as repetitious, or pure
Dada, but Rudner described it as "highly controlled and choreographed.
Very formal, very beautiful, very simple, very direct."

There were other eccentric gestures, but they became fewer, and were
always justified in relationship to the surrounding movement ideas. *Disperse*,
a twenty-one-minute dance from 1967, explored the idea of compression.
Each of the five sections used a successively smaller amount of space and
time. There was no music but the dancers called out numbers seemingly at

random. Blackouts signaled the start of each new section, and one reviewer thought Tharp was using "light and absence of it as a metrical accompaniment." The movement began with twisted turns and stops on relevé, each dancer using a slightly different speed and personal accent, and became more and more detailed as the dancers worked more tightly together. When the group had squeezed into a corner, Tharp brought out a red-painted wooden chair and smashed it. Later she said she was working on the idea of infinity: even when the space and time seemed used up, there would always theoretically be more possibilities. Breaking the chair, she said, represented "a little chaos in this pristine, artificially controlled world. Only the form of the chair was altered: its matter retained all its energy."

Discovering that Sullins College, where they were to perform in 1970, had a student body of girls and a faculty dominated by men, Tharp choreographed a solo for Graciela Figueroa, who was to dance it once topless and once bottomless. The series of solos into which this was inserted had an unpronounceable title taken from a newspaper misprint, *PYMFFYPPMFYPNM YPF.* The school threatened to cancel the performance, so when the time for the offending solo arrived, the dancers froze and Tharp clapped the appropriate counts. At intermission, Tharp announced that the piece would be repeated in its entirety, giving the fainthearted an opportunity to leave. No one left. She was trying out ideas of "duality," such as how the same movement would look with changes of clothing; perhaps nudity seemed a logical phase of the experiment. But even more daring and demanding, the movement itself had built-in contrasts. Rudner remembered a section in which the legs and arms were choreographed separately, at different speeds, and then performed together, in what they called the "slip phrase."

Like the rest of the avant-garde, Tharp had discovered that simple movement could go only so far in creating viable performances. Steve Paxton, Yvonne Rainer, and Simone Forti had exhausted pure pedestrianism in the first years of Judson. Having opened the audience's eyes to the diversity and even complexity of commonplace movement, they began to reattach theatrical elements: props and costumes, sublimated stories, references to animal behavior. The other downtown dancers adopted a wide range of devices for structuring ordinary, nontechnical movement in order to give the audience some thread of logic to follow. There were games, like Trisha Brown's *Falling Duets*, where one performer would start to fall without warning and another had to catch him or her before the first person hit the ground. There were tasks—performers had to build something or carry something, or, in one of the more elaborate plots, Ann Halprin's *Processions*, pick up objects that were strewn in their path and continue slowly across a predefined space as they coped with these encumbrances. Trisha Brown made dances where people had to maneuver through difficult environments. Deborah Hay made quasi—folk dances out of walking steps. Meredith Monk began to create childlike representations of historical characters.

All these strategies made for fascinating, often theatrical, experiences, but they conscientiously excluded the movement vocabularies of ballet and modern dance. During the '60s Tharp was almost alone in developing her work from a dance foundation. But she was in sync with the avant-garde in discarding conventional ways of constructing and presenting dance. She preferred nonproscenium spaces. She disliked thinking any one movement was more interesting than any other; she didn't work for rising and falling curves of excitement, dramatic climaxes, picturesque stage effects. If there was to be any thrill involved, it should come from the extraordinary range of challenges she threw at the dancers and the audience. What she was looking for was ways to move. The body plastique and externalized emotional states that had served the modern dancers didn't interest her, but ballet's rigor did. So did the expertise of athletes. Outside of a few French ballet terms, she talked about movement in everyday language, but she did not want people in her company to look like they had walked in off the street.

Tharp never organized her movement into a formal technique, and the concept of company class didn't exist for her dancers. They all took a daily class somewhere else. During the late '60s Tharp and several of the company members were going to the ballet teachers Richard Thomas and Barbara Fallis, who were noted for giving hard and intellectually provocative combinations. Working with her own dancers, Tharp was didactic, conceptual, smart. But also intuitive and exceptionally physical.

She would begin each day working in the studio by herself, trying out movement ideas to music. By the time the dancers arrived, she would have a set of notes, often accompanied by diagrams, drawings, and charts, and for the next several hours they would develop these ideas. She would teach a turn, for instance, and then the dancers would manipulate the movement—repeat it, do it in different directions or on opposite sides of the body, change the rhythm, do the segments of it in scrambled order, or throw the whole thing into retrograde. She drew on compositional techniques of music, film editing, and an acute instinct for pushing the physical envelope. All her dancers knew that more was being demanded of them than they had ever experienced. Jenkins thought "it was incredibly invigorating, and very very challenging to use the mind in that way." Dickinson was "very attracted to Twyla's almost mystical interest in math, in rational proportions and fractionalizing things. . . . I was extremely excited by that relationship, between the intellectual reason for dancing and the physical reason for dancing."

Tharp was making movement so highly developed that the dancers had to stretch to process it. Some were adept at picking up her train of thought as the ideas poured out of her body; others had to take the movement apart more meticulously in order to learn it. Theresa Dickinson and Carol Laudenslager, who were less kinesthetically quick than Rudner or Tupling, did master Tharp's complexities in their own ways. Dickinson remembers rushing into Merce Cunningham's advanced class with Laudenslager, late one afternoon after Tharp's rehearsal. Cunningham was teaching an exercise, and both of them did it immediately, twice as fast. Another time, after being invited to a rehearsal, dancers from the Cunningham company marveled at the speed of Tharp's dancers. "They said that we were working at a level that they didn't think they could do," says Dickinson.

An obsessive student and consumer of information, Tharp was creating material so fast that she had to develop some mental storage banks to allow her to change things without backtracking or interrupting the flow of collective invention. In college she had made use of the shorthand lessons her mother had pressed on her, by taking notes in class, then carefully transcribing them at night so that she would retain all the professors' words. She thought of choreographing as problem solving; she approached rehearsing and even performing as lessons to be learned. Early in the 1970s, when video recording equipment hit the market, Tharp acquired a primitive Panasonic and began taping rehearsals. This didn't necessarily save any time for her—when she was choreographing she would spend her evenings reviewing the day's output and extracting the useful material. But it did mean that nothing got lost.

When Tharp was picked by producer Charles Reinhart to do a split week at the Billy Rose Theater in February of 1969, with Yvonne Rainer, Meredith Monk, and Don Redlich, she had clearly arrived in another league. The Billy Rose concerts were part of a prestigious series of modern dance companies under the aegis of Richard Barr and Edward Albee's Theater 1969, and Tharp, Rainer, Redlich, and Monk represented the most important directions Reinhart thought new dance was taking. This was the first Broadway engagement for all four groups. Tharp made the cover of *Dance Maga-zine*, eccentrically bent into a right angle for *Tank Dive*, to publicize the Billy Rose series, and the younger generation scowled at photographer Jack Mitchell in a tense, historic family portrait for *The New York Times*, with Martha Graham at the center, and Merce Cunningham, José Limón, and Erick Hawkins completing the picture.

But downtown, according to Theresa Dickinson, "There was a little bit of contempt for those of us who counted and wore leg warmers. . . . We were not supposed to take ballet classes or count, anymore. That was out. Judson dancers wore regular clothes, dirty and tattered. . . . It was part of their ethos to not do these hyper-tight little tricky moves. That was exactly what they were legislating against. So in that sense we felt very isolated. I still see us as being in between cycles." *The New York Times* assigned its junior dance critic to the Tharp evening at the Billy Rose instead of Clive Barnes, and Anna Kissel-goff seemed caught on the edge between Tharp's "cool detached style" and "the high level of energy [that] left anything but a cool impression."

The Billy Rose season was immediately followed by a series called "Works for an Open Space," *Generation and Group Activities*, at the Brooklyn Academy Opera House. One of the important assets Theresa Dickinson had brought to the young company was her partner, Lewis Lloyd, then an administrator at the Cunningham Dance Foundation. Lloyd set up the machinery for the foundation to accept funds for Tharp, since she had no apparatus of her own for doing that, and he acted as an unofficial manager for a couple of years. In the fall of 1969 he became general manager at the Brooklyn Academy of Music, where a very active dance program was getting under way under a former modern dancer, Harvey Lichtenstein. Lloyd may have been instrumental in booking Tharp into the Opera House. As she had in Paris, Tharp dislodged the audience from its usual viewing seats. This time she made room for spectators right on the large stage with the dancers. This novel arrangement attracted attention in itself, but it also allowed the dances to be seen from two sides, in closeup, without the intervention of the proscenium and orchestra pit.

These two engagements established Tharp as a major player and a choreographer of repertory. Despite her assertions that repertory didn't interest her, she had by 1969 made five important dances in addition to *Re-Moves: Disperse; Generation; Excess, Idle, Surplus; After "Suite,"* and *Group Activities*. These were unapologetically dance pieces, exhausting and stark except for Huot's fine costumes. There was enough consistency among them for the audience to see Tharp's emerging movement style: highly flexible, exacting, objective, and unpredictable, with an inner-focused sensuality.

Generation was five solo dances performed together. At certain moments in the choreography the dancers had to coordinate their timing, but mainly they concentrated on their own movement rather than on interacting. Tharp thought of it as the first dance where she "dealt with movement as any kind of working material." She played Beethoven records—the *Apassionata Sonata* and the thirty-two Variations, Op. 191—while choreographing some of the solos, but the dance was always performed in silence. Tharp played music incessantly and almost indiscriminately, often basing her phrases or other structures on what she heard, then discarding the musical prompt. When Anna Kisselgoff saw *Generation* at the Billy Rose, she noted the "centered balletic movements."

Tharp was making *Generation* when Carol Laudenslager entered the company; she and other dancers later realized that Tharp had specifically been looking for someone with ballet training, and probably Laudenslager's solo was intended as a contrast with those of Rudner, Dickinson, Tupling, and Tharp. As Laudenslager/Lord remembers it now, she had a lot of ballet movements, speeded up and without the conventional orientation to a single front. "It wasn't really close enough to ballet to feel familiar in that sense," Lord says. "It felt foreign on me because it was a little freer and thrown around than I had been used to." She had trouble getting the "feel for the flow of the fall or the throw or the drop of the weight," but after months of rehearsal, she was comfortable enough to do a short improvised section at the end of the solo.

Huot designed sleeveless jumpsuits for the piece, in a different tone and texture of silver fabric for each dancer. They rehearsed it from the spring, after returning from the European tour, until its scheduled premiere in February of 1968. Bob Huot had secured them an engagement at his alma mater, Wagner College on Staten Island. *Generation* was laid out for the Wagner gym. The concert included a severe reconfiguration of that large open space, *One Way*, in which the dancers crossed and recrossed the floor with repeated preset stepping patterns, keeping within lanes like swimmers or sprinters, while Tharp zigzagged around and through them. The costumes were blue velvet tunics with long, Pierrot-esque sleeves.

After Wagner College there was another rehearsal period, leading to a performance at Notre Dame University in the spring. The new piece was *Excess, Idle, Surplus*, a "Quintet in three sections: 'Excess' being five 7-minute solos performed simultaneously; 'Idle,' a lyric stream lit by the projected beam of Hollis Frampton's 16 mm film 'Information' running overhead; 'Surplus,' an isorhythmic re-structuring of the movement in 'Excess'." Tharp may have been building on the ideas in *Generation,* or she may have actually folded the basics of *Generation* into the later piece. The movement for the first section involved traveling and then holding still for diminishing numbers of seconds. Tharp remembered it as "very very dancey and very complex movement."

In Part II the decor was by avant-gardist Hollis Frampton, a friend of Bob Huot, who made what film historian Gerald Mast called "logical exercises." The dancers remembered his film as a bright white beam coming from above. Jennifer Tipton, who had lit all of Tharp's work since *Tank Dive,* was credited with the lighting design, a cloud of smoke drifting across the space and into Frampton's projection. Lacking a smoke machine, the Notre Dame stagehands were instructed to exhale their cigars and cigarettes in the direction of the dance space. The dancers, individually twisting and turning, moved slowly together in a clump, down a diagonal through the smoky space. Morton Feldman's music accompanied this middle section. In the last section a tape of the dancers' voices during a rehearsal was the only accompaniment.

The dancers liked *After "Suite"* best of all the works of this period. A tribute to Merce Cunningham's *Suite for Five,* the piece once again brought out the attributes of the dancers in individually choreographed solos. Its main distinction was its spatial construction, ". . . performed in three adjacent squares. As each section of the work is completed, it is immediately repeated in an adjacent square as a variant of itself." The dance's overall form was to be an "arrangement of many situations—never completely developed at one time, constantly interrupting one another thus providing for repetition • variation • development." Tharp arrived at rehearsals with fiendish counted patterns, different for all the dancers. Rudner felt like an overloaded computer, processing all this "neurological information." There were flowing silk flesh-color pajamas by Huot, and no score except a metronome. At the Brooklyn Academy performances, Sharon Kinney, Tharp's old friend from her Paul Taylor company days, sat at a table and called out counts when a dancer asked for her place.

As choreographing for *Group Activities* began in the fall of 1968, Carol Laudenslager was becoming increasingly uncomfortable with Tharp's demands. She felt too inexperienced to keep up with the other dancers in learning the work, and Tharp let her know she would have liked a higher energy level from the newcomer. When she took Laudenslager out of *Generation* and replaced her with Rose Marie Wright, Laudenslager thought it was time to leave.

Wright was the ideal dancer for Tharp's needs at that point, and she soon proved invaluable in ways no one had anticipated. Gifted with impeccable technique and a willingness to try anything, she possessed an indelible memory for movement as well. She soon became the company's informal archivist, mental notator, and coach, a reference source for anything the rest of them had forgotten. Already a seasoned performer at twenty, Wright had been a teenaged member of the Pennsylvania Ballet, but she became stalled on the way to solo roles because of her height, six feet in flat shoes. Tharp spied her in Richard Thomas's class. She thought Wright would be too professional to bother with an obscure modern company that spent most of its time in unpaid rehearsals, so with Thomas's collusion she staged a fake audition and got Wright to attend. Wright found her way to the designated Harlem gym and saw immediately that this was serious dancing. She prayed that she would be accepted, and Tharp in turn could hardly restrain herself. She and Dickinson ran into the dressing room and made Wright an offer before she had time to get into her street clothes.

Two other new dancers arrived around the same time, Sheila Raj, a tiny Indo-English powerhouse, and Graciela Figueroa, a solidly built Uruguayan with folk-dance training. The roster stood at seven, and Tharp felt expansive. *Group Activities* started as a quintet but for the Brooklyn Academy performances she doubled the forces, adding a couple of extras. She herself didn't dance in the piece in Brooklyn; she was going through a period of sitting in the audience, finding out what her dances looked like to different eyes. For the expanded version of *Group Activities* she assigned each of the original five dancers an "analog" to whom the originator was to teach her part. The dance was made up of quite individual parts anyway, and this procedure spared Tharp from having to teach the whole thing herself. The device of doubling, apart from its practical advantages, became an effective choreographic tool in many later dances.

In its quintet-version premiere at the Philadelphia Theater of Living Arts, *Group Activities* impressed the critics, along with *Disperse* and *Excess, Idle, Surplus,* as "enigmatic but forceful," "organized spontaneity." But once doubled and released from the proscenium focus, at BAM, *Group Activities* became even more disconcerting. Tharp described a "Double quintet in which each group occupies a gridded area 20' × 40'. In order that one group will be an accurate duplication of the other, a metronome runs through the work's 40 minutes." From this tart description one might imagine two neat ensembles working companionably side by side, but Tharp refused to map out the dance so that it would be conventionally visible.

With the dancers facing different directions and moving individually but simultaneously, *Group Activities* didn't look amplified or inflated in any known stage sense. The twin groups intermeshed so that they became untrackable. The dance looked wayward, willful, scattered, but somehow fascinating. Cunningham too had abandoned strict frontality in his stage arrangements, but he left most of the other organizing rules of his game to be determined by chance operations, so his dance was in a way more consistent. Tharp's dance was contradictory and that gave it an extra edge. You couldn't dismiss someone who would choreograph an exacting structural scheme while at the same time exploding the stage's most trusted visual code.

Tharp liked the comment of Arlene Croce best of all the favorable reviews that followed the concert: "Watching a piece like *Group Activities*, one has the feeling of having emerged on the other side of some barrier to perception . . . brilliantly irrational to the eye. I know only two other choreographers who give the same effect, and they're Mr. B. and Merce."

These years generated a tremendous exhilaration in the dancers. It wasn't so much the successful performances or the increasing respect they were earning from the press, but the work in the studio with Tharp, weeks and months on end, exploring, exerting, exceeding themselves, that acted like a marathon runner's endorphin high. "We weren't thinking about getting famous, we weren't thinking about getting paid . . . we were just doing the work," says Wright. Dickinson had an "extreme moment of Nirvana" one day, working with Rudner on a piece she no longer remembers the name of. "Just the two of us, this endless kind of getting it right, counting it again, going over it again, making these little junctures in the pattern of the rhythms." And Tharp speaks almost blissfully about the fellowship that held the company together. "We knew one another's abilities and sensibilities so well that each of us became an extension of the others, moving as a genuine team of spirit as well as body." Rudner thought "The things we worked on were so inspiring for dancers . . . they weren't only dances. They were prayers. They were ways of investigating your own self."

3

The End of Amazonia
1969–1971

The avant-garde was spreading out. After finding alternatives to proscenium spaces in gyms and churches, they invaded outdoor plazas, college campuses, parks, forests, fields, and swimming pools. The definition of
dance opened up to make room for pretty much anything that moved with
a purpose, but technique was still taboo. When one looks back on the late
'60s and early '70s, it seems like a period of wonderful, eye-opening enter-
tainments and games—motorcycles paraded in formation, people slunk
across lawns like tigers, peculiar behaviors were enacted in skyscraper windows. Many prechoreographed dances got transposed into unorthodox
spaces, and many spaces suggested their own nondance movement. Trisha
Brown made the most dazzling synthesis of movement and environment, in
*Man Walking Down the Side of a Building, Walking on the Wall, Floor of the Forest,
Planes,* and *Roof Piece* from the early '70s. But however effectively they
stretched the perceptions of the audience, not even Brown's environmental
pieces represented an expansion of technical dancing. She returned to the
stage and to a self-invented dance vocabulary in the mid-1970s.

As the avant-garde was becoming less anarchistic, more serious and crafts-
manlike, the modern dance was receding. Established at Connecticut College
in 1948 as a successor to the pioneering Bennington School of Dance, the
American Dance Festival and its School of Dance now represented a modern

old guard, caught between the paroxysms of the counterculture and the perceived regressiveness of ballet. Two of the pillars of modern dance pedagogy had died, Doris Humphrey in 1958 and Louis Horst in 1964, but their teachings lingered on under the guidance of others. Martha Graham and José Limón controlled the school's faculty and dominated ADF performances. Merce Cunningham, Alwin Nikolais, and other mature dissenting choreographers made only rare appearances, and the younger revolutionaries hadn't been able to get a foot in the door. The festival and school were experiencing lower enrollments and smaller audiences. When Charles Reinhart took over the directorship in 1969, he acknowledged the shifting scene with a big overhaul.

Reinhart felt a clean sweep was necessary, and the committee of festival overseers gave him their blessing to try. All the staples of technique and composition that had served the School of Dance since its inception were swept away, though many of the basic offerings were later reinstated. José Limón reluctantly took the summer off from both school and festival, and his teaching disciples left the scene too. Martha Graham was represented by only two technique teachers, June Lewis and Richard Kuch, and the Graham and Limón choreography classes virtually disappeared, along with the compositional "forms" courses developed in the 1930s by Louis Horst. For the first time, ballet and jazz technique appeared, and an array of avant-garde–related courses took the place of the traditional curriculum for dance educators and musicians. Paul Taylor and Alvin Ailey, the youngest of the major modern dancers, held on to their presence, but the Festival wore a drastically different look. Ailey contributed the only important new stage work of the summer, *Masekela Langage*, while Taylor showed a work in progress as his only premiere. The other performances included works by outsiders Talley Beatty, James Clouser, James Cunningham, Yvonne Rainer, and Tharp.

Charles Reinhart had known Tharp since her association with Paul Taylor—he had been representing Taylor as a manager and producer since the early '60s. He recognized in Tharp's earliest work a rapprochement between classicism and the avant-garde, and as planning began for the 1969 American Dance Festival, he proposed Tharp for the festival's prestigious Doris Humphrey Choreographic Fellowship. The jury drew the line at this, and no award was made that year. Nevertheless he found a $10,000 commission, part of a larger grant from the National Endowment for the Arts, that brought the Tharps, as well as dancers from the companies of Rainer, Taylor, and Ailey, to teach on the campus for two weeks prior to their performance. This boon allowed Tharp's dancers to go on "salary"—thirty dollars a week, for twenty

weeks, long enough to qualify them for fourteen dollars a week in unemploy-
ment compensation. After rehearsals in New York, Tharp and the company arrived on the campus in New London, to work with thirty-three students from
the Festival who were to complete the expansive and beautiful piece *Medley*.

Following her emergence into the public eye at the Billy Rose and BAM,
Tharp had sustained the first serious attack of a malady from which she never
entirely recovered: the horror of stagnation. Having made four years' worth of
successful dances, she began to feel pinned down by them. She writes in her
autobiography that she feared "we would find we couldn't live up to our reputation; we would get too many proscenium opportunities and become caught
in our repertory, chewing the gum long after the flavor was gone; we would
lose our creativity, which maybe came only with being outside the system. . . .
I sensed we were spinning our wheels." To combat her own sense of impend-
ing boredom—it doesn't seem to have affected the dancers—she developed a
choreographic scheme for Connecticut that would not only showcase the
company but deploy a small army of performers across a vast empty field.

Medley began and ended without fanfare, or even punctuation. The
dance was in progress as the audience arrived to sit on the grass in front of
the college art museum, and it finished long after the spectators had left to
attend Rainer's gymnasium piece, *Connecticut Composite*, on the other side of
the campus. Tharp later said she wanted to blur the distinctions between art
and life. This was still a mantra of the avant-garde, but Tharp gave it a
unique interpretation. *Medley*'s casual beginning and ending made it seem
that the dance had been there all along, waiting for the audience to arrive
and turn it into a performance. The work unfolded in a series of set-pieces
meant to integrate performing into the open-field setting, to bring students
into a relationship with the members of the company, to incorporate the audience's movements into the choreography, and, in a final series of long adagio solos, to present each company dancer's special qualities.

In some notes written while she was working on the piece, Tharp wondered how to bring out what was natural to a dancer, how to provide technical challenges to each dancer's personal preferences. To what extent did the
choreographer's instructions enhance or interfere with the dancer's own presence? And if each dancer's choreographic material encouraged her to be
herself—or her ideal self—then how would this group of individuals be able
to relate to each other when dancing together, and how could you be sure
they'd all be equally appreciated by the audience? She considered "natural"
movement potentialities: improvisation, everyday gesture or action, tech-

nique done in the nude. She made the movement for one section by having the dancers "learn" their own movements from videotapes of themselves as they casually prepared for rehearsal in the studio. Each of the six dancers then became captain of a team of students, who learned the learned naturalism.

Influenced by Merce Cunningham's techniques of chance and indeterminacy, Tharp considered building in moments when the dancers would have to make split-second decisions, inevitably revealing their reactions and adaptations as "a dramatic situation." But everything would need to be formalized at some point or else the audience would become bored. She needed to "do away with the pretension that a 'new' piece is anything other than a continuation of all the work . . . a progression, development, standstill or denial."

Medley turned out to be a mind-bending experience for those who saw it—not only original but sensually pleasing. Tharp's exacting compositional structure seemed released in the huge open-field space, so that the piece looked more free-form than it actually was. After the preliminaries, including a pointe solo danced by Rose Marie Wright on a square of plywood set down in the grass, there were several mass effects. A group of students imitated Theresa Dickinson, who picked up the audience's actions as they arrived. Sheila Raj's "gnat" solo gave her the fastest movement possible, and a group of thirty students backed her up with "staccato chunks" of the variation. Tharp dubbed this the "movement machine." The most stunning effect came from a witty, contrary, typically Tharpian manipulation of movement. All six company dancers and thirty-three students spread out over the whole field. They were given a phrase that probably took less than a minute to perform, but each person used his or her slowest personal timing—Theresa Dickinson could draw it out to as long as forty-five minutes. The audience was confronted with a field of virtual statues, imperceptibly changing their positions. If you focused on one individual, the person would be moving too slowly to catch the change; only by looking away, then back, would any shift be apparent. The choreographed phrase simply disappeared, and the image emerged, satisfying and provocative.

Besides the planned indeterminacy in the piece, there were things Tharp couldn't control, and she felt it went wrong at the end. She had timed the entire piece so that the final Adagio solos would start precisely at sunset and end in darkness. This would have provided another perceptual revelation for the audience, the eye-opening effect of discovering how much one can continue to see in a gradually diminishing light. Not only did the audience leave for Rainer's scheduled performance but the dancers were attacked by mosquitoes and Tharp finally moved the remaining solos indoors. The dance finished in Windham House, a dormitory, where the postperformance party was going on. As Reinhart remembers it, he came upon Sara Rudner in a closet when he was looking for the men's room. Actually, Rudner was dancing for a few rapt onlookers in one of the dorm's public spaces, perhaps a dining room that had been cleared out for summer use as a studio. Tharp spent the rest of the evening in her room with a filched bottle of gin, inexplicably depressed and lonely for Bob Huot, who had stayed in New York. She hadn't danced in *Medley*. It wasn't the first time she'd chosen to watch her work from the audience, but this was the biggest thing she'd done and she felt she'd made herself superfluous.

Medley was a milestone in Tharp's career—not only because it succeeded so well as a dance integrated into a unique natural setting. It satisfied her appetite for gigantism, and she went on to imagine other large-scale projects, at least two of which were soon realized. But in spite of this success, environmental work wasn't really where she wanted to go. She spent the next two years exploring the conceptual questions that had come up while making *Medley*, never hesitating to put her research before the public in innovative formats both on and off the stage.

Tharp loved structure and she loved the working process. She could be in the studio six hours a day with the dancers, trying out phrases, then go home and write pages of new combinations. For example, her notes during the spring of 1969 could be simple:

> small relevés + head scratching sequence
> Balanchine 4th
> . . . back walk + slide bkwds
> sit on bottom
> dead kipp
> finger
> Look out for
> dance sequences
> that exist
> only for their
> complexity

Or minutely detailed:

Arrange 55 torso mvts 116 mvts of the legs for 30 people over 90 secs. Put moves into groups of 10 torso mvts/20 leg mvt. Leg mvts will be basically in place, but when they travel time must be allowed for dancer to return to place. Each set of 10TM/20LM (and leftover 5/26) will be distributed over 15 secs

Her tremendous capacity for invention was humanized by her unconde-scending inclusiveness. She thought football players and tap dancers moved beautifully. She liked to give vernacular names to things the dancers were learning; sections of *Medley*, for instance, were called "Street Moves," "Lay-outs (put-downs)" and "Audience pick-ups." She seldom visualized in terms of a technical dance vocabulary. She may have chosen the most exacting dance techniques for herself—ballet and Cunningham—but she respected whatever her dancers brought with them, as long as they could move with fluency from fundamental movement instructions. Not only the company dancers in *Medley* but students, audience members, and passersby could have their movements incorporated, subject to the utmost physical refining. For Tharp, the axiomatic pedestrianism of the avant-garde was not an end in it-self but a beginning of dancemaking. She thought in order to make dancing recognizable, it should be like "a near relative, not a distant European cousin," and that mirroring the daily movements of themselves or the audi-ence was the first step toward this recognition. "As dancers we had to first be mundane, before we could buy into the heavenly."

At the end of the summer, *Medley* was performed again in New York's Central Park, with an even bigger complement of extras. Contending with the usual occupants of the Great Lawn—Frisbee players, joggers, bikers, mounted policemen, ball games, and strolling civilians—gave the dancers a more realistic chance to test their art-is-life proposition. This time, Tharp's desired effect of having the piece end in gradually diminishing light was ac-complished, with an added flutter of alarm for some viewers, as darkness swallowed up the faraway dancers. *The New York Times*'s Anna Kisselgoff called the Adagio "a masterly coup . . . an impression of richness in sparseness."

As Tharp started the next big project, her working and living situations be-gan to change. Within half a year, four of the six dancers withdrew from the company. Sheila Raj and Graciela Figueroa were both having visa problems which would force them to leave the country by early 1970. Margery Tupling married and moved away. Theresa Dickinson, who had been with Tharp since

1966, was drifting away too. Dickinson relished the way Tharp combined rigorous dancing with pedestrianism. She was excited by the challenges Tharp constantly threw at the dancers' bodies and minds. But she felt "a mounting density of movement and images that was more pressured than I enjoyed." She saw Tharp's ambition as pulling the company toward theatrical dancing and respectability. "Twyla wanted to be famous and important. . . . She thought it was terribly important to be successful young, so that she wouldn't struggle for a long time in obscurity and then feel obligated to repeat a success when it happened." Dickinson reflects that the dancers themselves were changing. "We had acquired a certain amount of centrifugal force as a group . . . we were gaining power as dancers and as people, both because time had passed and because the work we were doing was so thrilling to us. . . . I think *Medley* gave us tastes of who we could be in other ways."

Dickinson was happy with parts of *Medley*, "the lovely long areas" of slowness and the "expansive, sort of running waltz material that was just beautiful beyond belief." But she dreaded going back to the confinement of long hours in the studio. Attracted to the more free-floating, hippie lifestyle, Dickinson wanted to leave New York. Her marriage to Lewis Lloyd was breaking up, and at the end of the summer, after *Medley* in Central Park, she took off for San Francisco.

Meanwhile, Bob Huot had received a grant from the National Endowment for the Arts. After some hesitation, he decided to keep it when friends convinced him that turning it back in protest over the Vietnam War would be a mistake. In September of 1969 he used it, together with a loan from Tharp's parents, for a down payment on a 215-acre farm in New Berlin, New York, a four-hour drive from New York City. Huot thinks Tharp didn't really want to move to the farm, but she agreed when he asked if she liked the big old house and its rolling fields. For the winter term he managed to compress his full-time teaching job at Hunter College into a three-day week, and after they moved upstate in January, he began commuting. He kept the loft on the fifth floor of 104 Franklin Street, where he and Tharp had been living and working. Putting her art-as-life concept to the ultimate test, Tharp hatched a spectacularly unrealistic scheme to relocate to New Berlin.

Before *Medley*'s second performance, she had started work on a new openspace piece, *Dancing in the Streets of London and Paris, Continued in Stockholm and Sometimes Madrid*, to be performed in Hartford, Connecticut, at the

Wadsworth Atheneum, a bastion of avant-garde arts in New England. Tharp's extravagant title seems to be a reference to another icon of modernism, the Blaise Cendrars/Sonia Delaunay *affiche*, *La Prose du Transsibérien et de la petite Jehanne de France*. Published in 1913 as the First Simultaneous Book, the seven-foot-long poem with color-swatch design describes a railway trip across Russia and its resonances. A cornerstone of collage aesthetics, the simultanist credo of Cendrars and Guillaume Apollinaire "requires that our minds entertain concurrently and without synthesis two or more contradictory propositions." Historian Stephen Kern calls Cendrars's verse "verbal montages [that] unite what is distant as if they were quick-cut camera directions," a collapsing of time and space made possible by modern engineering: "Now I've made all the trains run after me/Basel–Timbuktu/I've also played the horses at Auteuil and at Longchamps/Paris–New York/Now I've made all the trains run alongside my life/Madrid–Stockholm." Tharp had a similarly panoramic and contemporary project in mind.

None of the dancers remembers exactly how she got this opportunity, but the main connection was probably one of Bob Huot's admirers, Henry Geldzahler, who had become curator of twentieth-century art at the Metropolitan Museum of Art in New York. Geldzahler encouraged not only minimalists like Huot but experimental art, performance, and mixed media. He had appeared in happenings by Claes Oldenburg, narrated Jean Tinguely's "The Construction of Boston," and, as a friend and supporter of the Judson dancers, had also checked out Tharp's downtown concerts. At the end of 1969 he organized the Met's show of New York Painting and Sculpture 1940–1970, which was called "the last of the great '60s art spectaculars" by Calvin Tomkins, the chronicler of downtown art of the period. Around the same time, Geldzahler commissioned *Dancing in the Streets*, to be performed at the Met in January 1970. (Tharp says she talked him into it.) It's possible he made the contact for the first performance with James Elliott, director of the Wadsworth Atheneum, who was continuing the museum's avant-garde mission.

In Hartford, Tharp and the dancers took over the five galleries, and the auditorium passages, stairwells, elevators, and mop closets, according to one observer, for a variety of activities designed never to be seen intact because they would be going on simultaneously. Tharp thought of this polymorphic presentation as a dance analog to the pictures hanging in the separate galleries of a museum. Three cameras from Hartford's Channel 24 videoed the action like a news pickup, so the audience and the dancers could track it on monitors posted around the building. This in itself was a violation of the idea that a theatrical performance should occur in a sequestered space for the consumption of one privileged audience. Today, of course, lobby monitors are posted in major theaters for latecomers, and multiple cameras can broadcast live performances across the country. But this was unheard-of in 1969. Tharp gives several other reasons for using live television in the museum piece. For the big space of the Atheneum, she was acutely conscious of how few dancers she had, even with the addition of nine extra women. Video images would amplify the piece. The closed-circuit monitors would also reassure the crowd and encourage them to move around from one space to another.

Tharp felt that video gave credence to ordinary movement. "People are more accustomed to looking at movement on television and in film than they are [to] using their eyes on the street," she says. The frame of the TV screen rendered movement user-friendly, was her theory. She was still working out ways to make dancing more like life, or more acceptable as a life activity. A few days after the *Medley* performance at Connecticut College she was in Hartford "walking around the museum surreptitiously dropping moves, hiding them." She was acutely aware of the differences between conventional performance with its mandatory high audience visibility, and "invisible" dance, where the choreography would either be deliberately hidden (like the rehearsal inside the box in *Re-Moves*) or so minimal that the dancers would just seem to be casually moving around in sight of the audience. She mused about the psychic distance created when dancers were on a stage, and considered the intimacy that could occur when a dancer came upon a few people in a small space, "quietly watching a monitor or talking. Do a small something for them."

Tharp isn't fond of teaching but she's a dedicated explainer. She can be owlishly didactic—one of her dancers saw her as a nerd in disguise—and also lucid, erudite, ironic, funny, and occasionally profound in her attempts to disclose her methods to the audience. Confident that being "factual" about her choreographic designs would explain everything, she invited critics and friends to see studio previews of dances, where she gave rapid-fire expositions of the creative process that became legendary. Variants of this format appeared in lecture-demonstrations and in postperformance sessions, with the dancers present to answer questions and demonstrate. For the Atheneum, she distributed an eighteen-by-twenty-eight inch program sheet covered on both sides with hand-printed notes, observations, snapshots, company credits, and helpful hints for the audience. Embedded in the wordy text, she had thoughtfully laid out the elements of the choreography and set a timetable for the ninety-minute event.

According to the plan, the five company members, Rudner, Raj, Figueroa, Wright, and Tharp, plus four extra dancers, would work in the galleries and related spaces for two half-hour segments, while five more recruits performed excerpts from the repertory twice on the small Avery Stage in the basement. There would be a fifteen-minute intermission during which the company was to determine how they would restructure the same material for the second part. The audience got two five-minute opportunities to participate. They could dance the Audience Phrase, based on simple steps— walk, run, chassé—laid out in an Arthur Murray-type diagram on the floor. And in another gallery, Sara Rudner would be taking requests for anything the audience wanted to see her do. Rudner was hoping she'd be challenged to make up a modern version of *The Dying Swan* or the pas de deux from *Don Quixote*, but instead the requests were rather mundane: "jump off the window and land on your toes, and crawl across the floor on your ear."

Planned activities for the company included The Drift, a long, heavy phrase that was passed among the dancers and performed nonstop throughout the piece. The Traveling Phrase, which took them from one space to another, was "very dancey and steppy" according to Rose Marie Wright. Cluster Breakers, another set of choreographed moves, were used for infiltrating and separating the audience when it gathered together too tightly. In The Talky, Tharp and Rudner had a conversation while Rudner worked out choreographic problems that Tharp had given her. Wright had a specific dance for moving the audience away from a spot where she was going to perform. Her solo, the Wall dance, was a problem of leverage and balance, with her whole foot in contact with the floor on pointe, then on demi-pointe, and finally for her whole body affixed to a wall. Raj had fifty quiet moves, called The Parlor Phrase, to do in areas with low audience density. Fascinated with the rigor and precision, and the absolute objectivity, of gold medalists in Russian Olympic skating, Tharp made a phrase that would demand maximum exertion and no inflection.

Tharp had been making one minute of movement per day, which she put together for her own twenty-minute "diary" solo. After the Met performance, *Dance Magazine* critic Jack Anderson described it as "a spectacular solo study in energy flow and dynamic shifts, in which somnambulistic staggers followed staccato jabs; fierce lunges gave way to casual slides and dainty skips."

Besides the performance at the Metropolitan Museum of Art in New York two months after Hartford (22 January 1970), versions of *Dancing in the Streets* appeared in benefit performances that winter at the New York Public

Library for the Performing Arts Dance Collection in Lincoln Center; and at the Worcester Art Museum, preceded by a tryout showing in a lobby of the MIT administration building in Cambridge. While patrons at the public performances were prepared for something unconventional, partygoers at the benefits were taken aback by these casual young women in dirty jeans, rushing around and rolling on the floor near the skirts of their evening gowns. For each incarnation of the piece, which was never intended to be finished, the dancer population changed and material was added, eliminated, or adjusted to fit the space. For one of Tharp's favorite additions, the Drop-Bys, "we'd just walk by somebody and do . . . this little spurt of movement with the hope that we would be undiscovered and be gone before they caught us." At the library, Tharp and Figueroa put on their boots (it was snowing outside) and did their duet on Lincoln Center Plaza. Most dramatic of the site-specific segments was the dance on the Grand Staircase of the Metropolitan. Chains of dancers passed each other doing complex patterns of going up and down stipulated numbers of steps. Tharp created a new solo for Wright to do at the Met, weaving down among the chains.

By the time she made *Dancing in the Streets*, critic Don McDonagh thought Tharp had developed a distinctive style of "aristocratic movement with a vernacular phrasing." But despite the amount of precisely choreographed material, what people remember most vividly about the work is how "everyday" and unassuming it looked. In Hartford, one girl "chewed gum and did a sort of Swedish drill in the lobby." The Minutes specified that each dancer perform exactly the actions and words she'd been doing during two predetermined one-minute periods of a given day. During The Home Phrase, they read from a fairy-tale book and traded parts of their clothing. Counts were shouted from one room to the other, and in Hartford, "At the count of 42, the troupe, who had by this time all assembled in the Austin Gallery for calisthenics, collapsed on the floor and started applauding themselves."

The audience and the performers were to remain separate entities, even when the dancers adopted pedestrian movement or entered the audience's physical space. Although they were often packed tightly together and almost indistinguishable from one another, a certain reserve would always be maintained. Rosalind Newman, who joined the expanded company for the piece when it was done at the Metropolitan, remembers finding herself dancing face-to-face with one of her teachers, the modern dancer–choreographer William Bales. "I couldn't pass him and he wouldn't move and he kept saying, 'We did this stuff before. We did this stuff years ago. She can't tell us. . . .'" Newman's instructions, and her embarrassment, prevented her from answering him.

Newman was recruited for the piece by Graciela Figueroa. Tharp had given each of the company dancers the responsibility of signing up new people they thought were interesting—people who would be willing to come to unpaid rehearsals—to augment the New York version of the work. The company then acted as teachers and leaders of what would become different groups in the performance. Newman thought this was in part a strategy to shield the dancers from Tharp's peremptory manner. By this time many people had experienced problems with what several of them called Tharp's communications skills. Interposing the company as teachers and coaches not only broke in the new people faster, it took some of her boiling intensity out of the rehearsal process.

Tharp's gruff and tough demeanor was a way of showing fondness—she trusted close associates not to take offense. In choreographing and rehearsing, her goals were the proper execution of the steps, precision and accuracy in the ensemble work. "She'd tell us if it was working or not, or if we needed to do something here or there or phrase differently," says Rose Marie Wright. According to Rudner, "Twyla didn't come up to you and say, 'God, that was great.' She would not say anything. . . . When she watched . . . a rehearsal or a section, you could never tell what emotion she was feeling." Rudner attributed Tharp's reticence to a certain puritanism, the aftereffects of her Quaker background. The company at that time considered itself a "democratic dictatorship," according to Wright. They understood that Tharp was choreographing for their individual talents, and even giving them choreographic tasks to work out on their own, but she was a little bit more equal than the rest of them. "She encouraged me through giving me work to do," Rudner says. "Not by saying, 'Oh, you're really good at this' and 'This is wonderful for you, dear.' She'd say, 'Do this!'" Wright perceived her the same way: "Twyla, when she *loves* you, she makes dances for you. She gives you things to do, she gives you work. That's her way of showing love."

The unusual responsibilities taken on by the dancers and administrators in the early days gave the company a close-knit solidarity. The team formations in *Medley* and *Dancing in the Streets* were a palpable demonstration of the real bonding among the dancers. They felt they had a fundamental part in making the work, and they shared the company's success as well as hardships. Newman remembers some resentment and misunderstanding because Tharp insisted on nonstop rehearsals though she couldn't pay the dancers. "She really did care, that dancers should be getting paid, and yet somehow people didn't see that." The core dancers shared not only their work but sometimes their apartments and their miniscule resources. Says Tharp: "We shared adversities, welcomed sacrifices, created community much like a religious society. We were a bunch of broads doing God's work. The pleasure of those days of extraordinary and total equality is my ideal still." Tupling confirms this: "I always felt when I was looking at her that she was on the edge of a new frontier, and we were all working for that and had faith in her vision, even though we didn't know what her vision was." But the longstanding financial dilemma became more and more vexing as the devoted first cadre of dancers began to leave.

For the Worcester and Library benefits, Tharp supplemented the dancers' practice clothes with costumes borrowed from choreographer-designer James Waring. She was always scouting for rehearsal space she could afford, free if possible. *Dancing in the Streets* was developed in makeshift circumstances: a studio in Great Jones Street that belonged to Waring and Kermit Love, a forgotten mezzanine with a concrete floor that Tharp discovered in the City Center building, and the Metropolitan itself, after hours. The Met was undergoing renovation at the time, and in an attempt to disguise the dust of the construction work, Bob Huot came up with the idea of sprinkling an aluminum powder on the floor, so that when a dancer fell or rolled on it, she would be transformed into a "silver creature." Unfortunately, the paint turned out to be ordinary gray, and it was delivered too late to be taken back to Canal Street for exchange. He used it anyway, creating a ghostly effect.

Word had spread in advance somehow that the Metropolitan performance was going to be a big event in New York's cultural life. Tharp had no money for professional publicists or advertising campaigns, so she and the dancers mimeographed, mailed, and hand-delivered announcements to dancing schools, critics, universities, Bob Huot's contact list, and everyone else they knew. In addition to whatever the Met did to publicize the event, Merce Cunningham made his mailing list available to the company, and Lewis Lloyd let them use office facilities that the Cunningham company occupied at Brooklyn Academy. As a result, an unexpectedly large crowd arrived at the museum.

Tharp's timing and mapping of the simultaneous events, carefully rehearsed in the Met's deserted galleries, were demolished when the closed-circuit television failed to materialize. The crowd became disoriented. Anxious spectators milled around, and the dancers lost track of each other. Roz Newman remarks:

Twyla never figured out how to use crowd control. Or how to get the crowd to go from one spot to the next, or how we would even recognize who was one of us and who was one of the crowd during the piece. So . . . we were going, wait, where's Sheila? Wow, I see a little purple shirt, is that her? Are we supposed to start yet? Where is so and so? People would be trying to get from one room to the next to tell the next people to start their next thing or move, and there was no way they could get there on time. So that the timing got totally screwed up. Nobody knew where anybody was. We were just sort of wandering—I mean, things happened, you saw things. But it was totally not the piece that she had planned.

Tharp played Pied Piper, leading stragglers from one room to another, barking over her shoulder, "I know they can't see, so what?" At one point she had a long solo that she had never rehearsed with the company, and Newman remembers the dancers hesitating at the edge, not knowing where they should be or when to enter. She danced up to them and yelled, "Get the fuck back!"

Anna Kisselgoff of *The Times* was among the confused and frustrated members of the audience. All very well, Kisselgoff thought, for experimenters to try out new spaces. After all, that tradition went back to Isadora Duncan. But "It is nonetheless disappointing to see a previously disciplined and original talent . . . lose control of the performing situation . . . Her once-brilliant movement patterns appear less than interesting and smothered by an unpredictable participant public whose presence—if not obstructive—seems beside the point." Jack Anderson admitted that he found the trudging from room to room "wearisome" although he was intrigued by the relationship of the dancers to the architecture. Not everyone was put off by the discomforts of the situation. The work's unpredictability, its good nature and wit, and the evident fact that the dancers were often as unprepared for what happened as the viewers, made for a conviviality seldom found at an avant-garde event. Indeterminacy worked. Art met life in a cheerful, jostling accommodation, if not exactly adhering to the scenario Tharp had in mind.

The dancers found it satisfying despite its mishaps. Roz Newman remembers Sheila Raj's series of what seemed like a hundred phrases, with subtle dynamic shifts that capitalized on Raj's special abilities. They were like "unraveling a cloth of beautiful dancing." After Newman and some of the other extra dancers had learned these phrases, Tharp said they could spread out anywhere they wanted in the museum at the end of the piece, and do as many of the phrases as they wanted, in any order. "It was just like a mountain of material, it was like your whole life," Newman says. "Or maybe it was an encyclopedia of everything she's done since. . . . So I just remember doing my phrase and changing the order, and how that to me was *the* most amazing part."

By the start of 1970 Tharp was recognized as a major figure in the world of experimental dance, as choreographer, dancer, and developer of a distinctive company style. Important presenters and administrators like Reinhart and Geldzahler followed her work and opened up possibilities for it to be seen. She had been appreciatively reviewed by *The New York Times* and had received significant critical attention in the United States and England. In New York, where a new generation of writers was developing alongside the dance avant-garde, a strong and receptive press tracked her moves, notably Deborah Jowitt of *The Village Voice* and independent writers Arlene Croce, Tobi Tobias, Don McDonagh, and Laura Shapiro, soon to join *The New Yorker*, *New York* magazine, *The New York Times*, and *Newsweek* respectively. The journal *Dance Scope* featured a long profile by Tobias, a fellow Barnard alumna, and Croce's influential *Ballet Review* published the first of several Tharp-centered pieces, her minutely detailed notes for *Group Activities*. She had acquired an audience eager to see anything new she made, and she had received significant help in the form of grants and commissions.

Nevertheless, sometime in winter of 1969–70, without telling the dancers (consisting by then of Sara Rudner and Rose Marie Wright), she turned over the company records to the New York Public Library's Dance Research Collection. "I had every intention of quitting," Tharp says. She recalls being "very angry" at this point, but the gesture may have been disingenuous. Tharp had already shown she was capable of extreme actions on behalf of the company; a sign that she was closing it down might bluff potential donors into writing checks. Despite the performance opportunities being offered to the company, she still couldn't pay the dancers on any regular basis. She saw herself as scrambling to maintain an impossible compromise: although the company worked full-time all the time, it operated like a part-time avocation, with the dancers doing temp work and baby-sitting to support themselves.

Tharp was also very much under the influence of Bob Huot's "political declamations about war and taxes and let's not support this capitalistic society, et cetera, et cetera." Living on the farm and giving up the company seemed like a feasible alternative to struggling with the high cost of living in the city. She embraced Huot's pioneering ideas; they would grow their own food, restore the dilapidated house, and live a healthy life in the country. Agrarian communities had been constructing alternatives to American mainstream culture for a century, and in its benign aspects, the counterculture of the 1960s was an offshoot of this utopianism. Tharp's hometown of San Bernardino had served for a few years in the 1850s as a communal settlement for Mormons crossing California to their capital in Utah. And as recently as 1946, pacifist Quakers had established Tuolomne Farms in northern California, to carry on their businesses, farms, and schools in seclusion from what they considered the increasing militarism of American life. In California alone, historian Robert V. Hine identifies utopian cells devoted to dissident religions, sexual liberation, pacifism, health, mysticism, rural escapism, and social reform at the height of the counterculture.

For Tharp no gesture was too radical in pursuit of an ideal. She had taken on a strong secular moralism and independence from her Quaker grandparents, and nothing about her immediate family had been remotely conforming. Periodically she would be seized with the desire to go back to the land, to live in the idyllic simplicity she recalled from her earliest years in Indiana. Contemplating the inventiveness of nature inspired her to "go back in and do better." Now she persuaded herself that she could construct a good working life in withdrawal from the urban hustle. Dance for her was a kind of monasticism anyway; not so much a deliberate renunciation of other attractions as a single-minded immersion in the life of the studio. Huot adopted the rural lifestyle and was still running the farm thirty years later, but if Tharp ever thought about giving up dancing entirely, the vision lasted about six weeks. After a winter's retreat, she started dancing again and, almost casually, began inviting dancers up to the farm to work with her.

Nothing provoked Tharp's latent romanticism like the idea of New Berlin. She had her own dancing space, a big room at the top of the house that she and Huot fitted out with a new floor. She could work there as many hours a day as the household chores allowed; she didn't have to answer the telephone. Deep in domesticity, surrounded by nature, and pregnant by June, she saw herself as part of a huge process of biogenesis. "I made more dance that summer than I ever had before or since," she comments in her autobiography. In rhapsodic pages devoted to the early days on the farm, she describes grocery shopping, sheets drying on the line, making dandelion wine, raising and butchering cattle. Somehow, dancing merged with all of this in her imagination.

When the dancers arrived, first Wright, then Rudner and several others over the next months, they were less enthusiastic about the improvised living quarters, the severe weather, the housekeeping and gardening and paint stripping that were part of the package. Nor did they like leaving their families and social lives in New York City for unspecified periods of time. Besides that, they all sensed the displeasure of Bob Huot, who felt his home and his new work life were being invaded by these women. If this was utopia, it was a bit different from the fellowship of poverty they had shared in New York. But they still believed, with their leader, that what they were doing produced good in the world. "We were like people who went out and dug coal, and brought it up and made heat," Rudner told writer Laura Shapiro. "We were going into that studio and being laborers."

Isabel Garcia-Lorca had wanted to dance all her life. Her intellectual European family (she is the niece of the famous playwright) disapproved of dancing although they didn't stigmatize the other performing arts. By the time she was seventeen she was resigned to giving up her dream—she was too old, she thought, to begin training seriously. To satisfy her family, she got a liberal arts degree at Barnard. After graduation she was holding down an aimless job at the information desk of the Metropolitan Museum of Art when a friend invited her to Tharp's performance there. Garcia-Lorca was bowled over. "I thought it was fabulous," she says. "Plus, I thought, Well, I could do this. I could be one of those extras."

She made contact with Tharp first by phone, to invite her to participate in a benefit concert for Bobby Seale and the Black Panthers that was being arranged in St. Paul's Chapel at Columbia by Garcia-Lorca's boyfriend. Among the other artists were comedian Dick Gregory and rock-and-roll musician Country Joe. Tharp accepted. It was another opportunity to experiment. She laid out a space the size of a jail cell and put the dancers inside it: herself, Wright, Rudner, Raj, and Figueroa. According to Wright, she made several phrases, "some of them went on the ground, some of them were big, some were little and fast. . . . .And all five of us could put them together however we wanted to, but we were in this space all together, and of course *she* chose the big one. And it was supposed to make a statement about how to keep yourself mentally and physically together if you're in jail."

Garcia-Lorca says she doesn't remember much of the concert because she had decided to speak to Tharp afterwards. She nervously asked if there was any chance someone twenty-two years old, without any dance training, could still be a dancer. They had a long talk, during which Tharp discerned that Garcia-Lorca was highly intelligent and no dilettante, besides being unaffected, beautiful, and a natural mover. With intensive work it might be possible, she said. Garcia-Lorca would have to quit her job though, and come up to the farm where Tharp would work with her for two trial weeks. Garcia-Lorca agreed at once. The two weeks passed and Tharp didn't say anything. Garcia-Lorca went down to the city and got some more clothes.

From the spring of 1970 to the spring of 1971 the company flowed in and out of New Berlin. Breaking up the periods of intensive work were several important teaching residencies. For Amherst College in August Tharp made two country pieces, a "sowing of the seeds" piece and a forty-five-minute solo for Wright called *Rose's Cross Country*. Tharp's notes for this ambulatory variation include balletic steps that Wright excelled at, plus things like: "little drops enlarging, pick branch chew, slip fall, brush-off, twiddle hands s pattern, hand rhythms on leg maint s turning to back, 2 back falls." Then: "fouettés wiggle wiggle." Every day, Wright would dance this piece between buildings on the campus, trying to disregard the bewildered reactions of onlookers.

Following Amherst the company worked for two weeks with children's groups in three inner-city Boston neighborhoods: East Boston, Dorchester, and Hyde Park, leading up to Summerthing performances in three parks. Tharp didn't really know anything about juvenile dancers, but in New Berlin she invited two of the neighbor's children to come and learn some games the dancers were making up. According to Boston critic Jane Goldberg, during the workshop the Boston youths were quickly enlisted as teachers for newer arrivals.

The residencies, like the farm, served primarily as laboratory time for Tharp. She was making movement incessantly, trying it on dancers, putting it together different ways. She might not have had specific choreographic goals in mind, but the movement chunks would start to cohere and evolve, and eventually a dance would be made. Amherst saw the first performances of two unique works that have evolved over the years but have remained identified with her throughout her career, *The Fugue* and *The One Hundreds*.

Making up phrases was a discipline for Tharp, a task she set herself every day, like warming up or doing a barre. They poured out of her. During the spring before Amherst she taught Wright ten phrases a day, while also making movement for *The Fugue*. She was pondering contexts big enough to contain this flood of invention. Perhaps prompted by a dream of Margery Tupling's she had recorded in 1968, she was thinking about 150 combinations of eleven counts, maybe with three-second pauses in between. All 150 could be done by two soloists simultaneously, side by side, with the option of skipping the pause sometimes, or getting out of sequence by forgetting. Then five people would each do thirty of the phrases, without pauses, followed by 150 children doing one phrase each, simultaneously. Edited down by one-third, this colossal event became *The One Hundreds*, which Tharp subsequently put under the heading of "trying to get the world to dance so that they'd understand us." Tharp and Wright danced the first, marathon section; the five sets of twenty were done by Rudner, Garcia-Lorca, Douglas Dunn, and two apprentices who had been working at the farm, Elizabeth Fain and Sybille Hayn. The hundred civilians were rounded up and rehearsed when the dancers got to Amherst.

More densely structured but no less mind-boggling was *The Fugue*, a series of variations for three women. Tharp compared it to a man's game, like chess. Men had "the time and the interest to examine a process," a luxury she didn't think was ordinarily granted to women. *The Fugue* demonstrated that a dance can be abstract and compelling at the same time. Without musical accompaniment, three women (Tharp, Rudner, and Wright) danced a series of variations on an initial phrase. The rhythms ranged from rapid-fire tattoos to edgy suspensions and hair-trigger canons. With little upper-body elaboration, like tap dancers, they stomped out the intricate counterpoint patterns with a businesslike yet comradely efficiency.

The Fugue's original phrase is done twenty times, with the dancers in different spatial relationships to each other and to the audience. The phrase revolves in different directions, moves upstage and downstage. It retrogrades and inverts in sequence. It's done in double time and with different meters. Over the years it has acquired built-in ornaments and stylistic additives. It's a demonstration of invention and counterpoint, deliberately acknowledging Bach. Severe yet playful, *The Fugue* was seen by some of its early critics as a militant feminist statement. Since its first all-women version it has been danced by all-men and by mixed-gender casts.

In performance *The Fugue* and *The One Hundreds* represent contrasting ways to reconcile the art/life dichotomy. The movement for *The Fugue* cranks up everyday walks, turns, stamps, and slaps to acute levels of timing and structural virtuosity that only highly sensitive dancers can manage. In *The One Hundreds*, ordinary people get to approach a small task: mastering one nontechnical phrase that requires them to give extended, dancerly concentration to problems of coordination, timing, placement, and exact repeatability.

Tharp started work on *The Fugue* with Wright and Garcia-Lorca; she didn't intend to be in the piece herself. When Rudner returned to the farm from a trip to Europe with her then partner Douglas Dunn, who was touring with Merce Cunningham's company, Tharp decided *The Fugue* would be too demanding for Garcia-Lorca and finished making it for herself and Rudner with Wright. Skeletal and intricate, *The Fugue* was performed in an atmosphere of almost religious concentration. At Amherst it was done every day at three o'clock in a small meeting-house building. Tharp liked the sound of their sneakers on the floor and made a tape recording of it. At the end of the residency, when they performed it outside, she used the tape as accompaniment. For this performance, people turned on their car headlights as darkness settled over the field.

Tharp took advantage of every opportunity to perform. She usually gave titles to the phrase clusters in progress, so they could be shown in some kind of coherence even before they had totally evolved into dances. She used old dances as training material for newly arrived dancers, and in November of 1970 she showed ten minutes' worth of old and new work at Judson Church, where the downtown dance world was celebrating the publication of Don McDonagh's *The Rise and Fall and Rise of Modern Dance*. This was the first book on the Cunningham/Judson dance revolution, and Tharp was the subject of a whole chapter. All the major figures were performing, including Trisha Brown and Yvonne Rainer, but it was Meredith Monk who turned the occasion into a scandal. Monk had at first refused to take part; she thought the book had serious flaws. At the last minute she appeared. Dressed in white with her hair in braids all over her head, she played the Jews' harp and chanted a litany of McDonagh's offenses. The audience cheered. But Tharp was furious; she liked McDonagh and thought Monk's gesture was disrespectful.

For the Judson appearance Tharp rounded up some extra dancers, and either during the one-week rehearsal period or right after the concert, she held an audition. The people selected would go up to work with her at the farm. Two of her top choices had just arrived in New York to feast on the array of dance there. Kenneth Rinker danced with Tharp in the McDonagh tribute, but he was studying with Merce Cunningham and decided it wasn't the right time for him to take off. It wasn't until a year later that he joined the company, becoming its first male dancer. Dana Reitz had just graduated from the University of Michigan. She heard about the audition from Rudner at the Cunningham studio. When she saw Wright and Rudner dancing "fast and furious," she was stunned. This would be a great learning experience, she thought. She quit her job as a nanny on Staten Island and, with the rest of the group, drove up to the farm on Thanksgiving Day, as Tharp insisted they do.

This time, the dancers lived in a small house down the road. One person would stay at the big house with Tharp when Huot was away. They cooked huge meals for themselves after the long days of rehearsing, but the life was still hard. Reitz remembers that the attic studio was cold, and that her mind and muscles were stretching all the time to keep up with what Tharp demanded. There was no regular class, but after each person did her own warm-up routine in the morning, either Rudner or Wright would lead a ballet barre. Then they would spend hours learning phrases and working on them. Tharp was in the middle stages of her pregnancy, and she would demonstrate her ideas for a videotape, expecting the dancers to refer to it when she needed to rest. Reitz found this very difficult, but she was amazed at Wright's ability to pick up and translate any movement from tape, and then, as Tharp was demonstrating and inventing, "[Wright] could reverse it and invert it and retrograde . . . then remember that version, and remember the retrograde version."

When Tharp and six dancers went off to Oberlin College for three weeks in January, she had prepared a quantity of material called *The History of Up and Down*. It included the Exercise Book, which she thought of as a training manual for Isabel Garcia-Lorca, the member with the least dance technique. One set of exercises could serve for the beginning students at Oberlin and one would suit the intermediates. With Wright, Rudner, and the other dancers as teachers and captains, the company worked with students every morning and rehearsed alone in the afternoons.

The Oberlin residency was organized by Brenda Way, a graduate of the college who had just been hired to teach dance and create an interarts program. She had met Tharp in New York shortly after *Dancing in the Streets* and was immediately impressed by her intellect and the way she worked. For the free-form winter term, Way raised the money to bring in Tharp and company. The dance program at Oberlin, as in most American colleges at the time, had been struggling to gain status as an art discipline, and had finally worked its way out of the Athletics Department and into Theater Arts. Tharp thought this was a bad idea, says Brenda Way. "She thought I had made a terrible mistake . . . we should have stayed in the Athletics because that's where the money was." As if to prove her point, Tharp commandeered all the resources she could, and made two versions of the prepared material, one for the open space of the field house and one for the theater, with the same material rearranged by chance and minutely keyed to a computerized light plot. *The History of Up and Down* was a kind of choreographic nexus: at least three entities

THE END OF AMAZONIA 1969-1971   ∞ 49

wove together, exchanged information, and separated out again. Besides the Exercise Book, which the beginning and intermediate students performed along with the company in the field house showing, the movement came from the draft material Tharp called the Willie Smith series.

In New Berlin, with the cumbersome but workable videotape recorder she had acquired after the Amherst and Boston residencies, she aimed the camera on her increasingly pregnant self as she did her daily improvisation sessions. She was making up phrases as usual, and factoring the changing condition of her body into her creative investigations. For background music she happened to have on hand some records of stride pianist Willie "the Lion" Smith. At the Oberlin field house, in her seventh month, she performed the Willie Smith material as a solo. Brenda Way says that as a feminist during the Oberlin residency she was enthusiastic about the novel idea of a pregnant woman dancing. She remembers Tharp as a "solid round middle, and these legs flying all around. The strongest image I have of the whole residency is of Twyla dancing."

After the solo she led the students in a snake-dance version of the basic phrases. Accompanying this was another record from her stash in the attic, featuring the jazz pianist Jelly Roll Morton and his Red Hot Peppers. While the intermediate students did their Exercise Book, the company dancers went through the Willie Smith material. Spaced out over half the gym floor in practice mode, they did slow lunges and reaches with sudden arm gestures and fast head rolls, gradually building up the intensity into flinging turns and jittering step trills. Combined and reworked, these segments made up the dance called *Eight Jelly Rolls*. Willie Smith's music reemerged ten years later to accompany the suave ensemble piece *Baker's Dozen*.

Tharp was dancing and thinking even more expansively after her son Jesse Huot was born, on 10 March 1971. She thought pushing herself to move bigger and broader would be an efficient way to get back in shape. And she had taken on what was going to be the biggest of her nonproscenium pieces yet. Charles Reinhart had offered her a commission to do an environmental New York City work, and she decided nothing less than a dance that encompassed all of Manhattan Island would be appropriate. She wanted to put the dancers on a barge, dancing broadly enough so that people in apartments bordering the rivers could see their performance. When she encountered snags in implementing this scheme, she settled for three spaces, two in lower Manhattan and one uptown, all of them free and highly visible. The dance would surround a single day, 28 May, beginning in Fort Tryon Park at sunrise, continuing in Battery Park at lunchtime, and concluding in the evening at City Hall. Tharp, Rudner, and Wright performed the basic dance material for all three sections. The first was set to the Baroque music of Giuseppi Torelli, and *Torelli* became the umbrella title for the three sections, "Sunrise," "Midday March," and "Evening Raga."

Part One was, according to Wright, "a very exhausting little piece," where the phrases were first demonstrated in silence and then put together at the dancers' discretion, to Torelli's music. Wright remembers a "leg phrase, an arm phrase, a floor phrase and a fast little phrase." Hardly anyone showed up at Fort Tryon Park—not surprising at 6:30 A.M. No sooner had they finished the dance when a large group of spectators appeared, having first gone to the wrong place. The dancers repeated everything for this audience. At Battery Park, Tharp had enlisted a marching band from a Brooklyn high school to play Sousa in formations that intersected with the dance. Fourteen extra dancers rehearsed gratis for three weeks at Wagner College to augment the marches.

City Hall proved the biggest challenge. The city's official welcoming site, Tharp reasoned, was Gracie Mansion, the mayor's residence, but she couldn't persuade anyone to let her use it, so she accepted the elegant, Federal-period City Hall as second choice. She intended to have each dancer accompanied by her own musician playing Indian ragas in the rotunda, and a mechanical player-piano cranking out rags in another space, with the audience and dancers going between them. To interviewers for *Ballet Review* she gave a fanciful explanation of the connection between rags and ragas: the dance consisted of "fairly elaborate improvisations along the lines of things that are done in Indian palaces."

But there was trouble about Kermit Love's costumes—white pants with halter tops in a silky, quasi-Indian fabric, pink with gold embroidery— which were delivered at the last minute. These were the first real costumes made for the company since Huot's last designs, *Group Activities* and *After "Suite."* Tharp felt self-conscious about her body less than three months after giving birth. Rudner and Wright thought the costumes were too fancy and simply refused to wear them. So Tharp told the audience they'd decided the floor was too dirty to risk spoiling them. They performed, as they had for the past two years, in ordinary clothes.

In addition to the costume snafu, city officials wouldn't let the player-piano into the building—in these days of anti-establishment protests, City Hall could be a target for a slightly mad artist with a hidden bomb. The performance went ahead with the Indian musicians seated to one side of the City Council Chamber and the dancers punching a little tape recorder to play their piano-roll selections. All the movement was improvised.

In the months between Oberlin and *Torelli* Tharp's concentration was severely tried. Dancers came and went. There were difficult visits from parents after Jesse was born. Huot and Tharp's father had a couple of arguments, which Tharp suspected were a contributing cause of her father's death from a heart attack later that spring. Huot wasn't taking on as much of the responsibility for the baby's care as she had expected, and she regarded nursing and diapering as barely tolerable distractions. The stress of her double life increased, as she juggled the baby, the farm, the tensions with Huot, and her burgeoning career.

She and Huot were no longer on the same page artistically. At the start of their relationship they had shared searching discussions about the meaning and purpose of art, and Huot's already-established minimalism buttressed her initial goal of stripping away everything to get down to core dance values. Like him, she was unconventional, she didn't crave material comforts, let alone luxuries, and she had a highly developed conscience, a determination to live by her own ethics. But these affinities held them together for only so long. Huot wanted a wife whose main occupation was the traditional family he thought they were starting. Tharp knew another child would put an impossible strain on her career. She had given her marriage a heroic try but it was clear her heart was in her creative work.

At the same time as she was making the motions of closing down the company, Paul Epstein, an attorney and founder of the pro-bono Volunteer Lawyers for the Arts, had initiated the process of incorporating Tharp Dance as a nonprofit organization. After Oberlin Tharp let all the dancers go, but almost immediately following Jesse's birth, Wright, Rudner, Garcia-Lorca, Reitz, and two other dancers reappeared to start rehearsals. She tried commuting in to New York with Huot and Jesse, but the periods when she stayed in the loft grew longer and longer. During the summer she and the baby moved into 104 Franklin Street full-time. Essentially her marriage was over, although she didn't complete her divorce from Huot until 1974.

4

The Entertainer

1971–1973

At the farm Tharp had sampled utopia and discovered its limits. Now she embarked on another principled experiment, one that would be equally hard to sustain. She intended to find a path between remaining aloof from the culture of dance production and becoming enmeshed in it. To separate from Bob Huot and take up her life in New York again was only an initial move toward what she wanted, which was nothing less than creative independence *and* material success.

To Huot, the farm symbolized a rejection of the art world's career-building machinery. "I realized early on that I was going to have to be my own patron," he says, and by the end of the '60s he felt he no longer needed to cultivate moneymaking contacts or public visibility. In fact, one of his last projects, a series of sand paintings in homage to the Oglala Sioux, wasn't seen by anyone and couldn't be put on the market. In about 1971 he obtained the keys to the Paula Cooper Gallery, where he had exhibited in previous years. After closing time, he would go in with his sand and dry pigments, and create "these rather beautiful things" on the floor. Next morning, before the staff arrived, he'd return and sweep away the night's work. The only trace of it would be a small card he tacked to the baseboard of the room he'd worked in. "I think I was probably *the* most minimal minimalist," he says. Tharp was unwilling to take conceptual art to such an extreme.

Dancing in the Streets played hide-and-seek with the audience, but the dancing, after all, was what she most wanted them to see.

In the 1970s America experienced a period of unprecedented interest in the arts. Not only had the big funding structures been established on the national, state, and municipal levels, the tax laws made it attractive for individuals and businesses to channel significant dollars to art work and performance. The media reflected this healthy cultural activity with generous coverage and programming. Dance was routinely being mentioned alongside the other arts for the first time. Companies and schools that had never before developed strong institutional means for survival now became more stable. A broader, more knowledgeable public was being cultivated through touring performances and special shows on TV. The obvious course for any artist was to establish oneself as a nonprofit business and enter the subsidized world. In the case of a choreographer with a company to pay, studio space to rent, creative collaborators and managers to be enlisted, productions to be designed and built, this transition was mandatory.

Tharp made the necessary gesture. She had taken the first steps to qualify the company for public funding, and early in 1971 she met a young lawyer who wanted to help. William Peter Kosmas was starting an independent law practice after working for the firm of Greenbaum, Wolff and Ernst. He wasn't a dance fan, but through an associate who dated a dancer, he learned that Tharp might need a manager. He had seen the *Fugue* and the *One Hundreds* at the 1970 Delacorte dance festival in Central Park, and he was interested.

Between 1962 and 1980 the Delacorte Theater, an outdoor thrust stage built for Joseph Papp and the New York Shakespeare Festival, became an end-of-the-summer showcase for New York dance. Offering free tickets and a chance to see several different attractions in one evening, the series was extremely popular with the faithful, and lured new audiences as well. In 1970 Tharp and a group that included Rudner, Wright, Garcia-Lorca, Douglas Dunn, and two women they'd picked up in one of their Boston-area residencies appeared on a marathon evening with five other downtown choreographers. Tharp had asked for the closing spot. The Tharps wore their usual noncostumes, and the intricate *Fugue*, followed by the *Hundreds*, added up to an hour of uncompromising choreography. It was almost midnight before the company plus 104 extras delivered their eleven-second punch line. What remained of the audience broke out in cheers, hisses, boos, and loud arguments. Bill Kosmas didn't understand the controversy but he was intrigued with "this determined little figure . . . in sloppy sweatwear" who could provoke such a strong reaction.

She arrived at his office sometime in January or February of 1971. Pregnant with Jesse and probably dressed in her usual dumpy working attire, she made an incongruous entrance, lugging shopping bags full of canceled checks, bills, and company business that had never been properly recorded. The dapper Kosmas, who was wearing one of his handmade Italian suits, whisked "this beleaguered little person" past the disbelieving eyes of his office mates. They talked things over and he thought he could help her, although he refused to deal with her jumbled bookkeeping. "I was intrigued by someone who would make such demands and requests," he says, "and I thought it betrayed either great despair or a great sense of humor or chutzpah, or all of it." He doesn't remember a formal arrangement between them, but at the end of the meeting she said, "You'll do."

Company members and outside observers agree that it was Kosmas who turned the company around by convincing Tharp she needed to make her work more personable. He saw no point in forcing the audience to work so hard to see it. At first Kosmas regarded Tharp as a kind of savage, a strange young woman who was "sort of ashamed for not knowing how to walk around properly or what it meant to walk around properly." He thought a certain antimaterialistic primitivism had rubbed off on her from Bob Huot: "You don't wear nice clothes because that's decadent." The dancers' downscale style, on and offstage, was only partly attributable to their poverty-level income, Kosmas thought. They treated costuming "as though it were some sort of moral or ethical issue as opposed to what's most effective onstage. . . . I didn't think it was a question of good and bad, I thought it was a question of what would convey best what they were doing."

Whether prompted by Kosmas or not, after the birth of Jesse, Tharp was indeed evaluating her ragamuffin image along with everything else in her shifting life. Dana Reitz, who was rehearsing at the farm in the spring, watched Tharp building up a resolve "that she was going to become a famous choreographer. She sort of looked at everything and she said, I have to go for this. . . . She noticed that we were a mess and that she was a mess too. She made us clean up our clothes." The fastidious Reitz was dismayed. "I had worked so hard to get the look of the Twyla company, which was very disheveled." Tharp put Garcia-Lorca in charge of buying proper clothes for the dancers, no easy task in New Berlin. It was all part of the new plan. Says Reitz: "I think she just decided, no, she was not gonna be the housewife, in the country, with some dancers some of the time. She was gonna have to do this seriously."

The company had received another prestigious invitation, to appear in Paris at the International Festival of the Dance in November 1971, and in September they were booked at the Delacorte again. For the Central Park performance, Tharp scheduled a repeat of *The Fugue* and the New York premiere of *Eight Jelly Rolls*. Kermit Love made striking new costumes for *The Fugue*, which had been given before in motley clothes. The dancers wore black tailored jackets nipped in at the waist with three-quarter sleeves, and black pants in different lengths—short shorts for Tharp, knickers for Rudner, and calf-length gaucho pants for Wright. The miked stage floor amplified the shifting rhythms of their high suede boots. The *Jelly Rolls* were danced in the unused white pants from *Torelli* and brightly colored undershirts dressed up with little cutout holes near the neckline. Two Oberlin students joined the cast as apprentices. Kosmas insisted all six dancers get really good haircuts at Vidal Sassoon's salon—and let the public know about it. Professionally styled hair, even more than dressy costumes, signified Tharp's transit into a new sphere. She programmed the two pieces so that the austere and demanding *Fugue* would be followed by the affable *Eight Jelly Rolls*.

A series of videotaped records makes it possible to trace the development of *Eight Jelly Rolls* from its first performance in the field house of Oberlin College to its polished, possibly final form on a London Weekend Television broadcast three years later. These records, and other documentation of Tharp's early choreography, confirm how absolutely sui generis her dance was. It didn't look like the full-bodied, sculptural yearnings of modern dance, or the antitechnical perambulations of the avant-garde. It resisted both the musical theater and the dancehall, where jazz music normally accompanied dancing. It certainly wasn't proper and virtuosic like ballet, though it employed the ballet's vocabulary and strong, adaptable bodies.

In some notes for a lecture she gave at Oberlin, Tharp explained that she had not intended *Eight Jelly Rolls* as a stage work; it had been transplanted to the theater because a basketball game preempted the field house. Naturally, she could not present the dance on the stage the same way as she had in the open space, she said. So she had worked out a very elaborate way of coordinating the dance phrases, which she reconfigured by randomizing them on a computer and appending them to a "score" or lighting plot. Each of the eighty-six lighting instruments was correlated with "specific fractions of the dance materials." So when a certain instrument was in use, the dancers could do the corresponding phrase. This took long hours to put together and rehearse, and Tharp and lighting designer Lee Herman simplified their chart-making for the latter parts of the dance. What resulted was a fragmented, half-invisible performance. The audience accompanied it with derisive clapping. Brenda Way described "an excruciatingly specific time score that was connected to the light plot. And that of course was enormously exciting for us and completely irritating for the audience because there was no through-line. So all the artsy people thought it was fantastic, and the general audience thought, why did you bring this person?"

Eight months later, when *Eight Jelly Rolls* appeared on a stage for the second time, there would be no such experimental challenges. Tharp says she noted the places where she got laughs at Oberlin and cut out all the "technical problems" except ones that "were so fiendishly difficult that even the audience could delight in their perversity."

In form, the first four *Jelly Rolls* remained fairly constant throughout the dance's later evolution. At Oberlin Tharp incorporated the intermediate students to make a large ensemble, but in the company version three or four dancers backed up the core trio. Although the dance has no narrative, it does have a theatrical build. It begins with Wright dancing solo, then introduces Rudner and Tharp, completing the core trio. Rudner solos, the other members of the group enter and Tharp solos against them, there are small solos for the members of the group, a solo for Wright against the group, and a finale with everyone dancing their individual phrases simultaneously. The company thus emerges in a smoothly expanding sequence, and all the dancers complement each other in formal ways. Considering that Tharp hadn't really made a dance in the shape of a dance before, and that she hadn't abandoned her usual method of putting together phrases in no preconceived order, *Eight Jelly Rolls* is a gem of choreographic form.

But it was the movement, and the performers who created it, that captivated the audiences at the Delacorte. *Eight Jelly Rolls* is always referred to as a jazz piece, and the Jelly Roll Morton selections are authentic Dixieland, with a steady beat pumping behind successive instrumental solos and unifying choruses. Recorded around 1927, the music—grave, declarative, sometimes raunchy—comes directly out of the New Orleans funeral processions and saloons where jazz got started. At a time when the use of popular music of any kind was considered slumming on the concert dance stage, the *Jelly Rolls* astounded Tharp's Delacorte audience.

Tharp's relationship to music that carried so much cultural resonance was poorly understood. Although she quoted the Charleston, Suzy Q, shimmy, camel walk, Shorty George, and a dozen other steps, she put them through a process of metamorphosis and folded them imperceptibly into her own fusion style. For the 1974 broadcast of the dance on London Weekend Television, she explained how she applied techniques of inversion, retrograde, sudden changes of timing and direction, miniaturization and expansion, to render her sources almost unrecognizable. She further disguised them by eliminating the stops and starts between them, so that there were no obvious transitions or special emphases. Her dancers had become superb performers of this lightning-fast, multiplexed information. To her pre-*Jelly Rolls* audiences this loosely placed movement had often seemed untrackable or out of control. But when Tharp finally acknowledged the music, referring to and riffing on a regular beat, the whole enterprise gained coherence. The rhythmic variety, surprise, and humor that had been implicit moved out front. What had seemed intimidatingly cerebral in *The Fugue* and *The One Hundreds* now looked casual enough that anyone could do it.

Within this more accessible choreographic context, the core dancers projected as distinct personalities. Rudner was smooth and sensuous, and quick-witted. For the third Jelly Roll, she had a limited amount of material that she could put together however she wished in performance, so the solo was different every time. But whatever movements she was doing, Rudner always looked natural, composed. Rudner felt the *Jelly Rolls* was a watershed for the dancers because it brought all the improvisational possibilities into play. In a 1995 interview, she pointed out that Tharp disliked the casual connotations of the term improvisation: "I think she felt that it meant that we were making it up as we went along. When, in fact, they were like jazz improvisations. We had very specific material—just as you do with a song." For Rudner's solo, "Twyla said, 'Oh, everybody make a series of positions.' . . . So I put my arm here, I put my leg down there. And then she took me and she connected those positions, and we made an order out of them, which was the order that I had made them in. . . . [T]hat took up maybe one-eighth of the song. And the rest of the song was new combinations of time, space, and rhythm of that material . . . however I wanted them." Rudner remembered her duet with Wright in Number Two "had sections of intense unison and then . . . see how many of these arm gestures you can fit in before someone stamps their foot."

Wright, rebounding from her years as a ballet dancer, concerned herself with doing the movement, not with showing it to the audience. She says the transition from open spaces to stage performance was hard for her: "I hated that separation of audience and performer. And that's when I started questioning what I was doing separated from the audience. What I was doing up there, and they're in the dark. I always was about the process." Tharp thought of her as tough but trusting. "You don't mess around with a lady that big," she told the 1974 TV audience.

For her own solo, Tharp imported the experiments with weight and balance she'd made in the attic at New Berlin during her pregnancy. The first of several brilliant comic roles she played in her own work, the solo became a modern-dance analog of Charlie Chaplin's famous drunk scene in the 1916 two-reeler *One A.M.* Chaplin staggered and maneuvered through the clutter of what was presumably his own house, unable to recognize any of the objects or figure out how they worked. Constantly misjudging or making the wrong connections, he thought up shrewd but bizarre solutions, and finally went to sleep in the bathtub. Tharp performed her solo locked into a state of half-consciousness. On the 1974 video, she doesn't seem to know where she is or what her immediate surroundings might mean. The other dancers are doing their own somnambulistic slow dance behind her, a "drill" phrase of over one hundred counts, in which precise unison frays into individual interpretations of left and right. Tharp, in front of them, senses their momentum but can't figure out which one of them she should synchronize with. Weaving, skidding, lurching, flopping forwards or sideways and jerking upright again, she falls, has trouble assembling her limbs to get up. She dimly hears the music; its most emphatic notes jar her like a noise in the night, but she can't hang on to the thread of its rhythm. She staggers toward the wings, rockets back on a series of unpredictable cadences from the band, and finally collapses on her face.

Tharp, Rudner, and Wright danced with a certain inner focus at that time, which became part of the company's performing style. It was similar to the neutral performing attitude adopted by all avant-gardists. Besides that, the Tharp dancers had a lot of internal information and choices to pull together. They showed their concentration, but they also had rehearsed so long that the movement felt comfortable; they could be themselves. Rudner and Garcia-Lorca projected a fashion model's self-awareness; Wright seemed to want to shut out the audience and dance for herself alone; Tharp could look obstinate, challenging, and, in the Drunk solo, befuddled. Detachment, even alienation, might have served as a protective device for all the countercultural dancers, Tharp included, but for her, objectivity was a classical value as well. As the film historian Gerald Mast points out, one can't identify too closely with the audience one wants to reform: "The greatest film comedians are antisocial, but in this antagonism they reveal a higher morality."

Through some alchemy that clicked into operation with the *Jelly Rolls*, choreographic tropes that Tharp had used so often before to diversify the dance action now also facilitated personal interplay. Game structures, individual variations, unison, and the digression from unison, all reappear in the *Jelly Rolls*, but here they read as the activity of a slightly dopey bunch of people who find themselves together in a dance. As soon as they realize they're all doing the same thing, one of them veers off on her own. For Number Six, thinking of the way musicians in a Dixieland band step out and take solos, Tharp made little variations for each dancer apart from the ensemble. To make sure the audience won't be distracted, the backup group make their moves as small as possible. In the next section, Wright seems to noodle around languidly, and the group, behind her, captures and holds her shape in a series of "dots," or poses that they've learned by precisely imitating her performance on a videotape. Tharp may have borrowed the "dots" from Fred Astaire, whose backup chorus in the title number of *Top Hat* copied and held his first few moves. Even here, the Tharps make the transitions between the dots in their own ways. The last Jelly Roll is a companionable ensemble of solos, where the dancers have a pool of material they can draw from and structure on the spot.

On the London tape, the dance completed its transformation into stageworthiness with the addition of new and androgynous costumes by Kermit Love: black pants with backless tops made to look like tuxedo shirt-fronts, and patent-leather pumps. Kenneth Rinker, Tom Rawe, and Nina Wiener had joined Tharp, Wright, Rudner, and Garcia-Lorca in the company, and Tharp had made individual solos for all of them in the last sections.

With the 1971 Delacorte performance Tharp could no longer be written off as a brainy malcontent who disregarded the audience. In *The Fugue* and the *Jelly Rolls* she emerged as a choreographic giant who could command at least two different styles. Many of her most provocative gestures, like the box in *Re-Moves* and the nudity in *PYMFFYPPMFYNM YPF*, had been earnestly offered for the audience's own good, to open their eyes to more possibilities, and the *Jelly Rolls* were no different. She had simply decided to be entertaining. She wasn't a newcomer to jazz either, she just hadn't played it in performance. As more than one critic observed, *Eight Jelly Rolls* wasn't a drastic departure from what Tharp had been doing all along, but it did seem, in that single September performance, that she was releasing something she'd been holding back for a long time. At last she was fully acknowledging the music, the dance, and the audience, as necessary and equal components of her work.

Clive Barnes, who always seemed baffled by Tharp but wanted to believe, lost interest in *The Fugue* after the first few minutes, and he mistook the sound of the dancers' feet for a percussion accompaniment. But Barnes could see the *Jelly Rolls* was something different, "far more approachable," even though he overinterpreted it as "an essay in abstract jazz dance and urban despair." Critics for the mass press hated having to take Tharp seriously, and *Cue* magazine's Greer Johnson dismissed the Delacorte segment as "two gawky, interminable essays by the humorless (or deadpan?) Twyla Tharp Company."

Arlene Croce's admiring analysis appeared in the winter issue of *Ballet Review*. Tharp suited Croce's taste for nerveless brilliance: "Twyla Tharp's subject is not your life or hers, and in that sense she is a classical artist. She doesn't present herself as a force for change or as a vehicle for new ideas, and her aggressiveness is not the least bit hostile in its attitude toward the audience. She is radically different and radically new, but, whatever else you may think of it, after about a minute her kind of dancing doesn't even look strange. You find you can take more and more of it."

Tharp didn't appear in New York City again for a year, but the buzz circulated around the country as the company toured. The 1971–72 season was momentous for her. With the *Jelly Roll* material essentially shaped and put before the public, she began to process the personal crises she'd gone through—the birth of her son, the end of her marriage, and the death of her father—as she prepared *The Bix Pieces*. She had received her first significant funding, grants from the National Endowment for the Arts and the New York State Council on the Arts, and the first of two John Simon Guggenheim fellowships for choreography. *Harper's Bazaar* named her one of the hundred outstanding women in America. In April 1972 she won a prestigious Brandeis University Creative Arts Citation for younger artists— Merce Cunningham got the Medal of Achievement for his lifetime work. At the award ceremony at the Whitney Museum, Tharp gave her thousand-dollar prize, in two equal checks, to Sara Rudner and Rose Marie Wright. Later on she said, "You can't get to feeling safe and secure, or else you'll never get on with your work. I needed to pass on that money, and the dancers deserve it more than I do." She certainly wasn't taking her success for granted; she bit into it like a juicy plum.

Although *The Bix Pieces* became her second big hit, it started inauspiciously. The producers of the Paris International Festival had booked Tharp and former Cunningham dancer Viola Farber for two weeks on the 1971 program, partly on the advice of Bénédicte Pesle. Perhaps because both choreographers were reputedly avant-garde, they were assigned the Théâtre de la Cité Universitaire, a "less bourgeois" venue than the more centrally located and familiar Théâtre du Champs-Elysées, where the Batsheva Dance Company of Israel was to appear later on. Still operating on her antitheatrical instincts, Tharp wanted to perform in an open space, or a theater *and* an open space, as she told an interviewer, maybe hoping to fulfill her thwarted two-space plan for *Torelli*. She was given a huge gallery at the Cité Universitaire, while Farber appeared in a small theater with a company from Sunda, West Java, that was doing traditional Indonesian dance. All three groups shared the evening. Tharp was programmed last, and the audience balked at having to move to a new space for a performance that didn't begin until nine o'clock. What Tharp had in store was hardly designed to appease them.

Preparations didn't go well. The hall was too big and the floor was too slippery. Bill Kosmas hadn't arranged the season and this was his first tour with a dance company. While he anxiously argued with the sponsors about lighting and sound arrangements, Tharp watched rehearsals hunched at one end of the space with a towel over her head. The floor was scrubbed and doused with Coca Cola to eliminate excessive wax, and the dancers had to rubberize the bottoms of their shoes for safety. Nevertheless, someone fell at every performance. Tharp refused to dance *The One Hundreds* and Rudner had to step in for her. Normally the two initiators would perform side by side, relying on their kinesthetic radar to keep together, but Rudner only knew eighty of the phrases, so for security she and Wright faced each other. Though the *Bix* had been rehearsed in jazz shoes, Tharp decided on low heels for the women at the last minute, compounding the dangers of the slippery floor. "It completely destroyed the movement," Wright says. "We cried." The seats were arranged in sparse rows at each end of the long, narrow space. To compensate for the anticipated visibility problems, Tharp hit on the idea of stationing the dancers in separate spotlit areas for *Torelli* and inviting the audience to walk around them like sculptures. This didn't endear her to the unadventurous Parisians either.

The press was generally hostile to the whole Cité Universitaire program. Some liked Farber for her obvious technical authority and her connection to Cunningham, whom they dared not disrespect. The Indonesians had a certain exotic appeal. But Tharp offended nearly everyone, provoking the French critics to outdo each other with derisive remarks. *Le Figaro* announced that there was nothing but pretension in the company's humorless, unprofessional, and unspectacular performance. This was mild. "Poor Torelli!" mourned Jean-Pierre Barbe in *L'Aurore*. "How could they massacre such beautiful music! The dancers . . . with shocking vulgarity and heaviness, devote themselves to a sort of acrobatic jerk. . . ." He resented having to "endure this hairy and untidy outburst" and took the dancers in the spotlights to be a Happening, whose only advantage was that it allowed him to slip away through the ambulatory audience.

But there were proponents, principally Claude Sarraute of *Le Monde*, who appreciated Tharp's choreographic invention, the subtlety of the dancers' rhythm and their articulate bodies. The game-playing aspect of her work reminded him of the early days of abstract painting. John Percival came over from London and praised both Tharp and Farber, especially Tharp, for their originality. After the Festival was over, Kosmas waged a bitter fight with the sponsors, who accused Tharp of artistic fraud and refused to pay her fee until threats of a lawsuit forced them to ante up most of it. Tharp later acknowledged that the arrangements for the appearance had been unrealistic—the location too far out to attract a big enough audience to cover the sponsors' expenses in making the space workable. Her tour contracts after that became microscopically detailed.

For some reason, none of the French critics mentioned *The Bix Pieces* by name, which originally was *True Confessions*, or *Les Vraies Confessions*. The *Bix* contained Tharp's true confession—perhaps her first formal acknowledgment of what she was doing—a spoken script that accompanied part of the dance. Historically the *Bix* surfaces as a more important work than the *Jelly Rolls*, with the script to give it intellectual validation and an ongoing material existence. The two dances have chronological and stylistic connections, and they both were preserved and aired in professionally produced telecasts soon after their initial performances. Musically contemporaneous, they made a pair, one black jazz, one white. It could be argued that the *Jelly Rolls* is a more coherent and, for Tharp, a riskier work, a suite of dances in a unified choreographic and musical style, while *The Bix Pieces* mixes musical sources, dance ideas, and verbal narration. It's a collage, a lecture-demonstration in the form of a theater dance. Conceptually layered and inclusive, the *Bix* reveals Tharp's thinking more openly, if theatrically, than almost any of her other works.

As recorded for television's *Camera Three* in 1973, Tharp begins the dance in a follow spot, twirling a baton, a reference to her own overeducated childhood. Her solo distills a cluster of Americana references she would have absorbed as a cute, precocious little girl who spent a large part of her life in dancing school and at the movies. Her hair cut short with bangs screening off her gaze, Tharp wore another of Kermit Love's tuxedo-front tops, with short shorts in gray satin, sheer black hose and little low-heeled pumps that flattered her shapely legs. All the *Bix* costumes exposed the dancers' backs and shoulders, slyly drawing attention to their bodies. In most of Tharp's work from this point on, sex appeal seethes below the surface, subliminally heating up the cool performing atmosphere being cultivated.

Tharp was fantastic at playing two theatrical games at once. In her baton solo, she diluted the wiles of the music hall performer with the impassivity of the avant-garde trickster. To the legendary jazz musician Bix Beiderbecke playing his piano piece "In a Mist," she steps from foot to foot, keeping her body moving in slow shrugs, twists, and head turns. Without missing a beat, she catches a second baton thrown to her from off-camera, and briefly twirls two-handed. She drops one baton, glances at it, then catches another and another, trundling ahead like some gallant but maladroit comedian of the low stage. At one point, the offstage prop person goes amok and batons fly at her so fast she ends up with a fistful, which she drops. Finally she throws the last one down and leaves.

Like *Eight Jelly Rolls*, *The Bix Pieces* introduces each member of the company against the accumulating group, in four more bouncy recordings featuring Beiderbecke playing cornet, with Paul Whiteman's 1920s dance band and vocalist Bing Crosby. Tharp and Rudner begin a playful, girlish duet that slides in and out of a fox-trot. Tharp retrieves the drum-majorette struts and swaggers she hinted at in her solo. Rudner kicks, shakes her shoulders, and skips, with the innocent awareness of a Lolita. Wright is more purposeful, with spiky hand gestures and head jerks, as Rudner and Tharp do a sort of droopy chorus line around her. Garcia-Lorca's solo is the slowest of all, with luxurious leg gestures and tiny wiggles, against the trio's doodling.

When Kenneth Rinker appears, with Rudner, he uses less torso articulation but a lot of legs and arms. Wright and Garcia-Lorca join them soon to complete the ensemble. The dancers have appeared in the order in which they joined the company, a practice Tharp maintained in company listings and program credits until 1991.

Having gotten the introductions out of the way and pretty much dispensed with Bix Beiderbecke, Tharp now gets to the heart of *The Bix Pieces*, the extraordinary text called "Why They Were Made." The *Camera Three* video cuts to Marian Hailey, dressed in flowing white blouse with a bow at the neck, satin breeches, and black stockings and pumps, a modern adaptation, perhaps, of an eighteenth-century dancing master's costume. Hailey, a professional actress, was one of several narrators for *The Bix Pieces* over the years. Garcia-Lorca wasn't in this part of the dance, and she delivered the text frequently until she left the company in 1974. Tharp herself stood in for an indisposed Hermione Gingold at a performance in Brooklyn in 1977. The text was deadly serious, even sentimental, and Hailey's polished, technical way of delivering it warded off the laughter that Tharp's audiences were always ready to let loose during this period.

"I hated to tap-dance when I was a kid," she says on behalf of Tharp, who at first is tapping off-camera. The script goes on to a recital of Tharp's early classes, then comes to an abrupt stop with her father. "My father died this Spring and this dance was to commemorate the time when he was young." Tharp imagines the life of the '20s as relaxed, innocent, "concerned with style," like Beiderbecke's music. For Tharp, style is a way of evoking the past and all its associations. But her deeper point is that regardless of style, the real content of art doesn't change from one era to the next. "It seems to me that art is a question of emphasis. That aesthetics and ethics are the same. That inventiveness resides first in choice and then in synthesis—in bringing it all together. That this action is repeated over and over again, the resolutions being somehow marvelously altered each time." This credo still underlies her choreography three decades later.

Tharp/Hailey describes the main components of her dance: lyricism translated as a flowing, nonpercussive rhythm; the illusion of fluidity that results from compressing many small pieces of movement into a very short duration; the amalgamation of seemingly different stylistic ideas; improvisation as a process where the performer makes choices among very well-known materials; and finally the certainty that art has a long, unfolding life: "Can anything be new, original, private?"

After Tharp's baton-and-tap vignette, the company members arrive again—Rudner, Wright, and Rinker—while Hailey continues the lecture. Rudner solos to illustrate the idea of lyricism. Wright plunges into seventeen punchy numbered moves that Hailey commands her to assemble into a swift but nonlinear web, the edges rounded off by the speed of the transitions. Wright and Rinker demonstrate a sequence of steps that have balletic names but that can be executed classically by Wright and with modern looseness by Rinker. To eyes now accustomed to the conflation of ballet and modern movement, Wright and Rinker don't seem that stylistically divergent. But even when Tharp used classically trained dancers—Wright was the first—they were never cookie-cutter paragons anyway. Wright had enough individuality and Rinker had enough technique so that they already embodied the fusion Tharp perfected during the next decade.

After this lesson, Hailey/Tharp reveals that all the movement for the *Bix* was choreographed to the Op. 76 Haydn string quartets. According to Wright, the whole dance was built on four phrases. Performed to the initial Beiderbecke/Whiteman songs, they take on the gloss and lightness Tharp felt would evoke her father's generation. During the step demonstration with Hailey, the music switches to Haydn's Adagio Rondo on a folk theme, known during the pre-Hitler era as the German national anthem ("*Deutschland über Alles*"). The quartet begins another set of variations on the phrases, sometimes pairing off and later working together. There were instructions for each variation, but throughout, the dancers were supposed to stick to the original phrase material even when they were pushing each other around or lifting one another.

For example, Wright would start a phrase and Rinker had to respond with a different one. Then they'd trade roles and continue with a new set. It's unlikely that the audience could identify the original phrases. Even if they appear intact at any point—perhaps Rudner's phrase is number one, Wright's is number two and so on—the dancers borrow pieces of each other's movement from the outset, and Tharp has done her compositional play with the shape, timing, size, and placement of the core movements. Rudner's little two-handed digging gesture across the body flowers into Wright's sudden full-body evocation of a Greek nymph. During the ballet-modern litany, when Wright does a grand battement, Rinker throws an arm high instead of a leg.

A brief coda for Wright, Rudner, Rinker, and Garcia-Lorca uses the material again, this time to a chorus of "Abide with Me" arranged for brass by

Thelonius Monk. Staying in a tight cluster, they begin a phrase, then turn and gesture percussively toward the center. After an instant's hold, they pivot out, unfurl another phrase, lock together, spin out. In the short space of the music, they generate extreme and unpredictable changes of speed, emphasizing the stops and starts, in pointed contrast to the fluidity of all the earlier dancing in the piece. "Can anything be new? original? private?"

The company toured New York State, the Midwest and Los Angeles early in 1972. By the time *The Bix Pieces* came to New York, in September at the Delacorte Theater, Tharp had made another jazz piece, almost offhandedly. *The Raggedy Dances* to Scott Joplin and other composers was quite elusive. It was still unfinished when Tharp decided to show it, unannounced, as a "sampler" after the *Bix* at the Delacorte. It had its official premiere a month later on an evening Tharp shared with the Erick Hawkins company, part of a big modern dance series at the ANTA theater. Then she began to cut the dance, eventually dropping two-thirds of its twenty-four minutes, and took herself out of the cast. After a few years on the road, the reduction became known as the *Rags Suite*.

The slouchy, rhythmic Tharp style was now established, although each new jazz piece differed slightly from the others. *Eight Jelly Rolls* had delivered the shock of Tharp as musical and fun, and *The Bix Pieces* drew the audience's attention to individual dancers and then to Tharp's spoken manifesto. *The Raggedy Dances* seems more settled. Not only the dancing style but the look of the stage began to seem characteristic of Tharp and no one else. Once again she used separate, even wildly unrelated musical selections, but *The Raggedy Dances* seemed continuous. People entered while other people were finishing a section, did contradictory riffs, then left, seemingly ignoring the music's entrance and exit signals. There was one section of more or less conventional unison movement—the big finale—but instead of lining up symmetrically and facing the audience for it, the five dancers moved in a flock, using only one side of the stage. In fact, the dancers frequently didn't orient themselves to the audience at all, but worked facing their partners. Soloists often seemed self-absorbed, inwardly focused.

The idea of simultaneous but uncoordinated activities had pervaded Merce Cunningham's dance for decades, and Tharp took to it. The more dancing she could produce, the better she liked it. With Cunningham, the audience could make its own choices among the different activities going on at the same time, pick out particular individuals to follow. But Cunningham's theatrical randomness was intentional and largely unedited. Tharp always operated with some internal organization in hand. The dancers shared a limited amount of choreographic material, seldom falling into unison but resounding off one another in canons and other displaced timing. They were working with a musical impulse even when they worked in silence or when they'd learned the movement to different music. Tharp's stage could look busy, highly energized, but there was some principle at work keeping it together. It felt harmonious even when it looked crazy. William Whitener, who later became a Tharp dancer, has commented on the relation between her dance and New York street life: "It's the amount of traffic on the stage. The way people maneuver through space with large groups of dancers on the stage. I mean it's of course all choreographed, but so are the streets of New York in their way."

Simultaneity also assured that each dancer would be seen in his or her own right. During the early '70s, when Tharp was making the transition to outright theatricality, she worked at the problem of how to help the audience sort out the people on the stage—without assigning permanent rankings to the members of the company. In *The Bix Pieces* she speaks of affording the soloist some consideration as against the chorus, and to her formalist mind this usually translated into counterpoint. Working with six or seven dancers, or a corps of twenty, she didn't resort to the usual balletic tactics of positioning clumps of people to frame or mimic the important dancers in front.

The "dots" section of the *Jelly Rolls* was one solution—as the backup group captured and held Rose Marie Wright's movement in a series of poses. In *The Bix Pieces* and the *Rags*, solo dancers and backups are usually doing contrasting but equally interesting movement. Their floor patterns set them apart from one another. With the soloist stationary, one or more other dancers will circle around her or drift back and forth. Sometimes they're linked rhythmically or choreographically, but sometimes their movement is quite different. During Wright's solo in the first part of the *Bix*, Tharp and Rudner scurry around like windup dolls, strut like drum majorettes, chase each other with little skipping steps, show off with slow extensions and stretches. During Garcia-Lorca's sexy solo, Tharp, Rudner, and Wright periodically lounge and slide against each other.

Another important contrapuntal device was the crossover. Tharp used it early in the *Jelly Rolls*, in her fast, shadowboxing appearances with Rudner.

The background crossover was well developed in Paul Taylor's work. In fact, Tharp had been a resentful participant in at least two of them (*Scudorama* and *Junction*) during her short career with Taylor—both required anonymous, crablike acrobatics across the floor. Later, Taylor arranged crossovers to open up suppressed layers of psychological or cultural meaning, as in the war scenes silhouetted behind the swinging Lindy Hoppers in *Company B*. Tharp used the device as a choreographic tool to provide contrast, to showcase the small units of the company, and frequently to add comic possibilities.

The *Rags* started out with an ambling, companionable duet for Rose Marie Wright and Ken Rinker, and proliferated into syncopations and good-natured gamesmanship that carried through as three other dancers appeared. Rudner, Garcia-Lorca, and Nina Wiener comprised the rest of the company at that time, but the casting shifted constantly during its two-year run as a complete piece. Tharp created a strange solo for herself in a two-piece purple bathing suit, featuring the slow rotations and body-part isolations of a stripper. The title of the music, Scott Joplin's "The Entertainer," was ironically applied to the solo. According to critic Deborah Jowitt, "She dances for a long time, looking with every passing minute smaller, lonelier, tireder. A stripper seen through the wrong end of a telescope . . ." Garcia-Lorca soon learned the solo from Tharp, and without much prompting she understood "that it was somebody doing something that she didn't really want to do, but knew that she was good at. And got some satisfaction from feeling a connection with the person watching her. But ultimately felt very alone." Tharp was certainly aware of the conflicting agendas inherent in a stripper's performance, and indeed in any dancing for the public. She no doubt experienced ambivalence about it herself, and years later, when she was approaching forty, she did a similar but more aggressive dance within a longer solo called 1903, to Randy Newman's insidious, voyeuristic "Suzanne."

As she had in *The Bix Pieces*, Tharp once again pointed out the relationship between the popular and the classical idiom, this time capping the *Rags* with a duet to Mozart's variations on "*Ah, vous dirai-je, Maman*," better known as "Twinkle, Twinkle, Little Star." Nothing about the five-minute sequence, made on Wright and Rudner, violated ragtime's easygoing reciprocity and intuitive rhythms, which had been seen in the rest of the dance, but somehow the classical purity of Mozart invoked swifter footwork and unmistakable counterpoint. The Mozart duet was made as a birthday present for Bill Kosmas; Rudner and Wright performed it for him at a party in the studio. Tharp's personal references weren't meant to be identified by the audience, but the initial tone of cordiality and casualness, the playful cross-purposes of the later sections, plus Tharp's mordant "Entertainer," gave the work texture.

The Delacorte and ANTA performances brought more enthusiastic reviews. Clive Barnes loved *The Bix Pieces,* and after *The Raggedy Dances'* official premiere he remarked: "her work has a mixture of sloe-eyed innocence and intense professionalism that I find totally endearing." Ellen W. Jacobs, soon to become a successful dance publicist, surveyed the entire ANTA Marathon in the alternative paper *Changes.* Jacobs found the six-week, twenty-one-company season disappointingly mainstream except for Tharp. Noting that the project hadn't attracted the general public as hoped, Jacobs asked, "Are modern dancers eternally doomed to dance for family and friends?"

Jacobs, one of the many young writers Tharp inspired to eloquent prose, noted the deceptively spontaneous look of the company in *The Raggedy Dances.* She went on to probe Tharp's "Entertainer," so different in tone from the nonchalance of the rest of the piece. "Where a strip teaser's movements are expansive and outward, hers are stingy and minimal— though definite. I shudder, yet my eyes are glued. . . . Aggressive in her privacy, she is seductive only in the questions her performance provokes. If anything the work is anti-sensual. Who is she performing for?"

Entertaining had become a necessary part of Tharp's drive for success, despite her mixed personal feelings about it. After *Eight Jelly Rolls,* the company took its first bows ever, instead of simply vanishing at the end of the performance, and critics recorded the event. Anticipating a tumultuous reaction to *The Bix Pieces,* she had prepared the *Raggedy* preview as an encore. From the inception of Tharp's jazz cycle, the audience, on its own, began to acknowledge individual sections of a dance. This broke all the rules. You were supposed to take in a modern dance silently and respectfully until the end, even if it was made in suite form. A live performance videotaped in Minneapolis in 1972, a month after *the Raggedy Dances* premiere, records frequent appreciative laughter and applause.

Perhaps more important for Tharp than the added critical validation was the fact that Robert Joffrey attended the Delacorte performance in September 1972. His second company, the Joffrey II, was performing a piece that night by its director, Jonathan Watts, but, prompted by his partner, Gerald Arpino, and others, he was also checking out the up-and-coming Tharp. Since the 1960s the extraordinary Robert Joffrey had been building a small ballet company, and he was in the process of acquiring for it the most extensive repertory of twentieth-century revivals in the history of American ballet. In addition to restoring landmark works from Diaghilev's Ballets Russes, the English choreographer Frederick Ashton, and the Americans George Balanchine, Jerome Robbins, and Agnes de Mille, he mounted a few choice nineteenth-century items and programmed new works by himself and his resident choreographer Arpino, plus outsiders. Still, commissioning a new ballet from the unpredictable Tharp was a stretch of even his imagination.

Along with its devotion to archival preservation, the Joffrey Ballet cultivated an image of lively contemporaneity. Like Tharp, Robert Joffrey understood what he needed to do to survive, and he never presented the popular works any less respectfully than the classics. Though he started as a ballet purist, he fostered Arpino's glitzy eclecticism and brought back modernist experiments from the past, like Léonide Massine's *Parade*, which was revived in New York during the same 1973 winter season as Tharp's *Deuce Coupe*. *Parade* might be seen as a forerunner of *Deuce Coupe*, with its clashing elements, modern dress, low-culture milieu, and quasi-popular Erik Satie score. Robert Joffrey and Tharp approached contemporary dance fusion from opposite directions: Joffrey spreading out and diversifying a technical focus that had started with a solid ballet base, and Tharp infusing modern dance with the strength, mobility, and charisma of classicism.

The Joffrey repertory already included several jazz ballets, and modern dancers Alvin Ailey and Anna Sokolow contributed to early Joffrey seasons. But it was Robert Joffrey himself, an infrequent choreographer, who ignited a new wave of popularity with *Astarte* in 1967. A year before that, the company had taken up residence at New York City Center and had incorporated three ballets with special resonance for the troubled American conscience: Sokolow's 1955 drama of urban alienation, *Rooms*; Jerome Robbins's 1959 ballet in silence "about relationships," *Moves*; and the 1932 antiwar masterpiece *The Green Table*, by the German expressionist Kurt Jooss. *Astarte* tapped into the introspective sensibility underlying those older works, with a visual flamboyance borrowed from hippiedom and the peace movement, which were thriving on the West Coast as Robert Joffrey began developing the piece during a summer residency.

To a commissioned score by assembled-for-the-occasion rock band Crome Syrcus, an Everyman rose from his seat in the orchestra and strode, hypnotized, to the stage, where a woman enticed him from inside a psychedelic web of strobe lights and peacock designs. Four projectors threw a voyeuristic film of their own distorted images onto their actions. He stripped to his briefs and they made love with a cool eroticism. Then all the theatrical contrivances cleared away, and he walked out into 56th Street through the back door of the stage. Titillating but tasteful, *Astarte* was the first big mixed-media ballet, and it earned the Joffrey an eager new audience and a tidal wave of publicity. Arpino followed it up with several numbers featuring spectacular dancing and trendy trimmings. *Trinity* (1970) dignified a defiant virtuosity with ceremony—the dancers solemnly placed candles on the stage and left them burning as they exited to a pounding musical heartbeat. By 1972 *Trinity* had become the company's signature work.

Tharp had to come up with something to equal this. She says she studied the Joffrey repertory and audience during the fall season to assess the best way to make her mark. Without exploiting psychology, politics, or virtuosic display, she created something spectacular and immediate, something that transformed the dancers and made the ballet stage seem newly invented. *Deuce Coupe* was so successful that several performances were added to the season. And like a real American product, it had a built-in obsolescence; after only two years it had to be retooled before it could be performed again.

Robert Joffrey had already thought of the rock and harmony group the Beach Boys for a ballet, and Tharp welcomed the idea, although she'd considered the Beatles. The budget precluded having either group appear live. She used fourteen of the Beach Boys' recorded songs. Tharp by now had a lot of experience with putting together existing music, and she had no qualms about bending the Beach Boys to her purposes. Composer David Horowitz wrote four piano variations on "Cuddle Up," which she used as a kind of throughline for the dance, calling it "Matrix." The rest of the songs were subtly edited to make a coherent score on tape.

Deuce Coupe was probably the first ballet accompanied by pop records. The Joffrey's previous scores had included modern composers (Paul Creston, Lou Harrison, David Diamond), contemporary symphonic works with a jazz influence (Morton Gould), third-stream jazz (Kenyon Hopkins, Teo Macero), and the made-to-order rock of *Astarte* and *Trinity*. All of these had acceptably artistic dimensions. It was exactly the familiarity of the Beach Boys, their *not* being art, that was such an asset to *Deuce Coupe*. In his remarkable book about rock 'n' roll, *Mystery Train,* the critic Greil Marcus notes the lack of condescension in certain American pop artists, who have "hoped, no matter how secretly, that their work would lift America to heaven, or drive a stake through its heart." Marcus was launching a discussion about Randy Newman and the Beach Boys, but he might well have been describing Tharp.

Deuce Coupe became a phenomenal hit, but it had a stressful incubation, right up to its premiere at Chicago's Auditorium Theater on 8 February 1973. From the start of her discussions with Robert Joffrey, Tharp stipulated that her own company would dance in the work. This would be another first, for even in the legendary 1959 two-company encounter between Martha Graham and George Balanchine, *Episodes,* the modern dancers appeared in Graham's dance, the ballet dancers in Balanchine's, with a token crossover dancer in each piece (Sallie Wilson in Graham's dance and Paul Taylor in Balanchine's). *Deuce Coupe* was to be a fully integrated production, and this caused anxiety on both sides.

Tharp's dancers were in awe of the Joffreys' technical abilities. She broached the idea of the project to them before she took it on. Garcia-Lorca says: "I was not a strong technical dancer, which of course I knew better than anyone else. And being with these ballet dancers was a little daunting. A little scary." Rinker felt intimidated too, even though Tharp had already steered him into taking ballet class. He says: "I'm not a ballet dancer and never was and never wanted to be, but I tried to do it like I was." The prospect of being seen in the City Center Joffrey context was irresistible to the Tharp dancers, though, and Tharp worked out most of the movement on them in her usual way before Joffrey rehearsals began.

Beatriz Rodriguez was among the Joffrey dancers who welcomed the project enthusiastically. She had just come up from the Joffrey II and "I was just open to anything that came along! And it was a wonderful experience with her." But there was intense resistance from others. The more militant company members resented Tharp's jazz orientation and the "white" jazz of the Beach Boys. Besides that, she was an unknown, a funky downtown apparition in mismatching clothes, nothing like the star presences who'd come to them before. Once she began work, they felt confused and threatened. Richard Colton had recently joined the main company after two years in Joffrey II. He was understudying several roles in *Deuce Coupe* so he attended most of the rehearsals. He thought one source of the antagonism was Tharp's openness. She wasn't asking the dancers to imitate, to reproduce movement exactly, as they strove to do in their encyclopedic repertory of revivals. "Steps were being thrown out and you as a dancer were taking them and shedding a kind of new light on them. She was excited about mistakes or what things happened, and she was bringing a new breath and life, and a kind of spontaneity. . . . It was a company based on counting. There were no counts. It was just this great music."

People were grumbling in the dressing rooms: what *was* this? Tharp assigned Rose Marie Wright to lower the anxiety level. "I became Twyla's liaison between the dancers and the ballet. Because the Joffrey Ballet people really rebelled against this movement. I mean we went in there and they didn't know what to make of us. . . . There were dancers that Twyla wanted in the piece, and they didn't want to be in it. And I'm the one that said, Look, this is really a glissade, this is really an arabesque. . . . I was very excited because she was doing really interesting things with the ballet vocabulary. And it was really challenging to do and I was helping."

The project was hard on Tharp too. Added to her innate ambition and her struggles to realize this biggest project of her career, the Joffrey's plans for the winter season aroused her competitiveness. Preceding *Deuce Coupe's* City Center premiere by two weeks, there was to be a new ballet by Eliot Feld, to a symphonic-jazz score by Morton Gould. Feld, just a year younger than Tharp, was considered the rising young ballet choreographer of the time. He had as eclectic a background as Tharp, including performances with modern dancers Pearl Lang, Sophie Maslow and Donald McKayle. Like Tharp and company, he developed a close relationship with Richard Thomas, the guru of classically minded but unconventional young dancers. Feld had created the role of Baby John in Jerome Robbins's *West Side Story* on Broadway, but his first choreographies, as a member of American Ballet Theater, were classical, innovative, and very successful. In 1969, with strong support from Clive Barnes, Feld had started his own company at Brooklyn Academy of Music. Tharp too was eyeing this newly created dance venue, and she felt let down when Lewis Lloyd left Cunningham to work at BAM and shifted his concentration to Feld's new enterprise.

As Tharp and Feld rehearsed at the Joffrey in the fall of 1972, Tharp suspected—probably wrongly—that her rival was getting more rehearsal time, better dancers, and a bigger production budget than she. When money problems seemed about to curtail *Deuce Coupe* plans, Robert Joffrey supported her, and two Joffrey board members raised the money she needed. Feld's *Jive* turned out to be "a 1950's ballet in sneakers" according to Clive Barnes, one of the few reviewers who were lukewarm about *Deuce Coupe*. "It isn't half the ballet *Jive* is," he wrote in his first notice. A few months later, Barnes reaffirmed his opinion that Tharp's "choreographic squiggling" wore off quickly even if it had some initial appeal. Nevertheless, Feld's work disappeared quickly while *Deuce Coupe* became a landmark.

No one anticipated this outcome during *Deuce Coupe's* pockmarked journey to the stage. The day came when Tharp stopped rehearsal and announced that anyone who didn't want to be in the piece could leave; she wouldn't hold it against them. At least half the dancers walked out. Rebecca Wright was a leading ballerina in the company at the time. She had just been cast as Titania in Frederick Ashton's *The Dream*, but Tharp had passed over her for *Deuce Coupe*. When she heard about the mass exodus, she went to Robert Joffrey and told him she wanted to do Tharp's work. "I said, I think I can do that work really well, and I think she's in—I was so arrogant!—she's kind of in trouble, maybe I can help her out. Privately I was thinking I am going to *overwhelm*. I am going to be her saviour." As soon as she walked into the studio, Wright realized her mistake. "Oh my God, what am I doing here? I don't understand this stuff. . . . Syncopation I get, reversal I get, but putting this all together and watching Rose, watching Sara, watching these people do this work, rapidly!" Wright decided to stay with it, even practicing at home, until she could master the material. She became one of the three dancers who opened the ballet.

Deuce Coupe had a didactic subtext that reflected the actual circumstances of two vastly different dance companies working together. Though they came from opposing traditions, the two camps had a lot in common and were going to find a way of working together. Individuals would learn to accommodate to each other and submit to form. Structurally, the dance followed an exquisite Tharpian logic. Movement material came from the ballet lexicon, demonstrated throughout the piece by a soloist, Erika Goodman, who symbolized tradition and remained fixated on her own steps while the rest of the large cast surged around her. Additional phrase material was drawn from popular culture, rock 'n' roll, and Tharp's distinctive vocabulary, then shaped and mixed until it finally coalesced into a large, formal group section near the end.

The piece opened quietly on Goodman's first long sequence of steps, with Rebecca Wright and William Whitener behind her, doing a pas de deux to the first version of the Matrix, a romantic piano solo. The duet, confined to an upstage corner, began with small adjustments and port de bras, and expanded into leaps, a high lift, and a supported arabesque. Glenn White, Henry Berg, and Starr Danias appeared, and suddenly the Beach Boys' "Little Deuce Coupe" burst out as the rest of the dancers, led by Rodriguez, trouped in one by one across the footlights. The young writer Robb Baker later described this moment in *Dance Magazine*: ". . . out comes Beatriz Rodriguez, leading on a whole line of slinky/sleazy Joffrey/Tharp movement-makers. And the audience *knows* at once. Understands the juxtaposition. Whistles and cheers. By damn, it *is* the Beach Boys!" As the line advanced, one character cracked his knuckles, one shuffled forward with wrists dangling from outstretched arms and her head thrown back, one sauntered, one gazed into the audience. Movements repeated, and it became evident that they were all performing the same phrase, but in their own ways. On opening night in Chicago, the audience broke into yells of pleasure and recognition as this began to unfold. The dancers couldn't conceal their astonishment. Apprehension about the project vanished in that instant. The next day, defectors were clamoring to get back into the ballet.

The heart of *Deuce Coupe* consisted of "character" dances, where the accompanying songs inspired the movement. Dancers surfed across the stage in their socks to "Catch a Wave," hunkered down with caveman sluggishness to "Alley Oop." Rudner did an unforgettable sexy solo to "Got to Know the Woman." Tharp trotted around like a frisky calf begging to be roped and captured by "Long Tall Texan" Rose Marie Wright. There was a furious and funny mock battle-chase between Tharp and Gary Chryst that ended in an elaborate high-five truce. Several other individual dancers got a chance to stand out, sparked by Tharp's own tough, wry performing among them. Impersonating kids on the loose, leading the California life that Tharp had missed out on, they celebrated pals and play, reckless excitement, cars, sunshine, and pot. The audience adored them.

After the long, feisty string of variations, the exuberance subsided. "Don't Go Near the Water" and "Mama Says" introduced serious matters. The individuality, overload, and confusion must be disciplined and calmed down. Romantic love—"Wouldn't It Be Nice?" and "Cuddle Up"—brought the high spirits under control. Again a phrase, resembling the one introduced by Wright and Whitener at the beginning of the ballet, was passed among a group of dancers. This time they all stood facing the audience and politely waited while one or two at a time did a piece of the phrase. Tharp danced a brief solo version of Goodman's phrase. Then the whole group streamed across as they had in the first song, but this time they were doing the Matrix phrase, a fusion of ballet steps and expansive transitional movements. At a musical climax, the ensemble collected into a pose, with a girl held high in the air by several men as other dancers gazed up at her. Tharp had wanted this freeze to be lit in an explosive, blinding flash, but Jennifer Tipton couldn't manage it. She created a silhouette instead. The image evoked a news photographer's flashbulb event, like some tragic student demonstration in 1968.

Then the girl was slowly lowered to the floor and the others drifted away, leaving Goodman to go on with her lexicon. Like the eruption of "Little Deuce Coupe" at the beginning of the ballet, this denouement signaled a change and a continuation—perhaps the end of adolescence, an embarkation into a future of responsibility and order. Richard Colton felt at this point that the group was maturing. "If someone would run and go to the side, there'd be someone there for them. . . . There was this sense of being able to know yourself and your movement but also to . . . have this wonderful awareness of this community around you." According to Ken Rinker, by the end of the tempestuous rehearsal period, "it felt like we were all dancing together in the same manner." Tharp endeared herself to the dancers and reinforced the bonding process by gathering the cast in a circle before the opening night performance. She spoke to them while they all held hands. According to Christine Uchida, "She was one of us, we were all together. . . . She dropped that soon after that, which I always missed. But that was a really nice thing. And I think it really brought everyone together."

Tharp added one more brilliant stroke to the ballet—no one can remember whether it was in place for the Chicago performances. For a couple of years, an increasingly flamboyant display of graffiti had been appearing around New York, most prominently on the outsides of subway cars. By 1972 hot disputes foamed around these designs. Were they expressions of defiance against the Establishment? Wanton vandalism against public property? Or a refreshing antidote to the grim daily commute? This was the age of resistance and threats, claims to entitlement, and an exhausted fury at the waning debacle in Vietnam. It was also the age of Pop Art, junk sculpture, found objects, and musique concrète. Art was coming out of the cloister

and into a more public arena. Even nonpolitical work offended some people. The city put Sanitation Department crews to work scrubbing the paint
off the trains; next morning new decorations would appear. In fact, the graffiti contained few threats or profanity. Journalists eventually found the per-
petrators, who turned out to be youths from Spanish Harlem, writing and
embellishing their own noms de plume.

Tharp says she had a sudden inspiration for the *Deuce Coupe* decor while
riding the subway one day: "An ongoing upstage mural by adolescent boys."
What better way to equal the Joffrey's spectacular production values without imitating them, to project a timely image without resorting to Miliskin
or candles. An assistant in Bill Kosmas's office spoke Spanish, and she located the United Graffiti Artists, an agency newly formed to market what
the artists had been giving away to the city for free. The Joffrey Ballet hired
Rick II, Coco 144, SJK 171, Stay-Hi 149, Rican 619, and Charmin 65 for
each performance of *Deuce Coupe*. The street artists entered during one of the
first mass dance numbers and began spray-painting their designs on three
huge paper panels. As they covered the space, the paper rolled up to give
them more. When they left, before Tharp's Matrix solo, the paper continued rolling out, so that once again the background was blank at the end of
the ballet.

The bold, colorful graffiti made a lively setting for the dance and deepened its meaning. Tharp thought of the designs as a form of teenage identity advertisements, matching the Beach Boys' milieu. The writers in their
jeans and big hair reinforced the central conflict of the ballet by contrasting
street art with the rarefied behavior of studio-bred dancers. They could all
occupy the same stage, Tharp was insisting. But the graffiti also gave the
work a political edge. Just two years before, Tom Wolfe's famous piece
"Radical Chic" had captured a certain naive desire on the part of wealthy
and artistic types to support liberal causes that might be more dangerous
than they seemed. Like Tharp, who thought of *Deuce Coupe* as a commercial
proposition—"I never lost sight of the fact that Bob Joffrey was hiring me
to make successful art," she wrote—the graffiti writers were hoping to come
in out of the tunnels and get a piece of the money. *New York* magazine, ever
alert for a new blip on the culture scope, ran a cover story on graffiti three
weeks after the *Deuce Coupe* premiere, complete with a hokey competition
for the finest subway decoration and a five-page story by Richard Goldstein
on the whole phenomenon. The magazine's music critic, Alan Rich,
thought *Deuce Coupe* a great addition to the Joffrey's roster of pop ballets.

Tharp had rejuvenated an old idea with "the marvelously zany, insinuating, made-up quality of the ensemble, the flickering, rock-steady wit of it all, and, as that final little genius-ridden touch, the setting of the action in front of those inspired graffiti artists puttering and sputtering away at the backdrop."

Tharp certainly was not preoccupied with world or national politics, savvy as she was about style, nor was she aiming to improve life for the disadvantaged in Spanish Harlem. But employing these semi outlaws from the margins did have a feeling of rescue. The hippie lifestyle too had a certain exotic appeal for the audience, though in real life Tharp had now made a definitive turn away from impoverished bohemia. As a ballet *Deuce Coupe* made a soft but provocative and financially rewarding statement. It was hardly abrasive or threatening, like Anna Sokolow's *Rooms*, which offended so many people that it was pulled from the repertory. *Deuce Coupe*'s message of rapprochement and fun was one the Joffrey audience could embrace. If graffiti writing was politically provocative at all, given its origins in East Harlem and its association in people's minds to radical groups like the Young Lords, the artists of *Deuce Coupe*, like Tharp, had crossed over into a more pragmatic and materialistic world.

5

Local to Express

1973–1975

euce Coupe's great success intensified the pace and expanded the reach
of Tharp's career. She had more opportunities than ever, and she
wanted to accept them all. By the time an altered and more stable company
was functioning, in the spring of 1977, she had made new works for two
ballet companies; reconfigured *Deuce Coupe* for the Joffrey dancers alone; and
choreographed *After All*, to the Albinoni Adagio for Strings and Organ, for
ice dancer John Curry. She had worked for months on an abortive TV project at WGBH in Boston, completed professional videos of three major
dances, and taped the extant repertory for documentary purposes. The
Tharp company toured with the Joffrey and on their own during this period. They went to Europe three times and had productive out-of-town residencies as well as their first invited seasons at the American Dance Festival,
Jacob's Pillow, and Brooklyn Academy of Music. Most of the Tharp dancers
who had created *Deuce Coupe* left, and important new members arrived: Tom
Rawe, Jennifer Way, Shelley Washington, and the first of several defectors
from the Joffrey Ballet.

Tharp choreographed steadily for her own dancers, but only one company work from this period, *Sue's Leg*, endured over the years in its original
form. Everything else, about ten pieces, was soon scrapped, reworked, or
folded into another production. Deeply parsimonious, Tharp hated to

throw anything away. She had long made a practice of recycling choreographic material she hadn't quite used up. After 1973 she was taking more chances in more exposed places; there were more loose ends and delayed consummations. She made the first of several new models of *Deuce Coupe,* for the Joffrey dancers alone, early in 1975. Each of the later versions, with different numbers of dancers redistributed among the roles, retained some of the original material arranged in new sequences.

"I got on the Twyla Tharp train at a time when it was changing from local to express," says Ken Rinker. ". . . the wheels turning faster and the train getting grander and the stops being spiffier." Rinker had joined Tharp at the inception of *The Bix Pieces.* When she approached him earlier, he had his eye on Merce Cunningham's company and was seriously taking classes there. Rinker had studied modern dance while getting a degree in English at the University of Maryland, and when he arrived in New York in 1970 he'd already had considerable experience, dancing in the company of Ethel Butler and doing his own choreography. The only thing he remembers about his first brush with Tharp—as an extra in the 1970 Judson Church McDonagh book party and benefit—was being nervous because Cunningham was in the audience. Rinker eventually realized that he would never be bold enough to ask the imposing but noncommittal Cunningham for a place in his company. Just at that moment, the summer of 1971, Tharp's invitation came, and he accepted.

Rinker taught dance twice a week at the Brooklyn Ethical Culture school to supplement his hundred-dollar-a-week income from Tharp. Apprehensive at first about switching from Cunningham's work to Tharp's, which was so different, he found his bearings when he realized it was all right to dance *to* the music of *The Bix Pieces.* "Twyla was never the type to come out and say, We're doing a new dance and you're going to do a solo and it's gonna be a trio and I'm gonna use you, you, and you. No. We just sort of all got behind her and danced, and then the next day it was either the same thing or it wasn't the same thing. Or you were doing that and she was doing this, and then suddenly you were doing it with this music: Oh well, we'll try it with *this* music. . . ." Tharp could make tremendous demands on dancers but at the same time ignite and incorporate their individual contributions. Her challenge—not all the dancers who loved her work were up to it—was for them to accept her extreme resourcefulness in making up steps and then continue working the steps in their own ways. "The more I trusted myself in making decisions," Rinker says, "the more I felt like I was becoming like Sara

and Rose. Where they were doing Twyla's work obviously, but had a different point of view. . . . Twyla was very good about letting people go."

Initially Rinker felt like a pickup dancer. Tharp didn't make any long-
term commitment to him outright. When the company finished the Paris
engagement, he ran into Tharp and Kosmas at the airport. He told her he
was going back to New York after a visit to Berlin, and "She said, 'I really
like you.' And I remember there was a pause, like there was supposed to be
another part to this sentence and it didn't come. . . . It was her saying I'd
like you to keep dancing with the company. . . . I'd just *assumed* that I was
going to be dancing with the company." After this encounter Rinker felt he
had been admitted to the inner circle.

Tharp was chronically ambivalent about maintaining a permanent company of her own. What she really wanted was a group that would work
around the clock without expecting a salary. Not that she begrudged paying
them when money was available. But she saw herself being drawn into the
seemingly unbreakable loop that bound the whole American dance business. Touring would pay the dancers but interfere with making new choreography. Touring meant keeping a repertory of old pieces that presenters
could sell to their audiences and that the company could put up in new theaters with little rehearsal. Performing on the road and maintaining the
repertory while at home ate up the hours and held creativity at bay. Tharp
thought this was self-defeating and maybe even immoral. Ken Rinker
shared her concern about "getting stale, and not forging ahead. . . . How do
we do rep and not be a repertory company?" In some ideal world, a major
dance company would have a theater and working space at its disposal, and
be given subsidies so it could survive without debilitating months on the
road. This never really happened in America, not even during the "Dance
Boom" of the 1970s and '80s.

Twyla Tharp kept trying to circumvent the system she found corrosive
and demeaning. One way of getting the bodies she needed was to offer
young dancers the chance to work with her as a learning experience. She
tried this in various ways over the years—first with the group that went to
New Berlin in 1970. She experimented with adding the two Oberlin students as apprentices in 1970–71. At the beginning of 1972, facing a tough
schedule of tours to Upstate New York, the Midwest, and Los Angeles, she
signed on almost twenty young dancers as a "farm club." Sometimes these
schemes would yield a regular company member, but they were usually ad
hoc arrangements, financed by specific engagements or grants. She never

worked out a long-term way to keep some of the company in New York making new work with her while the rest trudged around the touring circuits to earn the company's living.

After *Deuce Coupe*, Tharp capitalized on her growing prestige and personal charisma to charge high fees for company appearances, for the use of her dances by other companies, and for freelance choreographing jobs. She was offered commissions; some were prestigious and even creatively interesting, like the ice-dance number she made for John Curry. These jobs earned income she could use for her company, but they also took her away while she worked on them. A certain pecking order had developed naturally within the company, with Rudner and Wright as trusted lieutenants and advisors. Everyone shared teaching responsibilities. On tour, one dancer would be assigned to keep track of the costumes, another made out the rehearsal schedule. There were group meetings where new members were evaluated and future plans discussed. But when Tharp was called away on independent jobs, the dancers missed her bonding presence.

Immediately after *Deuce Coupe* Robert Joffrey wanted another ballet, for his company alone. In the *Deuce Coupe* deal, Tharp had successfully traded weeks of contract work for getting her dancers on a payroll, and she often used this per-project strategy later on. But *Deuce Coupe* took a lot out of the Tharp dancers. Rather than dance in every piece as they did on their own programs, they had to wait through a whole evening to do their parts in that one ballet. Away from home on a tour that summer to the West Coast, there were whole empty days between *Deuce Coupe* performances. Tharp injured her foot and took herself out of the ballet despite her great success with the audience. Sitting out front and seeing her work alongside the Joffrey's repertory, which she felt was unworthy of *Deuce Coupe*, she wondered if the audience could really tell the difference between it and an Arpino pop number. She was also inspecting the Joffrey dancers with her next project in mind. A classical ballet, on pointe, seemed to her the logical follow-up, and she wasn't sure the Joffreys had the skills. This was hedging against her own uncertainty. Now that she had the chance to realize a great ambition, perhaps it was she who wouldn't measure up.

As Time Goes By premiered in New York on 24 October 1973, and it had almost as big a success as *Deuce Coupe*. It stayed in the Joffrey repertory for years, and brought several young dancers into prominence. Tharp made the choreography quickly but there were problems that taxed her in a different way from *Deuce Coupe*. Now she was all alone inside the Joffrey machinery, without any of her own dancers to appreciate her choreographic extravagance. For the first time she was experiencing the inner dynamics of a major ballet company—the rivalries among dancers, and among choreographers, all vying for the audience's favor; the gossip and rumors; the scrutiny of a national press. Robert Joffrey was making his first ballet in years, a heavy, romantic work to songs of Richard Wagner, and she suspected he was economizing on her production in order to finance his own. *Deuce Coupe* was still a box-office draw—about six performances were scheduled that fall—but Ashton's *The Dream*, a favorite among balletomanes, was coming into New York after a Joffrey debut on tour during the summer, and the repertory was laced with Arpino's classical and pop confections. Ballets were jockeying for placement even after the season started. There were discussions about an all-Tharp evening, with *Deuce Coupe*, *As Time Goes By*, and the Tharp company doing *The Bix Pieces*, but the Joffrey hadn't yet given such recognition to an outsider's work. Perhaps in deference to the resident choreographer, Arpino, the idea was allowed to evaporate.

As Time Goes By was set to the last two movements of Haydn's Symphony No. 45, *The Farewell*. Tharp began choreographing with a sextet, an intricate, fast, and spatially tight combination of individual phrases and partner work. Haydn's minuet set up what Tharp hoped would be a classical tone. Early in rehearsals, the dancers started to get uneasy. William Whitener and Pamela Nearhoof were ready to do anything she had in mind, but the other four weren't so trusting. Burton Taylor, perhaps the Joffrey's most finished classical male dancer, asked one day whether this was supposed to be a classical ballet. "Define classical," was Tharp's response, and she talked for a while about the aesthetics of art. To her mind, classicism didn't mean something frozen forever in one mold. She regarded Balanchine's *Agon* as a classical ballet for the twentieth century, and now she was going to explore classicism her own way.

But the dancers had more than aesthetic reservations—the Joffrey Ballet, after all, based its credibility on being able to reproduce any style of historic or contemporary classicism. But Tharp was pushing their classical technique to extremes. When one man considered taking jazz classes to prepare for her rehearsals, she pointed out that she wasn't asking them to throw away their classical technique but to extend it. For some of the older dancers, her off-center turns, transitionless changes, and fast adaptations meant overriding long-ingrained, safe body habits. The complicated spacing, daredevil partnering, and agile switches from individual to ensemble movement constituted a mental challenge that proved daunting too.

Eileen Brady remained but Burton Taylor, Paul Sutherland, and Denise Jackson withdrew, and there were weeks of uncertainty about this core casting. Beatriz Rodriguez and Joseph (Adix) Carman, recently elevated from the Joffrey II, were enthusiastic recruits for the sextet, but none of Tharp's prospects for the third man's part made it to the opening. There were injuries, doubts about the skewed movement Tharp was making, and besides, she thought, some of them were saving themselves for their featured roles in *The Dream*. Henry Berg, who'd assisted her on *Deuce Coupe* and whom she'd already named as regisseur for the Haydn ballet, danced in the first cast. Tharp slyly subtitled this section "Ten Make Six," a reference to the departed Jackson, Sutherland, Taylor, and Russell Sulzbach.

After the sextet, the ballet opened out into a large ensemble—she envisioned twenty-four dancers but ended with seventeen. What Tharp had in mind for the ballet was a series of subtle contrasts: harmony and dissonance; big, loose effects versus compressed, precise ones; unexpectedly quick versus unexpectedly slow movement. In the Farewell Symphony, Joseph Haydn is said to have been hinting to his patron, Prince Miklós József Esterhazy, that it was time to return to Vienna after the royal party's long stay in their summer quarters. During the fourth-movement adagio, the musicians blew out their candles and exited section by section, until only two violinists were left to play the final notes. Tharp thought it would be too obvious to duplicate this scenario, so she set the fourth movement with a commotion of exits and entrances, called "The Four Finales." Different subgroupings of the big ensemble played out each return of Haydn's presto theme in different ways. Each group retained dancers and movement elements from the previous sections. During the adagio after the fourth finale, a soloist, Larry Grenier, kept on dancing as the others gradually dispersed.

She had originally thought of the adagio as a trio, but she was so impressed with Grenier's particular qualities that she decided to feature him instead. And this meant rethinking the concept of the whole ballet. Grenier, accompanied by the disappearing group and the two traces of the trio, Ann Marie de Angelo and Christine Uchida, would suggest not finality but continuity, with his serene, looping, legato phrase. Haydn's reduction to the minimum would be represented at the beginning of the ballet instead, in a version of the phrase material condensed to less than a minute and danced with spiky intensity by Beatriz Rodriguez.

The duration of Rodriguez's solo was proportionate to that of the sextet that followed, which in turn foretold the timing of the four finales. The ballet had other inner workings that most audiences couldn't have detected. As each dancer crossed the stage and departed in the adagio, an element of Grenier's movement went too, but there would still be something left for him to do at the end of the ballet; in fact, the curtain went down as he was still moving. During the finales, Tharp built in moments when, within stipulated time slots and directions in space, the dancers could adopt any movement they liked from the material they'd learned. Says Richard Colton: "We knew exactly the direction but we would have to sculpt the movement to move in that direction, that was our job. But we'd have that freedom. And then she knew everyone would be picking movement that they would burst out with . . . and if they feel good doing it, they usually look good doing it." After the dancers' choices were made in rehearsal, the section was set and always performed the same.

In the intricately woven sextet, Tharp began exploring partner work. Without extending anything beyond a few measures, she made forays into the vocabulary of classical lifts and supports that required unusual trust and timing between the dancers. A woman launched into a low skid that would have ended on the floor if a man hadn't been there to stop her. You'd notice a woman high in a man's arms, then suddenly she'd be airborne for a second and end in another man's arms. No one stayed with the same partner, and in fact, by the end of the movement women were steadying other women on pointe and a man was caught in a lift by another man. Tharp simply disregarded the balletic prescription for stalwart males and passive females. Whenever she was quizzed about accepting Ken Rinker as the first man in her company, she replied that she was interested in using whatever skills dancers could add to her work—she'd just been waiting for one who was good enough. But she was aware that the audience has preconceptions. In *As Time Goes By* she deconstructed ballet's gender bias by refusing to differentiate the ensemble into separate male and female groups. Even more important, she chose Rodriguez and Grenier for the opening and closing solos because they could work against gender typing. They represented opposite ends of a spectrum, William Whitener thought, illustrating Tharp's concept of "the more feminine side to masculinity and the masculine side to femininity, and how it flipped in the ballet. Bea did very strong dancing and Larry was lyrical."

As Time Goes By constantly shuttles the audience between the satisfaction of beautiful form and the tension of form disrupted. If the dance looks chaotic or fuzzy, a moment later it locks into perfect balance. Its brevity alone was disorienting. Since Tharp didn't use the whole symphony, there were only about twelve minutes of music, prefaced by Rodriguez's forty-five seconds in silence. Yet in this short duration Tharp had shown the technical workings of a ballet company, the big and small units of the ensemble. She had focused attention on dancers who hadn't been singled out before. And she'd offered the chance for reflection and laughter.

With the exception of *The New York Times*, the reviews were appreciative. Tharp had tried to cultivate Clive Barnes, not very subtly, by inviting him out for drinks after a performance at Jacob's Pillow the previous summer. But he sent Anna Kisselgoff for the opening night review and then wrote a patronizing Sunday piece himself. Kisselgoff delivered the dubious compliment that Tharp had retreated from her recent audience-friendly pop phase to the "austere and highly interesting pure-movement style" of her prejazz days. Kisselgoff liked *As Time Goes By* but labeled it less accessible and entertaining than Tharp's recent hits. Barnes backed off his initial enthusiasm for *Deuce Coupe;* his pleasure in it, he said, "decline[s] markedly." And as for the Haydn, he liked it less each of the four times he saw it. Under the title "Ballets That Must Be Seen—Once" Barnes labeled *As Time Goes By* a "gorgeous putdown" of Haydn and classicism in general, comparing it to "the special cuteness of a moustache painted on the Mona Lisa." Like the stodgier Joffrey dancers, Barnes apparently resented Tharp's intrusion into classical music and, even worse, classical ballet. Rather than welcoming her efforts to revitalize ballet, he dismissed her as a serious classical contender:

> Miss Tharp creates for the moment. She would choose a Kleenex, with its registered trademark, rather than a lace handkerchief with its possibility of well-laundered permanence. Normally I would object to this. Yet I can see that ballets such as "Deuce Coupe" and "As Time Goes By" give a lot of surprised pleasure to people. People who never understood how much ballet could be like your friendly neighborhood discotheque.
>
> This kind of ballet is not so much to be savored as to be gulped. In the frenzied gasp of recognition you are expected to comprehend that all of classic ballet is nothing but a cute shuffle and a shamble. And totally unfrightening.

‗ *Re-Moves* in rehearsal at Judson Church, 1966. Sara Rudner.
(PHOTO: Robert Barry)

‗ *Jam.*
(PHOTO: Robert Barry)

⇒ *Disperse.*
Sara Rudner, Margery
Tupling, Twyla Tharp,
Theresa Dickinson.
(PHOTO: Robert Barry)

⇒ *Dancing in the
Streets* at Wadsworth
Atheneum, 1969.
Rose Marie Wright,
Twyla Tharp, Sheila
Raj, Graciela Figueroa
and audience.
(PHOTO: James
Elliott/Wadsworth
Athenuem)

꽃 *The Fugue.* Rose Marie Wright, Twyla Tharp, Sara Rudner. (PHOTO: Tom Rawe)

꽃 *The Fugue.* Tom Rawe, Raymond Kurshals, John Carrafa. (PHOTO: Nathaniel Tileston)

ଓଚ *Eight Jelly Rolls.* Sara Rudner,
Rose Marie Wright.

(PHOTO: Tony Russell, courtesy of
London Weekend Television.© REX
Features Ltd)

ଓଚ *The Bix Pieces.* Sara Rudner,
Twyla Tharp. (PHOTO: Tom Rawe)

ช๏ *Deuce Coupe.* Twyla Tharp. (PHOTO: © Migdoll 1973)

ช๏ *Half the One Hundreds* rehearsal at Brooklyn Academy, 1977. Twyla Tharp and civilians.
(PHOTO: Nathaniel Tileston)

☙ *Sue's Leg.* Twyla Tharp.
(PHOTO: © Midgoll 1976)

☙ *Push Comes to Shove.*
Mikhail Baryshnikov.
(PHOTO: © Max Waldman Archive.
All Rights Reserved)

✍ *Push Comes to Shove*. Mikhail Baryshnikov, Marianna Tcherkassky and corps de ballet.
(PHOTO: © Martha Swope)

✍ *Country Dances*. Tom Rawe, Shelley Washington, Christine Uchida, Jennifer Way.
(PHOTO: © Lois Greenfield 1977)

ᏪᏉ *Baker's Dozen*. Raymond Kurshals, Sara Rudner. (PHOTO: © Martha Swope)

ᏪᏉ *Baker's Dozen*. William Whitener, Christine Uchida. (PHOTO: © Martha Swope)

Later on, when the Joffrey Ballet showed it on tour, *The San Francisco Chronicle*'s Robert Commanday, much more susceptible to the overt romanticism of Arpino, thought *As Time Goes By* was "more to be censured than pitied." Calling Tharp's take on Haydn "vandalism," he called various parts of the dance "deliberately dissonant," "confusing to the eye," and "cheap and offensive."

But the new ballet had many powerful admirers. It prompted Arlene Croce, who had just become the dance critic of *The New Yorker*, to proclaim Tharp "the Nijinska of our time." Croce appreciated what Barnes did not about Tharp's work: "It seems to seek out first principles and turn them over with curiosity, finding new excitement in what lies on the other side of orthodoxy." Deborah Jowitt of *The Village Voice* was delighted to see Tharp retrieving "a whole range of dynamics that have slipped away from Western dance." She called Tharp the reigning queen of the new virtuosity.

During the same Joffrey season that saw the premiere of *As Time Goes By* and the reprise of *Deuce Coupe*, Tharp gained more visibility when the videotape of *The Bix Pieces* was broadcast on *Camera Three* one Sunday morning in October. For the next several months the Tharp company had a full schedule of touring and a date at New York's Town Hall. *Eight Jelly Rolls*, *The Rags*, and *The Bix Pieces*, with the women's *Fugue*, had become the standard repertory. A residency at the Walker Art Center in Minneapolis in January provided a chance to work on something new, *In the Beginnings*, in anticipation of the WGBH video. But no other new work was completed until the summer, when the *Bach Duet* for Wright and Rinker premiered during an American University–Wolf Trap residency in Washington. It was planned as the finale of the video.

Immediately after the two months of teaching at AU, the company went to Boston to do the filming. Titled *All About Eggs*, the video was to gather several big strands of Tharpian interests. She wrote rambling notes while working on it, exploring illusion, reality, and belief, and thinking about how to ask questions, how to deal with one's mistakes. Perhaps she was obsessing about her divorce from Bob Huot, which was finalized after much unpleasantness over the custody and care of Jesse, in November of 1974. It seemed life presented an overwhelming and inescapable assortment of dualities: "end begin, right wrong, perfect imperfect, yes no, red blue, today tomorrow—each part of the pair existent only in its promise of the other. Lifeless in itself and death to the other." And in another place: "This piece is an epistemological survey. Some things are known by association. Some things are known through physical perception. Some things must be taken on faith . . ."

While working on *In the Beginnings* she'd talked to Mike Steele of the *Minneapolis Tribune* with her usual bravado. "Staring success in the face is like staring down on death. To keep your integrity in the face of rankest commerce takes real mettle." About to film the repertory at the Annenberg School of Communications in Philadelphia, she figured she'd then have a working asset, like a Motherwell painting. She'd sell the Annenberg tapes as rehearsal aids to other companies that were willing to pay well to acquire her repertory. She thought she could beat the system, she told another interviewer later that spring. The company was popular enough to support itself decently, "but that means traveling about thirty weeks in a year and means forfeiting our standards and we are not prepared to do that. So it really amounts to going back to where we were in the beginning and not supporting ourselves by this work." She hoped television and videotape, being more tangible and mass-accessible commodities, would buy her way out of the loop.

The symbolism of eggs gave Tharp a way to ventilate these concerns in dance. She thought of the egg as idea, as creativity. But there might be no way to interrupt the chicken-egg cycle. How could you tell where tradition gave way to innovation, where inspiration lapsed into history? As she took her own wary steps toward fame, she was thinking about the dancer's fantasies, and she wondered which came first, the chorus or the star. She had always been committed to the individuality of each member of the ensemble; was the Cinderella spotlight creating false divisions within the dance company?

She liked the visceral associations between eggs and the female reproductive system, even if the consequences could be troublesome. Jesse, her very own chick, was supposed to appear on film somewhere in the video. In one of the three *Egg Stories* from *In the Beginnings* that were to open *All About Eggs*, Wright, wearing a white bandeau and briefs, does a series of gestures reminiscent of her Big Bang solo in *The Bix Pieces*. A fast-changing slide show runs on three screens behind her, like the unpredictable images on a slot machine: body parts, fruit, fried eggs, snapshots, a Renaissance painting, a bottle of pills for menstrual cramps. In a dry, stagy voice-over Tharp reads her own text about a sudden adolescent distaste for her mother's breakfast menu. She'd smashed eggs on the floor after a 1966 abortion, in *Re-Moves*, and one of her first critic-fans, John Percival, had titled his review in *Dance and Dancers* "Eggs Don't Bounce." Marian Hailey, who narrated the seven *Egg Stories* in Minneapolis, first broke raw eggs, then dropped hard-boiled ones, noting, "Some assumptions can be made; others can't."

Inspired as always with what new dancers could do, Tharp created a five-part fugue for Tom Rawe. TV technology would make it possible for him to partner himself. Rawe, who had joined the company the spring after the premiere of *Deuce Coupe*, spent most of the summer learning the choreography. "It involved a linear sequence continued throughout the piece with restated themes splitting off at points, with first a duet, then a trio, et cetera, until there was a short moment of five voices dancing at the same time," Rawe remembers. "Each point of a split was initiated by the same movement, which messed with my physical memory," and eventually he had to graph it on paper, but, "It was fun to do, and I think that it established me as a hard worker." The fugue was shot in Chromakey, the predigital process that allowed an unrelated background to be applied behind the central image. In the unfinished tape, which still exists, Rawe seems to be hatching out new versions of himself as he dances along in no-space.

At the end of the second and last day of shooting in Boston, an exhausted Wright and Rinker taped the *Bach Duet*. It was choreographed to the soprano-alto duet from the Cantata No. 78, *Jesu, der du meine Seele*. Wright recalls almost marking the dance in the very tight space of the TV studio. She and Rinker performed the piece again later on, but by 1980 it had disappeared, and Tharp made a different Bach work for dancers Whitener and Uchida, *Duet from the Third Suite*.

The Minneapolis critics were impressed with *In the Beginnings*. Mike Steele thought Tharp was "taking dance into a larger context of social space. She's dealing with fantasies, American mythology, with collective perception. She's using popular modes—even the music is full of patriotic and pop ditties—to penetrate that part of us that believes in popular dreams. She seems interested now in why she creates dances. As she probes deeper, disassembling and looking under the clichés, even banalities, of culture she's finding a poetry beneath. She's discovering fundamentals." Peter Altman saw her introspection beneath the entertainment, sunlight mingled with shadows.

For most of the year, Tharp had prepared not only the dance material for the WGBH adventure but the text, artwork, and film she wanted to incorporate. She expected to have a chance to work creatively with the television medium as well as with dance. This enterprise grew from so much self-examination that its sprawling, unruly elements got out of control. The production team at GBH hadn't anticipated a project of such complexity. The taping was a disaster and the video was never completed.

Tom Rawe and his wife, Jennifer Way, first encountered Tharp during the company's marathon one-day residency at Ohio State University in 1972. They were dazzled by the whole event—taking class, learning *The One Hundreds* and parts of *The Fugue*, and, during the concert that evening, absorbing the group's prodigious dancing. They became groupies, following the company to Antioch College and Minneapolis, and later driving all the way to New York in a yellow Volkswagen bus to see *Deuce Coupe* during its first season. Rawe had been playing the trumpet and dancing since his high school years as a student at the Interlochen Arts Academy in Michigan. His parents hoped he'd pursue a conventional career, but after earning a bachelor of science degree at Clarkson College of Technology, he returned to his first love, dance. Jennifer Way's mother taught dance in her hometown of Waverly, Ohio, and by junior high school was ferrying her daughter to study with ballet teachers in Columbus. Way enrolled in the Ohio State Dance Department after high school.

Rawe joined Tharp first. Having finished his M.F.A. in dance at OSU, he was driving a cab in New York in the spring of 1973. He heard about an audition at 104 Franklin Street and, with misgivings, decided to try out. He was one of three men Tharp provisionally accepted. For two weeks, Rawe was to work on getting the movement into his body: "She wanted to find out if I was able to get better. Was able to tolerate that work process." Rawe appreciated the fact that "I didn't have to show her my stuff in ten seconds, I could just work on the material." He thought the endless repetition in Tharp's rehearsal process brought about a feeling of such security that by the time the dancers got to perform anything, "it seemed improvisational, because it was like putting on an old pair of shoes. . . . We loved it. In the rehearsal studio it was good. It was a lot of work but that was good." Like others before him, Rawe didn't know when his trial period had ended. After rehearsing for the whole summer, he got up the nerve to ask whether he'd been taken into the company. He stayed for eleven years.

Way took classes during Tharp's American University residencies of 1973 and '74. The first summer she was earning the final credits toward her Ohio State bachelors degree. The next year dancers were leaving the company and Way filled in, teaching a ballet and a tap class. She wasn't sure Tharp had a clear idea who she was until the following fall in New York. Way was working in a health food restaurant and taking classes with Viola Farber when she went to a Tharp audition. After separate men's and women's tryouts, the dancers were paired up together. Way says, "I think it was only then, when I started dancing with this guy, that she saw something in me that she thought would work for the company. . . . I think she really liked the way I handled myself or handled him." She joined the company in early 1975.

Throughout the Tharp company history, dancers bonded intimately with Tharp and each other. They had chosen Tharp and stayed with her work because they felt it was stimulating and challenging beyond any other dancing available to them. Aside from injury or exhaustion, only extreme circumstances prompted them to leave. As happens in most modern dance companies, those with choreographic ambitions saw time rushing ahead and felt they had to break away in order to gain some different experiences and try their own creative ideas.

Sara Rudner became restless, partly for this reason, and left in 1974 after a difficult period of indecision. She and Rose Marie Wright had been not just long-term principal dancers, they had contributed as much as Tharp herself to the developing Tharp style, and to the strength and flexibility of a company that essentially had no formal organization. Rudner went on to a formidable career as a teacher and choreographer, but her imprint on Tharp's work was indelible. She returned, after a guest appearance in 1977, to create another series of extraordinary roles between 1978 and 1985. Since then she has remained a devoted friend, guest artist, and coach.

Nina Wiener, who had moved into the company after touring with the 1972 Farm Club, also had independent ideas. She didn't seem to fit in as well with the comradely spirit of the company, and there may have been some subtle element of competition between her and Tharp. Wiener was a gifted dancer but she sometimes held back. She could look merely correct when the others were putting their personal imprint on the material. At the request of Tharp and the company, Wiener left in June of 1974, and a short time later she formed her own dance group.

Tharp's unquenchable choreographic ambition kept pushing up the technical ante, and there were always dancers who felt pressured by this.

Powerfully attracted by something in Tharp's sensibility, they would find, down the line, that she had moved past what they'd initially embraced or even what they were prepared to execute. Isabel Garcia-Lorca's position was the most poignant of all. Twenty-five years after leaving the company, she wept when she talked about it. Admittedly without technical training, she'd been drawn to Tharp during the "people dance" phase. When Tharp brought her to New Berlin she'd worked hard to keep up with the others and learn the movement Tharp created especially for her abilities. Her long, elegant line and enigmatic composure were a great asset to the jazz pieces and *Deuce Coupe.* "When she was performing, it was like la créme de la créme," says Ken Rinker. "It made you look. You'd work with her, you watched her, you looked at her and you wanted to see more."

But increasingly Tharp craved a technical depth that only classical training could satisfy. She was grounding her choreographic invention in the ballet vocabulary rather than the "natural" locomotion and gesture of everyday life. The '60s avant-garde had rejected technique on principle and demanded dancers who looked like ordinary people. This programmatic pedestrianism was essential to their goal of clearing away excess and automatism. For laypersons like Garcia-Lorca, a window opened into a long-desired world of dancing and performing.

But choreography could develop only so far in the absence of technique. Judson anarchy quickly succumbed to simple organizing principles—games, worklike tasks, minimalist repetition. Tharp incorporated these along with anything that facilitated her innate sense of structure. But she quickly outgrew the overtly pedestrian inclusiveness with which she'd first assembled the company, and although she continued to look for individual qualities in dancers, she needed them to bring more technical skills into the studio. Garcia-Lorca saw the train speeding on. She was taking two ballet classes a day in New York, but when the company began working on *Deuce Coupe* she recognized a logical trend in Tharp's thinking. "It just makes sense," she says now, "that she would want to explore that vocabulary. . . . I just didn't have the technique. I mean fine, I was talented. . . . But the fact is, technically I couldn't keep up."

During the early part of 1974 Tharp, Rudner, Wright, and Rinker held discussions about whether to keep Tom Rawe, what to do about Wiener and Garcia-Lorca, and how to deal with a growing friction between Tharp and Bill Kosmas. Garcia-Lorca's fate was sealed, as she knew it would be. Her last performances took place at the Round House in London, in May, and after teaching a ballroom dance class with Rinker during the summer residency at American University, she left. She remembers a fateful meeting when Tharp seemed unable to tell her the painful truth. Garcia-Lorca bailed her out: "I made it easy for her. I said, I understand. I know what direction you're going, and I know I can't do it. So I know I have to go. She said, Right. That's it." It was the end of Garcia-Lorca's dance career. When she considered dancing for anyone else, she saw that other downtown choreographers hadn't yet taken on technical challenges, but she was underqualified for those with a conventionally demanding technique, like Cunningham. In any case, there was no other company that offered half the fascination of the work she'd been doing with Tharp.

Kosmas and Tharp conducted prolonged negotiations for the company's 1974 London season. Ten days of performances were booked for the Round House, an unconventional space formerly used as a railway turnaround. A thrust stage was built to afford some theatrical credence to the three jazz pieces, which were interspersed on two different programs with *The Fugue* and *The One Hundreds*. It was a risky venture—the company's fee wasn't guaranteed—and the advance publicity was carefully planned. Tharp spent a week in London in March, and an interview she gave to Peter Williams resulted in a four-page spread in the May edition of *Dance and Dancers*. The company arrived in London a month ahead of the season for workshops and open rehearsals. They had also arranged to make a one-hour video for London Weekend Television, and Tharp and Kosmas, looking to stimulate ticket sales at the Round House, hammered out a deal to have the completed video broadcast just before the season.

Both the video and the season were very successful. *The Financial Times's* Clement Crisp wrote two glowing reviews. *Dance and Dancers* sent Percival and two other critics, publishing nearly five pages of commentary with photos in July. Tharp's choreography disarmed Peter Williams, who, even after his interview with her, dreaded "encounters with American lady dance pioneers. It's all that dedication and intensity that worries us. . . ." Williams was greatly relieved to find Tharp putting forth no "portentous meaning, no hidden depths, but just what dance is all about and what American dance in particular is all about." Percival remarked that although many of his colleagues missed the point, the packed and cheering audiences got it. He expanded on Arlene Croce's Nijinska analogy, which he thought might have put off the English critics, for whom the Russian choreographer was a kind of totem: "Tharp now, like Nijinska in the '20s, produces ballets with a flip-pant, amusing surface concealing the meticulously worked structure; she has the same perfectionist approach to dancing . . . and like Nijinska she is a true innovator, therefore ahead of general taste."

The other major British dance periodical, *Dancing Times,* after printing a condensed version of Arlene Croce's *Eight Jelly Rolls* review in its May issue, offered its own rave. Mary Clarke chided those of her colleagues who thought Tharp needed taking down a peg or two. Clarke had had "one of my happiest evenings in the theater for years. The performance was totally exhilarating and I came out feeling that Isadora's dream had come true—I had seen America dancing." She disagreed with the critics who persisted in seeing Tharp's work as a put-on. "They are doing things which would be quite impossible for the classically trained dancer." Peter J. Rosenwald re-ported to the American magazine *Dance News* that the season had been an "unqualified success . . . If classicism in dance is about pointe shoes then Tharp's work fails by this definition, but in the broader context of authori-tativeness and traditional values her ballets are some of the most profoundly classical being produced today."

This set of reviews clearly established the critical battle lines from which Tharp's reputation would be assessed for the rest of her career. The British dance scene was still centered around its prestigious ballet tradition. Its strong ties to the Diaghilev era, including Nijinska, and even further back to the Russian Imperial school through revivals of nineteenth-century clas-sics, were a matter of national valor as well as aesthetic pride. Modern dance, on the other hand, maintained a faint presence within the field of British dance education, as a practice somewhere between recreation and physical culture, but with scant visibility on the professional dance stage. Some English critics, Clive Barnes included, went reflexively on the defen-sive whenever they saw Tharp venturing onto classical ground. Critics from the mainstream press—in America they were often not dance specialists—followed the conservative line about Tharp. Her jazz dances were great fun but anything that looked serious raised their suspicions.

But the "verbiage" some critics objected to in *The Bix Pieces,* and in the London Weekend Television production, was intentional, reflecting Tharp's determination to be understood as an artist and craftsman beneath her en-tertainer's persona. By this time she had mastered the lecture-demonstration format, developed by modern dancers early in the twentieth century to fa-miliarize audiences with their innovative work. Tharp blossomed in this environment. She could slide into an offhand mode with an audience of dancegoers or critics. Casual, irreverent, self-deprecating, she would speed through the intricate construction of her dances in a chatty singsong, interrupting herself to get up and demonstrate a phrase or two. These monologues took the sting out of her most austere works and gave credibility to the popular ones. *Twyla Tharp and "Eight Jelly Rolls"* introduced the English public to this brainy character with a collage of shots from the London lecture-demonstrations and rehearsals. Then it launched into a performance of the dance itself. The 1927 Jelly Roll Morton numbers were played by a band of English musicians under Max Harris, who had arranged and rehearsed every nuance.

In the documentary-demonstration part of the video, Tharp introduced the dancers—they too were smart, serious, and devoted to the work. Despite the obvious informality of her working process, Tharp came across as a perfectionist, articulate, unpretentious, interested in the history of her own dance as it fitted into dance history. By linking together images where she rehearses the company in the studio, presents them informally in dance examples to the theater audience, and describes the Jelly Rolls in some detail, the documentary captures the choreographer in different guises. After one chorus of the fifth Jelly Roll (the Drunk) running under the opening credits, the documentary leads off with Rudner musing:

> With Twyla it was the intelligence of it, the physical challenge and the great intelligence of it. I didn't know what I was going to be doing the next moment. All of those [other] situations, it was obvious to me what I was going to be doing the rest of my life. Sort of like run run run *arabesque*. And run run run *jump*. And this was different. This kept on changing. And it changed from being—the pieces we do now are nothing like the pieces we did then. But they're all rooted in the same integrity and intelligence and the desire to work and find out what dancing is and what we wanted to do.

A portion of the Drunk gets shown in a clip from a lecture-demonstration. By the time it occurs in the full performance, the viewer can savor not only Tharp's comic solo but the carefully rehearsed, disintegrating precision of the ensemble behind her.

Tharp came down with the flu on arrival in London and couldn't work, so the dancers spent several days going over the dance with director Derek

Bailey. The finished tape, made in consultation with Tharp when she recovered, defies the conventions of dance on film at the time. TV and tape cassettes were about to give dance wider public exposure than it had ever enjoyed, and by the end of the decade most misgivings about the camera had evaporated. But in 1974, dancers were still skittish about how they would look on the screen; critics and scholars still balked if the camera took any liberties with the choreography. From her years working at her mother's drive-in movie, Tharp had no qualms about the effects of the camera, and she was well aware of the difference between straight-on documentation of a dance and showcasing it for the screen. Already experienced with recording her work, she was eager to explore television further. She'd learned from the Camera Three *Bix Pieces,* produced by Merrill Brockway, and she probably picked up some more tricks from Bailey to add to her cache of expectations for *All About Eggs,* which was to founder in Boston a few months later. Along with *Eight Jelly Rolls* Derek Bailey taped *The Fugue* quite conventionally with the original cast, but only excerpts of this tape were included on the *Jelly Rolls* video, and neither tape was ever broadcast in the United States.

Twyla Tharp and "Eight Jelly Rolls" recorded not only the choreography but the seven-member company (Tharp, Rudner, Wright, Rawe, Rinker, Wiener, and Garcia-Lorca) at the peak of its form. Bailey filmed each section with a different stylistic treatment, avoiding the potential monotony of a single-perspective shoot. Number One, basically a solo for Wright, features the dancer against a white space. The camera frequently closes in on her legs and torso, emphasizing her size by peeking beyond her to Tharp and Rudner crossing in the background. In real life almost a foot shorter than Wright, they look even smaller because of the video camera's tendency to make objects exaggeratedly small as they get farther from the wide-angle lens. Bailey adds his own game of editing to Rudner and Wright's high jinks in Number Two. The screen periodically splits into two halves, keeping both figures in the frame as they separate from each other. The dancers pop in and out across an invisible dividing line, and sometimes there are two sets of them. At the end of the number they fade to white instead of exiting. Rudner is shot from above as she dances in a spotlight in Number Three. Her shadow on the floor shares the circle of light with her, and later a second shot of her upper body is superimposed on the long shot, lingering romantically on her arms and shoulders, and her expressive face.

Bailey's most controversial tactic occurs first in Number Four, when a giant film of the musicians fills the backdrop. This dance is the Tharp-Wright-

Rudner trio doing their three simultaneous solos. Busy already, and dwarfed by the Brobdingnagian musicians, the choreography gets reshaped further by sudden disappearances and reentries of the dancers. Rudner and Wright carry Tharp off after the unison final chorus, as the other dancers make their confused false entrance. The camera shoots Number Five, Tharp's Drunk solo, from all around, so that the viewer becomes as disoriented as she is. We see her falling and trying to balance, but we also see the group from her capsizing perspective, as they march inexorably and sometimes silently in the background, the foreground, and above her. For the individual solos in Number Six, we always see the soloist in harmony with all or part of the group. In Number Seven, the group fades to a doubled exposure behind Wright. This allows us to see exactly how they're copying the "Dots" poses from Wright as she lounges along. Toward the end, the group doubles again, reinforcing the choreographic idea of mechanical replication.

For the finale, the dancers do their nostalgic social dance steps, as giant black-and-white archival films of '20s dancers in night clubs and variety shows flicker behind them. Derek Bailey and the London team, with some help from Tharp, found the archival footage in their own library. Once the historical connection is made, the old films disappear and the dance finishes against a white space. The dancers exit, leaving Tharp to make a floppy bow.

The arrangements for the long and diverse London engagement put additional stress on Tharp's relationship with Kosmas. Bill Kosmas was the second man who exerted a crucial influence on Tharp's personal and professional life. The extent of their intimacy is hard to determine. Tharp is cagey about it in her own book—she admits to pursuing him with increasingly frustrating results. The dancers didn't know just what their relationship was; many people close to the company assumed they were not only lovers but were living together. Whatever their emotional attachments, she depended on his advice and managerial help during this period when her fortunes were changing dramatically. Kosmas contributed to her first public acclaim by insisting, from his first contact with her in 1971, that the company adopt a respectable, accessible image. At a time when downtown dancers, including Rudner and Wright, still clung to the moral authority of "poor theater," Kosmas saw straight down a more populist path to success. It wasn't until the end of the 1970s that countercultural stalwarts like Trisha

Brown, David Gordon, and Brenda Way's Oberlin Dance Collective decided to slick up their costumes and capitalize on their high-profile connections. By then, Tharp had been out of the pedestrian-dance business for a
decade.

Tharp was receptive to Kosmas's ideas of conventional art presenting.
They reflected her own middle-class instincts. She had, after all, grown up
in an early version of a trophy house, a sprawling place her father built for
the big family, where eight-year-old Twyla had her own wing. Her parents
were successful businesspersons, proud of the advantages they could give
their children. Twyla's mother, Lecile, provided her oldest with so many extracurricular lessons she became a driven professional instead of a cultivated
young lady. On the other hand, her parents weren't aristocrats who could
take their possessions casually. Lacking a built-in sense of entitlement,
Tharp worked too hard for what she thought she deserved, and then
doubted whether she had truly earned the rewards.

Kosmas, brought up in the professional world, thought the dancers
shouldn't have to do menial work like renovating the Franklin Street loft.
Rehearsing many sweaty hours a day was unusual, but Tharp, as director of
the company, should have a more privileged status than the rank and file.
He probably disapproved of her living and working in the same place. He
lived on Riverside Drive, and by 1974 she had also moved to the Upper
West Side. She could have afforded a beautiful loft in pregentrification
Soho or Greenwich Village, but instead she got an apartment high over
Central Park. Eventually she came to expect to be driven in hired cars and
put up in elegant hotel suites out of town. As soon as Kosmas started negotiating her contracts, they became detailed and overcautious. Working eight
hours a day with her own dancers in the studio was different from trying to
fit her extreme rehearsal needs into the schedule of a ballet company where
many choreographers were competing for the dancers' time, or a television
shoot where the crew had little experience with the needs of dancers. Presenters had to suffer through the combination of his lawyerly caution and
her gigantic imagination.

Kosmas not only dressed up the company's onstage and offstage appearance, he introduced Tharp to people outside the dance world who became
collaborators, like Kermit Love, Jeff Moss, and Marian Hailey. He understood the importance of social contacts and thought "showing up for an
event or being nice to people or going out for dinner" was part of Tharp's
responsibility. But this was never her strong suit. She could be rude to pa-

trons or drink too much and behave badly at postperformance parties. She didn't have the patience for obligatory socializing, Kosmas thought later. He wanted to protect and help her, of course, but he also had a personal stake in her social skills. She made him look bad, he thought, when she mishandled situations that he'd set up for her benefit.

Ironically, the more he facilitated her visibility, the more she was attracted to situations he disapproved of. She began a workshop at the request of theater director Andre Gregory. With Sharon Kinney as teaching assistant, she gave dance classes for the actors of his Manhattan Project and prepared material for them to show at a Tharp company performance at New York's Town Hall in April 1975. Gregory may have introduced Tharp to Richard Avedon, and she and the company were featured in two pages of his glamour photographs in the June 1975 *Vogue*. Along with people like opera director Sara Caldwell and painter Helen Frankenthaler, Tharp was one of that month's "People Are Talking About . . ." personalities, dubbed by an anonymous writer "the most decisive young American dance power today. What Jerome Robbins was to the 'fifties . . .'" The actors' project petered out, but Tharp and Avedon remained close friends. Perhaps Kosmas thought Tharp was headed for the wrong kind of stardom; perhaps the trajectory he'd started her on was zooming beyond his grasp. He began to feel that she was somehow compromising the quality of her work, and he "backed off and became less interested."

The professionalization that Kosmas set in motion meant that the company became less intimate and informal, at the same time that Tharp was having to acknowledge a responsibility as their boss. Even without the pressures of a high-profile career, modern dance companies inevitably undergo a gradual shift in the relationship between choreographer and dancers over time. Major figures like Martha Graham, Paul Taylor, Alvin Ailey, and Merce Cunningham all experienced the phenomenon. Every choreographer finds his or her own solution to the gap that opens with age and managing a successful business. Starting out as dancers themselves who've gathered friends around them to begin their group explorations, they all see new and younger members replace the original dancers. As their ideas mature and their opportunities expand, they dance less, yet the young dancers can do more. Their choreography becomes less a reflection of themselves than an idealization. Tharp continued to dance onstage well into her fifties, but her company was evolving fast. In a 1975 lecture-demonstration, responding to an audience question about why she chose the music she did, she reflected back to working on the *Jelly Rolls*. She felt a kinship with Jelly

Roll Morton and his Red Hot Peppers of the 1927 recordings: "I was out on a farm working [in New Berlin] and nobody knew anything about it, and here were these black guys that nobody had ever heard of in their time and they went through whatever they went through and they worked because they loved to work. . . . I responded to that feel about it." Now she was no longer unknown, and she and the dancers were working for a little more than the love of it.

Kosmas wanted to gain some distance, and since he was still conducting his law practice, he couldn't carry the role of full-time manager anyway. He saw himself as an executive producer, paving the way for Tharp's projects but keeping out of the day-to-day business of the company. Late in 1974 he and Tharp hired Rhoda Grauer, an enthusiastic young Vassar graduate who'd been working in the administration of the Spoleto Festival in Italy. Grauer had returned to New York to try her wings as a theater director; she didn't know much about dance but she'd been impressed with *The Bix Pieces* on *Camera Three*. Tharp met her at a party, and after a long talk she asked Grauer to come and work half-time for the same salary she'd made at Spoleto. Grauer was affable, practical, and the perfect administrator for Tharp at the time. In her years at Spoleto she'd worked with artists, dancers, big stars of the theater and music worlds. Famous prima donnas didn't intimidate her. She quickly decided that Tharp was unusual, that "She processed information in a way that is different from the way other people processed information. She thought differently. She was wired differently." Grauer wanted to devote herself to Tharp. "I thought, this girl is endless. . . . My life will be getting her whatever she needs to do what she has to do."

    Grauer put the company on a fifty-two-week salary, unprecedented in modern dance, inventing how to do it without excessive touring. She raised money, worked out contracts and bookings, and traveled with the company for important dates. She remembers making a deal with Harvey Lichtenstein, the director of Brooklyn Academy of Music, for the company's first big season at the BAM Opera House in 1976. Lichtenstein was apprehensive about the size of the audience, so Grauer agreed to a small fee and a large percentage of the box office profits. The season was a smash hit and the company made $90,000. It was Kosmas, a Minneapolis native, who established the initial contact with Suzanne Weil, director of programming at the Walker Art Center, for the first Minnesota residency, but Grauer implemented the more elaborate one that followed a year later. Everyone remembers the 1975 Twin Cities residency with pleasure. With cosponsorship from the Walker Art Center and the National Endowment for the Arts (both Weil and Grauer later became director of the NEA dance program), the month-long residency was to culminate in two performances, but the project was much more ambitious and community oriented.

Weil, Tharp, and Grauer drove around the Twin Cities to find a working space, and Tharp decided on the decrepit St. Paul Civic Center. This 1906 building housed a fine though half-abandoned theater and several other spaces, including a school for boxing. It was slated to be demolished and replaced by a more modern building. Tharp liked the offbeat reputation of the place, and disregarded the prickly politics of working in St. Paul while being sponsored by a major Minneapolis institution. Sue Weil arranged housing for the dancers, Jesse, Grauer, and stage manager Pennie Curry, welcoming them with baskets of groceries and pots of crocuses to ease them into the severe Minnesota winter. Grauer saw Weil as an ideal sponsor, who smoothed the way for the dancers and facilitated Tharp's most farfetched ideas.

As soon as the company arrived at the end of January, they set up a schedule of free, open classes and rehearsals every day, working in the king-sized, seventy-by-forty-foot Veterans Hall above the Civic Center Theater. They gave themselves class and rehearsed in the mornings, then invited the community in. The dancers thrived on this contact with the public. In addition to the open rehearsals and classes, they had sessions with local choreographers and public school teachers, they gave their own lecture-demonstration, and the day after the performances they appeared at a public evaluation session. They acquired a contingent of regular attendees who'd greet them on the street and talk about the day's work. Tharp was convinced that this kind of exposure to the working process was bound to enrich the experience of the future audience.

Initially there wasn't enough repertory for the final performances. Tharp had carried out her plan to mothball her old dances after making the Annenberg and London videotapes. Except for an early June repertory performance at the Henry Street Playhouse in New York, only *The Bach Duet* had been shown since London. In the fall, with the three dancers who remained, Wright, Rinker, and Rawe, Tharp had choreographed a new piece for the Walker, but there wasn't much else to fill in the programs. She came up with an elegant solution. During the daily two-hour open rehearsals over the month in St. Paul, she would create a new piece—she proposed to make a minute of movement a day. To fill in the rest of the program, they'd perform the other new dance twice. Sue Weil thought it was a great idea, and began advertising. Tickets for the performances went for a top price of six dollars.

Working on new choreography in public could be embarrassing and nerve-wracking, but the dancers were game for it. By the end of the residency, only eight minutes of new dance had been finished. Undaunted, Tharp staged *The Double Cross* to a series of radically different musical selections, with live readings of her meditations on performance and illusion, and *The Bach Duet* as a finale. Rose Marie Wright danced on pointe to the "Parade of the Wooden Soldiers," Rinker and Rawe did somersaults and pushups, and, according to Allen Robertson, who'd watched it being made, "The result is like a spinning trip down a radio dial band. A variety of contrasting choices, all of them usable but easily disposed of, are rapidly sketched in, glanced at and tossed away. . . . Given an overabundance of possibilities to choose from nobody knows where to go."

At the same time she'd been preparing for the residency, Tharp had reconfigured *Deuce Coupe*, which the Joffrey Ballet premiered as *Deuce Coupe II* in Chicago, 1 February, and in New York on the 26th, just after the end of the Minnesota residency. In addition to schedule pressures, Tharp was unhappy over the departure of Sara Rudner and her deadlocked relationship with Kosmas. *The Double Cross* as such disappeared quickly; Tharp filtered the movement material into her Chuck Berry piece, *Ocean's Motion*, which was coming up for a premiere at the Spoleto Festival in June. But *Sue's Leg* was a triumph. Easygoing almost to the point of negligence, it showed few signs of the difficult working situation that led up to Minneapolis. Tharp had found some choice old Fats Waller records, and she says she began making material for Wright, Rawe, and Rinker as a way of deflecting her gloom. In her autobiography Tharp asserts that the dance's final section, "In the Gloamin'," reflected "four desperate people clinging to one another for dear life," and there may have been other personal resonances or even a story. The title was a tribute to Suzanne Weil and a hint that the dance was intended as one "leg" of a three-part theater work that never materialized.

For the first time Tharp commissioned costumer Santo Loquasto—it's possible she used her 1974–75 Guggenheim Fellowship to hire him. Loquasto, who was a newcomer to dance, looked at a rehearsal and loved the dancers' idiosyncratic practice clothes. He decided to duplicate them, in elegant fabrics and tasteful shades of beige and brown. For the St. Paul performances, and again a few weeks later at Wesleyan University, the dance was repeated after *The Double Cross*, only this time in the original working attire. These costumes, so wonderfully suited to the dancers and to their movement, drew attention to the importance Tharp had always placed on what her dancers wore. Showing the costumes doubled, and redoubled when *Sue's Leg* ran twice in the St. Paul and Wesleyan performances, emphasized the idea that they were precisely *not* the clothes worn in the studio, but a theatricalized representation. They were neither the stark, black-and-white studio gear in which Karinska dressed Balanchine's modern ballets nor the fussy, skin-with-adornments of Willa Kim's many Eliot Feld productions. Throughout her career, Tharp used costumes as close to everyday clothes as possible, translated for the stage. Loquasto's layered jerseys and ankle warmers set a style for casual fashions in the world at large.

The *Sue's Leg* costume doubling itself echoed *The Bix Pieces*, where Kermit Love's little gray dresses, shorts, and pajamas for the Beiderbecke songs were replicated, for the lecture-demonstration and Haydn sections, in silky white fabrics. For the final quartet, "Abide with Me," Isabel Garcia-Lorca retained her gray costume. The white costumes were supposed to be the ghosts of the songs costumes, says Wright, and the final quartet "really is a recapitulation of everything that you've seen before, including the costumes. . . . So it's all, whatever the words are in the lecture-demonstration, it's all new again but it's also what has come before."

Sue's Leg, the last of Tharp's chamber-sized jazz pieces, had a close relationship to *The Bix Pieces*. Rose Marie Wright felt that the last Waller song, "In the Gloamin'," resembled the Haydn quartet section of the *Bix*. In both those pieces, four dancers worked closely together, entangling and freeing themselves in a continuous knot of movement. The difference for the dancers was that in the *Bix*, they had to make spontaneous choices from movement material that had been predetermined and rehearsed. Since all four of them were making choices that were unforeseen by the others, the whole dance became an improvisation. In *Sue's Leg*, the process of how they would work with each other was set, but the specific movement was not. "The material was much more mushy and nebulous," Wright thought.

Sue's Leg may be the last important piece in what's still considered—and lamented—as the definitive Twyla Tharp style. After only four years, the offhand performing attitudes and the loose, jazzy movement that seemed easy enough for anyone to do were verging on decadence, but her choreographic plan was still quite open and relaxed. After this her choreography became structurally tighter and clearer, more rooted in ballet technique, and more presentational. There wouldn't be so much breathing room. The dancers loved performing *Sue's Leg*—Tom Rawe called it a give-back piece.

Their performance was chosen to initiate the PBS *Dance in America* series, in a video directed by Merrill Brockway. Since the dance is less than half an hour long, it was supposed to be paired with a work by Eliot Feld. When this fell through, the producers prefaced Tharp's dance with a remarkable half-hour documentary on popular dancing, scripted by Arlene Croce. Uncannily related clips from *Sue's Leg* were spliced into the archival footage of square dancing, social dancing, tap dancing, chorus lines, marathons, burlesque, and ballroom. The documentary provided a context for Tharp's '30s nostalgia, but it may also have implanted the idea that her dance was simply a compendium of those old styles. Tharp reportedly was unhappy with the coupling, and Ken Rinker observed, "In my wildest imagination . . . I *never* related [*Sue's Leg*] to social dancing." Tharp certainly didn't elicit the dancers' recollections of popular steps, as she did in the last part of *Eight Jelly Rolls*, although the few minutes of archival footage on the London Weekend Television *Jelly Rolls* might have inspired the *Dance in America* treatment.

With its inner construction concealed under its goofy noodling-around behavior, and—in the video—overlaid by the historicizing documentary footage, *Sue's Leg* seems ultracasual, even thrown-away. Unlike the '30s performers on the documentary, the dancers aren't engaging in courtships, and if they're conscious of having an audience, they try hard not to play up to it. They seem to be pals or siblings, so intimate that they can trust each other completely, upstage each other without incurring offense, and fall in with foolhardy stunts and mischief. They may not have specific antecedents in Tharp's own four-sibling family, but they do play consistent roles. Wright is the benign big sister, tolerantly watching her two brothers act up. Rinker and Rawe are enough alike to be twins, but Rinker seems introverted, willful, while Rawe enjoys his own awkwardness. Tharp is at once the coy little sister and ringleader.

Most of the movement of the dance grows out of a walk that modulates from strolling to shambling to strutting, propelled by Fats Waller's bouncy theater organ and swing band. With their arms free, shoulders loose, torsos responsive to the possibility of twisting, they embellish the musical beat with understated shuffling and foot rotations. At times they break into overt tap dancing, but when Rawe goes into the shim-sham, accompanied by a tap soundtrack and an upbeat instrumental, he soon gets out of sync and proceeds with his own variation unfazed. Tharp has two solos, one very knowing, one naive. In the first, to "I Can't Give You Anything but Love," she peeps out from under her low-cut bangs and balances steady as a rock on half-toe, shimmying her shoulders, and twitching isolated parts of her body at the audience. Later, to Waller's clownish singing of "Ain't Misbehavin'," she could be doing the same movements, but as a professionally cute little girl. She alternates tiny, close-in attention-getting moves with huge assemblé turns and fast chaînés, inserting sudden scissors-jumps and drops to the floor.

All four dancers are featured in *Sue's Leg*, but they're equally memorable when they work in combination. Rawe and Rinker shadow each other in slightly-off unisons and canons. They circle around Wright and eventually engage in a shoving match with her. Later the three are gathered close together but looking away nonchalantly as one topples over against another. They seem to team up against Tharp as the outsider at moments, but they copy her as she shows an intricate step. They all link arms and bounce up and down together. In the windup, they begin scrambling over each other's backs, hoisting one another up, and suddenly they line up, taking a perfect preparation and joining hands for a bow. The music changes and they regroup for a fast chorus of "I've Got My Fingers Crossed," a sort of choreographed encore. They modulate from playful bouncing on two feet to tight step-turns and suddenly a replay of the hoisting and scrambling sequence. There's the lineup, the preparation, and finally they all bow while still holding hands

6

The Big Leagues
1975–1978

The company's engagement at the 1975 Spoleto Festival in Italy probably originated through Rhoda Grauer's connections, and it was Grauer
who booked the performances for the opera house, the Teatro Nuovo, instead of a smaller theater. This proved to be a miscalculation. The repertory,
consisting of *Ocean's Motion, Sue's Leg, Bach Duet*, and a reduced version of *The
One Hundreds*, eluded the high-culture European audience. But the engagement proved momentous anyway.

Tharp's career had been headed for an intersection with that of the extraordinary Russian dancer Mikhail Baryshnikov for several months. He had
defected from the Soviet Union only a year earlier. A phenomenon as a performer, a tremendous virtuoso and box office attraction, he had become a
regular guest artist at American Ballet Theater. By the time he met Tharp in
Spoleto he had danced eleven roles in the West, most of them classical, but
he was looking for new choreographic challenges. He was collaborating
with Charles France on a picture book, *Baryshnikov at Work*, and France, a
close friend of Arlene Croce, was a devoted Tharp fan who steered everyone he knew to see her work. American Ballet Theater codirector Oliver
Smith, always scouting for new choreographic talent for the company, had
his eye on Tharp. Early in 1975 her work was visible in New York both at

the Joffrey Ballet and at Town Hall in May, where her company did several small items and the New York premiere of *Sue's Leg*.

When Smith brought his codirector, Lucia Chase, and Baryshnikov to a performance of *Deuce Coupe II*, Baryshnikov was fascinated with the way Tharp made the dancers look: "sort of men and women on stage being in a way very whole and very themselves and very grounded and without playing a character, being the people of the streets." According to Tharp, Chase and Smith offered her a commission soon after the *Sue's Leg* debut. Tharp guessed that Baryshnikov had proposed the idea, and she scandalized the directors by naming a $10,000 fee.

In June Baryshnikov was appearing at the Spoleto Festival with Carla Fracci in a quasi–Martha Graham creation about Medea by John Butler. On the Tharp company's program the customary *Half the One Hundreds* mob scene, with a cast including Spoleto artistic director Gian-Carlo Menotti, was dubbed *The 49 Amici* for the occasion. Tharp decided to dance the introductory *Fifties* as a solo, she said, so that the dancers would have time to change costumes, but she wasn't naive. She knew Baryshnikov would be in the audience and she intended to win him over decisively, with her dancing. Seated in the Director's box with Grauer and Clive Barnes, Baryshnikov saw "how refined and delicate and impossibly difficult her vocabulary is." Later Barnes remembered that "they were both obviously amazed and astounded at each other. For Mr. Baryshnikov this was clearly a new world, and for Miss Tharp this was clearly a new dancer." After Spoleto, the deal with ABT was a fait accompli.

The artistic and personal relationship between Tharp and Baryshnikov that began at Spoleto stretched her fraying bond with Bill Kosmas to the breaking point. He resigned a few months later, before the premiere of the ballet that propelled her into superstardom, *Push Comes to Shove*.

Tharp began working in the studio with Baryshnikov after they returned from Spoleto, on what became the opening sections of the ballet. For hours they looked at films of black tap dancers and soft-shoe entertainers. "She was trying to explain to me where the movement comes from, it's not just like she invented it," he says. Tharp used the Bach Partita in D Minor for their initial improvising, and Baryshnikov thought she wanted to translate "the ease and grace of a flatfooted dancer . . . into a kind of virtuoso element." As in *Sue's Leg*, Tharp wasn't going to quote her vernacular sources so much as impose their temperament onto a different set of circumstances.

The ballet opened with a slouchy, sexy Baryshnikov, in another elegant Santo Loquasto practice outfit, just noodling to three minutes of ragtime. This Tharpian image was familiar enough by then, and the sight of the Russian prodigy goofing across the forestage, slinkily joined by ballerinas Marianna Tcherkassky and Martine Van Hamel, was both a shock and a delight to the audience. But when the rag and the prologue ended, the curtain went up on the real transformation. In rehearsals, by the time Van Hamel and Tcherkassky joined the work, Tharp had switched from the Bach Partita to Haydn's Symphony No. 82. Its subtitle, "The Bear," supplied an apt Russian reference, and it provided a spirited musical base for her revelation of the star, dancing classical steps in an unimaginably relaxed way.

The first movement belonged to Baryshnikov even though the women each entered and danced briefly. At first glance his solo seemed merely a string of alternating ballet steps and pedestrian movements, taken at maximum speed. He launched into ballet flash—multiple pirouettes, leaps, fancy leg designs and foot changes—interrupting this offhand virtuosity to rake his fingers through his hair or sink into one hip as if waiting for a bus. But in a sense, the street gestures are the least surprising thing about what he did. It's as if Tharp planted them there in order to establish an antithesis to the ballet steps, but what's in between is most interesting. Some part of each step is done in proper form, but the dancer's preparation, attack, and alignment reshapes it. Starting a pivot turn, he visibly initiates from his pelvis and throws his whole upper body and head back against the direction of the turn. He flings his arms across his body to change to a new stance, then finishes with exquisitely calm gallantry. He takes exaggerated preparations, or goes from one feat to another with no preparation at all. He whips from a set of hunched-over spins into a punch. He anatomizes a gesture by jerking through it one body segment at a time, what would be called "popping" twenty years later by hip-hoppers. When the music rears up and growls, he pitches forward into an upside-down arabesque, then springs upright.

With phenomenal control, he can uncork sudden speed or a sudden complete stop, accelerate or slow down in the middle of a phrase. He assumes the ballet body attitude: pulled-up torso, noble head, spread-out chest and arms, pointed legs and feet, assured address to the audience. The next moment he lets go of all this placement and relaxes into a comfortable, everyday slump. After a cascade of deranged beats, jetés en tournant, brisés, and combinations packed with steps, he ends with six pirouettes that decelerate into a perfect fourth position. You have the sense that he's thinking his way through the dance, choosing what to do, how to be. Everything is musical and everything draws attention to the classical dancer that he is, even when he's turning himself inside out.

Baryshnikov's appetite for new experiences, and his adaptability to them, made *Push Comes to Shove* possible. His personality and his role within the company became one theme of the many-layered ballet. *Push* was neither Tharp's first pointe ballet nor her first entry in the classical arena, but American Ballet Theater was this country's foremost traditional ballet ensemble. Since its founding in the 1930s ABT had maintained a contemporary wing, but its ongoing repertory of important classics asserted its connection to the great Russian/French heritage. The '70s were both an exhilarating and a demoralizing time for the company. By 1975 its roster was top-heavy with international stars. Besides creating a modern vehicle for Baryshnikov, Tharp set out to depict a company in which he and other celebrated guest artists dominated not only *Giselle, Coppélia, La Sylphide*, but contemporary works as well. Their every appearance enriched the box office, but when they were the main attraction, the other dancers faded into the background.

Playing on the double entendre of Baryshnikov as generic guest star and Misha as interloper and role model, Tharp developed a kind of fairy tale. Having lured the audience in with his name and gratified them with his pyrotechnics, she redirected the limelight to the rest of the company. Baryshnikov was known for his modesty during bows, the way he stepped back and let his ballerina accept the audience's ovation. In *Push*, he defers to his female partners in the first movement, leaves altogether for the two middle movements, and submits in the end to a rambunctious effusion of attention-grabbing stunts from everyone else. With this premise, *Push* became an insider ballet, in the tradition of Antony Tudor's *Gala Performance*, choreographed in 1938, and Jerome Robbins's 1956 *The Concert*.

During the preliminary rehearsals, as Baryshnikov was absorbing Tharp's casual style, she was quizzing him about ballet steps. Although she'd taken ballet class for years, she didn't know the refinements, and she needed a lot of information. According to Baryshnikov, "She was trying to understand how the girls go on pointe and what propels them around, and figure out classical coordination, where is croisé, what's éffacé, why it's écarté . . . and what's the difference between the first arabesque where it's flat and the fourth arabesque . . ." For the second movement of *Push*, she introduced a double corps de ballet, two groups of eight girls in identical short filmy dresses, one group in pale blue, the other in beige; led by Tcherkassky and a new soloist, Kristine Elliott. Recalling Robbins's famous Mistake Waltz in *The Concert*, they behaved almost properly but with misalignments and "wrong notes" that enlivened the static, secondary role traditionally prescribed for the corps.

Dance critic Laura Shapiro, writing in *The Boston Globe* shortly after *Push*'s premiere but without having seen it yet, remarked on Tharp's perennial choreographic "veneer of chaos." Shapiro felt that even when the audience couldn't see Tharp's underlying craft, it would always sense the form holding together her seemingly undefined activity and be reassured. The corps in *Push* initiates a long descent into this deceptive messiness. Tharp's vocabulary here consists of heeled-over ballet steps, multidirectional group poses, and port de bras exercises gone haywire. The two semichoruses alternate at first, working out Haydn's simple theme with several different floor patterns and subdivisions. The groups converge and appear to be trying to resolve all these designs into one, but it takes a lot of scrambled interweavings before they agree on four lines perpendicular to the footlights. Even this order is temporary, and they continue to rearrange it. When their movement finally unifies, they face different directions. As this brilliantly engineered machinery slips through its paces, the dancers disclose the boredom, competitiveness, and mishaps they usually conceal. A girl from one side somehow shows up in the other corps' territory and casually fades back into her correct place. Off to the side, the two lead sylphs claw at each other spitefully. Individuals saunter off when it appears they're not needed. At the end, only a few women are left to bow with their leader.

Egalitarian yet deeply respectful of rank and power, Tharp wanted every sector of Ballet Theater's population to be noticed. She told interviewer Jane Perlez that she didn't understand "alphabet dancing." That is, company rosters that listed all dancers equally. "Some dancers should be in the chorus—that's their level," she said, without intending any condescension, so she was making "trios and quartets which are very difficult and small featured parts for a dancer who can hold a small responsibility and excel at it."

Susan Jones was a member of the Ballet Theater corps when Tharp started rehearsals for the second movement, which was to be her showcase for the translated coryphées. "We were a bit afraid of working with her," Jones says. The usual dire preconceptions about Tharp had percolated through the company, but they were forgotten immediately. Tharp had worked out the corps movement and taught it to Jennifer Way, who came along as her assistant and demonstrator. Jones remembers: "From the very first day you had to be totally impressed with her, not just her pace but the homework . . . and her calculations of how long it would take for us to go across the room doing these complicated combinations, changing fronts and at a rapid pace, [it] was just unbelievable to all of us. It really blew us away." Jones noticed that Tharp had an uncanny ability not only to make up steps and groupings but to visualize how these would coordinate spatially and musically, before she taught them to the dancers.

Jones was given a tiny featured part, and a year later, after the untimely death of ballet mistress Fiorella Keane, took over the job of overseeing *Push* and most of Tharp's subsequent ABT repertory. She never lost her admiration for Tharp's work. "She crafted [that second movement] like the most highly crafted Petipa or Balanchine ballet. . . . It's like the bar is raised from the first minute of the rehearsal. . . . You rise to the occasion and you get in that zone and you work at the same pace that she does." Jones cherished her inside knowledge of the corps movement, subtle choreographic detail that she knew the audience probably wouldn't be able to discern. When she set *Push* on Britain's Royal Ballet several years later, Jones shared "secrets" with Monica Mason, then the Royal's ballet mistress, like the movement phrase that travels in a snakelike canon through the ranks of the corps. "You feel the effect of that wave getting bigger and bigger on the stage but you don't really see how it happens."

Not only did *Push* call attention to the hierarchy of dancers in ballet companies, specifically ABT, the piece had a shadow plot. Similar to the way Balanchine skimmed what he wanted from the classics, Tharp garnered the dance component from one or more actual story ballets in the repertory. She then reassembled these elements and reinvested them in a new tale of threat, dissension, and harmony restored. After focusing on Baryshnikov and his two female partners, and reinterpreting the corps, the "plot" moved on to a skewed pas de deux by Van Hamel and Clark Tippett, surrounded by male and female courtier types. As in some nineteenth-century party scene, the nobles—the men dressed like Baryshnikov and the women in long, somewhat dowdy dresses and turbans—enter in small groups, admiring and bowing to Tippett and Van Hamel, who grandly ignore them. Haydn's minuet serves as a processional, keeping all the nobles streaming across the stage behind the principal couple or posing in gracious attendance.

As the movement progresses, Van Hamel and Tippett's regal duet becomes contentious. Their timing goes slightly off; she hogs the spotlight and he contrives ways to be seen, burrowing under her arm, making extra gestures. Unnoticed by the principals, the nobles vie for the audience's attention with gratuitous bows and upstaging tactics. Tippett circulates among the courtiers while his partner waits for him temperamentally. Van Hamel is courted by three other men, who throw her bodily into Tippett's arms when he returns.

Tharp always resisted clichéd beginnings and endings; she loved movement that went on after the music finished, exits that didn't coincide with musical conclusions. Baryshnikov's second appearance, alone in the spotlight after the rag, deferred belatedly to his star status. At the end of the first movement, the women of the corps have already entered before the audience has stopped applauding his solo. As the music begins again, he leaves with a tremendous barrel turn into the wings. This is the first of three transitional interludes between movements. As the corps is petering out in the second movement, Tcherkassky brings Baryshnikov on for a flirtatious moment. In silence, they speed through a series of mistimed changes and lifts, then race off, to the audience's amusement. After the third movement, Van Hamel and her three courtiers saunter near the wings, passing a derby among them.

This hat, the only prop in the ballet, symbolically adds to the theme of competition and attainment. Baryshnikov is wearing it when he first appears. His two female partners snatch it, put it on, pass it between them slyly, like teenagers with a basketball hero's jacket. In the fourth movement, the derby becomes a desired trophy for everyone in the corps, and is tossed from one dancer to another. The hat doubles before the end of the ballet as the competitive activity takes over; Baryshnikov loses the symbol of his superior rank. When the dance was revived in the '80s Tharp made choreographic changes too, so that Baryshnikov, then ABT's artistic director, actually stepped back as the whole company acquired hats of their own. On closing night of the winter 1976 ABT season, with *Push* a certified hit, Tharp's fans orchestrated a surprise exclamation of derbies and deluged the stage with them.

The fourth movement begins with Baryshnikov leading two sylphs on for a bow. From there on, the ensemble and the principals dance in ever-mixing patterns, until the big finale, where they never quite get symmetrically organized. The corps women skitter on half-toe clutching their foreheads and making other desperate gestures. Even amid this planned breakdown, Tharp had encouraged the dancers to choose which choreographed phrases to do. But they finally assemble with Baryshnikov in the center on Haydn's volley of cadences, as if for a series of family snapshots.

The dancers knew *Push Comes to Shove* was funny, but none of them anticipated the ecstatic response that greeted the ballet's premiere, at the Uris Theater on 7 January 1976. Ovations are common on opening nights, but this was special. Tharp was brought onstage by Baryshnikov during the endless bows, and managed to grin while receiving bouquets and applause from the dancers. Friends said they had never seen her happier. Afterward, Gelsey Kirkland walked out shaking her head and saying "I'm never going to dance again. How could I be so stupid?" Kirkland, who had left New York City Ballet to dance with Baryshnikov at Ballet Theater, began learning the part that later went to Tcherkassky but withdrew after a few rehearsals, perhaps considering Tharp's movement too eccentric. *Hamlet Connotations*, the new John Neumeier ballet she and Baryshnikov performed that season with Erik Bruhn and Marcia Haydee, was dubbed "simplistically Oedipal" by *Time* magazine, and it quickly disappeared.

Although some critics still refused to take Tharp's comedy seriously, most of the press was delighted with *Push*. Clive Barnes unequivocally endorsed it. "It has charm, vivacity, humor, kinetic understanding . . . Miss Tharp has not merely done it again — she has done it better than ever before." Croce thought it was "a real work of art and an entrancing good time in the theatre," but almost too subtly balanced between real invention and spoof. The comic aspects of *Push* were so successful that they took over the ballet in many people's eyes. Pundit Roger Copeland objected to the "slapstick." The humor in *Push* was "facile and unadventurous" compared to *The Bix Pieces*, he thought, "not the result of delicately modulated sensibilities, but rather of a broad and rather obvious parody."

But Dale Harris saw the audience's spontaneous reception of the ballet—and of Tharp—differently. Unlike the "rites of personality worship" that cluttered the ABT repertory, *Push* made the audience understand "that [Tharp's] share in the evening's success was the determinative one, and, by extension, that first-class choreography is a rare and precious commodity." Hardly had the curtain come down when George Gelles of *The Washington*

Star declared Tharp "the hottest ticket in American dance today." Gelles thought that what some viewers saw as "jokey and facile" was in fact "parody of the highest sort . . . a combination of homage and criticism in one." ABT's own historian, Charles Payne, called it "a hit of such proportions as is apt to occur only once in a decade, and [it] went on to become the triumph of Ballet Theatre's 1977 European tour." Still, the company thought of *Push* as a comic vehicle for Baryshnikov, who "adjusted his classic technique unerringly to the grotesqueries" of Tharp's far-out ballet.

Despite the huge success of *Push Comes to Shove,* Tharp didn't make another company ballet for ABT until 1984, when Baryshnikov had become its director. Tharp's former associates can't account for this except to point out that she was working on other things—chiefly some big media projects and her own expanding company. But there were probably less visible issues.

Tharp was already notorious for charging high fees and insisting on other contractual perks that distressed the money-conscious ABT management. The company was committed to the star system at that time, an expensive practice that nevertheless yielded big box office and high prestige. Its paradigm had been set in the 1940s and '50s by Markova, Alonso, Bruhn, Youskevitch, Fracci, Lander, Serrano, and later by the defecting Russians Nureyev, Makarova, and Baryshnikov. From its inception, ABT set out to be the American company that would carry on the Russian ballet tradition— along with producing English and American works. Under Lucia Chase and Oliver Smith it had mounted full-length productions of *Swan Lake, Giselle,* and *Raymonda,* with *Sleeping Beauty* scheduled to go up in the summer season of 1976. Charles Payne relates in his company history that by the beginning of the '70s ABT had come to think of itself as a company with a repertory of standard works, vehicles for the great international stars, much like the Metropolitan Opera. Roving bands of dancers, singers, and conductors needed minimal rehearsal time to step into the schedule. Jet travel facilitated the process. As a touring company, without a permanent theater in New York or anywhere else, ABT achieved an alternative stability with its revolving supply of headliners, but its own principal dancers were constantly struggling to compete with visiting celebrities. Morale was dropping. Dale Harris took note of American ballerina Cynthia Gregory's resignation midseason (it turned out to be temporary) due to management's "lack of artistic encouragement." This state of affairs, of course, was the sub-text situation of *Push Comes to Shove*.

Baryshnikov in real life set out to reform the system during his tenure as artistic director of ABT (1980–89). He cut back the star system and further repaired morale by cultivating the in-house dancers, polishing up the indifferent technique of the ensemble, and summoning avant-garde choreographers to enliven the repertory. Ironically, when he left, the company was better able to produce the classics than ever before.

Despite shifts of economics and taste, ballet culture continues to privilege the classics and their top interpreters. Tharp herself partook of this mystique in her adoration of classical dancers. There was no point in taking on commissions unless she could begin her journey to the technical stratosphere from the tallest launching pad. "I cannot think seriously about a dancer who lacks technical control," she told Alan Kriegsman of *The Washington Post*. "But there are technically expert dancers who are terrified of dancing. . . . There must be a real passion to do it. And also a certain lust for adventure, the audacity to throw away any of that technique, to get beyond it." From the first Joffrey rebellions to French and English resistance years later, there were dancers who found Tharp's deconstructed classicism disorienting. Martine Van Hamel admits to needing time to master her unusual coordinations and timing. "You had to repeat it so it became natural. It had to get into my muscle memory." Her shruggy, comedic role in *Push* wasn't likely to add any luster to her ballerina's tiara either. Within ABT, a dancer of Van Hamel's stature did have the power to opt out, and by the time *Push Comes to Shove* was filmed in 1984 she had ceded her part to Susan Jaffe.

For Tharp there was one immediate follow-up to *Push*. ABT's annual fund-raising gala was scheduled for the New York State Theater in July after the *Push* premiere, and the management naturally wanted to showcase its prize acquisition, Baryshnikov. The ballet gala, a ritualized enactment of the ballet mystique, features invited stars and home talent in glamourous extracts from the repertory. Baryshnikov declined to trot out the expected pas de deux from *Don Quixote* or *Le Corsaire* for the 1976 extravaganza. Instead he asked Tharp to make something new. The two were just starting to work on a television project and she decided to double up assignments. The ABT commission would give her more time to work on the material for the TV taping. Besides, she couldn't resist the opportunity to choreograph—and dance—in the home of the New York City Ballet, what she called "Balanchine's stage." *Once More, Frank* turned out to be a notable failure—another possible reason ABT's management cooled to Tharp. It also touched off some of her greatest successes.

Eventually she got terrific mileage out of a dozen or so Sinatra songs that she selected from the durable crooner's recordings of the '60s, with their romantic Nelson Riddle arrangements. *Nine Sinatra Songs* (1982) was a Tharp company favorite for years; some considered it her all-time best dance. *Sinatra Suite* made its way into the ABT repertory, and it was danced by Baryshnikov and Elaine Kudo on the same commercial video that featured *Push*. In 1984 the Tharp company performed the *Nine* at the White House for President Reagan, and, as part of Reagan's 1985 inaugural events, Baryshnikov and Kudo danced the *Suite* with Sinatra singing in person.

For the 1976 ABT gala Tharp used "Something Stupid," "That's Life," and "One for My Baby." Dressed by Santo Loquasto in identical white jazz shoes, short-shorts and rugby shirts, with their small, compact, and superbly trained bodies, she and Baryshnikov looked like twins. *Once More, Frank* was never performed on a stage again, but twenty-six photographs by Martha Swope, published in *Baryshnikov at Work*, give some idea of what it looked like. Tharp took the idea of the pas de deux seriously. She made lifts, jumps, and parallel dancing for the two of them, but as in *Push* the classical ideas were either interpreted casually or gunned to extremes. He hefts her to his shoulder, where she puts on an anxious grin but points her feet in a kind of swan-dive assemblé. They slump against one another, spring up into circular jumps. In one photo, she seems to be pleading with him, like Giselle, while he edges away. In another, he seems to have just tumbled onto his back and is rolling with his legs in the air.

The gala audience had no taste for this, and the performance was loudly booed. Baryshnikov had to pull her on for their bow, and she ran from the theater in tears. He thinks now it was a "nice little piece," but the audience wasn't ready for it. They had expected to see a prince and instead they got two tomboys having fun. Baryshnikov found it interesting "to experience Twyla constantly changing from the authoritative figure the choreographer must be to the co-dancer whose psychological level was very much the same as mine." Charles France considered the idea too sophisticated: Tharp had miscalculated the degree of style-mixing the audience would tolerate, especially when she herself was dancing alongside the great danseur noble of the era.

But the gala was almost incidental to Tharp's real project. *Once More, Frank* was conceived to illustrate the dancemaking process as it related to television. David Loxton, director of the Experimental Television Lab at New York's public TV outlet WNET/Channel 13, had some funds to try new things, and he had offered Tharp his facilities. This suited her very well, because, having made primitive records of her work for years, she was eager to learn what professional television could do. She contributed a $100,000 grant for company development that she'd received at the end of 1975 from the Andrew W. Mellon Foundation. Loxton brought on board a young television director, Don Mischer, who welcomed the chance to work with a rule-breaker.

The project that became *Making Television Dance* was being documented in black and white by independent filmmaker Joel Gold, and his footage became a key element in the finished video. When Tharp and Baryshnikov were rehearsing the Sinatra, Gold captured their relationship superbly. (The unfortunate gala performance that was the ostensible end product didn't appear in the video.) Baryshnikov leans against a mirror, beaming and gasping with admiration as Tharp demonstrates a phrase to "That's Life." They practice lifts, trying tricky things. At one point she's nosediving over his shoulder, aiming for his outstretched leg. Laughing, she crawls down. On the next try, something goes wrong; he grabs her waist but she tumbles onto her head, to his dismay. He remembers that he just couldn't hold on to her when she giggled and let go. Tharp was fond of saying she didn't like to be lifted, it made her sick—but that was all the more reason to try it, and here she had the classiest escort in the business. Baryshnikov says she wasn't the easiest person to partner. "She was very spontaneous, of course, and trying too much to help the partner. And that's always wrong."

The edited sequence ends with "One for My Baby," shot entirely in sensuous close-up. Tharp explains in voice-over that the duet was intended to be very private, intimate, to be seen by a single viewer at home. You don't see the arms and legs because "I didn't make anything for the arms and legs. It was made for the void between us." She'd been thinking about close-ups two years earlier, as part of a multimedia production scheme for *Sue's Leg*. Six screens were to flank the stage, with previously filmed close-ups of the movement projected during the dance. Given the available resources and the capability of television at the time, the scheme proved unworkable, fortunately for *Sue's Leg*.

Don Mischer recalls that from the outset Tharp brushed aside the prevailing dictum that dance must be televised in a consistent full-stage shot with all the bodies visible at all times. They argued about it. One of her initial ideas was to "create dance with imagery that was not full-bodied dancers. She thought we could shoot close-ups of eyes or knees or fingers. Or elbows, and manipulate these images with video and create dance that way." The "One for My Baby" sequence was probably the best they could do with this idea, but she had plenty of others; some worked and some didn't. In a black-and-white shot early in the video, Tharp quizzes Mischer about the gadgetry in the control room. She wanted to use things television people took for granted, like the color-bar test pattern and the numbers that ran on top of the picture, counting seconds. She didn't care about the conventions of television, or televised dance; she wanted to see what the two media could do together. Loxton thought their trial-and-error process would be as interesting as the work, even when the idea failed, and midstream he brought in Joel Gold to record it.

Making Television Dance, still one of the most imaginative dance videos ever made, turned out to be a sort of anthology. There were three main segments with an epilogue, surrounded by Gold's black-and-white footage of the process—rehearsals, preparation, messed-up attempts, and commentary by Tharp, the dancers, and the crew. In addition to the Sinatra sequence, she choreographed "etudes" for the particular qualities or skills of four Tharp dancers, using video editing to underscore her compositional themes. Each etude was filmed in a different space, from the prehistoric Great Jones Street loft to Franklin Street to the ABT studios uptown. The square TV screen suggested an American square dance, which she turned into a group variation for herself—laboriously overdubbed eight times—and a company work that became *Country Dances*.

By the summer of 1976, Tharp's company had begun its evolution into the perfectly blended ensemble of modern and ballet dancers that created her work for the next decade. For *Making Television Dance* she was temporarily down to a quartet again. Ken Rinker didn't like the stop-and-go pacing of film and video work, so he declined the television project. Rose Marie Wright was taking some time off to care for a knee injury. At that point the first key players in the company's subsequent adventures, Shelley Washington and Christine Uchida, had arrived on the scene.

Washington was a student at the Juilliard School in 1973, apprenticing with the José Limón company, when she took Tharp's summer classes at

American University. The students had to learn one hundred numbered positions, do them on the right or left side, in slow motion, in retrograde, and be able to put them together in any order to make a dance phrase. Washington was dazzled. She was good at it too. Tharp even called her onstage from the audience to demonstrate the positions while the company conducted a lecture-demonstration. "All of a sudden, it was like every variable on your body and your brain," Washington said years later. She knew immediately that Tharp dance was what she wanted to do, but the company didn't have an opening until two years later, when she was dancing with Martha Graham. Washington auditioned for the dancers—Tharp wasn't present—and they invited her to work with them. It was a very big deal to leave a job in modern dance's most prestigious company for a small, ill-paid troupe that didn't even have separate dressing rooms for men and women. But, says Washington, "Something about the way Twyla worked in 1973, when I was seventeen years old or whatever, just . . . got me. I just had to do it."

Uchida, feeling stalled in the Joffrey Ballet, had left to try dancing in musicals. She'd loved working with Tharp and the company in *Deuce Coupe* and *As Time Goes By*, and she'd already let Tharp know she was interested in joining them. Tharp did call her but at a bad time, just before Uchida was about to leave on tour with a show that subsequently flopped on Broadway. Finally in the spring of 1975 Uchida heard Tharp was having auditions and decided to go. She got lost looking for Franklin Street and arrived late. But Tharp signed her up immediately, and she started learning Isabel Garcia-Lorca's part in *Eight Jelly Rolls*.

The etudes for *Making Television Dance* were ingenious one-to-two-minute miniatures, layered, Tharpian fashion, to display not only the dancers but the way choreography works, and the way television can both enhance and complexify dance. For "Speed" Tharp introduces Shelley Washington as a dancer with charm, warmth, and the physical courage of a big jumper. Washington spirals up into the air and down to the floor. In what Don Mischer calls "freezes with moves away," the camera captures the dancer at the peak of a jump or a turn, holding the dramatic moment over as she continues in real time, and then slowly fading out the still image. This is an almost uncanny adaptation of Tharp's old "dots" device, where the backup chorus arrested Wright's moves in *Eight Jelly Rolls*.

Tharp celebrates Tom Rawe's work ethic and endurance, his determination to analyze and conquer movement material, in "Repetition." Rawe jogs into some easy turns with his upper torso stretching and folding loosely; he runs in place with his hands flapping; he does pushups with handclaps. Much of the time he's accompanied by a shadow of himself, so he seems to be doing twice the work. Rhoda Grauer remembers that Tharp visualized Rawe "skipping rope, and then his body jumps out of his body, and then [he'd] keep skipping rope, and this other body that jumps out of his body goes over and does pushups, and then another body jumps out of that body. And Don going, it's not possible. Can't be done." But Tharp insisted until Mischer found a way to do it.

For "Focus" Jennifer Way performs the same phrase twice, simultaneously, as filmed by two cameras. She duets with herself and with the cameras, pulling the movement in close to the body and releasing it as one camera pulls back, and adjusting her space the opposite way for the other camera, which starts at a distance and zooms in. Before the shoot, Tharp and Way meet on the sidewalk near Columbus Circle, to go over the solo. Tharp is going to stand in for Way in rehearsal, and Way has to remind her how the sequence goes.

"Retrograde," says Tharp, is something only a mother could love. She then launches into one of her rapid-fire explanations as Chris Uchida gives a pristine demonstration of another doubled phrase. It's almost impossible to follow the words, the sequence, and the manipulation, but the gist of it is that in midphrase one Uchida starts dancing it backwards, while the other Uchida is filmed in reverse. Tharp wants to show the difference between mechanical and live retrograde. "Television can come closer to a conceptual rendition of movement in space than is actually possible," she remarks. "It's right—but it's wrong."

Tharp loved double images. Perhaps, as a child with twin brothers, she had realized early the advantages of pairing. In choreographic practice, the viewer would learn more, and enjoy more, by seeing two ideas side by side rather than one after the other. Ever since the days of Rudner and Wright, she'd deliberately put dancers of different styles and temperaments together within the same choreography. Wright and Rinker's demonstration of steps in *The Bix Pieces*, the duo that performed the first part of the *One Hundreds*, even the man-woman/ballet-modern symbiosis of *Once More, Frank*, all asked the audience to see contrasts within a finely tuned unit. Television was an ideal medium for this witty didacticism.

Although most of *Making Television Dance* was conjured up in the privacy of a studio, *Country Dances* needed a live audience. Conceptually, this brought a natural climax to the video process that began with one person dancing with herself in television no-space and ended in a stark coda where the outline of a dancer sinks and merges into a flat-line horizon. The circumstances of a proscenium theater wouldn't give the television crews enough freedom to do their work, so they booked a sound stage and set it up in arena style, for an all-day rehearsal and showing. Mimeographed notices were posted all over the city to summon the audience. It was Mischer who realized that after the first take the audience would be exhausted, and they came up with the slightly devious idea of scheduling two showings, both free. They'd set up in the morning and then tape a runthrough, which would serve as a dress rehearsal for the dancers and the crew. There'd be a dinner break, during which Tharp and Mischer could review the tapes and make adjustments. A second performance would be the actual take. Neither audience knew that this was the scheme. Both showings were booked solid a week in advance.

Tharp found a real bluegrass band, Snuffy Jenkins, Pappy Sherrill, and the Hired Hands, to play for *Country Dances*. On the video, she goes to South Carolina to hear them and select tunes for the dance, relaxing into a theatrical down-home accent as she banters with the boys. In New York the final rehearsals and performances began at 9:00 A.M. on a hot Sunday in August. In the backstage documentation, Gold's grainy, improvised black-and-white footage communicates the stress and exhaustion of this last phase of shooting. At the studio entrance Tharp is stopped by the guards and moans that she has no ID, someone will have to vouch for her. Santo Loquasto fusses with the costumes. The crew announces that the linoleum floor is bubbling; they decide to go with it, in hopes it will stretch out under the dancers' feet.

The careful schedule crumbled but the audience was patient. The first shift waited outside for half an hour, then listened to the band while the crew finished a mandatory break. Mischer warmed up the audience, encouraging them to respond with enthusiasm—stomp their feet if they liked. Tharp introduced the dancers, and a larger ballet began, as the videographer moved around the dancers, followed by a helper attending to his equipment, followed by Joel Gold and several assistants moving cable out of the way. Two cameras offstage filmed the whole thing. On the video, as Tharp is making her way out after the wrap, a man pokes his head out of the crowd, and says, "I don't like television but I like you a lot."

Country Dances set Rawe, Way, Uchida, and Washington romping to four numbers by the Hired Hands. The music seems to propel them into sketchy square-dancing steps and patterns—swing your partner, grand right and left, do-si-do. Way and Washington face each other in profile at the beginning. As the camera moves in, their faces become a frame, an open curtain, and they enter through it in an overdubbed shot. Woven among the quartet's swings and twirls and hopping there are ballet steps, lifts, including the racing dive Tharp did in *Once More, Frank,* and some lazy chumminess left over from *Sue's Leg.* The camera reads all this in edited long shots and close-up. When the music switches to an easy waltz, Rawe partners Uchida and Washington in turn, and the camera comes in to savor their odd, upside-down grapplings. The last number is fast and jittery; the dancers skid into slapstick. Washington lifts Uchida, and on the last split second, Way up-ends Rawe and they all gesture into a goofy final pose.

Mischer used his freezes with moving away, and something he calls "video lag, where an arm would sweep through the picture and there would be fifteen other arms just a split second behind it sweeping through." At one point Rawe starts a slow series of chaîné turns around Way and Washington. They pick up his step and are suddenly transformed into a fifty-woman Virginia reel. Mischer notes how labor intensive these effects were at the time. For the chorus line reel, and to trace the trajectory of some swooping lifts later on, the tape had to be stopped a few frames into the dancers' movement, recorded and fixed on the master tape, stopped again a few frames later, and so on. Mischer says it could take a whole evening to edit a single phrase. Today it would all be done digitally, in no time.

The live-audience segment ended with a short but intense solo for Tharp. Using some of the material she had sketched in her eight-part opening solo, she throws foot-slaps, jumps, ballet steps, and seductive shimmies into a casual stroll. After sixteen fast hopping fouettés with her extended leg gradually sweeping from front through side to back, and a few more wiggles and jerks, she glares, takes a giant step toward the camera, and disappears.

Making Television Dance didn't go on the air until October of 1977, but in the meantime Tharp turned *Country Dances* into a stage work. She first took it on tour with her company, to Edinburgh and Berlin in September of 1976. A month later it began a long transition where it slid between two companies, changed titles, and emerged with the addition of a showpiece for Wright and five men called *Cacklin' Hen.* Tharp had renewed her relationship with Robert Joffrey, and *Country Dances* became the first part of a longer piece, *Happily Ever After,* which premiered at the end of the Joffrey Ballet's fall City Center season. Her company was part of the initial package, dancing the quartet followed by her solo. A second quartet of Joffrey dancers did a slimmed-down version of the first, and the piece closed with *Cacklin' Hen*. This configuration occurred only once, on opening night. For the remaining three performances, the Joffrey presence diminished as Tharp withdrew their quartet section. She gave her own solo to Ann Marie De Angelo, the strongest technician Joffrey had. When the Joffrey took the dance on its winter tour, the Tharp company was gone; the quartets were gone; De Angelo's solo and the final sextet, led by Jan Hanniford, were all that remained; and the piece was renamed *Cacklin' Hen*.

The folksy-Americana mode was unusual for Tharp, although she was a great fan of country music and often used Hank Williams and Earl Scruggs recordings in the studio. The Bicentennial commemorations of 1976 fostered a certain amount of hayseed-chic, and *Country Dances* fit this sensibility. Robert Joffrey was planning to observe the Bicentennial by reviving George Balanchine's *Square Dance* with its original onstage caller, and by taking *Rodeo* into the repertory. Agnes de Mille's beloved classic would be a coup for Joffrey, appropriate for his young dancers, and doubly appealing to the audience because the choreographer was making a gallant recovery from a serious stroke. Bea Rodriguez danced the Cowgirl. The great success of this Western early in the season may have undercut Tharp's barn dances. Analyzing *Happily Ever After* in *The New Yorker*, Arlene Croce thought Tharp's initial quartet revealed a new dynamic amplitude that "makes an across-the-board difference: in momentum, which is now released to its fullest sway; in the legibility of the group dances; in the consistency of 'characterization' in the solos."

Tharp and Robert Joffrey must have hoped her dance would prove as durable as the remodeled *Deuce Coupe*, but the Joffrey Ballet was sliding into one of its periodic administrative abysses. Faced with serious financial trouble, Robert Joffrey canceled the spring New York season, so the final *Cacklin' Hen* wasn't seen in New York until the fall of 1977. *Country Dances*, with *Cacklin' Hen*, served as a repertory piece for Tharp's company until the fall of 1979. But she had little time to focus on it after it did its main job in the television project.

Besides keeping her own company in shape for touring—after BAM (May 1976), there were dates in Minneapolis, Europe, Florida, and Delaware—she made an exquisite piece for Olympic figure-skating champion John Curry. *After All* premiered at Madison Square Garden in November as part of Curry's Superskates show. Tharp never learned to skate when she was growing up. This wasn't the fault of the Southern California climate—she didn't learn to swim either, or drive—but her overscheduled childhood didn't leave room for recreational sports. Curry had wanted to dance before he became a skater, and he was an innovative boundary crosser himself. Dissatisfied with the rigidly defined figure-skating world, Curry started a company of ice-dancers and invited real choreographers to make ballets for it, beginning with Tharp.

She didn't think his challenge was unusual. "I've always wanted to have—it's sort of a fantasy—the 'glide factor' possibility," she told dance writer Amanda Smith. On the ice, where gravity didn't impede the dancer's locomotion, she could develop a new range of rhythms. With the piece she made, to the familiar Adagio from Albinoni's Concerto for Trumpet, Smith felt, "the dimensions of figure skating expanded so dramatically that . . . the seven-minute solo signaled a new era. . . ." Mary Grace Butler, a skater who served as a production assistant for Superskates, remembered *After All* as "dance, real dance, on ice skates, with theatrical lighting, in front of fifteen or twenty thousand people who usually saw spins and twirls. . . . I remember the hush of all those people holding their breath as John performed, and the explosive applause when it was over."

The country music pieces, the ice dancing, postproduction work on the video, and the busy company schedule of 1976–77 all proceeded alongside the biggest project Tharp had yet undertaken, her first Hollywood movie. The Czech film director Milos Forman had seen her work at ABT and invited her to set the dances for *Hair*. It took her a while to accept. "I wasn't sure that I wanted to be involved with a director, that I wanted to have to be put at the mercy of the project," she says now. She saw the opportunity as a turning point, not only in her career but in the life of her dance company. Commercial work offered financial rewards unheard of in the nonprofit dance world—Tom Rawe and Jennifer Way were able to make a down payment on a house in Brooklyn from their earnings on the movie. Tharp worried the dancers might be tempted to desert her after they tasted relative affluence. Finally she accepted Forman's offer. With Ken Rinker as her assistant, she was at work long before shooting began in New York, in October 1977.

The musical *Hair*, ten years old when Forman translated it to the screen, could claim several distinctions. One of the first successful rock shows, it started in a downtown workshop production directed by Gerald Freedman at the New York Shakespeare Festival. With successive renovations, it made its way to Broadway under Tom O'Horgan's direction, ran for 1,700 performances, then spawned innumerable regional and international productions and a best-selling record album. The show's nearly nonexistent plot uncorked a pageant of countercultural defiance—bad language, uninhibited sex, and antiwar outrage. Twenty-eight songs by Galt MacDermot, Gerome Ragni, and James Rado marked the era's turbulent politics and equally turbulent liberation. By the time the movie was made, the nation had climbed out of Vietnam and absorbed the best of the hippie lifestyles. *Hair* the movie made the '60s seem a colorful memory, much the way the music and dance of *Deuce Coupe* had romanticized other aspects of the period. Reviewing *Hair* after its release in March of 1979, *Newsweek's* Jack Kroll commented that it "treats the 'American Tribal Love-Rock Musical' exactly as it should be treated—as a myth of our popular consciousness."

With ballet and television under her belt, movies were the logical next challenge for Tharp, but her fears about relinquishing control over the product proved well-founded. So far she'd been fortunate to have sympathetic collaborators who understood her intentions and contributed to their fulfillment: the dancers especially, and Bob Huot, Bill Kosmas, Jennifer Tipton, Santo Loquasto, Rhoda Grauer. Professionals in other fields often learned as much from her as she learned from them. Don Mischer finally appreciated her radical ideas about TV dance: "She made me realize how much editing can affect what you walk away with. . . . I've learned a lot about questioning the rules and trying to do things even if everybody around me says, that won't work." On *Hair*, with Milos Forman making the ultimate decisions, the dancing would be an integral but subordinate element. The dancers felt that initially Forman undervalued them. "Milos didn't know anything about dance really, and Twyla educated him," Ken Rinker says. "Twyla made him give us some respect, not that he wasn't going to. He's not a nasty person or anything like that, it's just that dance for some people is like a costume. No, we really do work at this. We rehearse, we study, we know what we're doing, we have point of view, we can articulate it. She brought him to that point."

Making *Hair* was difficult for the dancers. Much of the movie took place outside, and the weather didn't always cooperate. Just as they were about to shoot the be-in on the Sheep Meadow it snowed. The crew was preparing to melt the snow with airplane engines and supply the dancers with ice cubes to suck so their breath wouldn't vaporize, but Forman managed to get the work suspended until green returned to the trees. During one period, the company was touring on weekends and returning to New York for all-night shoots during the week. On the set, there were interminable waits while the crew set up or reshot other scenes. All the dancers complained about the problem of keeping their muscles warmed up; they never knew when they would be summoned to perform. Some figured out how to stay in what Tom Rawe calls "a slight state of readiness," and then be prepared for retakes. On the day they finished the scene in the Sheep Meadow, a group of dancers, still in scruffy costume and makeup, went off to the upscale Café des Artistes for lunch with Tharp. They had a celebratory meal and many drinks—none of them had any money but the restaurant trusted Tharp to come back later and pay the bill. When they finally rumbled back to Central Park they found the crew desperately searching for them to shoot one more scene—which didn't make it into the film.

A great deal of the dancing was deleted during the editing, and Tharp never got over her sense of work wasted. Both she and Milos Forman were trying for a sort of through-danced scenario, but they approached that goal from opposite poles. He wanted to splice dance into the narrative. She wanted everything in the film to dance. Seven extended sequences involve the principal actors, Tharp's company, about forty additional dancers, and hundreds of choreographed extras. The dancers, together with horses, puppets, singing groups and soloists, are woven into the escapades of the hippie tribe. Tharp was already accomplished at making dancers look like ordinary people, and she gave the nondancing actors movement to do that blended them in with the dancers and singers. There was only one extended dance number made for a stage, and except for a few cryptic remnants, it was cut. But she did think in terms of self-contained dances throughout, and in the event, her choreographic coherence was sacrificed.

Conceptually, Forman adopted the hippie point of view: life, as they saw it, was a celebration, a deliberate disconnect from society. Transfigured by drugs, the runaways become performers, producers of illusion. Horses can dance. People can levitate. War can be stopped. The hippies do extravagant and risky things; the camera hallucinates even more flamboyantly, juggles time, fractures the landscape. Once released, the movie was very successful, and today it looks thoroughly permeated with dance. Years of MTV and high-tech editing have conditioned our eyes to negotiate its extreme jumps in continuity and sequence. Even Tharp might have approved the restless, sometimes surreal way the camera conveys the sensibility of *Hair* if she'd had a hand in it. In fact, three years later she used the technique of splicing to intercut two entirely different groups of characters, in one of her great stage works, *The Catherine Wheel.*

Milos Forman kept most of *Hair*'s original music; Michael Weller wrote a new screenplay that clarified the characters, gave momentum to the action, and instituted several spectacular setpieces. The movie's plot concerns a little family of hippies led by Berger (Treat Williams). Claude, a white-bread draftee from Oklahoma (John Savage), meets them on his way through New York en route to boot camp. The hippies induct Claude into a new way of life before he gets to the army, and in a macabre coda, Berger's most daring prank turns fatal. Having half-converted Sheila, Claude's debutante ladylove (Beverly D'Angelo), the hippies cross the country in a stolen car to visit him at the army base. Berger impersonates a soldier, gets into camp, and takes Claude's place for the night while Claude goes to meet Sheila and the hippies. It turns out to be the night Claude's unit is shipped overseas. In the last scene, the hippies visit Berger's grave at a military cemetery. Tharp went on location with the actors to the National Guard base in Barstow, California, where she staged the exercises for John Savage and 1,500 trainees. She did all the slogging and heavy drill herself, of course.

The film streaks through an increasingly bizarre progression of escapades and celebrations, and then pitches forward to its ironic denouement. It starts in the stark absolutism of an Oklahoma dawn, as Claude's father drives him to the bus stop. But the edges of reality grow ragged as soon as the draftee gets to Central Park. He rebuffs the hippies' first advances and they dismiss him as a square. But he quickly wins their respect by catching a runaway horse with tricks they've only seen done by fancy rodeo riders. They introduce Claude to marijuana, and the next morning it doesn't seem at all strange when Berger spots the face of the girl Claude noticed riding in the park the day before, right there on the page of a discarded newspaper. Or that the article tells them where to find her.

Just as hippie belief in magic can make amazing coincidences happen, film magic constructs the mythic journey that ends in the death of the antihero. A kind of cinematic counterpoint continually sets the hippies' freewheeling lifestyle against the conventions and enforcement of the uptight world. The hippies seem to beat the system with their brash disregard of the proprieties, and they persuade at least three characters to abandon the straight life, but in the end it's the charismatic, eternally confident Berger who gets destroyed.

Most of *Hair* was shot on location in Central Park. The huge spaces of the park—the Sheep Meadow, the band shell, the stone staircase near Bethesda Fountain—were a total contrast to the studio confines of *Making Television Dance*. For Tharp, the park had its own resonance, dating back to the New York rehearsals and performances of *Medley* in 1969. Intermittently throughout her life, Tharp looked back on her early childhood at her grandparents' farm in Indiana—and translated her nostalgia into dance. The prospect of a pastoral work-life persuaded her to decamp for New Berlin with Bob Huot in the '60s. Much later she spoke seriously—though not for long—about running off to live in the country with a lover as famous and sophisticated as she was.

Improbable as these schemes were, the utopian idea of free, natural living has informed a surprising amount of her choreography. Before *Medley* there had been the outdoor experiments during the idyll at New Berlin, with Rudner, Wright, and the volunteers working their way toward a style. There had been Wright mingling with the campus population in *Rose's Cross Country*. And on stage, the surfer allusions of *Deuce Coupe*, the whomping rusticity of *Country Dances*, and, as late as 1996, the sprightly Quaker exaltations of *Sweet Fields*. After quitting New Berlin and Huot's determined stance as an antiestablishmentarian, Tharp moved quickly away from the poverty and invisibility of the counterculture. Her later choreographic reflections on it preserved its romantic aspects but stepped around its liabilities. Democracy and inclusiveness were all very well but not when it came to implementing her choreographic ambitions.

Hair looked back to that festive era where life was a dress-up party and anyone could be a dancer. In an early version of the screenplay Tharp circled every reference to action with a green marker, intending to stage movement wherever she could. She choreographed gestures throughout the movie, basic training exercises, Frisbee games, and a massive peace rally. Her tactics ranged from full-out dancing to ingeniously scaled-down steps for the actors with limited dance ability. When dance scenes called for more than her nine company members, she would set their parts first, then distribute the additional dancers into their groupings. There were excellent dancers among the extras (Chris Komar from the Cunningham company, Christian Holder and Cameron Basedon from the Joffrey, modern dancers Marta Renzi, Mark Morris, and Deborah Zalkind, for example) but it was more efficient to work out the choreography on her inner circle.

The numbers are expansive, almost flung into space. In Claude's first view of Central Park as a perennial be-in ("Aquarius"), at the Sheep Meadow free-for-all where he takes his first LSD trip, and during the peace demonstration on the Mall in Washington, D.C., Tharpian looseness and spontaneity seems pushed to its highest level of abandon. Dressed in ragamuffin finery, the dancers race across lawns, skip in formation down a hillside, do flips and jetés, charge up and down a flight of steps like Bill Robinson. In spasms of self-absorption, they spin meditatively and practice tai chi. On the Sheep Meadow, Tharp gets tossed in the air by a group of men dancers.

But outdoorsy casualness isn't the only kind of dancing in *Hair*. When the hippies crash Sheila's coming-out party in Short Hills, New Jersey, Berger climbs on the dinner table and breaks up the banquet with the orgiastic "I Got Life." There's a heavily edited fight in the jail after Sheila's father has the intruders arrested ("Hair"). The disorderly gatherings and punchy jail fights are countered by a crowd of downtown businesspeople Claude sees when he heads for the army induction center. As he walks along the street singing "Where Do I Go," the corporate troops move in perfect formation, heading uptown, then downtown, then kneeling, then dispersing into all directions.

After this vision of the straight world's conformity, Claude reports for his army physical. The procession of naked draftees has a strange effect on the uniformed board of five black and three white inspectors. Grim and official, they display no reaction to the assorted bodies that come before them, but a raunchy montage reveals their subconscious thoughts. "White boys are delicious," sings a trio of miniskirted black women in the park, followed by three white women with a taste for black boys. The song cuts back to the army board, now rocking with pleasure. For the black officers' share of this homoerotic fantasy ("White boys are delicious"), the shot cuts to their legs, dancing in unison under the table. Since the officers' upper bodies didn't appear in the frame, Tharp was able to use five of her own dancers, male and female, for the routine. The dancers thought the idea was original with Tharp, but editing tricks weren't new to the movies. Before she started choreographing *Hair*, Tharp had studied a collection of movie musicals. Among them must have been the popular *Bye Bye Birdie*, choreographed by Gower Champion on Broadway and by Onna White for the 1963 film version. This movie, about a rock star's tumultuous guest appearance in a small town, has an almost fetishistic interest in feet. In one scene, kids are talking on the phone ("Goin' Steady"), and their legs, seen from the waist down, turn in and out in unison.

Hair reaches its phantasmagoric, psychedelic heights in the scene at the Sheep Meadow ("Electric Blues"), where Claude and the hippies kneel as if at a Communion rail, to receive cubes of LSD from a dealer with a painted face and dollar signs on his hat. Crowds of fun seekers swarm through competing singing groups, processions of giant puppets, chanting Hare Krishnas, and antiwar orators, and it all blurs into Claude's acid trip. He marries Sheila in a giant church (it was actually an immense film studio in Queens), lit by hundreds of candles, with white-clad ballet dancers in attendance. Tharp, once again taking advantage of high-budget technical opportunities, arranged the dancers on moving platforms and rigged them for flight. Rose Marie Wright, as the Virgin Mary, walks on air while appearing to sing in an otherworldly soprano. Tharp, in the front of the church, spins out of her clothes and into a pseudo-Indian robe, then seems suspended in midair like a Hindu deity as she intones the marriage vows. Sheila immediately sprouts a pregnant belly and joins the dancers, who are laughing and undulating like spaced-out devidasis in front of flaming incense burners. Eventually the madness melts back into the sirens and Hare Krishnas in Central Park, a reality only slightly less demented.

As shooting progressed, Tharp pressed Milos Forman for more dance, and he sometimes placated her by shooting scenes straight through with a second camera. The dancers realized this was going on, and many continue to believe that the outtakes still exist somewhere, preserving all the choreography that was cut from the film. The outtakes never surfaced, but Tharp did stage three of the deleted dances during her 1979 BAM season, just weeks before the movie's world premiere.

7

Hodge Podge Rummage
1976–1979

Immediately after the huge success of *Push Comes to Shove*, Tharp started to experience the downside of fame as well as the dividends. Everywhere the Tharp company toured that season, tickets were sold out, extra performances were added, and hopeful crowds lined up at box offices for last-minute cancelations. She and the company were featured in mass magazines (*People, Time, MS, US, Vogue, Rolling Stone*) as well as brainy ones (*Atlantic, The Nation*), often pictured adopting Richard Avedon's cheeky poses. *The New York Times* commented on Tharp's wedge haircut, along with those of Pia Lindstrom, Dorothy Hamill, and other notables. Media and entertainment personalities signed up to be in the cast whenever she put on *The One Hundreds*. She received her first honorary doctorate, from California Institute of the Arts, in 1978.

But only a month after *Push* premiered, when the company returned to Lisner Auditorium in Washington, critic Noel Gillespie announced that "the most inflated reputation in United States dance today is that of Twyla Tharp." Critics outside the orbit of her longtime supporters doubted that anyone could possibly be that popular and also that good. Some experienced Tharp-watchers began complaining she was repeating herself. "Tharp has created one good work [*The Bix Pieces*] and proceeded to rewrite it ad nauseum," said Gillespie. Even some of her most loyal critics thought they saw slippage. Alan Kriegsman of *The Washington Post* had scathing words for *Mak-*

ing Television Dance, calling it "one of the most disjointed, hectic, jumbled items ever to cross the screen, parading under the banner of creative innovation." Kriegsman blamed this on Tharp's "erratic sense of form" and said the show reflected "the same sort of indiscriminate frenzy that has characterized Tharp's choreography of late." *New York* magazine parodied her, alongside prominent politicians and athletes, in an alphabetical sendup of the year's municipal "Power Failures." Music critic Alan Rich wrote the jingle:

> Wiggle, waggle, twist that fanny—
> Twirling Twyla's not too canny.
> See one dance, you've seen them all.
> Modernism casts its pall.

Tharp's relationship to the company was changing too. In the spring of 1975, around the time of the *Deuce Coupe II* premiere, she indicated to *The New York Times* writer John Rockwell that she was feeling overloaded. She thought of her company as a workshop, she said, that facilitated "discoveries and advances . . . Artists must be allowed to wallow around in their own confusions, and that can lead to other, more finished things." Her working process had always been exploratory, but until the Joffrey ballets it had been her own company that brought the experiments to completion. Now, as the company handled the dual role of touring machine and laboratory, she started to work out ways to maximize its productivity, and her own.

She'd never flinched at delegating responsibilities to the dancers. When new members were taken into the company, they learned the existing repertory from videotape, and their colleagues often ran rehearsals. They talked to the media on tour, since Tharp usually didn't go along. She passed on invitations for extra jobs to them, both to increase their earning power and to make more efficient use of her own time. During residencies they did the teaching and often presided over lecture-demonstrations. For instance, during a multipart "residency" linked to the 1977 Brooklyn Academy spring season, there were master classes at Long Island University and a workshop for the basketball team at Brooklyn Polytechnic Institute. Tom Rawe gave classes to the team and organized a demonstration for an audience of eighty-five students and faculty members.

The tours were intense. Federal, state, and local funding for the arts was reaching its peak, and although Tharp was wary of the tradeoffs implicit in the nonprofit world, her company, along with the other major modern dance groups, became prominent on national touring circuits and subscription seasons. In 1977, with *Hair* set to begin shooting in October, the company went straight from its Brooklyn Academy season (12–22 May) to Minneapolis for two weeks, then on to summer festivals at Ravinia, Jacob's Pillow, Connecticut College/American Dance Festival, and Artpark in New York State. Between the end of September and the beginning of November they played Washington, D.C.; Boston; Wilmington, North Carolina; Detroit; Poughkeepsie; and Nashville. During the winter hiatus of *Hair*, in January and February 1978, they traveled to the Caribbean, Princeton, Philadelphia, and the West Coast, for eight engagements.

In May of '77, as she was preparing the movie and working on a television special with singer-songwriter Paul Simon, Tharp announced her withdrawal from dancing, "for now." She told *The Minneapolis Star and Tribune*: "I can't carry on this kind of schedule and also perform." This put presenters in a tricky position. Modern dance companies ordinarily took the name of their founder-choreographers, and now Tharp was highly marketable. Sponsors used her picture and her name in bold type, but they had to downplay the inconvenient fact that the company would appear without her. There were, inevitably, disappointed ticket holders. In Nashville, at least one newspaper preview claimed she would perform, and the sponsors then had to insert an elaborate disavowal into their advertisements. Comparing Tharp to Beethoven, the revised ad urged the public to view her as a great composer, whose creativity was implemented by her company rather than being dependent on her performing personality. "Informed dance fans know that to see her choreography is to see the woman and when you visit the Opry House on November third you'll see the greatness of Twyla Tharp. . . ."

Perhaps because she was preoccupied with bigger projects and the company was touring so extensively, she began filling out programs with short subjects—excerpts from older pieces, spinoffs from commercial projects, fragments or studies for longer works—that could be shuffled around to suit the company's immediate needs. During the period 1976–79 the company toured with three staple dances, *Eight Jelly Rolls*, *Sue's Leg*, and *The Fugue*. To these major works were added *Country Dances* and *Cacklin' Hen*, sometimes in their spliced-together form and sometimes as separate items; four small pieces: the *Bach Duet*, *Rags Suite*, *Half the One Hundreds*, and a seven-minute remnant from the Paul Simon special; and, for a season or two, *Ocean's Motion*.

Tharp's musical methods made it fairly easy to lift sections out of longer dances. She had always foraged freely in the musical repertory, and either

by brilliant synthesizing or intuitive good luck she could put together isolated pieces by the same composer (Jelly Roll Morton in *Eight Jelly Rolls*, Fats
Waller in *Sue's Leg*), or by disparate composers (Beiderbecke and Mozart in
The Bix Pieces, Joseph Lamb's "Bohemia Rag" and Haydn's 82nd in *Push Comes to
Shove*). In fact, her finished works are so musically persuasive that hardly
anyone has noted how seldom she's used a single piece of music for a whole
dance. With the exception of a few symphonic ballets and commissioned
scores later in her career, she has applied the cut-and-paste method ever
since early days. In her own mind she devised logical sequences, and sometimes even quasi-narratives, for her choices, but submitting to a composer's
throughline was another matter.

She never felt attached to her dances after she considered them finished;
repertory was an expedient at best. She would work on a dance—most often whittling it down—until it reached her idea of perfection and she had
learned what she could from it. She made large cuts in *The Raggedy Dances*,
for instance, and reduced the cast from five to two within three years of its
premiere. As the *Rags Suite*—the Mozart section sandwiched between two
rags—it served for years, often performed by Way and Rawe. The practice
of extracting self-contained numbers meant she didn't have to revive whole
dances; it might even be an improvement. She'd keep the best parts and
didn't need to bother anybody with the rest. As she once wrote: "the best
poems are sent by night letter—21 words counting signature and address."
This reductionist practice reached a peak on tour in fall 1976, with *From
Hither and Yon*, described as a compilation of excerpts from thirteen repertory
pieces since 1965, and its subsequent, further-refined version, *The Hodge
Podge*. Television was even better at collating the smallest recognizable tokens from the repertory, and in 1982 she glossed twenty-two items in the
hour-long PBS anthology called the "Scrapbook Tape."

At a time when the standard dance concert lasted about two and a half
hours, her programming began to look skimpy. One writer complained that
a 1977 performance at Lisner Auditorium took only two hours *including* two
intermissions. By the early 2000s she could program three miniature pieces
and one longer work, with an intermission, for a performance in a major
venue that lasted one and a half hours. She felt she was giving the audience
a lot for its money.

The dancers made the best of the touring. They stayed in decent hotels and
flew between dates instead of taking uncomfortable buses. They enjoyed interacting with the public in master classes and other events. Surprise castings and

bonuses kept the limited repertory from becoming routine. At the American Dance Festival in 1978, the *Bach Duet* was done twice, with two casts (Colton and Uchida, Wright and Kurshals), and *The Fugue* could sustain different combinations of men and women. Besides, the work itself was an ongoing challenge. "For me," says Raymond Kurshals, "it was such a treat to get out there and to do the work. . . . It was different every time." Even on tour, they kept working on the material in the studio. Anthony Ferro, who joined the company during *Hair*, felt a great sense of responsibility to the work, especially because Tharp was entrusting the dancers to present it on the road without her.

When the company had expanded to about twelve dancers, Tharp divided it into two units, the red and blue teams. She had conceived the ingenious scheme of sending one team on the road to earn money while the other team stayed in New York, where she could work with them on new material. This innovation addressed Tharp's chronic fear that the business of touring would undermine her creativity. She could keep on choreographing and preserve a personal schedule flexible enough to accept freelance projects. The dancers enjoyed the extra performing opportunities they got in the small ensembles, but the plan had stressful aspects.

The touring works had to be double-cast, which usually meant one person would be learning a part choreographed on someone else at a different time in the company's history. Given how closely identified Tharp's dances always were with the dancers who created them, a few rivalries took root and were stifled. Interpretations could change, but not too much. Technical problems arose when the original dancer's strengths were different from those of his or her replacement. Often one team would be rehearsed and ready to go on the road when Tharp would decide she needed a particular dancer for the ongoing work in New York. This necessitated frantic last-minute shifting or reworking. For the rehearsal directors, Way and Rawe in the latter years of the plan, the tours could mean nonstop rehearsing, performing, and teaching. Then, when both teams reassembled for performances in New York or another big city, there were hard decisions about which cast would perform. Not all the dancers disliked the team concept. Christine Uchida, who shared Tharp's role in *Sue's Leg* with Shelley Washington, enjoyed seeing the alternate versions.

It was in the creative process that these changes most affected the dancers. By the time he left in 1977, Ken Rinker perceived a subtle shift in Tharp's choreographing process. At one time, he thought, the movement had been simple but the treatment was complex; now the movement grew more complex and the treatment simpler. Rinker thought Tharp was using more balletic movement as she worked with ballet dancers, and that during her own company's reduced rehearsal time there was less problem-solving for the dancers to do. *Ocean's Motion*, which she made in 1975 before the company went to the Spoleto Festival, may have been the closest Tharp came to a potboiler in those days. Set to the music of rock-'n'-roller Chuck Berry, the dance used material recycled from *The Double Cross*. It didn't offer the dancers enough challenges, Rinker thought. She dropped it quickly, calling it "glib and facile." Five years later, she doubled the five-member cast and simply put one set opposite the other. They danced two whole songs in mirror image.

Tom Rawe and Jennifer Way discussed the evolving company with Mike Steele of *The Minneapolis Tribune* in the spring of 1977. While Rawe had spent his first year learning the repertory and performing only one section of the *Jelly Rolls*, rehearsing like that was now a luxury. New dancers had to have a strong technical background and be able to learn fast. According to Way, "Twyla has to concentrate harder now because she's doing so much more. Her new works are getting more and more complicated, but they're also more set. Dancers still get a lot of freedom, which is one of the great things about working for her, but she knows exactly what she wants now." Rawe added: "It's all more condensed. Where four phrases might have gone over a long period of time before, they will be done in thirty seconds now. There's more material in each dance."

For the company's first extended New York season, ten performances at Brooklyn Academy in March of 1976, Tharp offered a new "suite" dance, *Give and Take*. She used three seemingly incompatible modes of music: a prelude and fugue by the eighteenth-century composer Gregor Werner; four American marching band numbers; and the popular song "Willow, Weep for Me," in a recording by the great jazz pianist Art Tatum. Offsetting this apparent incongruity, the dance had several simultaneous throughlines. By manipulating the same movement material for solos and groups, Tharp laid out a company style that could hold its own against the most diverse accompaniments; and via that stylistic consistency she suggested there might be some relationships in the musical selections as well.

Trendy themes were invoked by the use of patriotic marches like "The Stars and Stripes Forever," which suited the American Bicentennial. Tharp cited George Balanchine's ballet *Stars and Stripes* with Sousa's music, and inserted a few movement quotations like the wedge-shaped formations adopted by Balanchine's perky ballerinas and cadets. She made explicit reference to Balanchine in a printed collage of words and graphics inserted in the program. The company announced it had invited the master to the opening and Balanchine did make a rare appearance. How he reacted to Tharp's tribute is not recorded.

As the six dancers assembled and dispersed, attended to the music or ignored it, *Give and Take* illustrated the tension between regimentation and freedom, conformity and individualism. Possibly these qualities needed their polar opposites to exist at all. The pulled-in, pulled-up strut of the drum majorette was countered by the far-flung, free-wheeling arms of the sports fan. The dance projected a familiar Tharpian casualness, but it was all neatly structured—the accidents choreographed in, the falling and getting caught in the nick of time, the "mistake" lineups where someone is facing the wrong way or moving on the wrong beat, the slightly ragged unisons. The dancers scuffled their way into the formality of the wedge patterns and ambled out of them.

Solos for Tharp, Wright, and Shelley Washington drew attention to each woman as a special component in the company's identity. Tharp opened the piece, introducing the movement vocabulary and the contrasting attitudes of rigor and nonchalance. Several times during Werner's Prelude she dropped whatever she was doing and started again after a cooling-off aside. Rose Marie Wright remembers that in the studio, while Tharp was making the dance, she was deluged with phone calls regarding her other projects and company business. She finally translated her annoyance into a thematic element. Interruptions punctuated her solo and the trio that followed for Way, Washington, and Wright. The group marches for the women, Rinker, and Rawe (originally there were four marches, but she soon eliminated one of them), and the solo for Wright that ended the dance, were full of unexpected stops and starts.

Without fanfare, in the midst of "American Patrol," Tharp brought Shelley Washington into the foreground. *Making Television Dance* had not yet been broadcast and these were Washington's first performances for the company's home audience. Her brief solo showcased a unique and accomplished contributor. According to Washington, Tharp had given her "everything that I couldn't do. Well, it turned out I had more this than that, more everything." The group faded away as she stepped out and crossed the stage with fast changes of arms and legs, and her star power was instantly perceived. The audience applauded her as she danced back to her returning companions, and on opening night Washington gave a nod of acknowledgment, right in time to the music.

Tharp's other generous gesture in *Give and Take* was Rose Marie Wright's final solo. Wright had been dancing in every company piece for years and had been Tharp's creative collaborator as well as keeper of the repertory. She felt miffed when the huge success of *Push Comes to Shove* seemed to fall exclusively on Tharp and the ballet dancers without a nod to the choreographer's longtime dancer-partners. Tharp may have gotten wind of Wright's feelings, and she dedicated the Brooklyn Academy season to her. After the marches in *Give and Take*, everyone left and the imperturbable, elegant Wright went through another reshuffling of the thematic material, to Tatum's rhythmically eccentric piano playing, demonstrating how she could make Tharp's stylistic contradictions seem perfectly logical. She ended on a long relevé in fourth position, then dropped the pose and walked off. After the Brooklyn performances Arlene Croce proclaimed Wright the season's dance heroine. "She has an unassertive style," Croce wrote, "but a clearly defined and exceptionally spacious one, and she warms you with her air of patient good sense." When Wright came on for a solo bow opening night, Tharp loped out from the other side of the stage with six dozen long-stemmed roses, a bouquet almost as big as she was, and nearly collided with the astonished Wright as she presented them.

Give and Take was set for the company's May performances in Minneapolis. Wright injured her knee in New York just before the trip. With the help of doctors and physiotherapists, she got through that run, then took a leave over the summer. She helped in the studio while Tharp finished *Once More, Frank* and made the men's movement for *Cacklin' Hen*.

Although *Give and Take* was the season premiere at BAM, it proved a lesser attraction than the repertory pieces. Croce thought: "As an audience piece, it's a courageous work for Twyla Tharp to have made at this moment—Twyla the toast of New York—because it's so unaccommodating. Not that it's unfriendly or anti-entertainment, but it just doesn't give away any secrets. It's anti-success." The other dances, *The Fugue, Eight Jelly Rolls, Sue's Leg*, the *Bach Duet*, and the *Rags Suite*, already had important reputations but they'd never been shown in such concentrated array for a big New York audience. So in a sense, the Brooklyn season consolidated Tharp's personal success by showcasing her own extraordinary dancers and the work they had made together.

⟨⟩

When the company returned to BAM in May of 1977, Tharp had only one new dance to offer, *Mud*, but she surrounded it with repertory works and festive events. Celebrities made guest appearances, dances were imported to the stage from the screen, and one-time-only gift packages were unwrapped for the audience. Paul Simon accompanied the medley Tharp drew from their forthcoming television collaboration. Before that show aired all the dances were dropped, but the *Simon Medley* on stage turned out to be fairly inconsequential. Tharp invited the press to rehearsals of *Half the One Hundreds*, enabling writers to spot participating luminaries like Estelle Parsons, Hermione Gingold, Milos Forman, Bobby Short, and City Councilman Robert Steingut, who would scarcely be visible among the throngs onstage.

For *The Hodge Podge*, Tharp strung together tiny excerpts from dances dating back to the '60s. In a way, the whole season was a kind of anthology, dominated by guest appearances and special happenings. It aroused great excitement but didn't encourage the audience to deepen its appreciation for specific dances. Arlene Croce thought things in *The Hodge Podge*, like smashing a chair (*Disperse*, 1967) and walking inside a large hoop (*Re-Moves*, 1966), were extraneous to the serious dance work Tharp had made even in the early days. Croce pointed out the uncompromising inwardness of lost dances like *Generation* and *Group Activities*, a quality she saw in evidence during the season only in *The Fugue* and *Cacklin' Hen*. Croce saw Tharp going overboard in her attempt to accommodate the BAM audience. "[R]eviving those antics today in the form of a montage tells us more about the taste of an era than it does about the emergence of Twyla Tharp," she wrote.

Far more momentous than the visiting movie stars and politicos was the return of Sara Rudner, dancing in *The Bix Pieces* and doing cameos from her early roles in *The Hodge Podge*. When Rudner left in 1974 she had already started choreographing on her own, and she wanted to try an independent career. She established a small group of dancers and gave concerts, as well as teaching and setting her dances for other companies. Her work was well received but the slow developmental process that she loved took a lot of energy and enterprise to sustain. She learned she had no taste for undertaking major touring or permanent payrolls, and this gave her a renewed admiration for Tharp. She agreed to come in for the final scenes in *Hair*—the rally at the Lincoln Memorial—when another dancer was injured. Rudner realized how much she loved dancing Tharp's work, and agreed to rejoin the company as a quasi–guest artist, with enough scheduling leeway to continue her own creative work. She moved to the bottom of the company's chronological roster and stayed until 1984.

Ken Rinker too was trying out an independent career, choreographing for his own group of dancers. He danced in the 1977 BAM season but then left permanently. As Tharp's first male dancer, Rinker had ignited what became a major energy source for her. Years later, the choreographer Rachel Lampert wrote in appreciation: ". . . when I first saw Ken dancing it was almost a shock. The precision and exquisite nuances the women could bring to the movement was perfect. Men dancers just didn't have that kind of finesse. . . . When Twyla added Ken to the company I think it changed how men danced from that time forward." And Richard Colton remembers Rinker in *The Bix Pieces*, the first time he saw Tharp's work: "I don't think I'd ever seen a male dancer move like that before." Perhaps no choreographer, then or later, equaled Tharp in creating male dancing roles that were both demanding and personal. After Rinker, she explored the potential of individuals as different as Larry Grenier in *As Time Goes By*, Tom Rawe in *Sue's Leg*, Mikhail Baryshnikov in *Push Comes to Shove*, and decades of others. With Rinker's departure, two important new men, Richard Colton and Raymond Kurshals, arrived in the company. A short time later, William Whitener joined them.

Colton's infatuation with ballet began at the age of seven, when he saw the spectacular Moiseyev Russian folk dance troupe at Madison Square Garden. Besides his strong, sturdy body, he had two big advantages from the start: supportive parents and a home just outside Manhattan, in Little Neck, Queens. Throughout his childhood and teenage years he studied with major Russian teachers, first at the Ballet Theater school, then at the Joffrey. While still in the High School of Performing Arts, Colton encountered the crossover artist James Waring. A great mentor-teacher and pioneer in the choreographic fusion of classical ballet and popular culture, Waring epitomized the aesthetics of camp in the mid-'60s, and he opened up the downtown dance world for Colton, who appeared at Judson Church in Waring's *Winter Circus* (1968).

Colton's commitment to Tharp developed gradually. He was named an understudy in *Deuce Coupe* as a young dancer in the Joffrey Ballet. He learned several parts but never went on in the original version of the Beach Boys ballet. Tharp saw his extraordinary technical ability and cast him for the Four

Finales in *As Time Goes By*, then later worked out much of the men's movement for *Cacklin' Hen* on him. That one-on-one session made a big impression on Colton. Tharp's choreographic detail, her unusual working out of the phrase, her "physical molding" of the body shapes rather than fitting shapes to an existing balletic norm, all reminded him of James Waring's compositional process. He felt his personal contribution to her choreography was as important as what he was learning from her. When he heard Ken Rinker was leaving the company, Colton wrote a note to Tharp from his vacation in New Mexico, asking her to save him a place. His colleagues at the Joffrey thought he was making a big mistake, but he stayed with Tharp until 1989.

Raymond Kurshals also entered the company via *Cacklin' Hen*. He was on layoff from Merce Cunningham's company in the summer of 1976, but he had succumbed to Tharp's dynamism years before. Kurshals had led a checkered young life in Honolulu and San Francisco—he says he attended half a dozen high schools and did some hanging out on the streets of Berkeley during the hippie years. As a floundering teenager he had a sudden revelation that dance was what he should be doing. By luck, he found his way to the Shawl-Anderson school, where the teachers provided a solid grounding in modern, ballet, and jazz techniques. He feels now that dance saved him from life on the street. "Dance literally gave me the discipline and the focus to change my life," he says.

When the Tharps came to Ohio State for their one-day residency in 1971, Kurshals was dancing with Ruth Currier in a small José Limón–influenced company affiliated with the university's dance department. He'd begun a friendship there with Rawe, Way, and Sharon Kinney. They maintained their connections over the years; Kurshals was best man at Rawe and Way's wedding and stayed with them when he arrived in New York in 1973. With Merce Cunningham (1975–76), Kurshals danced in the repertory and one new piece, *Squaregame*, but the Cage/Cunningham musical aesthetic didn't satisfy him. When Tom Rawe brought him into Tharp's rehearsals for *Cacklin' Hen*, he reconnected. She offered him a place in the company if he should decide to leave Cunningham, which he did soon afterward. His status not yet established, Kurshals wasn't allowed to perform *Cacklin' Hen* for the Joffrey season, but he danced it later in the Tharp repertory.

Tharp had a longstanding practice of pre-rehearsing—actors call it workshopping a piece. She made movement on herself each day before the dancers came in to work. But she began to need more bodies and she grabbed them whenever she could. In fact, even though the company was evolving into a more or less conventional organism, it was hard to separate "work" periods from what conventional workers call overtime. When the company went on a salaried basis, rehearsals still could extend into long hours. If the company was on tour, before the invention of the red and blue teams, she'd gather the best outside people available to develop new choreography. Sometimes the work attained a performable shape; sometimes it was warehoused until needed for a later project.

The workshopping process also allowed Tharp to try out new dancers before making a long-term commitment to them. With her extraordinary sense of inclusiveness, she could imagine her choreography beautifully realized by dancers as diverse as star ballerinas and Martha Graham neophytes. Many dancers lusted after her work, but not all of them could handle its demands, even some she thought were technically and temperamentally suitable. The company was entering a decade of relative stability, but it always had an outer ring of more-or-less temporary players. Dancers from other companies tried out and left: Joseph Lennon from Cunningham, Larry Grenier and Robert Blankshine from the Joffrey. People came in and stayed a year or two: Kimmary Williams, France Mayotte. Friends like Sharon Kinney and Gary Chryst lent their services in emergencies.

Tharp might have been directly charting this gift for diversity in the dance called *Mud*. Subtitled *Speed, Air, Fire, Water and Earth*, *Mud* was a wonderful dance about synthesis. Serious and comic, dense but concise, the choreography showed what the dancers could do together and as individuals. Once again Tharp was commenting on dance style, mainly ballet. With movement ranging from awkward to elegant, she showed what ballet is capable of encompassing, and how it can adapt. In the hodgepodge of the 1977 BAM season, *Mud* looked more like patchwork than it was.

Described in Tharp's official annals as "a dance in five movements for Adidas and pointe shoes," *Mud* began with the extreme contrasts promised by the footwear. The vernacular component was introduced by sneaker-shod Raymond Kurshals and Jennifer Way, who streaked across the space with a two-minute display of gender-linked ballet steps, attacked in fast, rough spurts. A trio of women in pointe shoes and white dresses were waiting to begin as they ran off. Tharp emphasized the women's dissimilarity by giving them basic classical steps, port de bras, and canonic patterns that, in any ballet company, would demand exact uniformity. Originally the cast was to comprise Rose Marie Wright, once a teenaged ballerina, who hadn't danced on pointe in over a decade; ballet-trained newcomer Kimmary Williams; and Robert Blankshine, a phenomenal Joffrey dancer who quickly found Tharp's complexities beyond him. Before the premiere, Christine Uchida replaced him in the trio.

Tharp arranged the trio's academic vocabulary into prim, in-place groupings, like a classroom demonstration, and the music was Mozart. But the dancers' bodies were oddly skewed at times, and their groupings veered off instead of interlocking. The audience laughed from their first moves, perhaps in stunned reaction to the clash with Way and Kurshals, or perhaps reading Tharp's witty comment as a sendup. Because of the discrepancy in the sizes and the off-key classical deportment of the trio, Wright was taken as a klutzy misfit, unable to keep in step with the others. Choreographed head motions made it seem all three were checking each other for cues. They were allowed some freedom in their timing, so one woman would finish a phrase a little ahead of the others and lapse into a waiting pose. The audience took all this for accidental ineptitude instead of a relaxed canon. Tharp's purpose was to show a unanimity among diverse dancers, not an imposed but simulated uniformity.

In an unpublished essay on *Mud*, Allen Robertson points out the extremes of rhythmic interpretation between ". . . Wright, [with] that uncanny ability of hers to be askew from the metronome rhythm of the music," and ". . . Uchida, so dead center on the beat that if she glides off of it the viewer is almost forced to swear that the metronome must have shifted tempo too." He thought Williams's neutrality left a hole where the "middle voice" should have been. Tharp's original intention of putting a man on pointe might have filled the gap with another dissonance.

New dancers kept appearing right up to the end of the dance, but each section contained holdovers from a previous section, so it seemed to develop organically despite its stylistic contradictions. Washington (now on pointe) and Kurshals were joined by Uchida and Richard Colton for the Fire quartet, a fast commotion of upside-down lifts, wheelbarrow promenades and fast switches in silence. With its topsy-turvy partnering, its ballet progressions begun, thwarted, and inserted when apparently abandoned, the quartet had echoes of the sextet in *As Time Goes By*. At the end of it Colton threw Washington over Kurshals's shoulder and walked away casually. Kurshals took her off while Uchida waited on pointe for him to come back and carry her away too.

A Mozart andante accompanied Colton's beautiful solo, Water. Colton has commented that the choreography "incorporates even the staccato movements into one long harmonious dance which emphasizes the long line of Mozart's music." The movement was balletic, as if Tharp had started with Colton's Joffrey Ballet persona, and then, applying twists, vigorous flings, and directional shifts to his attitude turns, jumps, pirouettes, and luxurious opening arms, she transformed him into her own adaptable, surprising, but no less virtuosic dancer. He was joined by Washington, minus the pointe shoes but wearing a feminine, off-the-shoulder dress and a Billie Holiday flower in her hair. After a short duet, they strolled off together. Allen Robertson saw their encounter as a fulfillment of Colton's "pensive yearnings . . . the most open and extended instance of emotionalism that Tharp has ever let flow."

To extinguish any possible indulgence, the final quartet was a precise rush of oppositions. Tom Rawe appeared for the first time, with Way, Wright, and Kurshals, in a stream of disagreements about positions and spacings. This section was also choreographed to Mozart, but was performed in silence. Colton described the way the dancers' muscles became imprinted with the music during this process: "The Mozart still served the movement in performance . . . in the manner that a clear container holds water." Finally the four dancers clicked into arabesque together. As if nothing more than this one move was needed to demonstrate the classical ideal, they melted into a twisted lunge and fell over in a pile.

Twyla Tharp Dance, like other modern dance companies, often arranged a day or two of local activities around its touring dates. These short stays gave the dancers a respite from traveling and brought them to the community in an informal way through master classes, lecture-demonstrations, and other activities. Every few years, Tharp was able to put together a longer residency—Amherst, Oberlin, and American University had set the precedent—and the two summers at Osgood Hill in North Andover, Massachusetts, were outstanding from her point of view as well as that of the company. Osgood Hill was built in 1886 by North Andover's Stevens/Osgood textile mill family, and was acquired in the 1950s as a conference center by Boston University. Initiated by Gerald Gross, a vice president of BU who loved Tharp's dance, the residency was designed to clear time and eliminate distractions so that she could make new work. For four weeks in 1978 and again in 1980, the entire company lived full-time at the old Victorian mansion surrounded by 150 acres of wooded parkland.

Tharp had a strong following in Boston. The company had appeared the previous fall at the 1,100-seat Hancock Hall, and all three performances were sold out hours after the box office opened, a hot-ticket record. When the Osgood Hill plan was announced, Boston dancers were ecstatic. The first year's scheme involved some intricate fund-raising and a rather large tradeoff in the form of teaching. Every day company members would drive the forty miles into Boston to give classes at BU's Sargent Gym for about twenty-five local dancers and dance teachers. A second group of twenty stayed at Osgood Hill. Some of the funding came from the National Endowment for the Arts, and the Massachusetts Council on the Arts and Humanities provided seven scholarships to dancers who auditioned for one of the two venues. A fifth week of performances and lecture-demonstrations in Boston culminated in a gala benefit performance of *The Bach Duet, Sue's Leg,* and *Half the One Hundreds.* Except for their classes and a one-day excursion to Osgood Hill, the in-town group didn't have any interaction with Tharp and the company.

Some of the Boston participants complained after the workshop was over that the project hadn't met their expectations. They got the ear of dance critic Debra Cash, whose account of the whole residency, "The Selling of Twyla Tharp," was featured in *The Real Paper* and touched off a controversy. Tharp was installed at Osgood Hill to choreograph; it was unreasonable to expect she'd involve herself in the Boston dance community as well. But BU hadn't made it clear, Cash thought, that Tharp wasn't going to be available. Angry letters appeared, but other participants felt the workshop more than fulfilled their dreams. Judith Cohen and Ramelle Adams, young Boston dancers, were both impressed with the repertory classes, where they learned phrases from *The Fugue* with associated structural manipulations, like reversal and retrograde. Cohen says, "I had never experienced anything like that and it was very intimidating. And it was very cerebral." Cohen felt it was a privilege to work with Tharp's "wonderful teachers. And to be exposed on that level, that very intimate level, to her repertory." According to Adams, "it gave a real insight into her work, and I've always really loved her work."

The schedule at Osgood Hill was demanding but there was time for play too. Tharp roused everyone early in the morning for a pre-breakfast run through the woods followed by a set of exercises she'd developed. Perhaps inspired by the basic-training sequences she'd been filming for *Hair,* this "boot camp" routine was more strenuous than any studio warmup although it wasn't exactly calisthenics. The dancers complained about it and started scheming to be excused. After ballet class, taught by Colton or Whitener, the rest of the day was given to rehearsals out on the lawn, and, for the students, repertory class. Once again *The Fugue* served as a teaching instrument. One of the scholarship students, Jeff Friedman, recalls "learning the twenty-count base phrase, so you absolutely do it forward, to the right, and then we would learn all of the different operations, and they would allow us to solve those problems for ourselves. . . . And that was definitely part of the purpose, to start to flex those muscles of kinesthetic intelligence." Friedman also remembers sessions devoted to learning repertory from videotapes. This had become so common a company practice that they'd discovered little tricks like turning the monitor toward a mirror to correct the video's reversed image. Tharp worked with these students, and with company members, on new material she was making.

Visitors arrived constantly, not only the dancers' families but professional writers, artists, and theater folk, who were curious about what was going on. The dancers remember killer volleyball games, relaxing in the pool, trips to local ice-cream stands and vegetable farms, and riotous evening charades. The dancers slept in the big house, while Tharp had her own quarters in a small building nearby, a former plant shed, with a big room on the ground floor and a loft above. There were no meals to cook, no laundry or housekeeping to do, and best of all from Tharp's point of view, no office interruptions. Touring, especially in the small red and blue groups, brought the dancers together, and the Osgood Hill experience bonded them even closer as a company. Tharp moved a little further away, psychologically as well as physically. She didn't always eat with the group, and she probably didn't take a regular part in the social hilarity. She stayed in her own cottage and listened to the Bach B Minor Mass late into the night.

The residency in 1978 folded some new members into the company. After months of missed connections, William Whitener had arrived. Whitener achieved outstanding success in the Joffrey Ballet's repertory of Tharp and Arpino works, as well as dancing Tudor, Ashton, Jooss, Balanchine, and the leads in *Petrouchka* and Flemming Flindt's *The Lesson*. He felt it was time to settle down with one choreographer. Whitener had been attracted to Tharp ever since *Deuce Coupe*. "First and foremost," he explains, "was the enjoyment that I received from working with her in the studio. I loved listening to her talk about dance. And was fascinated by her mind. I found the style challenging and unique. And felt that . . . she was in the process of redefining the male classical dancer." He wanted to be engaged in her creative process. "Her loft down there on Franklin was like a laboratory," he says now. "And I was ready." After talking with Robert Joffrey and affirming his decision, he danced his final performances at the end of 1977. At that point, *Hair* was in its postponed shooting stages. While Tharp was finishing the movie, Whitener joined the cast of Bob Fosse's *Dancin'* for a few months, but finally their schedules synched up.

John Carrafa was the other scholarship student at Osgood Hill the first year. Jeff Friedman accurately perceived the residency as a kind of tryout period for them, and he felt a certain competition and anticipation about the possibility of being taken into the company. Eventually it was Carrafa who was chosen. Friedman had protected himself from disappointment by applying to architecture school, and he later realized, as Tharp developed the partnering and character work she started at Osgood Hill, that she was going in a different direction from what had attracted him. Carrafa, who had recently come to Boston from Maine, had been accepted as a member of Concert Dance Company, a Boston-based group that did modern dance repertory. At the end of the Osgood Hill residency he remained with Tharp instead of taking up the job in Boston.

Katie Glasner had a protracted transition into the company—she calls it a "ghosting affiliation"—that went on for nearly two years. She'd been spotted by the ballet teacher Jonathan Watts during her freshman year at the University of Wisconsin–Milwaukee. Watts told her she was wasting her time in college and should go to New York to dance. She fixed her ambitions on Tharp after seeing a videotape of *Sue's Leg* in the Dance Department's library. Glasner flew to New York to audition for the 1977 Tharp summer workshop at City Center. She went on tour with the company, dancing in *Eight Jelly Rolls*, but both she and Tharp thought she was too inexperienced to become a permanent member at that time. Tharp hired her for the expanded choruses in *Hair* and brought her to Osgood Hill in '78 as a kind of apprentice.

Before the end of the residency Glasner fell into a hole while running in the woods and sprained her ankle badly. Once that healed she had just began working her way into the repertory when an unexpected surgery felled her again. The day she got home from the hospital in early June 1979, she learned that she was expected to be rehearsed and ready to go with the company to the Avignon festival in mid-July. Glasner met the challenge. "I was very drawn to this woman's dancemaking and then the kinesthetic power that it had," Glasner says now. "I wanted to move this way. I needed to move this way."

Among other things, the 1978 Osgood Hill residency saw the beginnings of a major work. By the time *Baker's Dozen* premiered eight months later, the company had expanded again, to include John Malashock and Mary Ann Kellogg. *Baker's Dozen* can be seen as completing and exemplifying the process of synthesis that had started with *Give and Take*. From this period until the company was dissolved in 1988, Twyla Tharp Dance represented the most successful fusion of ballet and modern dancers in the history of independent American dance companies. Without giving up her more visible exploits in films, TV, and freelance choreography during those years, Tharp made an astonishing number of original and challenging dances for the company, including *Short Stories, The Catherine Wheel, Nine Sinatra Songs, Fait Accompli,* and *In the Upper Room*.

Tharp has given many explanations for the genesis of *Baker's Dozen*. Years later she reflected on it as one of several "rebound" dances, responses to failed love affairs or tragic events in her life. *Baker's Dozen* followed the breakup of a doomed two-year romance, and she says she was beginning to suspect she "needed loss to create art." But this romantic construct greatly oversimplifies the inherent contradictions of her personality. Both sensual and puritanical, she craved love and stability but refused to let her own accomplishments attain a fixed identity. She fought for complete control of her artistic product but couldn't have realized the work without sympathetic collaborators. Beginning with Bob Huot, Tharp's sexual partners usually shared her professional life and contributed to it in important ways. The relationships didn't last, but she collected new reserves of creative energy from them. As one of her dancers from this period remarks, ". . . she quite often needs a new palette. And new dancers. For creativity to spark her."

Dancing in the studio was what kept her going; it made her happy and drew the dancers to her. Perhaps *Baker's Dozen* was a sublimation of the ideal family she'd never had in real life. Tharp had always buried her feelings superbly in form and abstraction. Some of her most heartfelt dances were perceived as formal, stylistic essays. *Give and Take* and *Mud* didn't stay in the repertory long enough for their subtle undercurrents to be appreciated. In these, and in *Baker's Dozen*, Tharp was offering the dancers a challenge and an opportunity. For her that meant offering them love.

Introducing *Baker's Dozen* on the videotape *Confessions of a Cornermaker,* made for the shortlived CBS Cable TV network in 1981, Tharp seemed to be rebounding as well from her disappointment with *Hair*. "I had been exposed to waste on a massive scale. No one's intention, but a project as large as a Hollywood picture seems destined to deny any fair correlation between investment and return. Therefore when I started to work on a new piece for my company, I was thinking a lot about economy. Nothing should be squandered or disregarded. As in Nature all things would be recycled and would accrue. A good cook wastes nothing. But this is not to be confused with stinginess. And so I named the piece *Baker's Dozen* in reference to a fair and generous measure." She unearthed the videotapes she'd made during her pregnancy, improvising to the records of Willie "The Lion" Smith. She wanted to project some of this footage as part of the new dance, and the "fair and generous measure," translated to the stage, meant that the audience was to get twelve dancers and a bonus—Twyla on tape with a baby, Jesse, in the oven. As the production went into technical rehearsals, difficulties arose with projecting the old video. When it was blown up to stage size it looked too blurry, and just before the premiere she scrapped it, along with the expensive set she'd had built to replicate the attic at New Berlin.

Baker's Dozen took shape in Tharp's imagination as a theatrical piece. The dancers were to enter in silhouette behind a scrim, and the videotape would appear between dance numbers accompanied by the sound of baby Jesse crying. Tharp even had a scenario of sorts. The harmonious work of the family (the dancers) kept being disrupted by the demands of this offstage infant. At one point Tharp, who was planning to be in the piece, "is trying to go on dancing with this kid crying and she finally exits to go take care of the kid." All the theatrical trappings, including Tharp's own participation, were discarded during a painful dress rehearsal at the urging of Santo Loquasto and Jennifer Tipton, her trusted collaborators. Loquasto says Tharp sometimes visualized more than the audience could keep up with. "Because of her own perceptions being lightning fast, the mortals can't keep up—Twyla, there's too much to look at." Cleansed of everything but the dancing, *Baker's Dozen* turned out to be perfect.

She had choreographed her own part on Shelley Washington, and she began rehearsing it. In the exquisitely calibrated universe of *Baker's Dozen*, Tharp provided herself with an amicable tribe of siblings, flexible companions who could be her life partners. Not since *Sue's Leg* had she actually danced on an equal basis with the rest of the company. Even in dances where she appeared to be one of the gang, like *Eight Jelly Rolls*, her irrepressible comic sense came to the foreground. Sara Rudner, who took over her role in *Baker's Dozen*, remembered her being "this one extraordinary comic, free spirit, messing everything up . . . like the kid who is so exuberant and everything has to revolve around her." Rudner thinks Tharp was wise to drop out. The dance needed precision timing and performing; it was a puzzle that the dancers needed the utmost skill to put together, and Tharp at that point was still in choreographing mode. "She didn't really know [the dance]," Rudner says.

Tharp has described *Baker's Dozen* as resembling a game of jacks, where you pick up an increasing number of pieces with one hand while your other hand bounces a little ball. This analogy captures the playfulness and dexterity of a dance that in fact is structured with geometric elegance. The dancers are introduced one couple at a time. They then group together in trios, quartets, sextets, and finally as an ensemble, out of which each member emerges for a small solo. Santo Loquasto dressed them in creamy white, the men in pants and collarless shirts, the women in slim, draped skirts with skimpy tops, over velour leggings. They all wore white jazz shoes, and all the clothes flowed beautifully with the movement. The costumes suggested the pre–World War I era of Vernon and Irene Castle, who popularized a more dignified social dancing than the risqué rompings of the turkey trot and the bunny hug.

Tharp took her primary cue from Willie "The Lion" Smith, a leading exponent of Harlem jazz piano, whose career stretched across the first half of the twentieth century. For the premiere at Brooklyn Academy, 15 February 1979, and as often as possible on tour, the music was played live by Dick Hyman. Smith's music was more embellished and orchestral, less predictable than the barefaced rhythms of ragtime or the regular beat of stride piano. Willie Smith may never have accompanied silent movies, but his compositions suggest the melodramatic, rapidly shifting moods those early musical improvisers had to establish. The four numbers Tharp chose for her dance, "Echoes of Spring," "Tango à la Caprice," "Concentrating," and "Relaxin'," flow almost untrackably through rippling arpeggios, trills, shifts of melody and key, hesitations, suspensions, and drastic tempo changes.

The dance too is a stream of invention and surprise, but the numerical sorting out of the dancers prevents the whole thing from becoming lost in continual novelty. You know the equation will fulfill itself even if you can't predict how. The dance begins and ends with couples in completely different configurations. First they enter one at a time in a strolling rhythm with a slight hitch step or skip. Each pair takes a different approach to partnering conventions, hinting at social dances, ballet dances, or children's games, and they each overturn the conventions in the same breath. When all six couples have come and gone, one or two dancers start to sprint on, as if they're too revved up to let the dance subside for even a moment; they're pulled back from behind the scene.

The tango section begins with large emphatic gestures and accents, slides to the floor, screwball lifts, long and short phrases with sudden halts. The trios comprise two men partnering one woman and two women with one man. This setup was used by Balanchine in *Agon*, one of the few ballets Tharp has publicly admired. Again she finds unlimited ways to play with the groupings, flipping from extravagant approaches and luxurious back-bending embraces to sudden releases and interruptions. The trios become quartets, with tight partner switching. The music goes into a softer variation of the tango theme, and the dance structure slides into the beginning of a long retrograde. The first quartet returns, then the remaining sets of four, and they in turn peel back to their original trios.

A new musical number begins, a chirpy, rippling theme, and the dancers fall into studied nonchalance, drooping and sliding against their partners, nudging and hauling each other about. For the first time a compact group of six crosses the stage, then another. The section ends in a series of escalating surprises. One sextet slowly unfolds into a unison pose, then, on an explosion of music, they all rip into a scrambling chase and vanish. Richard Colton is left alone looking bewildered. (Gary Chryst took the part in the *Cornermaker* video when Colton was injured.) He starts the solo section by shrugging off a woman who jumps onto his back, then another who topples into his arms from the wings.

As the fractional units have been accumulating and dissolving, the idea of ensemble grows stronger. When the group rises to its maximum organizational strength, in the unison sextets and finally a smart lineup that sweeps across the stage, Tharp counterpoints a solo for each person. Some are abbreviated; others are quite extended—Colton's riff on the romantic vignette he had in *Mud*, microexpositions of ballet technique for Whitener and Uchida, a stream of asymmetrical jumps for Washington. Only the part Tharp intended for herself has no special solo. At last the whole group threads casually in and out of a lineup to find their original partners, and like a movie going in reverse, they skip backwards couple by couple, and leave. When five pairs have gone off, it's Rudner, the Tharp-surrogate figure, who returns for the last, partnerless man (Raymond Kurshals) and leads him off by the hand. Shortly before the opening, when she was still in the piece, Tharp told Robert J. Pierce of the *Soho Weekly News*: ". . . theoretically the last passage is myself packing up that youngster and just walking off with him."

8

Family Business
1979–1981

Tharp has compared *Baker's Dozen* to Edward Hicks's well-known painting *The Peaceable Kingdom*, "a place where each dancer comfortably and naturally fits." She's also referred to the dance as "a society whose conventions are clear," a place where even a member who strays will be welcomed back into the fold. At the same time as she was envisioning this idyllic community, she began exploring the flip side of familial accord, a much less benign thematic territory. Osgood Hill in 1978 saw the first moves that led to *When We Were Very Young* and *The Catherine Wheel*. She had decided to confront the question of narrative, and some of the visitors to the 1978 workshop were prospective composers or script writers. Richard Colton remembers the balletomane and satirist Edward Gorey appearing and working with Tharp on what never got past being a skit: "Chris Uchida ran a Chinese laundry and I forget whether she hid me—there was some kidnapped boy, and I remember being in one of those rolling things, and the wheel fell out of it."

For a while there were only fragments. At the end of the residency the company gave performances in Boston, including a lecture-demonstration. After Tharp and Tom Rawe each took the dancers through a set of the dreaded daily calisthenics, there was a showing of material made during the residency, "a series of small allegorical studies" according to Christine Temin of *The Boston Globe*. The characters included two Evildoers (Rudner and Rawe); two housemaids, representing Chaos (Shelley Washington did something reminiscent of Tharp's drunk dance in *Eight Jelly Rolls*) and Order (Chris Uchida); Innocence (Jennifer Way with a pretend jump rope) and Authority (Rose Marie Wright in a long skirt). There was a seedy Greek chorus that, Temin observed, "do not further the plot, but are very good for getting rid of dead bodies," and a street scene with stomping punks played by some of the workshop students.

Tharp and the company had been listening all summer to the recently released album of The Band's farewell concert, *The Last Waltz*, and for a press showing at Osgood Hill, they did some of the new material using the song "The Shape I'm In." Without relinquishing the popular music idiom that had helped make her work look so contemporary and attracted such excited audiences, she was moving past the generalized types she had evolved—the kids in the schoolyard, the blasé sophisticates, the laid-back square dancers and hippies. Now she wanted to project more specific characterizations and action.

Baker's Dozen made its appearance the following winter during another packed season at Brooklyn Academy, along with four pieces from the repertory (*Country Dances*, *Eight Jelly Rolls*, *Sue's Leg*, and the men's *Fugue*) and three other new works. Tharp danced a powerful, introspective solo to three songs by Randy Newman, *1903*, a dance she referred to as "a study in genteel cynicism." She used movement from *The One Hundreds*, reinterpreted with a personal inflection that suggested she shared some of the hunger and disillusion in Newman's "Sail Away," "Suzanne," and "Dayton, Ohio—1903."

With the release of the movie *Hair* scheduled for two weeks after the BAM season, she laid claim to three dances from her edited-out choreography. In *Electric Blues*, she began as a playmate being tossed around by Rawe, Kurshals, Colton, and Ferro, and then metamorphosed into the hippie-deity who would preside over the film's hallucinogenic wedding scene. A big allegory, *3-5-0-0*, with Rose Marie Wright as a "macabre figure of death masquerading as a bride" and Tom Rawe stripping the valuables from the corpses of soldiers, was more than slightly redolent of Kurt Jooss's 1932 antiwar ballet *The Green Table*. In *What a Piece of Work Is Man*, Rawe danced with a drill team from the Army's Pershing Rifles Company. For the BAM performances of *3-5-0-0*, the company was expanded to include Deborah Zalkind, Richard Caceres, Kristin Draudt, and Mark Morris. An extraordinary dancer with a linebacker's physique, Morris auditioned more than once to join the company but Tharp hadn't figured out how to use big men.

A year and a half later Morris produced his first concert in New York and began his own history.

The fourth BAM premiere was the narrative work that had been in development since Osgood Hill, *Chapters and Verses*. It was introduced with a program note: "Three sections extracted from a larger piece, these dances are thought of as chapters published in advance of the completed novel." The dancers called it *Captured Nurses*. Though the five numbers bore some movement relationships, the work had the musical eclecticism and discontinuous throughline of Tharp's other "suite" pieces. As in some of her subsequent narratives, the characters fought with each other constantly but reconciled in an apotheosis of brotherhood. After a circusy opening, with the dancers leaping and grandstanding to a rousing march by Edwin Franko Goldman, the piece spun from one raucous episode to another, and then unwound into an almost monotonous disco sequence. Even when it looked most improvised, *Chapters and Verses* was choreographed on a musical beat. In the group sections canonic and counterpointed phrases piled on top of each other, but the musical high points emerged at the peak of the lifts and the emphatic phrase endings.

After the opener, "The Hard Circus," each part incorporated new Tharpisms. "Scenes from the Boy's Education" began with a condensed version of the Osgood Hill calisthenic workout. Tom Rawe bullied and harangued Kurshals, Ferro, Whitener, and France Mayotte, and they complained loudly as they labored through fast stretches, twists, bends, and sit-ups. Dancers didn't actually speak onstage at that time, let alone yell and scream. For Tharp, speech was going to be a component of drama. Though the dialogue in *Chapters and Verses* looked spontaneous, the dancers had memorized and rehearsed their lines along with the movement. Around the same time, she was getting them to work on hysterical laughter and oversized facial expressions, which made their way into *The Catherine Wheel*.

Without a pause the exercisers were joined by the rest of the company in a rowdy session of pushing, shoving, and belligerent vocalizing, set to Clarence "Frogman" Henry's "Ain't Got No Home," recorded by The Band. A real car, possibly a golf cart, drove onto the stage and as many of them climbed onto it as could fit. The rest followed it off. Cars, as an icon of youth culture, had been appropriated by Tharp as early as *Deuce Coupe*, and the arrival of a working model onstage caused a tremor of identification in the audience. She used the same device later in both her Broadway shows, *Singin' in the Rain* and *Movin' Out*.

She invoked another icon, along with fond memories of "The Nursery," with recordings of the theme song from the television kiddie show the *Mickey Mouse Club*. A small group marched in and out, leaving William Whitener behind to dance a solo. Wearing an abstracted expression, he glided through a string of balletic poses and extended transitions, most of the time keeping his legs in parallel position rather than turned out. In contrast to the aggressive physicality of the group, he seemed almost puppet-like. The effect was odd and sweet at the same time.

The fighting resumed in "Street from the Night Before," to disco music by John Simon, concert-music producer for the *Last Waltz* album, whom Tharp had enlisted to create the collage score. Richard Colton thinks the musical idea behind *Chapters and Verses* was to re-create the variegated energy of The Band's historic concert. For the last section Simon came up with a pounding, hypnotic number with a female singer doing gospel riffs on the theme of "Us Together," and a meter that shifted from four counts to three unexpectedly through the twelve minutes of the dance. Individual disco dancers swirled in and out seemingly at random while Sara Rudner maintained a calm ongoing presence. Gradually her centeredness seemed to smooth out the punchy hostilities everyone had exhibited before, and their movements became springy, even spongy, with bursts of quick accents. The tempo speeded up after a long time, and the dancers drew closer together. Packs of them were still moving when the dance ended.

Most of the critics were noncommittal about *Chapters and Verses*. It was, after all, offered as a work in progress, and on the BAM season it was overshadowed by *Baker's Dozen*, which everyone recognized as a major work. But two significant critical voices came out on opposite sides of the discussion about it. Anna Kisselgoff, who had succeeded Clive Barnes as chief dance critic of *The New York Times*, questioned Tharp's political credibility in a Sunday overview of the season. Kisselgoff had always admired Tharp's pure-dance works, and in *Baker's Dozen* she welcomed "the combined complexity of structure and ease of choreographic inevitability that mark Miss Tharp at her most creative and innovative." But she read "social commentary" into all the other new pieces and the musical pegs that held them together. *Hair* was mere "cosmetics" and *Chapters and Verses*, though sharper in tone, ultimately had a "soft center." Kisselgoff's colleague at the *Times*, Jack Anderson, had already noted Tharp's neutral stance toward provocative subjects. Perhaps she was "declining to sermonize" so she wouldn't offend anyone, he thought.

But Kisselgoff expected Tharp to dissect the social situations she portrayed; instead she was mythologizing them. Like a latter-day Agnes de Mille, Tharp was creating a "benign view of popular culture."

Nancy Goldner, then the dance critic of *The Nation* and five years younger than Kisselgoff, was no less appreciative of Tharp's compositional distinction, and she too saw *Baker's Dozen* as "obviously the great dance of this collection." But for her, the messier *Chapters and Verses* rang true, and she embraced the postures of adolescence warmly. Goldner loved the dance's boisterous humor, the awkward physicality, and "the marvelous excess of its content and form . . . Never have I seen anarchy so fully embodied or the bêtes noires of American life so wholeheartedly endorsed or sympatheti-cally examined." In the *Christian Science Monitor*, where Goldner was a regular contributor, she noted the emblematic car and the transistor radio that Sara Rudner clutched in her hand. But for Goldner these tokens of materialism added poignancy to the picture of kids trying to communicate: "In connect-ing teen-agerism with commercialism, and then celebrating both with such brio, Tharp has pulled off a coup de théâtre as well as a true comment on our times."

Tharp was gradually getting out of dancing as she neared forty, and it wasn't easy for her. Few people noticed that after *Sue's Leg* she'd either left herself out of new work entirely or made a singular role for herself within the dance: the yogic priestess in *Hair*, the soloist in *Country Dances* and *Give and Take*. After rescinding her plan to dance in *Baker's Dozen*, she made star ap-pearances when necessary, covered for company members in emergencies, and confined new roles to more or less overt reflections on her immediate personal concerns. Following her role as the mother figure in *When We Were Very Young* she choreographed again for herself only three more times: *Fait Accompli* (1983), a work of merciless difficulty, in which she confronted her own aging and disengagement from dancing; *Men's Piece* (1991), a menopausal reflection on sexuality and role-playing; and *Cutting Up*, for the celebrity tour she made with Mikhail Baryshnikov in 1992–93.

When We Were Very Young was a natural successor to the narrative investi-gations she'd been pursuing. Now she not only wanted to tell a story but to dramatize her own conflicts, about age, motherhood, and responsibility, in a more objective frame. She was looking for something literary, and she set her sights high. Through mutual contacts she was bold enough to approach writers like Harold Brodkey, John Updike, and John Irving for projects she was contemplating during this period. She had begun building the movement material for *When We Were Very Young* and even drafted a couple of scripts herself, when her agent at the Lantz office put her in touch with another of his clients, playwright Thomas Babe. A regular in Joseph Papp's unofficial stable of writers at the Public Theater, Babe hadn't worked with dancers before, but he hit it off with Tharp. He saw right away that the dancers were doing something more elemental than the literal treatment Tharp had written. He told John Rockwell of the *Times*, "The characters [in her scripts] were defined by facts, not feelings, but the dancing was *full* of feelings. . . . It was primitive, it was muscular, it was passionate. So, we started over." Babe, who had a poet's fondness for whimsy, found the A. A. Milne lament on childhood insecurity, "Disobedience," with its story about three-year-old James James Morrison Morrison, who warned his mother not to leave home without him.

Nine revisions later, they had a sort of composite memoir on the theme of growing up. The poem pointed the way to an exploration of role reversal, generational overlap, and some slippery questions of individuality, fidelity, and guilt. To Tharp "it seemed to make growing up the ultimate and cardinal sin." For practical reasons Tharp discarded the idea of giving the dancers dialogue to speak, and Babe wrote the script as a conversation between a father and daughter. In performance he took the father's role, opposite a child actress, Gayle Meyers. His own daughter was nearly the same age as Jesse Huot, and the final script was an impressionistic meditation on both his and Tharp's parental anxieties and defenses. The narrators traded roles so that the identities of mother, grandmother, parent, and child wrapped around one another.

Onstage the work was almost as diffuse as the text. The dancers shifted through time periods, characters, and situations with only tenuous reference to the spoken narrative, which often dominated the audience's attention. Santo Loquasto had devised a set made of large cardboard packing boxes; the dancers shoved them around to create settings for different scenes. Tharp had made two discrete cadres of dancers. For the four main characters—a son and daughter (Raymond Kurshals and Katie Glasner), a brother/husband (Tom Rawe), and the perpetually dissatisfied mother/child, Jane—she developed an exaggerated acting style that carried over into the next and more successful version of the tortured tale, *The Catherine Wheel*. Then there was an anonymous ensemble that supplied additional characters to the wispy plot. Whitener's Mickey Mouse solo and the disco dance from *Chapters and Verses* were incorporated in abbreviated form, as were the company calisthenics. There was a Little Match Girl (Washington), a juggler (Carrafa), a thirty-ninth birthday ruefully observed, a twenty-six piece orchestra, and the lines from "Disobedience," chanted in march cadence by dancers crossing the stage like squads of recruits. The noise and fractured activity rose to a crescendo as Jane/Tharp discarded the clothing and symbolic objects she'd accumulated during the journey and casually dropped off the edge of the stage into the orchestra pit. "I could hear the intake of breath in the audience, the eight times we did it," Babe reflected later. "You got us, you moved us, the audience said; you left us, and we care." This response confirmed what Tharp had always wanted for her work.

Arlene Croce, though she deemed the dance a failure, acknowledged that Tharp had reached the audience, "a genuine, pleasure-seeking Broadway crowd [which] behaved as if being up to its eyes in murk were perfectly normal" and granted its "hearty approval" at the end. The following fall Tharp explained to Susan Reimer-Torn of *The International Herald Tribune*: "I do want my work to be in the mainstream of people's lives. Great composers, like Brahms, for example, have always picked up on the social dances and music around. . . . When my dancers do the impossible developed from the possible, it gives people something to connect to."

When We Were Very Young was the centerpiece of a big gamble for Tharp, her first advance onto Broadway. Having won acclaim with her concert dances and television work, she now embarked on a new phase in her lifelong campaign to attract bigger and broader audiences. Instead of returning to Brooklyn Academy where she could count on a loyal following and some subsidy, she booked the Winter Garden Theater through her own foundation for three early-spring weeks of old and new repertory. Ticket sales were excellent even though the season coincided with a subway strike. The Tharp company, now numbering fifteen dancers, was in peak form. In addition to *Baker's Dozen*, *Eight Jelly Rolls*, *The Fugue*, and *Ocean's Motion*, the repertory included a revised version of *Deuce Coupe* and another new work, *Brahms' Paganini*.

Set to Book I and II of the Variations on a Theme of Paganini (the same theme that later inspired Rachmaninoff), the Brahms began with a Tharpian tour de force, a twelve-minute solo that pushed its alternating dancers, Richard Colton and William Whitener, to extreme limits of technique, endurance, and performing ingenuity. Following the solo, she set one of her

minutely engineered quartets, with Jennifer Way as a recurring outsider figure. In form the dance was odd looking. Way's solitary figure was like a distant echo of the first solo, but she was elusive against the quartet's frenetic
changes and soaring, perilous lifts.

Nancy Goldner thought the quartet was "about the strenuousness of
partnering. It dwells on rough edges, near misses, and harsh bodily impact.
Canon structure usually produces buoyancy. Here it produces a jagged,
bumpy ride." But Deborah Jowitt saw the movement as a double-edged
metaphor: "Ironically, it is through cooperativeness and considerateness and
skill, which have to figure in any dance this difficult, that this work creates
an illusion of debating, fighting, yielding, winning, and turning to enter a
new competition." Tharp told an interviewer at the time that she was finally
dealing with passion, a subject that had always embarrassed her. "I acknowledge the difficulty of getting through—your life. That's what it's all about as
you get older. The man's variation is a heroic undertaking. . . . And the
quartet shows the underside of romance, a lot of unlovely stuff."

Tharp had choreographed different parts of the solo on Colton,
Whitener, and John Carrafa, whenever one of them was in town between
tours with the red or blue team. For Colton, these choreographing sessions
were among the most stimulating moments of his career. Tharp's foot was in
a cast at the time from an injury, and she trusted the dancers to follow her
suggestions since she couldn't demonstrate. Colton also taught the solo to
Mikhail Baryshnikov, in anticipation of a special appearance on opening
night. Baryshnikov was up to the technical demands, but he'd been shooting a movie and didn't have the stamina to get through it just then, so
Colton danced the premiere.

The solo was a breathtaking stream of invention. Characteristically,
Tharp packed so much into it that the casual viewer, dazzled by the performance itself, could take in only the rudiments of her composition. A tape of
William Whitener in performance reveals just how much she was able to say
about dancing without resorting to mime or literalism. While Whitener
does a repertory of fairly conventional steps—pirouettes in various positions, high open jumps and small hops and staggers, tight spins, wide balances, and skids—his upper body is equally active and consistently
unpredictable. You have the sense that you've never seen these steps before,
and that perhaps you'll never see them again, because whenever they repeat,
the whole body is shaped, phrased, and focused differently. He goes from
relaxed to precise energies, and as he becomes more exhausted this range

widens, to include a drooping or dangling of weight and flung motions of the whole arm or leg. The gestures seldom look placed or stopped. With typical articulateness, a Tharpian dancer of that period could make small initiating moves with shoulders, chest, neck, head, even the whole upper torso. Instead of being held and proper, the body could twist against itself, spiral around to the back, make small adjustments. Whitener and Colton's movement never halted between the fourteen musical variations, effectively stifling any applause until the end.

Later Whitener told Texas critic Josie Neal that the solo "encompasses just about everything I know about dancing and endurance and theatrics and performance. That's the most satisfying role I've ever danced." Colton says he didn't feel competitive with Whitener in the role because each of them danced it in his own way, and the critics saw this too. Colton felt that Whitener represented the Paganini, or classical, side of the music while he himself danced the more romantic Brahmsian aspects. Critic Deborah Jowitt contrasted the two interpretations: "Whitener is a superb dancer. A trace of sharp, almost foxy intensity keeps him from being unbearably elegant. . . . But if I hadn't seen Colton perform it, I don't think I would have seen quite as much in it. Colton is capable of changing the nature of a gesture in the middle of it, of beginning to let a particular quality take over one part of his body while something else is still going on in another part. Perhaps because he is a small man, he has taught himself to expand immensely in space, to prolong a gesture with almost voluptuous lyricism, even to jump slowly."

Tharp disliked double casting a new piece. She wanted the dancers to make the steps their own, "to breathe and behave," in Colton's words, before setting the choreography and transferring it to a second cast. It's a common rehearsal practice for alternates to shadow the first dancers from the sidelines, but Tharp found this distracting during the creative process. She didn't like teaching old roles either, and she had no reservations about entrusting this task to the dancers and the videotapes. Tharp did envision two dancers sharing a role choreographically. In fact, she utilized doubling so often and in so many ways that it could be called a major aspect of the way she looked at the ensemble.

Her younger twin brothers, who had made up their own private language, provided early lessons in the behavior of bonded siblings. She had noted her "fascination with duplication" as a choreographic ploy back in 1969, in her program notes for *Dancing in the Streets*. The same year, she put together the overlapping double-quintet version of *Group Activities* for the stage of the Brooklyn Academy Opera House. Her analytical mind found endless structural possibilities in this simple idea. She loved setting two dancers, or two groups of dancers, against each other doing the same things. This device could act as a formal element of design, like the two female anchors in *In the Upper Room*. It could impose a formal rigor on a dance that might be perceived as just another youthful romp (*Ocean's Motion*), or teach the audience to take note of the dancers' differences, like having two dancers demonstrate the one hundred phrases side by side in *The One Hundreds*. To create a nonstop frame around the long last section of *Known by Heart* she made a marathon shuffle for a team of male dancers, perhaps in fond remembrance of the two-of-a-kind soft-shoe numbers she'd cut her teeth on in the old Gene Kelly movies. When she wanted to poke a little fun at ballet's vanities, she split the corps into two gangs of feckless ladies (*Push Comes to Shove*).

Tharp even carried the notion of duplication into costuming. The device could be didactic. The gray costumes turned white in *The Bix Pieces* to signify that the ghosts of history are always with us. The white-to-black-to-white outfits in the 1995 ballet *How Near Heaven* imposed a shadow of death on the community. It could be a charming trick. In *Sue's Leg* the four dancers' dressy versions of their own practice clothes made a witty comment on the porous borderline between studio and stage, with another layer of reflexivity added when the dance was repeated on a single program in the original work clothes.

Tharp was well aware of the drama inherent in competitive twinning, and she fully exploited the other compositional tools that called for exact imitation: canon, mirroring, and repetition. *Uncle Edgar Dyed His Hair Red*, one of the smaller offerings of 1981, was built entirely on the idea of six women dancing in pairs. Wearing black tank suits and sneakers, the side-by-side couples began in unison and proceeded to a full panoply of duet manipulations. There were trompe l'oeil sections where pairs swept through the space and left with different partners. Behind an upstage scrim, couples passed by in silhouette, sometimes mirroring other couples in the foreground. The movement was unforgiving, with bodies skewed into slow twisting falls, or arms and legs levering in monolithic motions reminiscent of the women's aquatic exertions to "Don't Go Near the Water" in *Deuce Coupe*. Tharp told an audience at a preview showing of *Uncle Edgar* that she was thinking up "new ways to torture the female form." When it premiered in New York in the fall of 1981 Anna Kisselgoff thought it was one of the season's best. She appreciated the dance's exploration of "formal movement problems—not coating them with attitudes or social comment."

As a producing experiment, the 1980 Winter Garden confirmed to Tharp that she could escape what she considered the confines of assured dance venues and take her work to a less specialized audience. Self-producing, with contributions from independent backers and promoters, she exited the BAM reservation and traded the college touring circuit for legitimate theater situations whenever possible. She opted out of Brooklyn Academy's prestigious and handsomely funded annual Next Wave series. That would have required her to accept commissioning money for new choreography with inevitable strings attached, and besides, she disdained being just one among a cluster of performing groups marketed together as each year's new thing.

In 1981 she formed a relationship with rock promoter Bill Graham. She booked the company into Graham's Warfield Theater in San Francisco, antagonizing the biggest Bay Area dance presenter. The Committee for Arts and Lectures at the University of California, which administered Zellerbach Auditorium on the Berkeley campus, insisted on securing an exclusive on the company's appearance. This would have prevented them from going into any other theater within thirty miles. Tharp considered Zellerbach a suburban enclave. "Brooklyn, like Berkeley, represents something slightly outside the center of things," she told *The San Francisco Chronicle*. "A campus is not a city." She withdrew from the Zellerbach series, incurring a small scandal and threats that she'd never be booked there again. Tharp was also uncomfortable with the guidelines imposed under National Endowment for the Arts sponsorship, and she wasn't reluctant to share her displeasure with the press. "We get the same fee whether we're dancing for a 300-seat house or a 4,000-seat house. We can fill a theater like the Music Hall in Detroit. We should charge our Endowment fee while somebody else is taking all the box office? It was getting to the point where I couldn't afford the Endowment."

Tharp's activities during the early 1980s were so prolific that the business became increasingly complicated. The Twyla Tharp Dance Foundation handled the company business, booked tours, and raised money for projects. Twyla Tharp Enterprises was the corporate entity under which Tharp negotiated her independent work—movies, choreographing commissions, and other outside assignments. Tharp would receive a separate fee for doing a movie or video, but she would try to get the dancers hired on the project wherever feasible. A small administrative staff worked with the foundation's board of directors to facilitate her work. For years, the two company units toured relentlessly and worked with her, while she took on extracurricular jobs, projecting her protean selves out into the world as choreographer, filmmaker, television director, theater director, and super-energized celebrity.

Going into theaters where dance hadn't established a beachhead was one way of getting the work out to more people, but film and television were even better. In the first half of the 1980s Tharp worked on four Hollywood movies and four in-house videos. She contributed incidental dances to Milos Forman's *Ragtime* and Woody Allen's *Zelig* (for which she didn't take a credit). These were essentially period pieces—turn-of-the-century waltzes, chorus lines, and popular dances for *Ragtime*, and a pseudo-Charleston called the Chameleon among other trifles for *Zelig*.

Forman called on her again to do *Amadeus*, and this was more substantial. Tharp choreographed the dances and staged the operas for Peter Shaffer's fantasy on the life of Mozart as told by his rival Salieri. *Amadeus* was shot in Prague over a period of months. The music was recorded in London under Neville Marriner's direction, but Tharp needed people who could move credibly as well as lip-synch the singing. For the comic operas she ignored protocol and enlisted members of Prague's popular-theater company; she considered them more flexible than the classical singers at the National Theater. After checking out the local ballet dancers, she arranged for her own company to come over and appear in two of the big opera scenes.

She delegated Shelley Freydont to research the culture of the late-eighteenth-century Viennese court. Freydont had concentrated in ballet and art history when she was getting a masters degree; she'd taught undergraduates in California and danced with Louis Falco in New York before joining the Tharp company following a 1979 audition. Freydont was able to decipher the old dance notations, and with the help of period dance specialist Elizabeth Aldrich she reconstructed examples of the galop, schottische, ländler, and other dances for herself. Then Freydont would fly to Prague, where Tharp was directing the opera scenes. She'd demonstrate some of the possibilities she'd found, and after Tharp made her choices Freydont would go back to New York and teach the material to the company. When the dancers arrived in Prague, Tharp staged the material for the camera. Freydont also set some of the social-dance scenes that ended up in the background of the movie. She says she had such a great time working on the set that she didn't mind being listed only as one of the Tharp company dancers.

Tharp also choreographed for Taylor Hackford's film *White Nights*, the thriller about a dancer who accidentally finds himself back in the Soviet Union after defecting, and is then used as a political pawn. Mikhail Baryshnikov starred, with Gregory Hines as a disappointed American tap dancer who's emigrated in the opposite direction. Hines is assigned to befriend Baryshnikov and persuade him to stay in Russia. For the scene where they face each other down in the studio, Tharp made one of her fusion dances. Each man tries to outdance the other in a tap-ballet competition and they end up in mutual admiration. She started choreographing the scene where Baryshnikov returns to the empty Maryinsky Theater and dances his farewell, but Baryshnikov felt he needed something more personal, more Russian, to express the Mussorgsky music, so he took over making the dance and she offered her advice. Hines choreographed his own tap solos.

Each of the four videos of this period demonstrates a different solution to one of Tharp's ongoing dilemmas: how to preserve her repertory so that she wouldn't have to keep maintaining it in performance. *Confessions of a Cornermaker* (taped in late summer 1980 and first aired in October 1981) was a camera-adapted documentation of three important dances, *Short Stories*, Uchida and Whitener's duet from the Bach *Third Suite* (both choreographed in 1980), and *Baker's Dozen*. Like the London Weekend Television *Eight Jelly Rolls* and *The Fugue*, *Cornermaker* not only preserves prime examples of Tharp's choreography, it showcases the extraordinary Tharp company dancers at their peak. Tharp doesn't dance in this video, but she appears in it as mastermind. Wearing a fisherman's sweater and jeans, she's filmed on a blustery beach, introducing the dances with provocatively quotable commentary she scripted with Allan Robertson. At the end, she confesses that working with the human body's "passion and precision" seems as close as she can come to "nature's righteousness." Then the camera pans past her to look at the ocean for a full minute before going to black.

The *Cornermaker* project, first broadcast on 13 October 1981, was conceived as a first dance offering by the new CBS Cable Television network. For that brief moment, the arts seemed a workable premise for television, and CBS Cable was launched with great optimism. Merrill Brockway joined the venture as executive producer of arts programming. He thinks he was offered the job partly because he could bring stars like Tharp and Balanchine to the table. Although he had directed many shows at *Dance in America*, Brockway wanted Tharp to do her own directing for the CBS Cable show. As usual, she was incredibly demanding—she worked with the cameraman for a week before the shoot in Nashville—and as usual she defied the rules.

Both *Baker's Dozen* and the *Bach Duet* were filmed in a completely white space. The no-space white background had become a trademark of Richard Avedon's fashion photography. With the "horizon" line erased, the dancers appeared suspended in some utopian void. She edited the Bach dance freely but discreetly, and did the whole first half of *Baker's Dozen* in one long take, using the screen as a proscenium frame for the dancers' frequent entrances and exits. For *Short Stories*, a much darker dance about destructive relationships, she used a black background, lighting that smoldered like a half-extinguished blaze, and camera closeups that zeroed in voyeuristically on the dancers' bad behavior.

Tharp got paid $50,000 for the *Cornermaker* work, and the company negotiated a deal for half the net profits on future uses of the show. CBS Cable featured Tharp in a full-page ad announcing the network and its roster of forthcoming attractions: "When you want an original, go to a master!" But the new venture started to lose money right away, and within a year after it went on the air it announced it was folding due to insufficient advertising revenues. It reportedly lost $30 million. The government was starting to pull back on arts funding but hopes for television as a cultural medium didn't die immediately. Five public television stations announced an alliance to produce the *Great Performances* series, and this coalition contributed funding for Tharp's 1983 video remake of *The Catherine Wheel*.

For ARTS cable, another commercial television venture at the time, Tharp put together the *Tharp Scrapbook*, clips from her extensive video archives, with a voice-over about the way the dances were developed and related. Besides generous examples of dancing, the compilation included interactions with interviewers and celebrities. Tharp plays straight man to Dick Cavett, who's trying to learn one of the *One Hundreds* in a 1979 PBS episode. There's a bit of an ice-dancing solo she made for John Curry, and a segment from the Gene Kelly special *Dance Is a Man's Sport Too*. This curiosity was another compare-and-contrast duet, for New York City Ballet star Peter Martins and Pittsburgh Steelers linebacker Lynn Swann, joined briefly by Tharp. It had aired on the ABC *Omnibus* series 15 June 1980. According to Don Mischer, who cocreated the segment with her, they marked out yardlines on a black floor to simulate a football field, and Tharp gave the men jumping and throwing movements that each would do in his own way.

In 1984 the whole American Ballet Theater cast went up to Toronto, for reasons of economy, to film *Push Comes to Shove*, *The Little Ballet*, and *Sinatra Suite*, under the codirection of Tharp and Mischer. It first aired on PBS in October of 1984, and this time Tharp was nowhere to be seen or heard, except as the choreographic force behind it. The video was intended to showcase Baryshnikov, both as star of the three ballets and as a genial host who presented a kind of ballet primer with helpful illustrations by the other dancers. It was issued as a videocassette and stayed on the market for years. *Baryshnikov by Tharp* won an Emmy and was later retitled *Baryshnikov Dances Sinatra*.

Reflecting on the 1980 Winter Garden season, Arlene Croce didn't think the Broadway challenge brought out anything in Tharp that her fans hadn't already seen. Perhaps, having taken the craft of choreography as far as she could go in *Brahms' Paganini*, observed Croce, Tharp was trying to develop "a fresh area of expertise," but in *When We Were Very Young* "she gets nearly everything wrong, and when she's right—for Broadway—she's terrible." Notwithstanding this brickbat from one of her staunchest admirers, Tharp wasn't about to give up on conquering the commercial theater. It took twenty years and several expeditions into "Broadway" territory until she succeeded fully with *Movin' Out*.

After the Winter Garden (24 March–12 April) and some tour dates, the company returned to Osgood Hill, undaunted by the critical failure of *When We Were Very Young*. Thomas Babe was there too, with his daughter, to work on a new project, for which, he said later in an affectionate program essay, Tharp had only a vague idea. John Philip Sousa was to be the hero of a new tale with a cryptic title, *Gat Dickers*. Babe and Tharp worked together on a script for a few weeks, trying it out day by day on the company. No one remembers anything about it except some bathroom episodes and scatological sound effects, and to the dancers' relief it was dropped.

Osgood Hill was the sole base of operations for the 1980 workshop; there were performances in Boston before it began. With forty students in North Andover, classes and rehearsals took place in a tent on the grounds of the mansion and overflowed into the Grange Hall in town. At a final lecture-demonstration Tharp tallied the number of sprained ankles and hours worked—the company rehearsed for 163 hours during the month, she said. An interviewer for the *Boston Herald-American* asked her how she liked Osgood Hill's baronial arrangements. It was nice, she told him. "Her voice was neutral, like that of an oilman admiring a profitless patch of daffodils. 'The best thing about all this is that it's paid rehearsal time.'"

Despite the derailed Babe project, she emerged from the residency with several new dances. She set the Third Orchestral Suite of Bach for the full company, but edited it down to Uchida and Whitener's duet when it got a poor critical reception in Paris. From two retired earlier dances she extracted material she couldn't bear to give up. *Assorted Quartets* comprised the "Fanfare," "Clap," and "Manners" quartets from *When We Were Very Young* and the final quartet from *Mud*, which had already migrated into *Chapters and Verses*. Danced to silence and varying selections of music, *Assorted Quartets* became a serviceable addition to the touring repertory for the next several years. The dancers worked hard to bring off the seemingly reckless partnering of these fast, brief sketches, and they called them *Sordid Quartets*. *Short Stories* and *Uncle Edgar* also joined the repertory for the next intensive touring cycle. Before *The Catherine Wheel* made its debut in the fall of 1981 the company had done another season at the Warfield in San Francisco, toured the West Coast and the Midwest, and made two trips to Europe, appearing in Belgium, Paris, Milan, London, and Holland. When John Curry presented Tharp with the Dance Magazine Award in the spring of 1981, she called the dancers to the platform to share the applause with her.

Tharp now took the biggest financial and creative risk of her career. The first Winter Garden season had recouped its expenses and made a small profit for the company. Buoyed by this outcome she headed back to Broadway. The company booked into the Winter Garden again for four weeks, with the full-length *Catherine Wheel* as the centerpiece, plus two programs of old and new works including the first New York performances of *Short Stories*, *Uncle Edgar*, and another new version of *Deuce Coupe*. Although this plan resembled previous concert seasons, when Tharp thought "Broadway," she thought "commercial theater," and she intended *The Catherine Wheel* as a legitimate show, a hit of course. For several reasons, this didn't happen. The cost of the production itself was high, with its elaborate scenery and costumes by Santo Loquasto. She commissioned the music from David Byrne, the brainy young leader of the Talking Heads band. With the month's associated back- and front-of-the-house costs, she had to do capacity business in order to recoup her expenses.

In 1981 the Broadway musical was shifting away from the traditional book show with interpolated music-dance numbers. Jerome Robbins, Michael Bennett, and Bob Fosse had brought dance forward as an integral conveyor of plot, and with shows like *Black and Blue*, *Follies*, and *Jerome Robbins' Broadway*, the plot became nearly nonexistent. *The Catherine Wheel* should have fitted into this fluid picture, but as a product of the dance field rather than show business, it was judged as choreography, not as theater. Probably its closest analogue at the time was Stephen Sondheim and Hal Prince's *Sweeney Todd*, which was winding up a highly successful two-year run. Like *The Catherine Wheel*, the experimental *Sweeney* was a macabre epic about corruption and violence. It too had cumbersome, mechanistic scenery, extravagant characters who engaged in bizarre behavior, and a contemporary score that didn't easily fall into the popular idiom of musical comedy. Sondheim's monstrous hero is redeemed at the end when he finds out his grisly rampage has been a mistake, and he breaks down in remorse. Tharp's characters never did acquire a human dimension; redemption was only possible when they lost their personas entirely and became dancing angels in the *Golden Section*.

The Catherine Wheel foundered under its densely layered symbolism and over-the-top presentation. Tharp admitted that "My company has never done anything as complicated as this." Everything about it was shouted through a megaphone. Tharp piled her own contradictory dance resources into the piece. Instead of finding a way to reconcile her recent narrative preoccupations with her genius for pure dance composition, she kept them severely cordoned off in distinct sections of the piece. She restored the family from *When We Were Very Young* almost intact, replacing herself with Jennifer Way in the mother's role. Now the autobiographical implications resided, much less obviously, in a new character, the leader of the chorus, played by Sara Rudner. Once again, Tharp says, she had planned to dance this role but gave it up so she could work on the piece from the outside. Rawe, Glasner, and Kurshals returned as the father and children. Two of the allegorical sketches from the 1978 Osgood Hill workshop, Chaos and Order, matured into Shelley Washington's Maid and Christine Uchida's Pet, and John Carrafa's Juggler in *When We Were Very Young* became a Poet.

Instead of being awkward, unfocused, and lovable like their predecessors, the *Catherine Wheel* family were mean and grasping cartoonish exaggerations. They danced in a simplistic, almost slapstick mode. Hardly models of domestic harmony to begin with, they soon begin bickering over a pineapple given to them by Rudner. Tharp saw this object as not only the traditional domestic welcoming gift that turns into forbidden fruit, but as a symbol of escalating ambition for material possessions, and a destructive device that looks like a hand grenade or a bomb. As the family grows increasingly greedy they pummel and abuse each other. The mother teaches the children to tap-dance so that they can become street beggars. The father chases the Pet, gropes her and mounts her from behind. The Maid shrieks and mugs hysterically. When the Poet arrives, he fondles the pineapple in awe. He's momentarily attracted to the Pet, but later attacks the fruit in an orgiastic binge.

Throughout this frenzy, Rudner and a cadre of anonymous figures surge in the background, unseen by the family, commenting on their actions and perhaps accepting punishment for them, like a Greek chorus. Santo Loquasto's scenery and Jennifer Tipton's lighting situated all this in a harsh and threatening environment—a forest of twenty-four metallic poles planted on the stage, and a network of sinister machinelike objects that hung overhead and sometimes descended with clanking noises—and the family's action was echoed on back curtains by doppelgängers, in a life-size, even more exaggerated shadowplay.

As the perversion and aggression mount nearly out of control, the parents try to bury the hatchet with a duet of social dances in period styles—waltz, bunny hug, jitterbug, twist—but the contentious children keep pushing between them. By this time the pineapple, grown as big as a person, has been torn to bits, swept up by the chorus, and stuffed in a trash bag. Rudner tries to dispose of it by shoving it into the most menacing of the overhead machines, but is almost impaled herself.

Finally, three-quarters of the way through the seventy-five-minute piece, the madness exhausts itself. The machines and the poles fly out, the light turns warm, and the two groups are united. Transformed into a splendid ensemble in fancy gold sportswear, they end the work with fifteen minutes of the fastest, most airborne, and closely coordinated dancing this company of virtuosos had ever done. *The Golden Section* went into the repertory two years later as a self-contained piece.

David Byrne's music—twenty-two short numbers in different styles—was a propulsive mix of recorded electronic, instrumental, and vocal performance. For the musical material, Tharp didn't give Byrne more than a general idea where she was going with the piece, nor did she specify counts for each number. Byrne figured that "If I made music that was rhythmically multilayered and busy, then the dancers would link to beats anyway, though not necessarily the most obvious ones." He would bring his musical ideas into rehearsal and adjust as needed, so the score grew organically, the music and dance influencing each other as they went along. Byrne was interested in West African music at the time, especially the ways in which rhythm can both reflect and reinforce community. One of his mentors was the ethnomusicologist John Miller Chernoff, author of the groundbreaking study *African Rhythm and African Sensibility,* and Chernoff supplied basic rhythms for some of the tracks. Byrne did the main lyrics (only seven of the numbers had words), a spacey commentary on life slipping "through the cracks."

The musical and dance numbers had different titles. The company produced a big fold-out program, with construction plans for Loquasto's scenery on the back, to crosslist how the dance numbers corresponded to the music. This probably created another source of confusion for the audience because both sets of titles were evocative in oblique ways. For instance, "The Leader Repents," a dance for Rudner and four men of the chorus, was accompanied by Byrne's "Big Business." "Think you've had enough/Stop talking, help us get ready," he sang. For each number the program meticulously identified the dancers, the musicians, and the eclectic instrumentation, which included guitars, Western and African drums, synthesizers, calliope, gongs, flutes, and homemade percussion. For "Cloud Chamber"/"The Poet's Decline" Tharp played the water pot.

Byrne, like Tharp, had a reputation for stretching his own boundaries, and both of them had developed specialized ensembles to perform their work. But they were both big creative egos, and though they found *The Catherine Wheel* a good working collaboration, the performance was imprinted with their divergent temperaments. The collaboration generated pre-performance buzz in both the dance and pop music columns. *The Catherine Wheel* was the first score she commissioned from a rock composer, and Byrne was working with theater dance for the first time too. She already knew what a drawing card pop music could be for the audience. Hooking up with contemporary composers could also bring her visibility outside the dance field. In the next few years she commissioned three prominent avant-gardists (Glenn Branca, David Van Tieghem, and Philip Glass), with predictably attention-getting results.

The *Catherine Wheel* score was released soon after the season. It was chosen as one of 1981's ten best recordings by both *The New York Times* and the *Soho Weekly News.* At the time it struck listeners as loud and abrasive; two de-

cades into the age of multicultural techno-fusion, it seems intriguing and almost lyrical. David Byrne says: "I was hugely proud of being involved in the
piece. It was like nothing else out there," and he was pleased when *The
Golden Section* was spun off as a touring piece. Byrne and Tharp had been in-
separable during the creation of the dance, but they quarreled bitterly over
ownership of the score, and they severed their relationship. A complicated
disposition of the rights was worked out, allowing Tharp to use the music
while Byrne retained ownership. She had foreseen that commissioned
dance music might have a life of its own, and indeed, all three of her next
new scores came out as audio recordings.

The *Catherine Wheel* reviews were mixed. Anna Kisselgoff seemed dis-
turbed the morning after by the "message she has so purposefully muddled"
and the atmosphere of "youth culture," though the golden denouement of
the piece was "Tharp at her best." Following up with a Sunday piece, Kisselgoff was even more critical. Tharp undermined her formal brilliance with
"lapses in seriousness that greater choreographers would not. Most of Miss
Tharp's immaturity takes the form of platitudes she expresses as social commentary." The more positive weekly critics didn't get into print until late in
the season. Arlene Croce called *The Catherine Wheel* "a major event in our theatre," but even she saw the first part of the piece as murky, overloaded with
alternative references. *The Golden Section* saved not only the characters but
the whole piece:

> Tharp's abrupt alchemy substituting harmony for chaos is almost painful in
> its honesty. It's as if she were substituting art for life, knowing that no solu-
> tion to the palpable terrors she has invoked is possible. Art, less than a solu-
> tion yet more than a consolation, offers terms she can settle for; it's the great
> alternative to the dilemma of life, the only other reality that isn't death. "The
> Golden Section" is the classical "white" ballet, with all its implications of re-
> demption intact.

Afterward Tharp claimed that *The Catherine Wheel*'s twelve scheduled performances weren't enough; one more week would have allowed it to build a
solid audience and recover her outlay. But a revival of *Camelot* was already
booked into the theater and she could neither extend her run nor move the
cumbersome *Catherine Wheel* elsewhere. The production's size and complexity made it unfit for touring. When the Winter Garden season closed, the
piece was essentially gone and Tharp was left with a $200,000 deficit. She

and some board members underwrote a loan to cover it and she didn't get out of debt for several years.

Tharp was disappointed by the reaction to *The Catherine Wheel*. She'd counted on it to be a Broadway success; she'd even invested some of her own money in it. Not only had she lost out on the economic gamble, she felt she hadn't molded her ideas into a suitable package. The critics all saw the dichotomy between what Kisselgoff called the "Bumstead" narrative and the cathartic idealism of *The Golden Section*. It was a problem of conflicting aesthetics— expression versus abstraction, hot versus cool. Tharp felt she simply hadn't made her thesis clear. With her usual tenacity, she made two further stabs at the problem in addition to salvaging *The Golden Section* for the repertory. After drastically revising the dance for video, she staged a condensed version in 1984 during the company's Brooklyn Academy season.

Even those critics who scratched for a path through the underbrush of meaning interpreted *The Catherine Wheel* in terms of the Guignol story and its golden antithesis. According to Janice Berman Alexander in *Newsday*, *The Golden Section* "sets forth the idea that once you abandon that archaic family structure, life can take place." Linda Winer of the *Daily News* wrote: "[It] begins as a grim epic of sensory overload and family torment. Then, without clear explanation, everybody gets happy and unbinds in a golden abstraction of just about every hurtling impossibility on the Tharp physical high-wire."

Most of the critics, pro and con, skimmed over the masked chorus and their leader. But Sara Rudner's character, more than anything else, embodied the notion of purity being eroded, destroyed, and finally reclaimed. As a dancing figure she glowed and suffered while the family acted out the perversion, greed, and misogyny her gift of the pineapple had ignited in them, and she disappeared when the others ascended to the exalted plane. To Tharp, clarifying this figure would fix what was wrong with the dance. She enlisted Rhoda Grauer to produce and fundraise, made a coproduction deal with the BBC, and enthusiastically began rethinking the dance for video.

Tharp had done considerable research into the fourth-century martyr Catherine of Alexandria. The religious zealot was executed amid purported miraculous events, for refusing to marry. According to an elaborate scenario Tharp constructed, Catherine was both flawed and admirable, "a woman of extraordinary spirit and adventure whose sole desire is to seek the truth in all things and thus, control the world." Tharp's story line, like a Hindu epic, describes how Catherine steals the symbolic pineapple in her desire for power, thus disrupting the world's balance and bringing about destruction. The family, inheritors of this war and chaos, bicker among themselves for the pineapple. Their increasingly horrid behavior thwarts Catherine's efforts to restore order. She steals the remnants of the symbolic pineapple from them, tries to restore it to its place of origin, but is unable to reassemble its pieces. Finally, she renounces her own ambition and acknowledges her guilt. The overlapping cycles of suffering come together and a great release of energy allows everyone to be free.

As a character in search of superhuman perfection, Catherine might have resembled any rigorously trained dancer, but on-camera in the preface to the video, Tharp admitted that no mere mortal could have achieved such heights. To represent this "anti-physicality" she used a computer-generated animation. On-screen the Computer Catherine looked like a bundle of lines assembled into human form—perhaps an early version of what we now know as motion capture. This animated figure became one aspect of the creation/destruction myth that Tharp had tried to combine in Rudner's part onstage. So when the family misdeeds became intolerable for Rudner and the ensemble, the Computer Catherine would appear and teach Rudner an idealized movement sequence to calm their ravings. According to Tharp, Rudner's character in the original dance "was too complex to work theatrically, because she was both her own undermining and her own inspiration. Now the Catherine figure, the computer, teaches Sara the theme that she uses to make something from. It's not that she simultaneously has to invent and take apart."

Despite this effort to clarify, on tape the story line wasn't any more lucid than it had been in the stage version. By the time she videoed The Catherine Wheel, Tharp was quite experienced in television technology. She plotted every shot ahead of time on a storyboard, so that she only needed a single camera for each take. But she'd then have to move the setup for the next take. She incorporated as much of Santo Loquasto's scenery as she could, then tried for even more complicated effects with it. Having used most of the twelve-day shooting schedule on these time-consuming arrangements, she filmed the whole Golden Section on the last day, with insufficient lights. During the editing she added other new elements—interpolated fireworks, a flashback through the family history in retrograde, shots of Rudner striding across a hilltop toward an ancient castle, a tricky final ascent for Rudner before *The Golden Section,* and a slow-motion final leap into the stratosphere for Uchida.

The video premiered at the end of January 1983 on the BBC's *Arena,* and two months later on PBS's *Great Performances.* There were some good reviews, but the video was even less coherent than the dance had been on the stage, and in videocassette release it failed to achieve the commercial success Tharp was hoping for.

At this point she was becoming more and more pessimistic about maintaining a dance company. The Winter Garden season in 1981 had been a downer for her, not only because of the dubious fate of *The Catherine Wheel.* Before the season Rose Marie Wright had conclusively retired from dancing. With some reluctance Wright accepted the role of rehearsal director and Katie Glasner learned her roles, but she was a great loss to the company. The long season on Broadway brought financial burdens and injuries. Tharp wasn't happy about stagehands she didn't feel were conscientious enough. One night during a performance, a street woman got past the front door and wandered onto the stage. For several anxious minutes no one knew what to do. Whoever was supposed to be manning the act curtain wasn't at his post to bring it in. While the music continued playing, the dancers weren't sure if the woman was dangerous or not. Tharp went on stage prepared to wrestle the intruder into the orchestra pit, but the curtain finally went down. The woman slipped away and was caught by the police outside the theater. At another performance before this unnerving event, the show had to be stopped because of a small fire. Tharp was so disgusted she left town before the end of the season. A month later she was vowing not to make any more stage dances until *The Catherine Wheel* was safely on tape.

Television had long seemed a solution to the problem of repertory. Soon after the release of *Confessions of a Cornermaker,* she told a writer for *The Wall Street Journal:* "It's quite clear that the future of dance economics is in the recorded medium." If she could commit the dances to tape, she could reach the public in a controlled way, and use the dancers to make new work. *The Catherine Wheel's* escalating chaos, the glamour and sensual provocations of the dancing and the music, may even have invited the deranged woman onto the stage, she thought. She longed for a way to make her own working life replicate the fable, she wanted the responsibilities smaller and the thinking time quieter.

In June of 1982 Harvey Lichtenstein made a generous offer that seemed to answer her prayers. The company had been rehearsing in some unused spaces at Brooklyn Academy for some time, with its administrative offices housed at BAM as well. Now, through a new BAM agency, the Local Development Corporation, Lichtenstein proposed that Tharp take over the former Strand Theater, a city-owned building two blocks from the Academy. The company would renovate the building for studios, offices, and a television production center, and perform as usual in theaters, principally the BAM Opera House. When the scheme was announced, Tharp Dance Foundation manager Steve Dennin estimated that the foundation would have to raise $4 million for the work, but in the long term, the opportunity would give the company permanent rehearsal space and allow Tharp to realize her dream of opening a school.

Within a year, the scheme had collapsed. Besides the financial commitment, Tharp had strong objections to locating the company in downtown Brooklyn. It was a long commute from the Upper West Side of Manhattan, where she lived, and the seedy Brooklyn neighborhood made her nervous. Lichtenstein had seen BAM as the anchor for a revitalization of the area ever since he took over the Academy, but in the 1980s the process seemed stalled. BAM was surrounded by blocks of parking lots and demolished or deteriorating buildings. Tough and street-smart as Tharp was, she couldn't face subjecting herself and the dancers to that environment every day.

9

Romance and the
Opposite
1982–1983

Despite the mishaps at the Winter Garden and the divided press for *The Catherine Wheel*, the season was a success with the audience. The old repertory drew former admirers and attracted new fans. As for new works, each one was a surprise. With her horror of repeating herself and her unquenchable imagination, Tharp seemed to reconceptualize the choreographic act every time. Naturally, there were certain useful tropes she returned to—the flying, tumbling episodes of partnering and partner switching, the mirroring and canonic imitations, the pedestrian gestures and attitudes, the retrogrades of everything from step combinations to entire dramatic encounters. By now the dancers shared a movement vocabulary and an easygoing, articulate, and fearless approach to dancing, but the look of each dance was always different. The hooty synthesizer music and the formal pairings of the tank-suited women in *Uncle Edgar* was a far cry from the urban romances of *Short Stories*, set to rock songs by Supertramp and Bruce Springsteen. Both *The Golden Section* and *Baker's Dozen* may have pictured utopian harmony, but the ensemble of one dance could hardly be mistaken for the other. *The Bix Pieces* taught lessons about the interrelationship of art forms; *Deuce Coupe* taught the same lesson for a generation that spoke in another idiom.

When she deliberately recycled material, she gave it new surroundings. For 1981 *Deuce Coupe* returned in a new, fourth version, with ABT star Cynthia Gregory in the ballerina role and a new "composite" ballet-modern role for the effervescent longtime Eliot Feld dancer Christine Sarry. The street graffiti writers were back, and a supplementary ensemble of seven young ballet dancers surrounded Gregory. Anna Kisselgoff called it "an abstraction of her original pop ballet," and many people thought it the best *Deuce Coupe* since the first model. *The Catherine Wheel* looked unique even though it had evolved out of several previous works. All of its predecessors had disappeared except for the seedlings in *Assorted Quartets*, and few spectators noticed those connections.

Tharp insisted that repertory was a dead issue for her once she had learned everything she could from a dance. Then she was done with the piece and didn't need to see it anymore, even if this was the point at which it could serve the repertory most effectively. As the company prepared for performances in Frankfurt and at Vienna's Theater an der Wien early in 1982, she didn't see the need to check on how the dances played with European audiences. Sometimes she gave in to sponsor demand and made an appearance when the company was touring to some especially important venue, but she begrudged the time she had to spend to do it. She had Rose Marie Wright to oversee the repertory and the administrative staff to do the office work, but: "My priority has always got to be to ignore them and to make dances . . . in a way that is challenging to me creatively and that makes sense to an audience."

The company continued touring intensively. They did two international trips and seven months on the road in 1982; three trips abroad in 1983 plus several other dates and a summer residency; four months of tours, two of summer festivals, and a trip to Germany in 1984. All this activity began to have a synergistic effect. With the New York and international press coverage drumming up interest, the company was avidly anticipated and widely covered. They developed a faithful constituency across the country, which in turn stimulated interest whenever they had a New York season. Many new works were shown on the road, so that they would be well broken in and cleaned up before premiering in New York.

Tharp submitted to telephone interviews with eager local journalists during these years, but frequently the dancers were delegated to deal with the press. Along with the extra responsibilities of residencies—teaching master classes, running lecture-demonstrations, giving their own company class—most of them now became spokespersons. Self-possessed, thought-ful and lively personalities, they could reflect on the work they were doing. Wright, Way, Rawe, and Washington had years of experience dancing and teaching Tharp's work to draw on. Colton was especially insightful about the choreographic process. Linda Shelton, who was company manager dur-ing the '80s, usually worked with local sponsors to identify who should be interviewed. It might be the newest dancer in the company, someone who'd grown up or gone to school locally, or someone with a featured role in a new dance. These interviews and feature stories brought the dancers special attention and of course made the performances even more appealing.

The mounting success didn't make Tharp happy. Committing to the BAM/Strand Theater project might have solved some of her chronic dis-contents, with a permanent home for the company and a laboratory for her creative work. But putting down roots in Brooklyn would have tied her firmly to the long-term life of the company and committed her to the school she knew she needed but couldn't take the time to establish. Though Tharp didn't like to teach, there were excellent teachers in the company. As long as they could wedge master classes and short-term workshops into their residencies, they could still perform, but a school would have drawn them off the stage or required former Tharp dancers to sign on as a regular fac-ulty. She had never codified a technique to be taught on a predictable basis. Any established classroom technique would be doomed to obsolescence be-cause Tharp was always moving on in her technical demands. As she saw it, with a home base the company would have to get bigger, the budget would get bigger, and she would have to do more to hold it all together, not less.

Once she gave up the Strand opportunity, touring was the surest way for the company to earn its livelihood. While she was preparing to rescue *The Catherine Wheel* from its imperfections, the company was winning rapturous audiences and great reviews across the U.S. and Canada, Germany, Austria, Israel, and Japan, their visibility bolstered by the release of the videos and films they'd made. The period between the fall of 1981 and the spring of 1983 saw the premieres of *Confessions of a Cornermaker* (13 October 1981), *Ragtime* (18 November 1981), and the *Scrapbook* tape (25 October 1982). In New York, waiting for the dancers to return to the studio, Tharp carried on her extracurricular activities. She collaborated and appeared with Andre Gregory in *Bone Songs*, a misbegotten off-off-Broadway play. By mid-1983, she was planning the movie *Amadeus* and she'd reestablished her relationship with American Ballet Theater, where Mikhail Baryshnikov was now artistic director. During this period Tharp also made two of her most unusual dances for the company: *Bad Smells*, which nearly everyone found repellant, and *Nine Sinatra Songs*, which became its signature piece.

Tharp was better at capturing the events of a relationship than she was at showing how a story unfolded. As early as *Chapters and Verses*, Richard Colton noticed she was creating a "world of vignettes . . . little pieces that didn't yet have any kind of narrative flow but were evocative. . . . It was character without building a story." These vignettes often had to do with the past, Colton thought, but they weren't an indulgence in nostalgia. Tharp made more than one "Dance of the Ages," stringing together successive period dances like a movie montage, to show the passage of time. In *Short Stories*, she illustrated how the same group of people could behave differently toward one another at different times. Dispensing with narrative connections, she simply looked from different angles, the way one turns a stone over to view its facets.

Short Stories never attained the iconic status of some other Tharp dances. Like *Nine Sinatra Songs* it was a portrait of moods rather than a continuous story. Both works used social dancing as a baseline for human interaction as well as physical display. All the dancers in *Short Stories* were dressed in pants or shorts and polo shirts, but viewers usually thought of the first group as teenagers and the second as twenty-somethings. The three couples in Part I (Supertramp's "Lover Boy") are show-offs, riding the music and amplifying their slow-dancing with flamboyant circular flings, dips, lifts, head tosses and backbends. When Shelley Washington openly flirts with the other men, her partner, William Whitener, pulls her in possessively. This doesn't restrain her, though, and her extroverted behavior infects the others (Katie Glasner and Raymond Kurshals, Mary Ann Kellogg and John Carrafa on the *Cornermaker* tape). Their circular dance moves bring them into eye contact with each other and they begin switching partners. The switches seem casual, but there are competitive tensions, threatening glares, momentary failures to synchronize, more switches. What started as playfulness builds to hostility.

After a standoff, the song ends and begins again. Kellogg is alone, moving inwardly, as if to distance herself from the others, who are now dancing with open aggressiveness, still exchanging partners. Carrafa tries to bring Kellogg back from her reverie, and they dance together intimately, erotically, for a short time. Then, for no apparent reason, he backs away from her. She goes limp and the men slide her from one to another. Soaring, dramatic lifts and intimate holds have escalated into brutality. When they're done with her they leave her on the floor. The dancing continues, pausing only momentarily as one person or another glances down at Kellogg.

In Part II, the two couples (Sara Rudner and John Malashock, Jennifer Way and Tom Rawe in the video) seem older, more serious. They too switch partners, fight, go back together, dance passionately, but everything is more intense and more personal. (The music is Springsteen's apocalyptic "Jungle Land.") The couples seem committed to each other, spouses or roommates. Their duets seem like domestic love scenes. They jog in squabbling, and after dalliances, fights, and reconciliations, they leave, in choreographed retrograde, the same way they came.

What's remarkable about *Short Stories*, apart from the extraordinary dancing, is that the drama going on between all these people arises out of the way they're dancing in Part I, or the way they're arguing while they enter in Part II. The characters were temperamentally disagreeable, and the dance acquired a downbeat reputation. Anna Kisselgoff called it unpleasant, derivative of Jerome Robbins. Tharp used "clichéd youth culture as a pretext for delving into relationships." Tharp herself may have done it no favor with her over-the-top introduction on the *Cornermaker* tape: "Its people are out of sync with themselves. Their love seems incestuous and somehow devious. Intimacy is a threat and their only recourse is to split, whether literally, as in the first of the *Short Stories*, or more subtly, simply to withdraw, as in the second."

But the dance also was handicapped by underexposure. Less than thirty minutes long, it seemed pedestrian at first viewing, not heavily choreographed, too much like other Tharpian takes on young people and social dancing. Tharp often wanted to disguise her craft and evoke the audience's emotional response by making movement just a little more artful than everyday behavior. Stealthily she could close the distance between "verbs that we all know and recognize" like walking, running, pushing and shoving, and the abstract vocabulary of ballet. Perhaps *Short Stories* was too deceptive in this way for its own survival.

Its truncated career also illustrates the way Tharp handled repertory as an expedient. Before its stage premiere, in Ghent, Belgium, in the fall of 1980, she had already translated it to videotape for *Confessions of a Cornermaker*. Its first U.S. performances were given on the West Coast in March of

1981, and when it appeared in New York during the 1981 Winter Garden season, it was overshadowed by *The Catherine Wheel* and further upstaged by the *Cornermaker* tape, which was broadcast before that season came to an end. *Short Stories* served in the touring repertory for about three years, but when only part of the company was on the road Part I was omitted and the pocket-size Part II was performed alone. By the time the company appeared in New York again (Brooklyn Academy, early in 1984), *Short Stories* was gone.

Nine Sinatra Songs carried a working premise similar to that of *Short Stories*: the rhythms and attitudes of social dance evoked real-life behaviors and temperaments. Sometime after she had made the *Sinatra*, Tharp said it was meant to show the stages in a relationship. It didn't need any thematic rationale, though, and achieved its success as nothing more than a glamorous suite of romantic dances. Tharp had been working with Frank Sinatra recordings for several years, and she reused all three songs she'd choreographed for her disastrous duet with Baryshnikov, *Once More, Frank*. Now she had a magnificent company of dancers, and instead of setting out to overturn convention, she mounted a full-scale ballroom dance extravaganza, with the men in tuxedos and the women in Oscar de la Renta cocktail dresses, and a mirror ball revolving above the stage.

In comparison with the choreographed intricacies of *Assorted Quartets*, *Uncle Edgar*, and *The Golden Section*, or the steamy revelations of *Short Stories*, *Nine Sinatra Songs* was stunningly straightforward. The company was now big enough to yield seven couples. Tharp chose recordings from Sinatra's glossy Nelson Riddle period and gave each couple one number. Midway through the dance and again at the end, they assembled to the effusive "My Way," recorded at different times. But there was no partner switching and no group work at all. Each pair danced its own variation and focused on its own partnership. Overall, the dance achieved its continuity through Tharp's sequencing of the numbers. As always, she brought out the strengths of the individual dancers. She worked out the early material on Sara Rudner, Keith Young, John Carrafa, and then the other members of the blue team, Shelley Washington, Mary Ann Kellogg, and John Malashock. When the red team returned from tour, she assigned the rest of the roles and they began developing the partnering and the personas that went with each duet. The dancers felt it took over a year for the dance to find its feet. Premiered on the West Coast in late 1982, it didn't reach New York until the Brooklyn Academy season of January–February 1984. Early reviewers felt Tharp was working below par, and some may have been put off by the piece's uncharacteristic romanticism.

Amy Spencer, who'd had extensive ballet training and worked with downtown choreographers, particularly Rudner, had joined the company in 1981, after *The Catherine Wheel* was choreographed. At that time Tharp was expanding the company's red-and-blue capability, and Spencer learned the repertory. She remembers the *Sinatra* as one of the first roles Tharp choreographed on her. She saw that the dancers had a big responsibility in bringing it off, perhaps because the material was less intricately structured than some of the other works: "[*Sinatra*] had to have inner life . . . another layer to it, to make it more than just some flip ballroom piece. And I think it took everybody a while to get a handle on it." Performing the piece over time also gave the dancers a sense of "how the narrative ran in the audience mind." This "narrative" was more like an expressive throughline that carried over from one duet to the next. Tharp made some small adjustments and one major change to improve the flow of the action. As the dance was performed by successive casts, in Tharp's company and others, it gradually grew tighter, jokier, and more flashy, but the creators of the roles were never equaled. Unfortunately, their performance wasn't professionally filmed.

The piece opened on a bare stage, dark except for the revolving mirror ball, and the audience often screamed with the first bars of the music. Shelley Washington and Keith Young, the original lead-off couple, appeared as Sinatra began "Softly as I Leave." Their dance seemed to float on waves of expectation, dipping and rising in a single line from beginning to end. Toward the end of the song, the moves became more pressured, the mood more ecstatic. As they left, Mary Ann Kellogg entered with Gary Chryst. (John Malashock, on whom this dance was created, was on a leave of absence at the time of the first performances.) "Strangers in the Night" was a pseudo-tango, packed with close embraces, averted eye contact, and tight supported turns. There were intricate, over-and-under lifts, and changes of positions with crossed hands. These tricky moves expanded into some upside-down lifts and other oddities near the end.

Rudner and Carrafa's "One for My Baby" ignored the singer's morose tale of rejection, except for his slow, relaxed tempo. Like two affectionate drunks, they slid and climbed over each other, clasping together almost by reflex and groping for whatever limb was nearest when they drifted out of contact. Nearly unfocused, they seemed drawn together by instinct, and determined to keep manipulating each other as if that were the only way to

❧ *Brahms' Paganini.*
William Whitener.
(PHOTO: © Martha Swope)

❧ *Brahms' Pagnini.*
Richard Colton.
(PHOTO: © Martha Swope)

♔ *When We Were Very Young.* Tom Rawe, Twyla Tharp, Raymond Kurshals, Katie Glasner.
(PHOTO: © Martha Swope)

♔ *The Catherine Wheel.* John Carrafa, Christine Uchida.
(PHOTO: © Paul B. Goode)

℀ *The Golden Section.* Stephanie Foster, William Whitener, Cheryl Jones. (PHOTO: © Monroe Warshaw)

℀ *Short Stories.* William Whitener, Raymond Kurshals, Shelley Washington. (PHOTO: © Martha Swope)

ॐ *Nine Sinatra Songs.*
Jennifer Way, William
Whitener, Richard
Colton, Barbara Hoon.
(PHOTO: © Martha Swope)

ॐ *Bad Smells.* (PHOTO: © Paul B. Goode)

℘ *Fait Accompli.* Keith Young, Sara Rudner.
(PHOTO: © Tom Caravaglia)

℘ *Bach Partita.* Robert La
Fosse, Cynthia Harvey,
Cynthia Gregory, Fernando
Bujones, Martine Van
Hamel, Clark Tippett.
(PHOTO: © Martha Swope)

℘ *In the Upper Room.* Jamie Bishton, Cynthia Anderson, Daniel Sanchez,
Isabella Padovani, Kathleen Moore, Kevin O'Day. (PHOTO: Marty Sohl)

శ్రీ *Octet.* Allison Brown, Kevin O'Day. (PHOTO: © Martha Swope)

శ్రీ *Men's Piece.* Twyla Tharp, Kevin O'Day. (PHOTO: © Martha Swope)

శ్రీ *Demeter and Persephone.* Christine Dakin, Terese Capucilli. (PHOTO: © Tom Brazil)

৵ *Noir a. k. a. Bartok.* John Selya, Stacy Caddell. (PHOTO: © Tom Brazil)

৵ *How Near Heaven.* Kathleen Moore, Susan Jaffe.
(PHOTO: © Jack Vartoogian/FrontRow Photos 1995)

৵ *Known By Heart.* Ethan Stiefel, Susan Jaffe.
(PHOTO: © Tom Brazil)

❧ *Sweet Fields.* (PHOTO: © Jack Vartoogian/FrontRowPhotos 1997)

❧ *Surfer at the River Styx.* John Selya with Elizabeth Parkinson, Benjamin Bowman.
(PHOTO: © Tom Brazil)

❧ *Variations on a Theme by Haydn.*
(PHOTO: © Tom Brazil)

keep from passing out. This duet was probably the last of Tharp's low-key, befuddled comedy dances.

After the three-couple "My Way" Christine Uchida and Richard Colton were a sweet, almost demure duo in "I'm Not Afraid." Tharp felt this number didn't provide enough contrast, and when Uchida left the company she re-did the section for Colton and Barbara Hoon as fumbling kewpie-doll characters, to Sinatra's "Somethin' Stupid." This dance was almost a burlesque of the complicated linkages and extravagant yearnings of the other couples. Then the goofiness gave way to a sedate but intimate duet ("All the Way") for Amy Spencer and Raymond Kurshals. At moments the woman took the lead, but despite their physical contrasts—Spencer was tall and refined, Kurshals strong and rugged—they conveyed a partnership of equals. Their turns and lifts were closer together, less outwardly demonstrative, and their moves leisurely enough for them to unfold into supported attitudes and arabesques. The tempo turned upbeat again for "Forget Domani," a quick, frivolous step dance for Jennifer Way and William Whitener. Tossing the skirt of her shocking pink dress with deep ruffles on the hem and neckline, she flirted and led him on. Both of them bobbed up and down with small steps and syncopated skips.

The last duet before the ensemble finale was Tom Rawe and Shelley Freydont's "That's Life," which Tharp called an apache but which had almost no dance steps in it. Rawe was the antihero whose shopworn but sexy girlfriend likes to be treated rough. These types descended from a long line of movie toughs—James Cagney and Shanghai Lil, the hoofer and the striptease girl in Balanchine's *On Your Toes*, and endless reworkings by Astaire, Kelly, and others. Rawe played him lanky and hardnosed. Deadpan, Freydont submitted to all his abuse and finally flounced away, only to change her mind and dive into his arms just as he was putting on his jacket to leave. She thought of it as a French nightclub dance. In the final "My Way" number, all the couples returned for a ballroom scene that gradually opened up and out, until the lifts were rising and cresting in overlapping waves, and then subsiding as the couples ambled away and the music died down.

Tharp said she'd been inspired by films she'd seen of Vernon and Irene Castle when she was researching the period dances for *Ragtime*, but *Nine Sinatra Songs* owes only an initial spark to the stylishly decorous Castles. It draws on the sweeping, sophisticated escapades of Fred Astaire and Ginger Rogers, the lovelorn yearnings of Gene Kelly, and the annals of physical comedy from silent movies to Lucille Ball and Betty Hutton. What was innovative about the dance was the volumes of new lifts and partnering possibilities. Tharp's ice-dancing experience let her try some skimming, swooping mechanics on dry land. Using the momentum of turning, running, or two-stepping, the couples created a lexicon of lifts and falls. The men could sling a partner to the floor and up again into locomotion or twist her into a behind-the-back or over-the shoulder revolution, while she unfolded her legs or changed the shape of her whole torso. One partner could act as a fulcrum to wheel the other at arm's length or link into a set of spins. They could lean or fall or even jump with their full weight, into each other's arms or against each other's bodies. Their trust and sensuality was what saved the dance initially from its own excesses. After one break-in performance in Los Angeles, Burt Supree of *The Village Voice* remarked on "the careful, faithful interdependency that permeates *Nine Sinatra Songs* and creates its atmosphere."

Riding the creative high of working with David Byrne on the new score for *The Catherine Wheel*, Tharp had remarked to the *New York Times* music critic Robert Palmer that she didn't intend to use previously recorded music for a dance again: "Older music has all its connotations in place; everyone knows what they think about it." But the cost of commissioning new music was significant. Within months she was choreographing to Sinatra. The question of live music versus recordings had troubled modern dancers throughout their history. Only Martha Graham in her later years had the resources to commission composers and hire orchestras on a regular basis. Until at least 1950, the modern dance was notable for its small scale musical ingenuity, and its aesthetic was very much influenced by the experimental composers it attracted: Henry Cowell, Harry Partch, Dane Rudhyar, Lou Harrison, and others. In the early days Louis Horst composed chamber scores for piano and one or two other instruments. When tape recorders and synthesizers arrived, choreographer Alwin Nikolais was the first to make his own electronic scores. But existing music on tape, often overamplified in an effort to simulate acoustic sound, became the standard modern dance accompaniment. One thing that distinguished Mark Morris as a major player from the outset was his resistance to this alternative.

Tharp was just as constrained by her financial resources as other choreographers. A musical sophisticate, she started her career with a sparing use of the classical material that inspired her in the studio and provided so many structural ideas. For the first ten years, silence or seemingly offhand quotations accompanied her dances. Recorded Haydn or Mozart were slipped in bashfully next to archival jazz; recorded Bach was permitted because it was supposed to be used in a video (*All About Eggs*). She didn't fully employ classical music on stage until she had an orchestra to play it, for *As Time Goes By*. Then came recorded excerpts, collages, and pastiches, and it wasn't until the *Brahms' Paganini* that she used a complete classical work on tape.

The jazz and rock artists and arrangements that established her reputation were so inimitable no one would have wanted live substitutes, and their prior credibility took her halfway to success. When she could afford live musicians, she had the material transcribed: the Willie Smith numbers played by Dick Hyman for *Baker's Dozen*, the English jazz band on the *Eight Jelly Rolls* video. If she had to perform to tape, the original Beach Boys or Chuck Berry were fine with the audience; these records were part of their lives. But jazz and rock had a creative bite, an antagonistic edginess. Tharp avoided soft popular music—the sentimental, the hummable—until the *Nine Sinatra Songs*. And probably nothing else of hers clicked so successfully into the taste of a broad population, until the Broadway show *Movin' Out*, with its reconstructed recordings of Billy Joel.

Nine Sinatra Songs became a Tharpian trademark, even though it was virtually unique in relation to her other work. For the same reasons that it was so popular, it became a target. The newly critical field of "dance theory" attacked it as a purveyor of heterosexual gender stereotypes and a blatant bid for audience approval that didn't even have the saving grace of satire. Feminists and some critics objected to the way she portrayed women in the *Sinatra*. Music editor Michael Fleming of *The Fort Worth Star Telegram*, for example, commented that "as the dance progresses, the female member of each pair seems to become trapped in one of two obnoxious roles—either a seductress or an emotionless rag doll. . . . There was something sinister lurking in the background, something all the more frightening for the glamorous sheen that covered it."

What scholars also found alienating about Tharp's dance around this time was its use of virtuosic technique and its theatrical staging. Some early devotees were troubled by Tharp's evolving popularity. Writing in *Dance Magazine*, Joan Acocella sensed a "relaxation of concentration" in the *Sinatra* when Tharp took it to Broadway in the summer of 1984. "Most of the subtleties were removed, replaced by mugging," she thought. Fans fell away and new ones arrived, but the intellectuals' disapproval stigmatized her for a generation. The *Sinatra* may have been "something like a panorama of Middle America in middle-age" according to Arlene Croce, but it would take its place alongside *Sue's Leg, Baker's Dozen,* and *Eight Jelly Rolls* as "a masterpiece of Americana."

Before the *Nine Sinatra Songs* had seen its first New York performances, Tharp imported five of the songs to a reconditioned *Sinatra Suite.* This version, for one couple alone, went into American Ballet Theater's repertory in December 1983, and had its PBS premiere on the video collection *Baryshnikov by Tharp* in October 1984. The *Suite* preserved and even strengthened the romantic tone of the *Nine,* with the gorgeous Elaine Kudo partnered by the danseur who was every woman's heartthrob. For the video, the songs were given a Hollywood frame: a cocktail party is in progress, Baryshnikov and Kudo lock eyes across the room, and exit through a garden trellis to begin the dance.

Again the songs track the progress of an affair, and the choreography is drawn closely from the *Nine Songs.* Spread over seven couples, the dances were like variations on a theme of love. As danced by only one couple, the theme becomes more of a story. Camera close-ups draw attention to their mutual attraction and gradual divergence. When Kudo walks out, Baryshnikov dances his pain and disbelief to "One for My Baby." After Tharp's two earlier settings of the song, this solo for the first time brings to mind a much angrier dance, Fred Astaire's barroom breakdown in the 1943 movie *The Sky's the Limit.* "One for My Baby" was written for Astaire by Harold Arlen and Johnny Mercer. Distraught over his decision to jilt Joan Leslie for her own good (he's an air force hero on furlough from the war), Astaire drowns his sorrows, then smashes up the bar. Baryshnikov works up a series of ever more anguished pirouettes but eventually becomes resigned to his disappointment and leaves the party.

In one or the other of these two versions, the *Sinatra* dances became a perennial gala attraction. Baryshnikov and Kudo did the *Suite* as a tribute when Frank Sinatra received the Kennedy Center Honors in 1983. The *Nine* were performed in the East Room of the White House at a state dinner given by President Ronald Reagan for the Grand Duke of Luxembourg, in November 1984. Tharp's dancers performed them for a company fundraiser in 1982, at New York's famous Rainbow Room atop Rockefeller Center. The company rented itself out in February 1985 as part of the floor show, at a bash for three hundred guests to celebrate the opening of a high rise condo development, a "billion dollar section of the European Riviera on Florida's Gold Coast." And Tharp succumbed to the ill-considered notion of dancing the *Suite* herself with Baryshnikov, for the closing-night benefit of the company's Brooklyn Academy season in 1984. Whatever her gifts as a dancer, they did not include playing a glamour girl. Some critics tried to ignore the embarrassing moment. Anna Kisselgoff deplored what she considered a deliberate parody, with Baryshnikov as "a beleaguered straight man grappling with a version of Carol Burnett."

Reviewing a 1982 Tharp Dance performance at Meany Hall in Seattle, critic Laura Shapiro marveled at the close coordination among dancers that made Tharp's pieces work, the intimate and the fractured ones alike. In *Short Stories*, "Suspicion, nothing better, is what sparks the choreography; but the movement remains bound by trust." None of the antisocial action in that dance could have happened "without a perfectly tuned ensemble, and that ensemble is always shaping our vision of the violence." The same performance included *Nine Sinatra Songs* and Tharp's devastating new pursuit of the violence, *Bad Smells*. During this period Tharp was in the grip of dark imaginings. She'd created the ruthless family in *The Catherine Wheel*, but atoned for their cartoonish menace with *The Golden Section*. For the less compassionate and more realistic *Short Stories* she'd depicted a "tribal bloodletting" and a "community of cannibals," according to her own clinical introduction on *Confessions of a Cornermaker*. But the characters in *Bad Smells* weren't even a dysfunctional community, perhaps they were no more than "nature's darker forces." The dancers, dressed in shredded thrift-shop underwear and wearing makeup that looked like smeared mud, had no graces to save them; if anything she boosted their heartlessness into a lurid spectacle.

In her autobiography Tharp says she started thinking about ritual sacrifice on a visit to Mexico. She visualizes priests peeling the skin off their victims and then tells how she used this horror for a dance, to work off her anger over her breakup with David Byrne. Tharp may have made the antithetical *Sinatra* and *Bad Smells* as therapy, but the self-expressive implications in both dances took second place to grander theatrical visions—in the case of *Bad Smells*, pitiless ones. Tharp says *Bad Smells* was conceived through the violent and disorienting point of view of the television camera. By the time it aired on ARTS Cable as part of the *Tharp Scrapbook* tape, in October 1982, a stage version was touring the West Coast with *Nine Sinatra Songs*.

Tharp never did things in moderation. She was capable of pushing her ideas over the brink after they'd reached perfection. Starting out as a "stark, austere minimalist . . . resentful of physicality," wrote the critic Roger Copeland in a 1982 *New York Times* Sunday piece about women and modern dance, she worked her way to a "lush, virtuosic physicality," and many other postmodern choreographers followed. "Apparently," thought Copeland, "after proving that dance could be unmistakably brainy, it then became ideologically acceptable to be 'beautiful' as well." Reviewing a Washington performance the same week, critic George Jackson called *Baker's Dozen* "a caprice for beautiful people." But after *Baker's Dozen*, what was beautiful ripened into the artificial glamour of a Hollywood escapade, in *Sinatra*. Similarly, once she broached the subject of misogyny in *When We Were Very Young*, she dug into that pit until she scraped bottom.

There was more than ritual torture in the background of *Bad Smells*. Tharp still wanted to deliver large-scale dance to a large-scale audience. The problem was how to magnify the dancers without losing the effect of their immediate presence. Film could do it, especially in close-up, as she'd already demonstrated. But filmed dance wasn't live dance, no matter how compelling you could make it. Putting the two together would risk reducing the live dancers to Lilliputian scale. She had used big effects on stages before with the graffiti writers in *Deuce Coupe* and the film-scaled scenics in *The Catherine Wheel*. She was thrilled with spectacles, like the enormous but fictional peace demonstration in the movie *Hair*, where thousands of extras had been rounded up to see her dances and a rock concert on the Washington Mall. Now, in late 1981, she was thinking about how rock concerts could be amplified to reach an almost unlimited audience, and about how rock's intense noise levels could release flamboyant and possibly lawless behavior in both performers and spectators. Around this time, live video came into use at concerts and large sports events, where the audience was too far away to see the faces and action details routinely captured on the home television screen. Tharp's plan to add a video component to *Baker's Dozen* was derailed only because she was ahead of the technology in 1979.

She commissioned one of the loudest avant-gardists of the day, Glenn Branca, to write a score for *Bad Smells*. Branca, whose concerts of massed electric guitars had been called "sonic onslaughts," wanted his music to induce a kind of mystical ecstasy. He told John Rockwell: "I always think of my own music as absolutely pure and beautiful. Sometimes it sounds distorted and disgusting, but the *idea* is for it to be beautiful."

Another important film dance, Merce Cunningham's 1979 *Locale*, preceded *Bad Smells*. *Locale* had been made for—and with—the handheld camera of Charles Atlas. At a time when film was thought of as a poor substitute for live dancing, Cunningham took a chance and programmed a film evening during his company's 1980 New York season at City Center. *Locale* was screened together with *Roamin' I*, a small documentary about *Locale* in the making. Projected in the theater, *Locale* was disorienting, a shocker. Cunningham and Atlas used a choreographed moving camera that shot the dancers from different angles, traveled among them, changed focal distances and speeds. The continuity was further disrupted with jump cuts and editing devices. *Locale* couldn't have been shown as a live dance, and Cunningham reworked it for the stage.

Bad Smells also began as a film project, with Tom Rawe wielding the camera. Three takes of the dance were superimposed and edited. "Finally no one liked it," Rawe told Minneapolis critic Mike Steele. "So maybe it was inevitable from the beginning that it would go back to being a stage work instead." In the stage version Tharp took the camera's ability to reconfigure live dance a notch further by superimposing one on the other; in fact, she put the whole process on display at once. Anticipating the motion-capture techniques of the early 2000s, she longed for a camera that would "blossom and make abstract shapes from things." She would have liked an overhead computerized camera to photograph the dance from the grid, but such a thing hadn't been invented yet either, so Tom Rawe shot the dance as it was being performed. The live video was projected simultaneously on a huge onstage screen.

Rawe's moves were as carefully choreographed and rehearsed as the organized frenzy of the dancers. Usually moving downstage of them with his back to the audience, he sliced his camera up and down their bodies and probed into their faces. The dance, seen alone in studio showings and archival tapes, was obsessive, robotic, a hellish bout of jogging and calisthenics and dance warm-ups. Branca's deafening guitars whanged and crashed, detonating sour tone clusters and pile-driver thuds. Tharp had given the dancers morbid images to work with. They chanted "Me, Me, Me, Me, Me!" and she told Barbara Hoon to imagine "dog carcasses and three-legged horses in the doorway," according to an observer of rehearsals. For one lift, where a man circled with a woman gripped horizontally in his arms, she wanted them to think of helicopter blades slicing close to the ground. There were hideous seductive gestures and halfhearted vaudeville turns, and a woman slowly somersaulting over men's rolling bodies. Mary Ann Kellogg, the victim in Part I of *Short Stories,* was once again beset and, at the end, she was throttled or murdered by Raymond Kurshals.

Despite their apparent similarities of approach, *Locale* and *Bad Smells* were very different in effect. In his anthology devoted to Merce Cunningham, Richard Kostelanetz has noted that Atlas's camera in *Locale* stands in for the audience, making it possible for the viewer to move around and look at the dance from many vantage points. Rawe's camera isn't at all detached or objective. As another moving body, Rawe becomes part of the choreography, and the camera itself enters into the dance. Stretching and tilting, bleaching and blurring the dancers' bodies, veering from amputated limbs to spasmodic laughing faces, raking over them in myopic close-ups, it creates a new dance. Like an X-ray it seems to be trying to get under the skin of the dancers, probing for their poisoned alter egos. Terrible as the dance is, the video shows us one that's even more terrible.

Cunningham's companion documentary, *Roamin' I,* revealed the complicated mechanics of *Locale:* the cameras with their cranes and dollies, the tangles of cable and the helpers who whisk the cable out of the camera's path, the dancers scurrying to get into position for the next shot. Tharp had given viewers a look at this dance of the techies in the public taping sessions for *Country Dances* (1976). *Bad Smells* was something else. The ten-minute *Scrapbook* version includes only the video footage, but the stage version, one-third longer, was a total production with three elements that could not be disentangled once they were assembled. Most viewers in the theater felt split between the dance and the video looming above it, but synthesis did occur later on, in the form of metaphor.

Bad Smells was like a news documentary, with Tom Rawe as the intermediary, the facilitator, the one who slants the news to favor his own point of view. It graphically demonstrated the dehumanizing effects of mass media. Arlene Croce thought the stage production less effective than the dance alone: "On the stage, it becomes a chunk of curiously deflected raw sensation. It's all about itself—about things of horror and how the reporting of these things keeps us from experiencing them." Burt Supree of *The Village Voice* didn't share the audience's enthusiasm for it at an early performance, but he saw enough "political, totalitarian, post-nuke resonance" to justify the feelings Tharp was exploiting. He thought such protracted violence and compression of emotions went past credibility, though. In real life they were "never so relentless, so frozen, except perhaps in some psychotic frenzy."

When the dance played New York in the 1984 BAM season, Anna Kisselgoff hit on another probable source for the production when she likened it to "clubs in which disco dancers are simultaneously reproduced on a large screen by a television camera." Mistaking Tharp's deadly design, she saw the piece as "an unintentional comic takeoff." Laura Shapiro accepted the pairing of *Bad Smells* ("deliberately repulsive") with *Nine Sinatra Songs* ("deliberately luscious"), and Tharp herself thought they made a balance between politesse and amorality. Shapiro welcomed the choreographer's radical resistance to pigeonholing. *Bad Smells* was "a dance that spans the imagery of savage chaos from primitive to punk, a dance that reduces anything human to puniness in comparison with the vivid, hungry screen, a dance that instantly, and easily, overwhelms both dancers and audience, a dance that hurts to watch."

Perhaps *Bad Smells* was Tharp's attempted exorcism of the marauding bag ladies and listless stagehands who'd haunted her Winter Garden performances, but she hadn't achieved catharsis yet. *Fait Accompli,* the company piece that immediately followed, was a dance of death, a dance about facing the onset of menopause and the end of her performing career. Tharp hadn't been dancing consistently for a couple of years; now she got herself back into shape by taking boxing lessons and a private ballet class with Rebecca Wright. She was in a fighting mood. She intended to be the first person to deal onstage with "the physical, factual entity of a dying body." She relished telling interviewers about her studies of "concentration camps, life after death, war, bombing, airplanes going down and flight recorder boxes." The dance was to be about "what the implications of dying are, and how people see fit to protect themselves," as she told dance writer Eric Taub. She also spoke about totems, and the power of the supernatural to fend off evil forces. She, in fact, was to symbolize that resistance: "The last part of the piece is a single figure against an overpowering mass . . . which can't be held back."

Fait Accompli was one of the few dances Tharp referred to publicly in such metaphorical terms. The dance itself, premiered in Austin, Texas, in November 1983, turned out to be the largest, most severely formal work she'd ever made: forty minutes of highly structured dancing for seventeen people. It didn't hold this record for long; a month after its first performances, the jumbo-sized *Bach Partita* made its debut with American Ballet Theater. In the

long run *Fait Accompli* was overshadowed by the dance it directly anticipated, *In the Upper Room*, but it was actually a more interesting work, more
unified in style and more original in concept. Admittedly reflective of
Tharp's state of mind, it gave her a platform for a late hurrah, and it earned
wild audience approval as a star turn and a company gut-buster.

The first part of the dance is another of Tharp's quartet inventions. The
dancers wore identical black tank suits, athletic socks, and sneakers. Santo
Loquasto, following Tharp's fetishistic indications, originally had wrapped
them from head to foot like mummies. She may also have had a metaphor
for birth in mind, perhaps thinking of Balanchine's Apollo being unwrapped
from swaddling cloths. This symbolic opening scene had been deleted from
the New York City Ballet production of the ballet, to intense controversy,
when it was revived for Mikhail Baryshnikov in 1979. Tharp abandoned the
idea when it proved unworkable. They also tried the dance on a Mylar
floor, which had worked for the videotape version of *Bad Smells*, but it was
discarded as too slippery and dangerous.

One by one the groups of four enter in formation. With an almost math-
ematical dexterity, Tharp brings them in and out, works them in squares and
lines, adds in new units, reorganizes the units, sets up counterpoint patterns
and canons. The aggregate pattern goes from two to sixteen dancers. Every
dancer works in tandem with at least one other dancer and every subunit is
always related spatially and rhythmically to every other unit on the stage.
On paper this sounds stupefyingly compulsive, but on the stage the patterns
evolved from one engaging design to another as the solid cadres regrouped.
Big ranks crisscrossed, creating strange effects like a camera going in and out
of focus. Tharp set a seemingly rigid but inventive vocabulary of calisthenics; fighters' sparring and feinting moves; large stiff-armed and stiff-legged
gestures; precipitous jetés, spins, and extensions; recuperative flop-overs,
stretches, and heaving breaths. The dancers were in constant motion, glued
to David Van Tieghem's propulsive techno-disco score, but varying the beat
by doubling, suspending, and syncopating their relation to it.

The movement was unforgiving. Tom Rawe remembers he would knot
his stomach at the beginning and stay clenched, just to be able to get
through it. The company worked on it in the attic studio at Brooklyn Academy during hot summer days, with the doors and windows closed, the
dancers sweating and dehydrated. Mary Ann Kellogg thought Tharp
wanted to push them to the point of exhaustion, but somehow, performing
the piece, a mysterious bonding took place. "What you were feeling inside,

that kind of total excitement and drive and push, that the audience was also getting that. . . . In a way I felt that we weren't so much dancing it for you all out there in the house as that we were dancing it for each other. . . . Being on that stage with those incredible dancers and working with each other and feeling each other and the physicality, it was orgasmic."

Jennifer Tipton supplied a fabulous environment for the dance, after Tharp complained one day that theaters weren't designed for upstage entrances and exits, only side ones. Remembering an effect created by lighting designer Jules Fisher in the Bob Fosse show *Pippin*, Tipton adapted the idea of a "curtain of light," using banks of stadium lights beamed down from behind the dancers and onto a manufactured fog, to create such a bright forestage that the background would vanish. When the dancers made upstage appearances and withdrawals, they seemed to materialize out of nowhere and then evaporate again. Tipton created the same fog-and-light-beam effects later in *In the Upper Room*, using the more economical, standard lighting instruments instead of 144 overhead PARs.

After twenty-five minutes, the whole dance shifted, from a formal group structure to an expressive, personal narrative. Tharp appeared and danced out the struggle of a lifetime. Lit by a follow spot, she summoned up the men in the company for another, more concise edition of her "phases of love" duets, while the rest crossed in the dark with faltering steps, like prospective or rejected partners. Tharp was lifted and tossed over shifting clusters of men as the light faded in and out, a star—idolized but controlled by others. She did a tight, internally focused solo dotted with trademark moves from some of her earlier dances. Then the group reprised its biggest counterpoint pattern in the brightest lights, and retreated into limbo.

Tharp faced the audience for a moment, shuddering, then turned upstage just as a row of footlights at the back flared into the eyes of the audience. With a skater's deep, lunging glide—only checked by the traction of the floor—she dissolved into the blaze as the curtain came down. Interpretations varied as to whether this symbolized Tharp's retirement from dancing or her determination to keep it up. When *Fait Accompli* entered the repertory of Hubbard Street Dance Chicago in the '90s, the whole second part of the dance was dropped, perhaps for practical reasons. Or perhaps this was one role Tharp couldn't transfer to another dancer.

Reviewing *Fait Accompli* when it premiered at BAM in early 1984, Anna Kisselgoff inferred a theme linked to some half-intelligible words in David Van Tieghem's score—an announcer reporting the recent shooting down of a Korean airliner by a Soviet plane. Neither Tharp nor Van Tieghem intended any such narrow Cold-War reference; the score's intermittent voice-overs suggested many other tense, threatening situations. Kisselgoff's interpretation cast a pall over what she acknowledged was an otherwise fine piece: "And so the end of one dancer's career is equated with the shooting down of nearly 400 civilians in an airliner. Somebody's scale of moral values is off here." Croce, who appreciated Tharp's elegant handling of the groups in Part I, thought the spectacular production was bigger than its meaning: "The fiery Wagnerian beauty of it all is so impressive that we may lose sight of how little is actually being said in the choreography or else attribute a sacerdotal meaning to its extreme asceticism."

But for theater critic James Leverett, reflecting on a dismal New York season of playgoing, *Fait Accompli* was a triumph of dance and theater, "a retrospective so energetic and incisive that it contains the future as well." Leverett discussed the physical, social, and metaphorical meanings of *Fait Accompli*, ventured that "merely by sharing the planet with Tipton and Loquasto, we live in a golden age of stage design," and interpreted the ending as an unmistakable image of "the ageless metaphorical bond between the stage and the world, theatre and life."

If *Fait Accompli* was a logical development in Tharp's stream of creative thought, it can also be seen as a pivot into a new direction. The layouts and floor patterns, the group-versus-soloist hierarchy, and the stage scoured of any clutter or peripheral information, all suggested a more balletic emphasis. *Fait Accompli* staged a Tharp company the audience had never seen before. In her previous dances, even the "abstract" ones, there was always a sense of individuals working together, often in physical or eye contact. If necessary they sacrificed visual clarity for the pleasure of their game. In *Fait Accompli* they forged designs through their adherence to the beat, their obedience to the lineup, and the uncanny ensemble radar they had developed, but there was no sign of the individual imprinting so customary in the Tharp canon. The performing style resembled the style of the first *One Hundreds*, flat, expository, and depersonalized. The movement was tough and relentless; they seemed to be doing it only to prove they could do it. But that, in a way, added to its theatrical power.

Tharp's popular success rested largely on the character and social-dance pieces, and in the '80s on her spectacular stagings. She wanted this success and she deliberately went after it. But at the core of all her dance, always, was structure and the act of dancing. *Fait Accompli*, with its expressionistic lighting effects, formal group section, and quasi-narrative conclusion, fused the two tendencies. Tharp thought of herself as a classicist, but whenever she trespassed on classical territory, she was accused of parody or viewed with distrust by some observers. "The ballet is something we all depend on," she told an interviewer for *Dance Magazine* around this time. ". . . we *use* the ballet, we don't *present* the ballet." But she was penetrating the ballet world in a big way, *her* way, and few other choreographers could equal her resources for crossing over.

In the early '80s Tharp fed the repertory from time to time with small, demanding, but disposable quasi-ballets that could be done by the chamber-sized red or blue company. Richard Colton calls them "ballet being done with interesting counterpoint and interesting textures and layers and behavior." *Third Suite*, set to the most familiar of J. S. Bach's orchestral pieces, was made at Osgood Hill in 1980. An informal showing after the residency constituted what was probably the only complete American performance. The dance made its debut at the Théâtre du Champs-Elysées in Paris in October. It didn't fare well there. For four couples, it was a fabulous but possibly overchallenging application of technique. The live orchestra proved a liability. According to Shelley Freydont the conductors' tempi were unreliable, and Tharp pulled the piece midseason. On the archival performance video that exists, the score is played at breakneck speed and the dancers hurl themselves into it quite recklessly.

The dance begins with a catalogue of subverted ballet moves: tilted balances, heel walks, upside-down supported arabesques, women flying into the men's arms, where they're less likely to open into beautiful extensions than to crumple into a ball or drop like a sandbag. These moves are threaded into a continuous spool of action. In a small duet interlude, Uchida and Whitener alternate spinning phrases, Whitener whips off immaculate pirouettes and air turns, and Uchida does ballerina steps on half-toe. When the group reenters—too quickly for the audience to applaud—the music's original fast tempo seems almost languid. After the slow, measured second-movement duet, the music suggests expansive leg swings and jumps, and dotted-rhythm chassés, skips, and hops. The whole dance takes on this buoyant idea, with jazzy dips and the partners lilting side by side like skaters.

What's noticeable even on this ghostly performance tape is how strong the dancers are technically. *Third Suite* featured fast, exacting legwork for men and women—turns, batterie, step combinations, everything except pointe work. But their technical abilities, subsumed into the articulate flow of movement, hardly looked exceptional. Few people appreciated the inventiveness with which Tharp utilized the ballet training she'd always prescribed for herself and her dancers. After the early modern dancers' severe disconnection from ballet, the generation of choreographers emerging from postmodern austerity in the 1980s were finding new fluency through increased technique training. But no other modern dancers at the time had so confidently absorbed the ballet vocabulary and embraced its musical environment.

Soon after the residency at Osgood Hill, Christine Uchida and William Whitener's *Third Suite* duet, to Bach's Air for G String, was taped for *Confessions of a Cornermaker*. As a stand-alone piece it remained for several years in repertory as the *Bach Duet*, a showpiece for these two superb Tharpians who'd started life in the Joffrey Ballet. Whitener's elegant line, his seemingly effortless turns and beats, Uchida's daring allegro and stop-on-a-dime balances, and the musical flexibility they shared, transformed the classical adagio into a suspenseful dialogue, an exploration of the ways two people, not necessarily lovers, could come together and go apart. In each of a dozen or so meetings, conventional lifts, poses, and promenades became reconfigured, gender roles got traded. The approaches and retreats were made on "everyday" walking, hurrying, or delaying steps, and created an exquisitely personal frame for the dance interactions. Without "acting" tenderness, disaffection, appeal, hesitancy, or decision, the dancers told a story that ended with an embrace and a farewell.

Tharp drastically reshaped the idea of a pas de deux here, from a series of self-important gestures to a conversational, almost casual relationship between people who might pass each other on the street every day. When she filmed it for television, she tried an alternative to zooming in and out, the usual way of keeping both dancers in the frame. As they separate and move closer, the screen splits, with one camera on each of them, then knits back together. You see what Uchida and Whitener are doing, but you lose the dance's continuity and its story, which lay in the distances between them.

Through archival videotapes it's possible to see both Bach duets Tharp did for the company, the *Third Suite* duet, in what was probably a Paris performance, and the first *Bach Duet*, danced by Rose Marie Wright and Ken Rinker outdoors at the Delacorte Theater on 7 September 1974. A lot had happened in six years. Alongside Uchida and Whitener's suave, balletic colloquy—only a shade less romantic than Baryshnikov and Kudo in *Sinatra*

Suite—fusion pioneers Wright and Rinker look spiky, a bit awkward, but easygoing. They seem younger, less comfortably attuned to each other. Their vocabulary of pivots, châiné turns, slow lunges, extensions, and swings gets disrupted by pedestrian punches, shrugs, pushes, and shoves, and arms that churn almost of their own volition. The issue between them seems to be one of dominance. Through games of leader-follower, woman-man, big person–small person, they lightly dance out a real situation in the company's history. Wright, the teacher and coach, is patient and affection-ate; Rinker, once the new kid in the group and the first man to join Tharp's enterprise, stifles his resistance and lets her show him the way.

At the beginning Rinker spits on the floor, then rubs his shoe in the spot for traction. This behind-the-scenes business caused nervous laughter when it recurred later as a dance gesture. Rinker's two-fisted temper fits and de-fensive flat-of-the-hand moves—the kind of irreverence Tharp was soon to interpolate with such success for Baryshnikov—also took the audience by surprise. The fact that this *Bach Duet* was set to a prayer probably added to the indignation of Tharp's critics. By the 1980 *Bach* she had suppressed her need to épater le bourgeois and the audience had gotten used to her free-wheeling mixture of refinement and coarseness.

Telemann made its appearance early in 1984 during the Brooklyn Acad-emy season that brought *Bad Smells*, *Fait Accompli*, *Nine Sinatra Songs*, and sev-eral older works to New York. It was very accomplished, maybe too skillful to be persuasive, as Arlene Croce believed. It starts out "a perfectly charm-ing, diverting little piece and ends up a mad game of Ping-Pong between Tharp's baroque sensibility and Telemann's." A serviceable program opener for the next year of touring, it was always overlooked in favor of the more dazzling items in the repertory. With three only slightly misbehaving cou-ples dancing to an unexceptional score, *Telemann* was an exercise in symme-try and academic variations. Revisited twenty years later it's one of the few things Tharp ever made that could be called bland.

Another little ballet for the company from that period, *Sorrow Floats*, re-volved around a solitary male character and quickly disappeared in the wake of its distant cousin, *The Little Ballet* (1983). *Sorrow Floats* premiered at the Amer-ican Dance Festival in July of 1984. Tharp had received one of four handsome commissions ($40,000) the festival made that summer for new work. She didn't exactly blow off the commission, but she was probably cruising on overload, even for her. She'd spent the spring on her important collaboration with Jerome Robbins for New York City Ballet, *Brahms/Handel*, taped the three ballets on *Baryshnikov by Tharp* with ABT in Toronto, and was in the last stages of postproduction for *Amadeus*. She had four ballets up and running at ABT. Around this time she also choreographed *The Hollywood Kiss*, then discarded it unperformed (she retrieved some of the material later on for *In the Upper Room*). Work on the movie *White Nights* was beginning in the summer. The Tharp company was coming off three months of touring. Besides the American Dance Festival, their summer schedule included a teaching residency in Lake Placid, New York, and a bonus two-week run of *Nine Sinatra Songs* and *Fait Accompli* at the Gershwin Theater on Broadway. At the ADF Tharp was not only premiering *Sorrow Floats*, which had previewed in June on a tour to Germany, she was back dancing her old role in *Eight Jelly Rolls*.

Sorrow Floats did give the impression of a sketch. John Carrafa played a Pierrot-like character, with Shelley Washington, Jennifer Way, and Katie Glasner as figments of his drooping imagination. Tharp had wanted to make a piece for Carrafa and according to local critic Linda Belans, "the success of *Sorrow Floats* depends heavily on Carrafa's gift for mime." The dance's title echoes a motif in John Irving's 1981 novel *The Hotel New Hampshire*. Disaster after disaster plagues the characters, but they keep reassuring themselves that as sorrow keeps floating to the surface, so does love.

The dance sustained a couple of mishaps at its premiere. Before the end, something in the sound system malfunctioned and the music (Georges Bizet's *Jeux d'Enfants*) abruptly ceased. Carrafa improvised to cover, until the curtain came down. Over the audience's loyal cheering everyone could hear boos from the balcony. It was Mark Morris, in residence at the festival for a Young Choreographers and Composers conference. Morris, then enjoying a reputation as the Bad Boy of modern dance, followed up his outburst at the end of the evening, yelling "No more rape!" after *Nine Sinatra Songs*. Morris apparently was reacting to the rough handling Shelley Freydont received from Tom Rawe in "That's Life." *Sorrow Floats* ran in its entirety at two subsequent Festival performances, but the dance was too insubstantial to last much longer. Tharp had persuaded American Dance Festival director Charles Reinhart not to videotape *Sorrow Floats*. Looking for a record of it ten years later, she was disappointed to learn he'd carried out her wishes.

First titled *Once Upon a Time*, *The Little Ballet* also focused on a dreamer and his muses and, like the Carrafa piece, it had a score from a chapter of musical literature Tharp had skimmed over. The waltzes by Alexander Glazunov were suggested by Baryshnikov. Tharp probably found the music congenial because it resonated with George Balanchine's multiple stagings of

Glazunov's *Raymonda*. Tharp started choreographing it late in 1981 as a duet. Three coryphées were added later for amplitude, but it ended up only a twelve-minute piece anyway. Where *Sorrow Floats* had featured the expressive acting of John Carrafa, *The Little Ballet* centered on Baryshnikov's pliability, his seemingly effortless technique, and what Dale Harris called the "vulnerability and introspectiveness behind the confidence and bravura." Baryshnikov describes it as a "nostalgia piece" about the elements of Russian classicism as seen by modern man. Young Dierdre Carberry and three other ballet women, possibly imaginary, drift in and out, wearing filmy, flowery-colored dresses of indeterminate period. He wears pants and a shirt, collar unbuttoned, sleeves rolled up, a tie casually knotted. He molds and propels Carberry as if she's just a thought. Alone, he seems wistful but never at a loss for dance ideas.

Arlene Croce contrasted Baryshnikov's persona with the one Tharp made for him in *Push Comes to Shove*. Tharp had been subtly revising *Push* ever since its premiere, with some fairly significant adaptations for the TV version. By 1983 Baryshnikov was head of ABT, not a curious interloper, and she reworked the last movement to emphasize his new relationship to the ensemble. He had adjusted his dancing too, Croce thought. "The changing imperatives . . . no longer find Baryshnikov pretending to be at their mercy. He now meets the tactical switches Tharp has devised with a nonchalance that is twice as funny as his former bafflement." In *The Little Ballet*, "he's a reflective figure steeped in the tradition of Russian ballet, pursuing its chimerical sylphs down one hopeful path after another."

Dale Harris pictured the ballet as "a succession of memorable dance images in which a thousand meanings are contained." To critic Laura Jacobs it not only evoked iconic works from "ballet's collective consciousness" but portrayed Baryshnikov "isolated within his star persona, and within the romantic classics that he's so eager to go beyond but which still reveal him to us in the most potent dosages." With a poet-and-muse pretext that suggested *Apollo*, it's not inconceivable that Tharp also wanted to pay homage to Balanchine, who died on 30 April 1983, a month before the ballet's debut, and to honor Baryshnikov's recent attempt to put himself under Balanchine's tutelage.

10

Three-Way Stretch
1983–1990

Misha Baryshnikov had always been Tharp's strongest advocate at Ballet Theater. Baryshnikov left ABT in 1978 to dance with New York City Ballet, as perhaps the one place in America where he thought Russian ballet had a future. Calling Balanchine "an incredible symbol of uncompromised creative genius," he looked forward to learning new ballets and repertory from the master. It was late for this; a heart attack had impaired Balanchine's health and initiated his long final decline. Baryshnikov learned twenty-two roles at NYCB, but the situation proved less fruitful than he'd hoped. Balanchine coached him in ballets he'd done with ABT, *Apollo* and *Prodigal Son*. He learned other Balanchine ballets, most successfully *Rubies*, but few of the extreme modern works and no new choreography. Baryshnikov found the technique hard on his body—unlike Tharp's more eccentric but less angular style.

At the end of the 1978–79 season Lucia Chase retired from ABT and Baryshnikov was offered the directorship. It was a difficult decision, but he probably realized he wasn't absorbing what he had gone to NYCB for. Robert Garis, an intense observer of the New York City Ballet, felt that, only months after showing an early aptitude for the style, "he looked like someone who had given up on a project that he had been well on the way to mastering." If the dancer had been twenty when he arrived at NYCB,

Garis thought, he might have adjusted more easily. But he was thirty, and he never quite lost his "foreign accent" in the company. He resigned from City Ballet in the middle of the 1979 fall season, and became artistic director of ABT the next year.

It took a couple of years for Baryshnikov to effect his transition from a famous dancing star to company director with authority over the repertory, the personnel, and the ever-endangered budget. Tharp was gradually reinstalled, first with a revival of *Push*, and seven months after *The Little Ballet* (May 1983), *Sinatra Suite*, and *Bach Partita* had their premieres in Washington. The company could now mount all four Tharp ballets on a single program, and this package began appearing on ABT's touring roster early in 1984. Christine Temin of *The Boston Globe* thought the program represented "Tharp's bid to become . . . the first great classical choreographer of the post-Balanchine era." She was good for business, and for company morale. When ABT put on the all-Tharp program at the Metropolitan Opera House in New York, the *Times*'s Jennifer Dunning reported that it "filled the theater with affectionate excitement." Dale Harris remarked that Baryshnikov understood "how desperately his company needs the challenge of Ms. Tharp's uncompromising originality," and after a round of internal dissension and high-level administrative shakeups, rumors were circulating that Baryshnikov might appoint her codirector. He had always hoped to bring about a permanent relationship, but her notoriously high fees were a stumbling block.

Bach Partita was audacious in several ways. Tharp seized the opportunity to employ a large ensemble; the ballet leapfrogged its immediate predecessor *Fait Accompli*, with a total of thirty-six dancers, strictly deployed according to rank—three principal couples, seven demi couples, and a corps of sixteen women. The leading women were Ballet Theater's top ballerinas, Cynthia Gregory, Martine Van Hamel, and Cynthia Harvey (alternating with Magali Messac), partnered by Fernando Bujones, Clark Tippett, and Robert LaFosse. Against this formidable array Tharp had the nerve to set a solo violin, playing the Bach Partita in D Minor, which she'd used in the studio with Baryshnikov years before during the early stages of *Push Comes to Shove*. *Bach Partita* became a shifting play of unequal forces, during which the dancers kept redistributing themselves against the violin's inexhaustible line of melody.

The *Washington Post* dance critic Alan Kriegsman thought *Bach Partita*'s "sheer density of action and intricacy of configuration are as much of a Tharp name tag as if she'd embossed her signature on the dancers' backs."

"The object is to raise allegro dancing to a speed and clarity never seen before," wrote Mindy Aloff of *The Nation*. The press took special notice of the enlivening effect Tharp had on the company. According to Martha Duffy of *Time*, Tharp provided "the role Gregory has waited a career for," and Dale Harris thought all six principals "dance with new-found enthusiasm—like people released from a lifetime of drudgery."

Throughout the ballet's twenty-seven minutes, the groups streamed in and out in surprising combinations, reordering space and augmenting the music in Balanchinian ways. Playing with scale, she began with just a few dancers, replacing, adding and subtracting small units in quick but unpredictable relays. This suited the proportions of the music, but gave the stage space an elasticity, a capacity to expand, shrink, and open out again. She could then build from close-in focus on a few dancers to larger episodes: the solo women backed by the sixteen coryphées, a supported adagio for seven couples. But she avoided the symphonic device of assembling all the dancers onstage at once, which might have overwhelmed the violin. Magically, she kept the tone intimate and grand at the same time.

Tharp's movement vocabulary was entirely classical, except that the dancers were traveling most of the time. The couples resumed the supersonic flying double-work she'd been developing with her own dancers in works like *The Golden Section* and the *Bach Third Suite*. Individual steps—arabesque, attitude, brushes, leg extensions, and beats—were taken on the run or en tournant. The landscape reeled with pirouettes and chaîné turns. Both the individual enchaînements and the counterpointed groups elaborated rhythmically on the musical line.

In a long appreciation of Tharp at the end of the '83–'84 dance season, Arlene Croce called *Bach Partita* "an enormous, whirling, weightless ballet." Like several other critics, Croce noted what a triumph it was for the Ballet Theater dancers, as possibly "the hardest ballet [ABT] has ever danced," although she wondered how long the piece could remain in active repertory without technical erosion. What Croce saw as Tharp's great distinction was her Baroque sensibility, her talent for "seeing movement in a new light." It was probably this quality that most invigorated dancers in her ballets. The difference between dancing Tharp at ABT and at New York City Ballet in *Brahms/Handel*, her collaboration with Jerome Robbins, was that her demands weren't far from what the City Ballet dancers met every day: "In N.Y.C.B. repertory, certain ballets feed certain other ballets, and the style for such a piece as *Bach Partita* is in the dancers' bones. In A.B.T. repertory, it's anomalous." But neither *Bach Partita* nor *Brahms/Handel* gained a lasting purchase in its respective company.

Tharp and Jerome Robbins were friends of long standing. They'd met in 1973 through Rhoda Grauer, who at that time was working as an assistant on Robbins's "Celebration—The Art of the Pas de Deux" for the Spoleto Festival. Robbins had long wanted to collaborate, according to his biographer Deborah Jowitt. After persuading Tharp to do it, he put the project on New York City Ballet's spring 1984 schedule. The company was going through its own difficult transition, sorting out its power structure after the death of Balanchine. Robbins and Peter Martins had assumed codirectorship, and Lincoln Kirstein, no fan of Tharp's, remained a potent influence. Over the next decade Robbins gradually withdrew and Martins gained control. To date, Tharp has made only one more ballet for the company, in 2000.

Brahms/Handel was a hit, though a challenge for the ensemble, headed by Merrill Ashley, Ib Andersen, Maria Calegari, and Bart Cook, and inevitably short-lived in the NYCB's huge repertory. The collaboration gave Tharp access to a large contingent of twenty-eight excellent classical dancers. Public perception may have cast the choreographers as similar—they both flourished in many genres and applied a contemporary, eclectic sensibility to the stage. Robbins was probably the closest thing to an artistic prototype for Tharp. But their working processes and product were very different. They began the Brahms project schematically. Each of them directed half the group, with costumes color-coded, setting alternate stanzas of the Variations on a Theme of Handel orchestrated by Edmund Rubbra. But as the piece grew, they infiltrated each other's work, interconnecting and splicing material, trading dancers, breaking up and recombining the groups, and making variations on each other's variations. Their compositional process was a bit like a postmodern game with instructions by John Cage.

The ballet turned out to be an exploded version of a theme both collaborators had used before: the amiable competition. In their core behavior, the blue and green teams started out like alien tribes—Robbins's blues with smooth, elongated tendu port de bras, reminiscent of Balanchine's *Theme and Variations*, and Tharp's greens working in tandem to subvert the norms with splayed legs, flexed feet, tipped-over and rocking lifts, and displays of female bravery. As the lexicons collided and combined, references to ballet repertory flashed by, a frame or two of Balanchine, moves from old Robbins and Tharp favorites, hints of ballet classics. The teams intermingled, partners crossed over, neat floor patterns shattered into odd clumps and onslaughts. Women toppled or dove into the arms of moving masses of men. The two principal men did a challenge dance—I'll do this hard thing, see if you can copy it—an idea taken up by the principal women and then by the two couples. The whole ensemble gathered for the first time one stanza before the final fugue, with partners from the opposing side. The teams separated out again for the finale, each doing its own theme on either side of an invisible fence, and then they formed a picturesque traditional lineup behind the principals, who posed with arms linked in a quote from Balanchine's *Four Temperaments*.

Brahms/Handel, with its deliberately dualistic agenda, looked more cluttered than *Bach Partita*, more self-conscious. The color coding invited the audience to track each choreographer's contribution, and underscored the amount of information sharing they'd done. It made the ballet clearer, and perhaps cuter. But what no one disputed was how invigorating it was. Tharp hadn't made a big ballet so exhilarating and funny since *Push Comes to Shove*, and perhaps never did again.

Parenthetically amid this tremendous activity and success, in the spring of 1984 she started thinking about the twentieth anniversary of Tharp Dance, which she dated from her first choreography, *Tank Dive*, in 1965. She hatched a scheme to mount a one-day retrospective in the summer of 1985, spread across the New York venues where the works had first appeared, with buses to take the audience from place to place. *Medley* would be done in Central Park, *Torelli* in Fort Tryon Park, *Dancing in the Streets* at the Metropolitan Museum, *Eight Jelly Rolls* at the Delacorte, *Yancey Dance* and *Re-Moves* at Judson Church. The celebration would wind up with a Broadway show. It would take more dancers than just the Tharp company, and maybe they could use young nonprofessionals for the earliest works. Tharp sent Sara Rudner along with company executive director Steve Dennin to propose this extravaganza to her board of directors. According to Rudner, they weren't willing to take on the financial and logistical burden it would require.

In 1985 the cavalcade skidded to a halt. Over a period of five years Tharp had completed ten dances for her own company, four new ballets, four videos, two movies, two specialty dances, and two makeovers. She produced two big Broadway seasons of repertory, and additional engagements took place at BAM and the Gershwin Theater. The Tharp company was playing to ecstatic audiences on tour. The ballets were such big box office that ABT programmed lucrative all-Tharp evenings. But the Tharp company was beginning to feel the effects of heavy touring. The innovative two-team system and its requisite double-casting made for some resentment over the ownership of roles. Tharp wasn't touring, and the dancers felt a widening separation from a leader increasingly occupied with outside projects. Some even saw a disparity between their dancing and hers when she rejoined them in *Fait Accompli*; she was coming back to the stage in her forties after a layoff, while they were in top form as an ensemble and as individual dancers.

Rose Marie Wright left decisively in 1982, and Tharp struggled to replace her. No one knew the repertory better or could teach it more conscientiously than Wright. Rudner didn't want to take on the responsibility. Rawe and Way helped, and Rebecca Wright went along on some tours as ballet mistress, but these weren't permanent solutions. Setting the repertory pieces on new casts was always hard. As the older company members retired, new divisions appeared in the company. Arriving too late to learn the repertory from the creators, the younger dancers were aware they weren't tapping into the source. The responsibility to approximate original interpretations began to douse the excitement of learning the roles.

Tharp made no secret of how burdensome she found the company's upkeep. In a 1985 interview with Jennifer Dunning she spoke "with despair of maintaining a company in a culture she feels is not receptive to dance." While Steve Dennin struggled to convince her that the nonprofit model was a reasonable way to keep the company going, she still believed commercial enterprise was "not merely compatible with but essential to the survival and progress of art," as she told Joseph Mazo in 1984. And although she hardly lived on a grand scale, she probably saw the celebrity lifestyles and incomes of famous friends like Richard Avedon, Paul Simon, and Woody Allen as indicative not only of success but of social approbation. She thought she and her dancers deserved as much.

At that point the Broadway prize she still hadn't claimed seemed to surface within reach. A successful stage version of the beloved 1952 Gene Kelly movie *Singin' in the Rain* was running in London, produced by the Chicago team of Maurice and Lois Rosenfield and starring the English musical star Tommy Steele. After falling in love with *Nine Sinatra Songs* at BAM in early '84, the Rosenfields approached Tharp about directing and choreographing a New York edition. She went to London to see the show in June, then agreed to do it, provided her company was signed to dance "the lavish production numbers." The dancers' contracts covered the first six months of the show, which was scheduled to open at the Gershwin Theater in June 1985. After that, a hit would ensure their continuing employment. As Tharp saw it, "I would be able to park my company in the show for several seasons, providing not only an alternative to our frantic touring but also, once the show was running smoothly, the opportunity to rehearse new dances during the afternoons." Besides that, a benefit bash planned for opening night was going to wipe out the company's nagging deficit.

Tharp was apparently the only one who had no misgivings about the scheme, but the company and staff threw themselves into making it work. She assured the dancers there would be jobs for them after the show ended, although board member Lewis Lloyd told Bay Area critic Janice Ross just before their last performances, at Zellerbach Auditorium, ". . . this is a time of transition. . . . One of Twyla's great aggravations in life is that a company like hers doesn't run a surplus. In the future she wants to run [it] more like a business." No further touring was booked until January of 1986. During the period of downsizing the company's activities, longtime manager Roddy O'Connor left, along with Steve Dennin. Linda Shelton held the fort as company administrator, with a small office staff. "That worked just fine," says Shelton. "And then once the show opened . . . we were in place ready to go."

Some of the dancers were shocked when Tharp announced the plan; others had long sensed that things were beginning to unravel. They finished up their touring commitments, which stretched until February of '85, with the final runout to Berkeley in April. Those who elected to be in the show began tap and singing lessons. Fearless, they plunged into the new experience. In separate interviews with Nancy Goldner, Washington, and Rawe were excited about working in tap shoes, and all of them relished the idea of being based in New York for a decent period of time. Eleven company dancers were integrated into the show's cast of thirty-two. But a substantial segment of the company fell away. Chris Uchida had been withdrawing, and by 1983, after *Third Suite*, she had essentially left. By the time *Singin' in the Rain* rehearsals got under way, Rudner, Freydont, and Way had all become pregnant, much to Tharp's annoyance. Way stayed on to assist Tharp on the show but the women's portion of the repertory would have to be rebuilt when the company reassembled. So once again Tharp was jackknifing off the high board without much of an idea where she'd surface.

Even Tharp admitted later that *Singin' in the Rain* was a fairly unworkable idea. Not only had she had no experience directing in the legitimate theater, she would be stacking her work up against one of the icons of American cinema. Although the show seemed to release her from the dance company's dependency, it quickly snared her in another trap. In one of the only sanguine statements she released during the ordeal, she told *Playbill* writer Sheryl Flatow that she viewed the show as continuing the legacy of the movie: "It should be a part of our living theatre tradition." Her job was to translate a classic, with its affectionate plot about the early days of movies, into a medium that resisted the very premise of movies.

She decided to re-create some of the original choreography and make completely new settings for other numbers. This plan hurled her into a paradoxical situation. Preserving the original script, songs, and choreography guaranteed a nostalgic audience for the show, but her transposition of Kelly and Stanley Donen's cinematic montages to theatrical shtick invited unflattering comparisons. In her autobiography Tharp argues that the reason she left the original numbers alone and didn't do much new choreography was that the producers held the rights to the show's "original choreographic materials," and she didn't intend to relinquish ownership of her creative property to anyone else. She concocted collages of outrageous elements: eighteenth-century French peasants on roller skates, a tango, a cowboy and a stage horse that did a brush step copied from the police stallions in the movie *Hair*, a tap-dancing cavalier, and a movie-montage number with dancing dolls. If she had an overall concept for staging the movie, it was probably too brainy for Broadway. She was reported to have said she would do the show like a movie, "with the audience as the camera." She told one interviewer that the movie's chorus girls "look like they're trained dancers. In reality, those people had no training. So what you have to do is *untrain* sophisticated and technical dancers—and then get them out of unison." No Broadway critic was going to fall for this.

Besides, however brilliantly she cast it, *Singin' in the Rain* would be competing with the memorable performances of Gene Kelly, Debbie Reynolds, Jean Hagen, and Donald O'Connor. Although some big stars were considered for the Kelly role (John Travolta, Kevin Kline, Treat Williams, all unavailable), she cast Don Correia, a good dancer without a star personality, and relatively obscure actors for the other featured roles. In the few scenes from the show that have been preserved on videotape, the actors adopt a broad, overemphatic style of delivery, roughly equivalent to the hyperexpressive mode of the family in *The Catherine Wheel*.

Tharp's inexperience, plus the indulgence of her theatrically naive producers, made for a fatal combination. She called for extravagant effects and the Rosenfields acceded. The budget escalated alarmingly—topping $5 million by the time the show opened, according to a searing six-page investigation of the "turkey that refuses to lie down" in *New York* magazine three months into the run. The real rain, a must for the title song and dance, necessitated onstage plumbing and a floor with a special drainage system. One number boasted a trolley car and a replica of a classic Bugatti. Tharp ordered a life-size locomotive that never worked. A film sequence was commissioned from top cinematographer Gordon Willis, who'd worked on *Zelig*. By comparison *The Catherine Wheel* was a backyard skit.

The Rosenfields came up with extra financing when things started getting out of hand, but money wasn't the only thing that made for apprehension. Tharp brought in as many trusted collaborators as she could. There were sumptuous sets and costumes by Santo Loquasto and Ann Roth. Jennifer Tipton did the lighting. Shelley Freydont researched social dances of the 1920s. John Carrafa learned tap routines from the movie and taught them to the chorus as dance captain. But she was contemptuous of theater veterans who could have helped. The original screenwriters, Betty Comden and Adolph Green, were dispensed with when they tried to adapt the script instead of preserving the movie's scenario verbatim. Like many subsequent critics, they felt Tharp hadn't really reconceived the movie as a stage show. Two more writers worked on the show after they decamped, and were fired in turn.

Discontents sprang up all around, mostly due to Tharp's inability to establish authoritative command and her refusal to compromise. She was out of her depth. Supplying physical cues and imagery might work with her dancers, but the actors needed specific direction she didn't know how to give. As things started going wrong she clammed up and left them to work things out for themselves. Tharp's theater chums Mike Nichols, Harold Prince, and Jerome Robbins began showing up at rehearsals. If they gave her advice they weren't credited. Three successive press agents and an acting coach were called to the rescue. After previews began in May it became clear that the show needed serious doctoring. Tharp was never officially replaced but Albert Marre, who had directed *Man of La Mancha*, was hired. He refused directorial credit but he made important changes over Tharp's objections, putting most of the movie reconstructions into Act I, with the spectacular rain scene as a closer. Tharp's production numbers were stuffed anticlimactically into the second act, with almost no plot left to hold them together. The opening was put off twice, from June 13 to the 20th, then to July 2, which downgraded the long-planned Tharp company benefit from a glamorous first-night happening to a preview perk.

The reviews were devastating. The Broadway press didn't welcome this lady intruder from the art stage any more than the actors did. Frank Rich of the *Times*, the kindest of the daily critics, decided "Miss Tharp and company have turned a celestial entertainment into a mild diversion that remains resolutely earthbound." "'Singin' Down the Drain" blared the *Daily News* headline. The Rosenfields were ready to close the show immediately, but they caught the proverbial Broadway spirit. The audience had responded enthusiastically, and—assured by Shirley Herz, the last of the three publicists, that with more time it could be saved—they put up another million dollars. Expenses were shaved, the actors took a cut in pay and ballyhooed the show at the Times Square TKTS booth. They relaxed into their roles and business improved. In the end, *Singin' in the Rain* ran for almost a year, closing on 18 May 1986 after 367 performances and thirty-eight previews. "Call it an honorable mistake," wrote *Newsweek*'s Jack Kroll, almost the only major critic who had anything good to say. "Broadway needs the new blood of an artist like Twyla Tharp, but it needs her own ideas, her own energy, her own sensibility. Why hire Picasso to copy Matisse?"

Shattered, Tharp fled to California. In her autobiography she describes herself as suffering a near breakdown, but she may also have helped finish up work on *White Nights*, which premiered at the end of the year to lukewarm reviews. Eventually she pulled herself together and returned to New York and to choreographing. She started working during the day on new material with the dancers in *Singin' in the Rain*.

Tharp's huge productivity of the early '80s may have been driven partly by an effort to recoup the *Catherine Wheel* deficit, or at least stay abreast of it. *Singin' in the Rain* hadn't been a financial bonanza and she still had money worries. Issuing a call for new dancers in *The Village Voice* during the 1985 startup period, she required a $10 audition fee. She'd heard that orchestras charged a cover fee for people to audition. She paid for rental of the hall and other expenses, after all. Those who survived the audition were to become unpaid apprentices and then presumably join the company, a tryout practice Tharp had been using one way or another with new recruits for years. The dance world never got over this. The audition fee constituted "an unheard of request and a dangerous precedent for struggling young dancers," huffed *Ballet News*. People told the story, greatly inflated and with great disapproval, twenty years later. But Linda Shelton counters that Tharp's tough business practices and high fees raised the standards for the chronically downscale dance field. She had indeed set another precedent. Twenty years later a quarter of the U.S. companies listed in the *Dance Magazine* Auditions Guide were charging an audition fee.

Tharp winnowed out just two dancers from the hundreds of hopefuls who auditioned, Jamie Bishton and Liz Foldi. Bishton had danced with two of his dream choreographers, Bella Lewitzky and Lar Lubovitch, after graduating from Cal Arts in 1984. Tharp was his third ambition. In the callback sessions after the first cattle call, Bishton remembers working in small groups with company dancers on new material that later surfaced in *Bum's Rush*. "I was just in joy because here were these little pods of three people all over the studio, with Twyla choreographing on us. It was like a master class." He thought the audition fee was pretty outrageous, but the chance to work with Tharp, even for a day, was worth it. Tharp never charged for auditions again.

The reconstituted company wasn't officially announced until May of 1986, about the time the show closed, but the group had been gradually coalescing. Amy Spencer and Richard Colton had left *Singin' in the Rain* in December. Spencer joined choreographer Martha Clarke's innovative physical-theater work *Vienna Lusthaus*, and Colton stayed with Tharp. Mary Ann Kellogg had won a small speaking part in the show, and when it closed she set off to explore acting and other kinds of work for a while. Raymond Kurshals also thought it was time to move on, and instead of going back into the company he turned to an acting career. William Whitener passed up the show, returned to the reconstituted company, then left again early in 1988 to transition into a career as a choreographer and ballet company director. Once again Tharp's technical aspirations outdistanced some of the dancers' training and instincts. Katie Glasner thought she wouldn't fit into what she sensed as a more balletic company direction.

When the dust settled, only four of the former company members had returned: Colton, Washington, Whitener, and Carrafa. Tom Rawe was forty and after the show ended he reassessed his career. Performing the same material eight shows a week hadn't been his cup of tea. "I like to develop movement—to work on it together with dancers, to keep it alive, to try it different ways," he told Nancy Goldner just before the new company's debut in Philadelphia. Rawe decided to stop performing but he rejoined Tharp Dance as a teacher and coach. Uchida, Kellogg, Way, Rawe, and Spencer all came back to dance for brief periods during the next few years, but the company balance now shifted. New members Kevin O'Day and Jamie Bishton became key players, and the sixteen-member roster was filled out with ballet-trained young dancers.

Perhaps to celebrate the restart with a financial boost, or perhaps to stage another attack on a lingering deficit, the company threw a big benefit at the downtown discotheque the Palladium in May. For one thousand dollars plus a pricey ticket contribution, patrons could have their picture taken by Richard Avedon. The main event was a preview of the piece Tharp had been working on, with music by Philip Glass. *In the Upper Room* became one of Tharp's biggest hits and was eventually performed by several ballet companies as well as her own ensemble.

In the introduction to a *Dance in America* video of *In the Upper Room* made in 1996, Tharp tells one version of the dance's genesis, as a "secular mass." In her deadly-serious lecturing style she says she'd been using Glass's music in the studio for years and found it perfect for her intentions, the way it was "constantly unwinding from itself, as though scheming endlessly." The dance title came from a Mahalia Jackson gospel hymn that Tharp used while Glass was composing the new score. Jackson's melodic line "modulated relentlessly upwards." It "seemed to climb so high it pushed through the roof," and reminded Tharp of "an empty attic, a place of last resort, where one takes out one's treasures and puts them up for very special public view." This statement is packed with startling personal implications. Tharp seemed to visualize her work spiraling upward, from the idyllic days in the New Berlin attic into the glare of post-Broadway scrutiny, and beyond that to a heavenly reward. *New York Times* critic Jack Anderson supplied a New Testament reference to the Upper Room as the place where Jesus and his disciples experienced the presence of the Holy Spirit. Tharp may well have thought of dancing as an act of spiritual ascendancy, but she'd never been so explicit about it.

However literal or self-referential these clues might be, *In the Upper Room* struck most viewers as either pure composition or pure energy. Christine Uchida, who had married and moved to Vermont, returned to the newly formed company long enough to create one of the two leading roles. Sensing that Tharp would pull her back into a full-time commitment, Uchida left again, only to do the New York premiere in 1987 as a guest artist. "That to me was the ultimate," she says. "I loved that piece. I absolutely adore that piece . . . it didn't really matter if there was anybody out there. It just felt like there was so much involved. Focus and discipline, and really being aware of what was going on. Getting into the movement . . . And just to accomplish that and make it a whole piece."

Conceptually *In the Upper Room* was about contrast: men/women, modern dancers/ballet dancers, the air and the ground, high voices/low voices, foreground/background, all reflected against Glass's layered chord progressions. Two women working in tandem (Shelley Washington was the other original) began the piece with a scan of the Tharp movement lexicon— calisthenics, attitude turns, vaudeville shuffles, circular leg gestures in the air and brushes fore and aft, shoulder shimmies, punches and jabs, high extensions, baseball pitches—set on a jogging pulse (Stompers, the dancers called them), along with five others in sneakers. The twin leaders' movement served as a blueprint for variations and thematic reprises during the rest of the dance. Two women on pointe (they called themselves the Bomb Squad or the Pointers) with their partners, represented the ballet half of the contrast, contributing more and more precarious supported adagio to the mix. One woman floated between sides. The groups shared the vocabulary to some extent, but preserved their stylistic differences.

One persistent question about *In the Upper Room* is why Tharp revisited this aesthetic debate, after she'd resolved it so ingeniously in *Deuce Coupe, Push Comes to Shove,* and *Brahms/Handel.* For one thing, she could now do it entirely within her own company. Amy Spencer felt Tharp was trying to prove something by going back to things that had worked so well in *Fait Accompli:* "She *knew* she could make a piece that was gonna totally blow the audience away. And it seemed that she had looked at the elements she had developed and she knew exactly what she was doing. She was going after making a hit."

In the Upper Room had the audience in its grip as soon as the two Stompers emerged from Jennifer Tipton's luminous mist. As the temperature rose, from the slow, meditative opening music through successive intensifications of the vocabulary and the dynamics, the dancers shed layers of designer

Norma Kamali's costumes. Starting in black-and-white striped coveralls, the women went to red tank tops with little flared skirts for the Pointers and red unitards for the Stompers. The sneaker men ended up barechested and the danseurs wore white shirts. The music grew louder; the lights got brighter; the fog swallowed the upstage entrances and exits. Forty minutes later the music slammed to a stop and the two Stompers pulled down their fists triumphantly and jogged backwards into the void. Nancy Goldner described the tremendous effect: "what one imagines pure oxygen to be like—that's how exhilarating the dance is."

During the summer of 1986 the company worked on *Upper Room* and another new ballet, *Ballare*, to Mozart's two-piano sonata K. 448, during a seven-week residency at Skidmore College in Saratoga Springs, New York. They performed there and at the Ravinia Festival, then went off to Europe. By the time the New York public got a look at the company, in a month-long Brooklyn Academy season in February 1987, the new material and the new dancers were broken in. The generous repertory included *Baker's Dozen*, *Nine Sinatra Songs*, *The Fugue*, a revival of *As Time Goes By*, and a recondensed *Catherine Wheel*. Critical reaction to *In the Upper Room* and *Ballare* was mixed, and most longtime Tharp watchers took the opportunity to consider the company's new dimensions in terms of her whole career.

By incorporating hard-core ballet into her modern-dance sensibility Tharp had made another breakthrough. This was different from setting her eclectic dances on a ballet company or making fusion pieces for a mixed company with varying degrees of ballet training. Even before this big shift, writer Matthew Gurewitsch had put his finger on a crucial aesthetic question in a *Ballet News* essay. Tharp's determinedly nonhierarchical temperament, and her inclusive montage technique of putting the elements together, he observed, worked against organizing the material into one system, one classical framework. "She cannot assign rank and order. . . . The world as it offers itself to the mind is a jumble." This resulted, Gurewitsch thought, in a "lack of an ethical dimension in her aesthetics." Traditionalists perceived Tharp's dance as transgressive, but though it was physically complicated, spatially trackless and sometimes frenetic, it was never unprincipled. Tharp had inherited a postmodern aversion to value systems. A moralist without the certitude of doctrine, she refused to shape her imagery around given classes or classifications. To gain entry into ballet's most elite ranks she would have had to abandon her unique choreographic voice.

Arlene Croce was open to Tharp's eclecticism but the refinements of classical style still mattered. In a 1987 roundup of ballet crossovers Croce rejected Lincoln Kirstein's theoretical closure of the academy's doors to all but the New York City Ballet's insiders. "Might it not be time for another essay, called 'The Curse of Balanchine,' in which it would be shown how the great choreographer created twentieth-century ballet and put it off-limits at the same time?" Although Tharp hadn't yet mastered it, "she could be the first [modern dancer] to acquire pointe technique and make something new of it."

Tobi Tobias went further in assessing Tharp's use of pointe work. Her new dancers could go on pointe but they hadn't internalized the transitions between pointe steps. "Put the performers in pointe shoes, and—instead of growing lighter, fleeter, their range extended—they become awkward and ponderous," said Tobias of *In the Upper Room*. The four-woman, three-man *Ballare*, a "ballet blanc," was reminiscent of Balanchine but got Tharp into "big trouble," wrote Tobias. She didn't mind being jolted when "obstreperous Tharpisms intrude into the atmosphere of elegant decorum" but she felt the choreographer hadn't worked out a "rhythmic continuity" between the two idioms." Mindy Aloff assumed Tharp's contrarian pointe effects were intentional, "to give weight to a dancer's rhythm, as an exclamation interrupting her headlong attack and, perhaps most difficult, as a brake to a speeding phrase." Echoing Gurewitsch, though, Aloff asserted that "To use pointe implies that one has certain philosophical positions about grace and line. . . . Ease, authority, calm, fleetness without urgency," qualities Tharp had yet to acquire within her own aesthetic.

Anna Kisselgoff was even more harsh about Tharp's new direction in a Sunday piece entitled "Twyla Tharp and Ballet—An Uneasy Match." The BAM season had been "the most successful ever in terms of popular appeal and packed houses. Still this has been a hollow success—a case of an important talent less confident about an artistic imperative than about her ability to widen an audience." Croce saw the same opportunism more sympathetically. *In the Upper Room* was crude as a ballet, Croce thought, "where the points are only a means of advertising the newly constituted company and what it can do." But that work was undeniably important; "with it, Tharp reaches a new public and takes out insurance for her experiments in classicism."

Singin' in the Rain had left another coat of distemper on Tharp's grouchy frame of mind. Around the time of the BAM season she was telling interviewers New York had better shape up and support her or she would leave town. "We feel compelled-slash-obligated-slash-pleased to present the company in New York," she told Janice Berman, "but I'm seriously thinking about making this the last year, because it's just so expensive." With ABT, Eliot Feld, and Alvin Ailey about to take over the rental studio spaces at 890 Broadway, she would have nowhere to rehearse. And then there were the New York critics, who often were intentionally destructive and had "very little real imagination." She wasn't planning a fall season there because she wanted the repertory to be perfectly broken-in and foolproof before taking it to the "product-oriented" New York press. She even offered to move the company to Dallas for part of the year if someone there would come up with $2 million. She was beginning to portray herself as a businesswoman, as if she couldn't afford to get anyone else to lick stamps, do publicity, or fundraise. "It's not an easy job," she told interviewer Lois Draegin just before the BAM season. "But I do it because it's been necessary to ply these other trades in order to dance the way I wanted to, to develop my own platform."

The audience had no problem with Tharp's ambition. Immediately after the BAM season the company embarked on a touring marathon: twelve weeks in American cities in the spring of '87, South America in the summer. There was another summer workshop at Skidmore; then they spent the fall and winter crisscrossing North America from Anchorage to Boston, six weeks in Australia and New Zealand, more American cities, and a trip to Portugal in June 1988. Tharp danced in repertory on the early part of this tour, but stayed home for the Australian segment, much to the sponsors' disappointment.

Skidmore had produced more difficulties. After the South American tour, six dancers left the company. Most of them had been among the new recruits, but John Carrafa also decided to embark on his own choreographing career at that point. Once again almost half the company had to be replaced. Amy Spencer returned, and Elaine Kudo and Gil Boggs left Ballet Theater to join Tharp. Four new dancers were taken in, and the residency focused on learning the repertory. Tharp was doing two hours of weight training before each day's class and rehearsals. She was determined to dance *Sue's Leg* and *Eight Jelly Rolls* again. Jamie Bishton told a local paper that seeing Tharp coming back into the old repertory pieces "that are Twyla—the way she moves" was a phenomenal experience.

A special workshop had been planned for high school and college students, led by Tom Rawe and Jennifer Way, with Rose Marie Wright to help teach. As soon as Wright arrived, she was snatched away to bring back the style of *The Fugue* for the new company dancers; then she was pulled into more and more repertory coaching. Rawe and Way found their workshop arrangements getting shifted around to make room for the company rehearsals. By then their daughter, Hannah, had arrived, and after the planned Australian tour they decided not to go back on the road. Way realized she couldn't work administratively with Tharp, although she danced on and off during the next period and remained a faithful Tharp reconstructor and teacher for years.

Preparations for the Australian tour were complicated, and the result was outwardly a huge success. Tharp Dance was invited to visit several cities in honor of the Australian Bicentennial. The company was handsomely accommodated on the tour and paid well. Tharp received a very generous choreographic commission, with only one stipulation: the commissioned dance had to be set to music of an Australian composer. She knew nothing about Australian music and she started listening to everything she could get her hands on. Linda Shelton hired an assistant to comb through the record stores, while Tharp was working on the new piece. Rather late in the game, she discovered Bruce Smeaton, a well-known composer of Australian motion-picture and television music. Tharp thought Smeaton would know just how to make a score to fit the dance she had under way. Smeaton, on the other hand, knew Tharp's reputation as a groundbreaker and saw the commission as a chance to do some serious experimenting of his own. For once he wouldn't have to score someone else's work. They met once in New York, but their ideas never connected.

A month before the tour's February 2 opening, Tharp was still waiting for the score. She told *The New York Times* the dance material was ready. It had to do with "my frank admiration for the Marx Brothers and for that approach to the dilemmas of life." Smeaton was experimenting with "human voice. Grunts, yawns, gurgles and snorts . . . plus some snatches of unintelligible language," and he wasn't sure if Tharp would like it. When she got it, she found it unusable.

There was no good way out of this situation. Tharp had already spent most of her commission during the months of making the dance and it was too late to rethink. There were internal discussions about giving back the money, but that would probably have meant canceling the whole tour, since all the publicity had been built on Tharp's making a special Bicentennial piece. Finally Linda Shelton suggested there might be some other Tharp material suited to Smeaton's concept. *Assorted Quartets*, already a recycled product, proved adaptable again. Rawe and Way, Colton and Spencer, did most of the work to cut and splice, and to apply portions of Smeaton. The piece was retitled *Four Down Under*. The composer was understandably crushed when he discovered Tharp was only using two of the fourteen movements in his fifty-minute score. But he went to rehearsals in Melbourne and graciously threw a dinner party for the dancers on opening night.

Four Down Under wasn't presented as brand-new. Fudging tactfully, Shelley Washington told an interviewer the piece was "an ideal introduction to Tharp's work. . . . It doesn't have an Australian theme, it's simply the highlights of eight or nine years of work." Washington did identify the source after the Australian tour, when *Four Down Under* was performed briefly on the West Coast. Melbourne critic Neil Jillett described *Four Down Under* as "vigorously gymnastic fun and games accompanied by bursts of silences and part of a score (dabba-dabba-doo vocals and twangings from a Jew's harp, set to a vaguely didgeridoo beat)." As a bonus for the Australians, Tharp premiered the new piece she'd been making under the title *Untitled*, accompanied by a collage of musical selections ranging from Michael Jackson to Spike Jones. Neil Jillett called it "one of Tharp's elegantly devised choreographic grab-bags," incorporating break dancing, a classical solo to Bach by Gil Boggs, hysterical laughing, and blue jokes. Throughout the tour the company was rapturously received. *Nine Sinatra Songs* and *In the Upper Room* were the biggest hits, but *Untitled* got good reviews. A year later it morphed into *Bum's Rush* at American Ballet Theater.

The company threw one of its inimitable benefits midway through the winter-spring tour, at the Silvercup Studios in Queens, on 1 May 1988. The feature of the evening was a Tharp dance choreographed for the company and then taught to the patrons, with a few civilians assigned to each dancer. After rehearsal, the dancers stepped off the floor and let the patrons perform the dance. Longtime Tharp admirer and donor Patsy Tarr remembers having a hard time keeping up with the movement, and at one point grabbing on to Kevin O'Day's belt so she wouldn't get lost. Despite the upbeat celebrations and the months of well-received touring, the future of the company was more problematic than ever. A two-week July workshop in New York was announced, with Rudner, Rose Marie Wright, and Stacy Caddell of the New York City Ballet teaching alongside the company. At the end of June they were just back from performing in Spoleto/Charleston and Portugal when *Newsday* reported that the company had "temporarily disbanded," with the dancers on salaried vacation and no further performances scheduled. Late in the summer the public learned what was in store. As of August 22, Tharp was to become an artistic associate at American Ballet Theater. Mikhail Baryshnikov announced that "core members" of the Tharp company would join ABT with her.

Tharp had revealed the dramatic move to the whole company in a meeting, but instead of offering them a chance to come along, as she'd done in earlier rollovers, she had already decided who would go with her to ABT. "It was a harder moment," says Richard Colton. Tharp then met individually with the dancers; Amy Spencer received a check for several months of salary and returned to Martha Clarke. Rawe and Way had been edging out of the company for a while and took the opportunity to make their exit. The rest of the dancers were recent arrivals and, except for Daniel Sanchez, they were let go. Tharp took up the new post with Sanchez, Bishton, O'Day, Washington, and Colton, as well as ABT crossovers Kudo and Boggs.

Baryshnikov pushed to implement this unusual plan. The dancers were given one-year contracts. It took some intricate negotiating to install them at the highest levels possible without alienating the ABT dancers. Kudo and Boggs resumed their former soloist rankings. Longtime Tharp dancers Colton and Washington also became soloists, along with ballet-trained Kevin O'Day, who'd danced with the Joffrey II before joining Tharp in 1984. Bishton and Sanchez entered at corps de ballet level, since both of them were primarily modern dancers. Tharp's dancers were apprehensive about becoming members of a premier ballet organization, but as usual they relished a new challenge.

Total integration of the two companies didn't quite happen. ABT had a history of embracing but effectively marginalizing elements that didn't assimilate to its classical image. There were Negro and Spanish units in place at the company's inauguration in 1940, for instance, and Agnes de Mille brought in a package of outstanding African-American women for her 1965 ballet *The Four Marys*. The Tharp unit did the Tharp ballets, of course, and found slots in the rest of the repertory. The arrangement was hard for them. They weren't dancing nearly as often as they were accustomed to, but it took constant work to stay in shape for high-powered pieces like *In the Upper Room*. Although they weren't strictly classical dancers, they took character roles in the ballets. Shelley Washington mimed a memorable Madge the Witch in *La Sylphide.* Bishton and O'Day were paired as Sancho Panza and Don Quixote. O'Day danced in Paul Taylor's *Airs,* one of the modern dances Baryshnikov had acquired for ABT. Bishton remembers the sojourn as a wonderful opportunity to get a ballet education. He appeared in all the Agnes de Mille works and enjoyed playing townsmen in the big story ballets. He even danced in the corps of white-tight ballets like *Sleeping Beauty.*

Not all the ABT dancers learned the existing Tharp repertory, but she choreographed some of them into all four of her next new works. *In the Upper Room* and *The Fugue* entered the repertory right away. Then she decided to stage an evening of new ballets that would showcase what she could do with the exemplary dancer resources at her disposal. Baryshnikov gave her carte blanche. The company began phasing in *Everlast, Bum's Rush,* and *Quartet* during its winter tour, and the program made its debut at the Met in June of 1989. The effort cost a fortune and was tepidly received by the New York press. Baryshnikov enlisted his patron, the Howard Gilman Foundation, to cover the reported $575,000 cost of the venture with a loan to the company. The new program was a survey of Tharp styles from ballet to Broadway to bizarre, and the Tharpian suavity that the public loved in *Sinatra* and *The Little Ballet* was missing. *In the Upper Room* brought the evening to a heady climax.

Quartet was set to "G Song" by the important postminimalist composer Terry Riley, who was working in a more meditative vein than the stentorian Glass. The eleven-minute set of continuous variations on a G-minor scale, against a descending four-note basso ostinato, was played by the Kronos Quartet on tape. Tharp's first-cast quartet of dancers comprised ballerinas Cynthia Gregory and Cynthia Harvey partnered by the young classicists Ricardo Bustamante and Guillaume Graffin. *Quartet* made a striking counterpart to the *Upper Room*—compact and almost austere where the Glass was extravagant, quiet rather than aggressive and noisy. Like Jerome Robbins's duet *Afternoon of a Faun,* another small ballet that drew a big stage around itself, it achieved a rare feeling of intimacy. Chance encounters consolidated into brief social exchanges and tiny quadrilles. The dancers sailed through Tharp's transitionless step combinations, jumps, and leaps, completing the step with generous arm gestures that swept across the body or spiraled upward, a bit like Spanish dancing.

Quartet was downplayed by all the critics. Perhaps even Tharp thought of it as a trifle among the flamboyant attractions of the rest of the program.

With *Everlast* she was making another try at a Broadway show, perhaps to atone for *Singin' in the Rain* and cull what she had learned from that bitter experience. During the waning days of her own company she'd audited screenwriting courses at Columbia University's film school, searching for a way of putting a narrative together in dance form. The solution, which she applied again thirteen years later for her first true Broadway hit, *Movin' Out*, was to stitch together a line of existing songs that would convey the emotional tone of the story and leave the dancers unencumbered by dialogue. For *Everlast* they were Jerome Kern songs, familiar and unfamiliar, performed by an onstage trio of singers. Tharp expected that *Everlast*, as a condensed musical, would herald a future full-length popular ballet that would "be a financial godsend for the company several seasons from now."

The plot unfolded through solos and small ensemble dances marked with personal traits and narrative development, just as in a traditional story ballet. At Columbia she'd met film writer James Jones, who supplied a scenario, no flimsier than the average Broadway show or story ballet, and the plot made only enough demand on the audience to see it through forty minutes of dancing. Kevin O'Day played a famous prizefighter hooked into a betrothal of convenience with a financially embarrassed debutante (Susan Jaffe). O'Day's adoring fan (Anne Adair) masquerades as his sparring partner, knocks him out by accident, and is eventually recognized as his true love. The wedding in shambles, Jaffe pairs off with one of her many playboy suitors and everyone joins in a joyous finale.

Tharp slipped in ballet references, without making fun of them as she'd done in *Push Comes to Shove*. Just when Jaffe and O'Day are about to be married, Adair hovers around them and distracts the hero, who runs off after her like James lured by the Sylphide. O'Day discovers the cross-dressing ingenue is a girl when her cap is pulled off and her long hair tumbles down. But for the happy ending she has to exit and come back in a dress, recalling the transformation of the tomboyish heroine in de Mille's *Rodeo*. Once the plot is untangled, the whole ensemble struts downstage in lines, to the song "Who" arranged in march time, a windup worthy of *Stars and Stripes*.

Everlast worked like a show, and like a story ballet. But Tharp's dance style by now had traveled some distance from the casual resilience of her *Baker's Dozen* days. She'd worked up a vocabulary of fighting moves and tough-guy attitudes during her comeback/farewell period around *Fait Accompli*, and along the way the style had lost some of its wittiness. In absorbing pointe work the dancers' bodies had somehow grown more upright and less articulate. This didn't matter in a formal dance like the *Quartet*, or a tough, spectacular marathon like *In the Upper Room*, but it didn't suit the light, rhythmic score for *Everlast*. Arlene Croce analyzed the work in terms of the music. Jerome Kern's songs evoked the Princess shows of the jazz age, but Tharp's treatment lacked their charm.

Bum's Rush had been developing for almost five years. Even before the tryouts on tour in Australia, Tharp had taken up the subject of her family again. Jamie Bishton remembers working on phrases when he first joined the company, with himself and Kevin O'Day as the twins and Liz Foldi as Tharp's sister, Twanette. Tharp was to dance in it then too, and John Guare was on the scene to write the libretto. The sibling story was abandoned, but the material carried over into *Bum's Rush*, and resurfaced again in *Movin' Out*. "It keeps coming back, this autobiographical piece," says Bishton. Rhoda Grauer remembers the dance as "all anger, fighting, being bamboozled. All bum's rush." Tharp and the dancers gave a preview at the Guggenheim Museum as a part of the "Works and Process" series. In all seriousness and amusement, she told a crowd of connoisseurs that the Madhouse Trio (Bishton, O'Day, and Sanchez in place of Foldi) was "exactly what life in my household was like," only more disciplined.

Bum's Rush was a dance about death, about farting in the face of death. The last thing a corpse does, Tharp had learned, is to break wind. For Kudo and Boggs she made a Wind Duet. "With death just around the corner, cruelty doesn't seem so unthinkable." The cruelty she meant was found in burlesque comedy and the nasty games of children. Washington and Colton were hobo-clowns, making funny faces and bopping each other around. Ever since *When We Were Very Young* Washington had developed extreme acting skills, and she had no problem with being grotesque; she threw laughing fits and pushed Colton down while yelling the name John! for as long as she could, then the whole sequence went into retrograde: Nohhhjjj! ABT dancer Sandra Brown appeared on pointe inside a B. F. Goodrich tractor tire. Danny Sanchez did a break dance number and told dirty jokes, which were excised after the Chicago premiere. Colton and Boggs had a leaping duet. The piece was a jumble, a surrealistic cartoon. Croce thought it brought out the Katzenjammer Kid in Tharp. The audience was puzzled but entertained.

As the 1980s drew to a close, values were shifting in the dance world. Baryshnikov, like Peter Martins at New York City Ballet, had taken on the leadership of a major ballet company from its founders. Reorientation was inevitable but so was resistance to change. Many critics still didn't approve of the way NYCB was evolving, and Martins was on the defensive in the late '80s as he tried to preserve the Balanchine tradition but invigorate the dancers with new choreographic energy. ABT supporters were divided about Baryshnikov's virtual elimination of the star system and his invitations to choreographic outlanders like Mark Morris, Karole Armitage, and David Gordon to do new ballets. He took a lot of criticism for his own big ballets, an expensive *Cinderella*, co-choreographed with Peter Anastos, and a new *Swan Lake*.

After nine years with ABT, Baryshnikov was restless. Now forty, he was moving out of the demanding virtuoso roles. Running a big company, with its associated administrative and fund-raising burdens, was as unappealing to him as it was to Tharp. He began withdrawing from the company's day-to-day operations, acting in a Broadway production of Kafka's *Metamorphosis*, and spending more and more time in Europe. Rumors surfaced that he was considering a post at the Berlin Opera Ballet. In another startling crossover, Mark Morris had moved his modern dance company to the Théâtre de la Monnaie in Brussels in 1988. Baryshnikov found Morris a congenial working partner. He'd made an attractive new piece for ABT, *Drink to Me Only with Thine Eyes*, with a role for Baryshnikov that suited him splendidly. In the fall of '89 Baryshnikov danced in the premiere of Morris's *Wonderland* at the Monnaie, and they soon co-founded the White Oak Dance Project under the patronage of Howard Gilman. White Oak was essentially a continuation of Baryshnikov's summer touring ensembles, oriented to contemporary and postmodern dance rather than ballet.

Right after the all-Tharp program in June 1989, Baryshnikov announced his resignation from ABT. He planned to stay another year, to see the company through its fiftieth anniversary celebrations, but internal conflicts with executive director Jane Hermann grew worse and he left suddenly, on 25 September. Tharp and fellow artistic associate Kenneth MacMillan resigned rather than keep their posts during the search for a new company head. It's pretty clear that Tharp wanted to play a bigger role at ABT than resident choreographer with an in-house stable of dancers. She pictured herself as a mighty Robin Hood of the dance world, a lone individual standing up to the big institutions and entrenched adversaries of true art making. She characterized the three new ballets, in retrospect at least, as calculated to conquer American Ballet Theater's established fiefdoms: "American" (*Everlast*), "Ballet" (*Quartet*), and "Theater" (*Bum's Rush*). She expected the company to appreciate what she was doing for it. Not only did her ballets have cachet, she assured writer Sasha Anawalt in a *New York Times* interview, they were good for the dancers. Still, even before the collapse of the shelter Baryshnikov had provided for her, in April of 1989 she had forebodings. "*Bum's Rush* stands for finality," she told the "Works and Process" audience. "We're all bums at the mercy of the history of death. Being thrown out. Forcible ejection. Abrupt dismissal."

Once she dropped off the company roster, Bishton and O'Day were left with jobs in Ballet Theater and no Tharp company as refuge. Shelley Washington had essentially stopped dancing but she remained as ballet mistress for the Tharp repertory. Her staging of *Nine Sinatra Songs* premiered in early 1990. Richard Colton and Amy Spencer, who had married during *Singin' in the Rain*, accepted an offer to teach and choreograph at Concord Academy in Massachusetts.

For the fiftieth anniversary gala, 14 January 1990, a three-hour marathon of live and filmed excerpts from Ballet Theater's history, Tharp prepared a fast-paced video survey of the eight dances she had made for the company. She also offered excerpts from her newest work, ironically titled *Brief Fling*. As a delightful bonus she made a surprise appearance substituting for the departed Baryshnikov in the last movement of *Push Comes to Shove*. Was she modeling herself as a candidate for the real-life role of artistic director?

Brief Fling began as a straightforward exposition of the building blocks of ballet. To a drumroll, small groups entered one at a time and displayed their goods: ballerina and danseur, corps de ballet, character dancers, and stompers. It was Tharp's mixed gathering again, only here the stompers were the interlopers, "these modern people that were plowing through this ballet world," Jamie Bishton thought. Fashion designer Isaac Mizrahi gave them funky outfits in color-coded imitation tartans. As soon as the introductions ended, the principal couple began a prim little variation to Percy Grainger's *Country Gardens*. From there the ballet went on to explore its own resources, with the groups interweaving and exceeding their own limits. Although it preserved its plotless formality, the ballet worked its way through dramatic and unexpected possibilities, greatly aided by composer Michel Columbier's juxtaposition of Grainger's settings of folk tunes with his own postmodernist rhythms and moods. The whole thing ended with a fugue for each of the group voices and a procession of the clans, entering across the footlights in a slow farandole reminiscent of *Deuce Coupe*.

Tharp has referred to *Brief Fling* with cold pragmatism: "It was a success but it offers no discoveries. Everything happened the way it was supposed to, just as in commercial work, because that's what the company required." But it was a great success with the audience and the critics. Arlene Croce thought it was the hit of New York's spring season and "an exhilarating statement of classicism reëngaged." Tharp had finally bowed to the power of hierarchy by sorting out the ranks in order of technical competencies, Croce thought. She had also made inspired choices of dancers, with the Argentinian prodigy Julio Bocca and the young risk-taker Cheryl Yeager as the principal couple. *Brief Fling* looked random and unpredictable at times, but the groups finally came together "in a vision of vernacular/academic parallelism as persuasive as the last act of 'Raymonda' or—the more evident source of Tharp's inspiration—[Balanchine's] 'Union Jack.'"

When the ballet premiered officially at the Met later that year, Deborah Jowitt noted: "The audience's applause amounted to a mandate to ABT's new directors. I hope they listened well." But Tharp had serious temperamental and artistic differences with Jane Hermann. The budget-minded administrator was going in a conservative direction—Croce thought it looked "as if she would rather appeal to the audience's weaknesses than to the company's strengths." Money was a big issue with Hermann, who later complained to the *Times* that Tharp's ballets could cost the company $100,000, three or four times what other choreographers charged for a work. There was no question that Tharp had enormous talent, energy, productivity, and foresight. She could make successful ballets and inspire dancers. But her brief fling had proven once again that neither she nor her ballets fared well under the severe schedules and harried personnel, the economies and box office pressures, of touring repertory life in America. After getting *Brief Fling* safely launched, she let the licenses on her ballets lapse. She didn't make another work for American Ballet Theater for five years.

II

The Anti-company
1990–1995

The long process of freeing herself from company responsibilities was now complete. It had been five years since Tharp put a hold on the touring and diverted the dancers into *Singin' in the Rain*. While the company was retrograding toward its planned extinction, she made comparatively few in-house dances—*In the Upper Room* and *Ballare,* and the four ABT ballets. In between, she was rehearsing what it would be like to have a different life, as writer, filmmaker, freelance choreographer.

Toward the end of 1985 Tharp asked the writer Laura Shapiro to work with her on an autobiographical book. She had started documenting her career at least twice before, with writers Don McDonagh and Allen Robertson, but neither effort progressed very far. Shapiro, one of Tharp's most devoted fans and an outstanding member of the new generation of dance writers, had been reviewing Tharp's work since the '70s, from Boston, then Seattle. Now based in New York, she had become the dance critic for *Newsweek*, where she also wrote about books, women's issues, and food. She had just finished her first book, *Perfection Salad—Women and Cooking at the Turn of the Century*, a sparkling contribution to cultural history. For the collaboration, Tharp would do a set of interlinear comments on a narrative by Shapiro. They worked closely together and within three years both components of the book were finished. Shapiro doesn't remember if they settled on a title, but as co-authors they held a contract with publisher Henry Holt.

Late in 1988 Tharp circulated the manuscript among some respected associates, among them Jacqueline Onassis, then an editor at Doubleday. Tharp wasn't happy with the editors at Henry Holt and began looking for another publisher. Shapiro isn't sure of the time frame, but Tharp at some point wanted to make their book less journalistic, more of a comprehensive in-depth study. Shapiro felt this ran counter to her own intentions, and Tharp terminated the deal, withdrawing the book from Henry Holt in the process. It seems to have been Onassis who encouraged Tharp to write the whole book herself. She started over from the beginning to write her life singlehanded, from a more personal standpoint. She also came to think of the story as a guidebook for women who aspired to a career in the arts. *Push Comes to Shove* was published in 1992 by Bantam Books, a division of Doubleday.

Shapiro was devastated not to see the original work come to fruition, but she understood Tharp's thinking. "I was writing a portrait of a fabulous artist in midcareer," she says now, "but it wasn't a monument to her genius." Shapiro considered herself a journalist who'd undertaken a shared project, and, with perspective, the cancelation seemed "more like losing a job than losing something I had made myself." In any case, the project had allowed her access to Tharp's rehearsals during the making of *In the Upper Room*, and that had been immensely satisfying. "I had such a crush on her work," she says. She remained friends with Tharp but vowed not to work with her again.

Push Comes to Shove turned out to be a curious but highly readable document, part memoir, part confessional, part psychoanalytic bubble wrap. The story of Tharp's choreographic trajectory is there, festooned with hyperbolic flashbacks and steamy bedroom revelations, encounters with the culturati and accolades for her dancer cohorts. It reads like an extended script for one of her videos—smart, sardonic, outspoken, entertaining, and deadly serious all the way. Margo Jefferson, who reviewed it for *The New York Times Book Review*, thought "it uncannily captures the sensibility of her dances. That teen-age girl with the flashlight [Tharp inspecting the cars at her mother's drive-in], voyeur and analyst, parsing the spectacle and longing to invade it, is the adult choreographer we've come to know so well."

Always attracted to movies and moviemakers, Tharp did a tradeoff in 1987 with Robert Redford, staging some folk dances, uncredited, for his activist film about Latino farm workers struggling against developers, *The Milagro Beanfield War*. In return, Redford lent his name as honorary chair for her company's benefit party on the opening night of their 1987 BAM season. The gossip columnists fussed over whether he would show up—he attended the performance but not the party. During a hiatus in a tour that fall, the company stayed at Redford's Sundance film colony in Utah, rehearsing for a big AIDS benefit concert at the New York State Theater. It looked as if Tharp and Redford might have some larger project in mind, but although she returned to Sundance for a while to work on her book in 1990, nothing materialized. Around that time, Tharp was also auditing classes in screenwriting at Columbia University's film school. She says this study taught her how to tell a story in dance; it may also have helped her plot the autobiography.

Shortly after moving to ABT, with the company rehearsed for *In the Upper Room* and a leg up on her three-part ballet evening, she headed for Paris, where Rudolf Nureyev, then artistic director of the Paris Opera Ballet, had invited her to make a new work. She took Richard Colton along to stage *As Time Goes By* for the French dancers. *Rules of the Game* had its premiere on 18 February 1989, alongside revivals of Léonide Massine's *Les Présages* and Balanchine's *Agon*. Once again Tharp violated the rules of ballet hierarchy by giving featured roles to young dancers as well as étoiles in her cast of four soloists with a four-man, four-woman corps. She was particularly taken with Lionel Delanoé, "a young man from the lower ranks of the company," according to Dale Harris, but "a potential star." The project was not without scandal. The prodigious Sylvie Guillem, whom Tharp had made the centerpiece of the ballet, suddenly refused to participate and later left the company to join the Royal Ballet. Tharp said she had to rebuild and recast the work in a week.

Rules of the Game, like *Push Comes to Shove*, poked a little fun at the mores and mannerisms of the host company. Tharp used a Bach violin sonata, augmented with fully orchestrated variations by Michel Columbier. After an opening procession of haughty solos, the ballet proceeded to a Tharpian take on classicism. "Her phrases twist, hiccup and backtrack, bodies move in several different directions and at several speeds at once; serene classicism and utter chaos meet at every moment," wrote the London-based critic Barbara Newman. Anna Kisselgoff thought it was a "serious and fine work" despite its jokey references to the costume and design conventions at the Opéra. Kisselgoff noted perceptively that ". . . despite all her attempts to integrate herself into the world of classical ballet, Miss Tharp remains an out-sider looking in—a modern dancer who does not take the classical idiom for granted, and who cannot resist examining its parts under a microscope." The Paris audience adored the ballet, "rhythmically slow-clapping Tharp and cast through a long series of curtain calls," according to Allen Robertson.

Back in New York, the ABT politics were heating up to a boil. But Tharp had something else on the fire. During this uneasy sojourn after the demise of Tharp Dance, there was no vehicle for producing her repertory, other than those items deemed suitable for ABT. The popular early dances like *Sue's Leg* and *The Golden Section* had no current interpreters. Tharp claimed to have no interest in maintaining the repertory herself, but perhaps she could cultivate an existing group of dancers to perform her works credibly. That way, she wouldn't have to support a company but the dances would be seen, and would be producing income for her and the reconstructors she dele-gated to oversee them.

By now she had enlisted several dancers to help pass works on and re-hearse them: Rose Marie Wright, Jennifer Way, Shelley Washington, and Richard Colton, as well as the ballet mistresses Rebecca Wright and Susan Jones. Through Linda Shelton's contacts, Tharp worked out an arrangement with Hubbard Street Dance Chicago, a medium-size company of excellent modern dancers specializing in contemporary work. The deal started with a $300,000 three-year contract for *The Fugue* and *Sue's Leg*. Hubbard Street's artistic director, Lou Conte, a longtime Tharp fan, became even more ad-miring as he saw the depth and musicality of the way she worked, and he thought Tharp's unusually high price was well worth it. Jennifer Way and Rose Marie Wright rehearsed the company but Tharp made six trips to Chicago during the summer to initiate the dancers and supervise the pro-cess. The dances were shown for the first time in August 1990, at Jacob's Pil-low. Eventually, under Shelley Washington's direction, Hubbard Street did six Tharp revivals over a ten-year period, plus an original, *I Remember Clifford* (1995).

Washington had begun to feel uncomfortable with holding down a soloist's rank and salary in Ballet Theater. She was dancing only *Brief Fling* and the odd character part in the ballets and Tharp works. She hadn't thought of herself as anything but a dancer, but she was in her mid-thirties and she realized she couldn't continue to dance as intensively as she had in the Tharp company. With Richard Colton she had been in charge of the Australian tour, and her acute memory and enjoyment of detail proved to be an asset in devising rehearsal and performance schedules. She asked to be named a ballet mistress at ABT, first acting as Tharp's assistant on the revivals and new works. "She kind of just guided me," Washington says, "and then, when they decided they were gonna do *Upper Room*, I just took it and did it because I knew it. I knew what I was doing." She eased into the Hubbard Street assignment in the second phase of the project, with *Baker's Dozen*, and directing for Tharp became her full-time occupation.

A frequent winner of awards and citations, Tharp now began to collect some big ones. In 1990 the American Dance Festival gave her the $25,000 Scripps Award, an annual prize established by generous benefactor Samuel H. Scripps to recognize a choreographer who makes a significant lifetime contribution to the field. Tharp didn't have a company to do a performance, and she resisted traveling to North Carolina to accept the award at the festival, now based at Duke University. Finally she agreed to a solo residency and asked the festival to hold a square dance so that the whole community could celebrate with her. Director Charles Reinhart arranged for the invitations, music, and decorations. According to legend, Tharp gave a severe lecture to the students, which she would not allow the festival to record, danced a few sets at her square dance party, and went straight to the airport. Reinhart says Tharp's eccentricities never offended him. "She's gonna give me what she's got, at the time. But the love is always there."

A year later, after ABT had given its last all-Tharp program (a blockbuster: *Push Comes to Shove, Nine Sinatra Songs,* and *In the Upper Room*), she was named the first recipient of the $50,000 Wexner Prize. Given by the Wexner Center for the Arts at Ohio State University, the prize was set up to honor "a living artist whose career has been one of constant exploration and innovation." The prize was underwritten by Columbus businessman Leslie H. Wexner, a major donor to the spectacular modern art museum designed for the campus by Peter Eisenman and Richard Trott, which had opened in the fall of 1989. The Wexner Center took Minneapolis's Walker Art Center as a model for sponsoring creative work in the visual, media, and performing arts. Along with the Wexner Prize, Tharp received one of three first-time Residency Awards. She started assembling a company and planning for a complex, six-week assault on the campus that was to culminate in two public performances at the three thousand-seat Mershon Auditorium in the fall of 1991.

Kevin O'Day, feeling restless in ABT, had called Tharp early in 1991 to see if she wanted to get back in the studio and work. They started making duet material in a space at City Center. A new group piece, *Octet,* also got under way. By the end of the summer she had assembled a sixteen-member ensemble with a finite life span and the title Twyla Tharp and Dancers. In addition to her old associates O'Day, Bishton, Keith Young, and Shelley Washington as ballet mistress, she pulled in a stellar assortment of ballet and modern dancers. Thrilled to work with Tharp again after their experience on a 1990 revival of *Brahms/Handel,* New York City Ballet dancers Stacy Caddell, Shawn Stevens, and Allison Brown joined up. Robert La Fosse, then a principal at NYCB, took an extended leave to work with Tharp. She "borrowed" Lionel Delanoé, Stephane Elizabé, and Delphine Moussin from the Paris Opera Ballet. Jodi Melnick, a gifted protégée of Sara Rudner, and six other dancers with varied résumés completed the roster. The company was perceived as ballet oriented, perhaps because of the prestigious backgrounds of the ballet contingent, but it was in fact another fusion group. Tharp's next new dances were pointe ballets, but she also brought back some of her pre-pointe works, with the ballet dancers assimilated into them.

Officially the Ohio residency began in August, with a special workshop in the Dance Department given by Rudner and Mary Ann Kellogg, who had moved to Tucson and was heading into film and television work. In addition to repertory and video studies, a daily technique class included body-sensitive Iyengar yoga work with Kellogg. When the company arrived early in September, *Octet* was nearly completed. Washington taught repertory— the two different Mershon programs included another revision of *Deuce Coupe, The Little Ballet* with La Fosse in the Baryshnikov role, *The Golden Section,* and the two new works. Meanwhile Tharp continued working with O'Day and the men. She intended to dance in the men's piece herself—she hadn't really performed since the pre-ABT days of her company—and she began each day giving herself a warm-up, then improvising and dancing privately for a video camera. For several hours she worked with the men, separately and in groups, and after a late afternoon visit to the gym, she reviewed the morning's taped phrases in her hotel room to skim off the usable parts. She toyed with several titles—*Solid Men to the Front, The Men We Love*—called it *Untitled* in Columbus, but settled on *Men's Piece* when the dance was given in New York.

There were other activities on campus, including open rehearsals and a Wexner-sponsored Tharp film series. A performance of *The One Hundreds* almost got squeezed out of the schedule but Jamie Bishton learned the first fifty phrases and five other company members headed teams of five students each. Tharp made a highly publicized payback to the university by donating her archives to OSU's Jerome Lawrence and Robert E. Lee Theater Research Institute. At a press conference she likened the gift to a Native American potlatch, the custom of returning one's good fortune to the community. Besides her files of press clippings, choreographic notes, company records and correspondence, photographs, costumes and designs, and her personal collection of books and music, the Institute was to get her hundreds of rehearsal and performance videotapes—as soon as they were copied from their original, perishable formats.

Tharp presented the Ohio State performances of *Men's Piece/Untitled* as a work in progress, and also as a "World Premiere." By this time what started in the studio as an informal exploration of partnering had acquired several layers of performance ideas, and Tharp was not reticent about revealing them. *Men's Piece* contained three interlocking forms: a series of duets for Tharp and Kevin O'Day, a structured and rehearsed work session with Tharp as the choreographer and Bishton, Elizabé, and Young as her willing crew of dancers; and a lecture-demonstration in comedy-club style. Tharp thereby got to play all three of her roles at once: dancer, choreographer, and conceptualizer.

After improvising alone to the Gershwin song "Love Is Here to Stay," she gave a scripted running commentary on the rest of the piece. The twenty short duets she'd made, she said, centered around the question of partnering—what did it mean for a man and a woman to dance together in the '90s? Besides that, there was the matter of work and play, illustrated by a tape laid down the center of the stage floor, with the O'Day duets on one side and the three-man drills on the other. Could they be made to coexist? These questions touched off hilarious philosophizing and one liners about the most serious issues of her life. Tharp had concocted this professorial, half-mocking tone very early, in *All About Eggs* and the open rehearsals, to entertain the audience while making sure they understood her highly serious purposes. As she danced less, she found more ways to use this talk medium.

The gist of the narrative was Tharp's pursuit of a kind of equality between men and women. She was no outspoken feminist although she'd had great success as an independent artist and entrepreneur. Somehow, in both the duets and the ensemble sections, her dance overcompensated. The three men followed her lead but ended up looking foolish. She probably wanted to send up traditional role patterns but instead she reversed them, becoming the macho boss to their submissive workers. Bishton remembers one sequence he had with Keith Young where "she wanted us to go from really strong, military, very masculine, and then drop it and come downstage in this whirlwind flurry, and just dance dance dance and go back upstage and become militarist again."

In the O'Day duets, she proposed various unworkable formulas for men and women to dance together in one another's arms, after the depredations of the Twist, "which is what tore men and women apart and put them into the disco's little *podulettes* of randomly gyrating egos." This funny line, accompanied by film clips of terribly refined, bouffant-headed twisters from the '60s, sidesteps the liberating effect that the Twist actually had on American culture, not to mention its influence on Tharp's own dance style.

In a yodeling duet, or canon, she followed O'Day's movements, but this didn't work because it was built on only one theme. She tried a "bar scene" pickup and he brushed her off. They burlesqued a role-reversal episode, she as a beer-swilling football fan, he in frat-house drag, pushing a mop. Astaire and Rogers represented only a romantic fantasy: "It would be perfection to think you could calculate every move [but] love includes an element of uncertainty." Finally, they worked out an "isometric improvisation" in which, she said, they would exert opposing but equal forces, like Romanesque vaults in buildings engineered to withstand earthquakes. She concluded with one of her greatest aphorisms: "Love is the art of constant maintenance." As the critic Tullia Limarzi noted, Tharp was a little late in her attack on sexual clichés. A younger generation of "Contact Improvisation, gay, lesbian and straight experimentalist choreographers have already come up with many more exciting and original variations on dance coupling."

Tharp had now been working on the duet form for fifteen years, since *Once More, Frank.* The culminating *Men's Piece* encounter evoked the intimate 1976 Sinatra footage on *Making Television Dance,* except that unlike the young Baryshnikov, who shared her sensuality, Kevin O'Day approached the problem in a pragmatic, objective way. Tharp now was a more cautious dancer. They might have been doing equal amounts of work, but most of the time he was hefting and hauling, while she hung on to his back and slithered round his body. Visually she was his dependent, even his incubus, despite the matching inner mechanics. Tharp's movement style by now was vastly different from what her dancers were doing, and not only because she was fifty. She was proud of the number of pounds she could bench-press, but it wasn't her muscular definition that made her a classy dancer. She moved from the center and close to the center, with innumerable small articulations and rhythmic subtleties, a dynamo of variable energy. Audiences sat spellbound during her solo, but the final duet provoked laughter.

Some of Tharp's range of small-movement possibilities carried over into the *Octet*. She now had enough ballet women of her own to develop what she'd started at ABT in *Quartet*. Dressed by Loquasto in severe black—halter tops and shorts for the women, pants and tank tops for the men—the dancers maintained a strict male-female division except when they sorted themselves into couples. They flashed reversed-gender gestures as the ballet began: the women slinking on with muscle-man arms, the men leading into a step with a shoulder or a hip, their arms akimbo. But these were mere affectations; what Tharp proposed was another exploration of partnering. She seems to have taken several Balanchinian lifts and balances as a text for elaboration.

The choreography was completely formal, but Edgar Meyer's music for electric guitar, double bass, and percussion ("The Plumed Serpent") went from funky, bluesy rhythms to misterioso tensions and agitato bow work, and created a dramatic atmosphere in which you could almost detect a story, tinted by David Finn's moody lighting. Partnered mostly from behind, the women seemed enmeshed in elaborate games of capture and escape. The dance became more and more strange, as the women wrapped their limbs around the men and were sprung into splits from behind and lifted into billowing arcs. After barely fifteen minutes, the music jittered up and up, and the women bourréed backwards, threading their way through the leaping and turning men. As the music reached its stratospheric high note, they rejoined their partners for one final supported spin, then snapped into a face-to-face embrace just before a blackout.

After a break, Tharp gathered the company together in New York for a two-week City Center season (28 January–9 February 1992) followed by a late-February tour of Japan. Then the group was scheduled to disband. At City Center they presented the same repertory as in Columbus, with the addition of *Nine Sinatra Songs*, *Ocean's Motion*, and two more new works. In exchange for the three Paris Opera dancers, Tharp had created a showpiece for étoile Isabelle Guérin and Patrick Dupond, who had succeeded Nureyev as director of the Ballet. The two stars danced *Grand Pas: Rhythm of the Saints* on opening night in New York; then Guérin stayed on for the rest of the run to dance it with Lionel Delanoé. She also appeared in the *Sinatra Songs* and Tharp's other premiere, *Sextet.*

The *Grand Pas*, a variant of ballet's showstopper format, was in some sense a miscalculation. Tharp set her duet to selections from Paul Simon's recent foray into Afro-fusion, "Rhythm of the Saints." Within what was supposed to be a high-tech display, she inserted unpredictable stops and starts that squelched applause, as the dancers put on everyday moves and over-the-top attitudes. The audience was confused. Nancy Goldner thought the false endings were intentional, that Tharp had gambled on the audience to play along with her super-campy effects, but most of the other critics passed over it lightly. "An egregiously empty bit of fluff," reported Jennifer Dunning.

Sextet was similarly lightweight, although Anna Kisselgoff thought it "an inspired piece of work, a laid-back tropical equivalent of the love dances she created in her big hit, 'Nine Sinatra Songs.'" *Sextet* was originally commissioned by a pickup group of New York City Ballet and ABT dancers who were planning a tour led by NYCB principal Damian Woetzel. The cast included Susan Jaffe partnered by Woetzel, Kelly Cass and Guillaume Graffin, Isabella Padovani and Keith Roberts, just the kind of adventurous and technically terrific dancers Tharp loved. According to Jaffe, before Tharp settled on the music, the tour was canceled, and after a studio showing—probably in the summer of 1991—the original cast never performed it. They do appear, rehearsing with Tharp, on PBS's prestigious *Dancing* series. Another of Rhoda Grauer's brainchildren, *Dancing* aimed to survey world dance in eight installments. Program Seven, "Modernizing Dance," covered the evolving notions of the twentieth-century avant-garde, from Isadora Duncan and Ruth St. Denis through Digahilev, Balanchine, Graham, Cunningham, and the postmoderns, using Tharp as a kind of throughline to articulate the unflinching individualism that seemed to define the whole century of tradition breakers.

Transferring the *Sextet* to her post-Wexner group, Tharp commissioned a carnivalesque, Latinoesque score from the eclectic composer Bob Telson, and the dance blended balleticisms with flouncy, sexy display. Robert La Fosse and Delphine Moussin held center stage, backed by Allison Brown and Lionel Delanoé, Guérin, and Elizabé. Alastair Macaulay, who was filling in while Arlene Croce took a leave of absence from *The New Yorker,* didn't see much substance in the music ("a suite of bubble-rock/Latin numbers that keep up a somewhat relentless pulse and have little fluctuation of tone") or the dance ("the piece creates its own clichés"). But Joseph Mazo compared

Tharp's Latin adaptations to the character dances in classical ballets: ". . . she takes them further from their origins and deeper into classicism than the Russians ever did."

New York was delighted to have a good look at Tharp again and the season did well. For the last four performances the City Center management opened up 568 balcony seats that usually went unsold. Anna Kisselgoff, in a year-end roundup, named *Octet* and *Sextet* as "Premieres that Restored Faith in Twyla Tharp." But some of the old loyalists had misgivings. Linda Winer, in her *Newsday* "Limelight" column, wondered about the viability of the pickup-company concept for Tharp's work. "Dancers, no matter how virtuosic, cannot learn [her style] overnight—especially if they are trained exclusively in ballet. Although some of the old pieces looked terrific, others seemed much too careful, too placed."

Tharp fell into a period of public introspection, prompted in part by her work on the autobiography. Alongside the very private individual who was most comfortable in the studio with her dancers, she constructed a more formidable, outer-directed presence who had a higher calling, a role to play in the greater scheme of American dance history. Balanchine's death had left her without a master to interrogate. She saw herself, as did many critics, as the only successor to Balanchine—with a mission, not to carry on his tradition but to carry it forward. When Martha Graham died in 1991 she felt a new responsibility to the modern dance lineage she had mostly discarded. But Tharp was always more of a dissenter than a leader. Once she broke the rules, others saw new ways to go, but she had little patience for cultivating her own sphere of influence. She spoke of the need for a school and an organization to propel her work, but she had often and openly declared her distaste for the apparatus of institution maintenance. She thought art should be marketable and competitive, and that her dance should be compensated on a par with the work of businessmen and sports stars. But she gradually priced herself out of the market. Every ballet company wanted her dances; few could afford them. Dancers got paid well for her projects, but they had no security and sometimes they worked for free. In 1992 she received a MacArthur "genius" award, with a stipend of $310,000 over five years. The grant did nothing to assuage her restlessness; if anything, she was more determined than ever to preserve the freedom of project mode.

Tharp thought of the *Men's Piece* as a definitive turn toward more dramatic work, although she didn't abandon the pure-dance idiom she was so good at. The *Men's Piece* shifted and refined the parameters she had set in the autobiographical pieces, *When We Were Very Young, The Catherine Wheel,* and *Bum's Rush.* As in *Fait Accompli,* her role in *Men's Piece* both disclosed and fictionalized her personal preoccupations about love, life, and dancing. In an analysis of the parallels between Tharp's career and that of Martha Graham, Arlene Croce compared *Men's Piece* with Graham's self-parody in the form of a rehearsal, *Acrobats of God.* By giving herself a speaking role, Tharp could make her concerns explicit. She took naturally to the role of master of ceremonies, a duty she had often performed in her videos, lectures, and open rehearsals. This funny, brazen, crankily lovable persona could convey some of her most earnest thoughts. Like the narrator of the autobiography, a theatricalized version of herself could elevate her insights and observations into lessons that would benefit everyone.

She even found a way to theatricalize the rehearsal process. In 1993 she hosted a two-week City Center season of repertory, new material, and surprises. Every night she'd invite volunteers onto the stage from the audience, to learn a new phrase along with the company dancers as she demonstrated it. Beginning in 1998, she expanded the *One Hundreds* into a pageant, a retrospective on the '60s, with the original dance concept embedded in a celebration of community. As always, recruits learned their phrases ahead of time from company dancers, but Tharp presided over an evening-long show, talking about her own history, showing videotapes, and conducting audience-participation games and costume competitions. Once the one hundred volunteers had swarmed onto the stage for their eleven-second climax, Tharp would get out in front and do the first several phrases, "teaching" them to the multitudes behind her.

During the early 1990s Tharp continued to juggle several projects at once. She was famous and successful but elusive. Her work became even more spread out. The project companies did limited repertory and new works, sometimes in provisional form. They didn't always play New York, so the critics there either had to travel to her touring venues or miss entire chunks of her development. Her ballet commissions, film, and video work received limited exposure. The public to whom dance mattered—the New York audience and critics she loudly disdained—were still the arbiters, and they were seeing more of Mark Morris and William Forsythe and Pina Bausch than Tharp.

In 1992, after the City Center season and the tour to Japan, Tharp spent some time in Boston overseeing Boston Ballet's revivals of *Brief Fling* and *In the Upper Room*. She then headed off to Hollywood with Jodi Melnick, Jamie Bishton, Shawn Stevens, Allison Brown, Stacy Caddell, Keith Young, and Michael Whaites to make a movie with writer-director James L. Brooks. *I'll Do Anything* was intended to be a groundbreaking musical. Tharp and Brooks rejected the clichéd romanticism of the 1950s MGM model, as well as the more recent Bob Fosse style of kinky pessimism. They wanted to find an upbeat but contemporary way of integrating dancing and singing into a story. None of the leading actors—Nick Nolte, Albert Brooks, Tracey Ullmann, and Julie Kavner—could dance, but the show-business story line seemed to allow for musical numbers. Jodi Melnick remembers scenes in a disco and a restaurant, and a sequence where patrons waiting on line to buy movie tickets suddenly broke into a tap dance.

Tharp looked up her old associate Sharon Kinney, who was living in Los Angeles, and asked her to assist with the staging. Kinney says Tharp was under some pressure at the time because she was already working on her next project. Kinney admired the way Tharp could hold her own among the all-male production team, often showing them how they could shoot the dance numbers effectively, and reshaping her choreography for the cameras. Tharp taught her, Kinney says, "as an artist, woman, dancer, that you go in and you try to make the situation work for you." Despite everyone's high hopes, the movie didn't gel as an integrated piece. When it was shown to preview audiences, they liked either the musical parts or the dramatic parts, but not both. Before the film was released, all the musical numbers and transitions were deleted.

I'll Do Anything was Jodi Melnick's only opportunity to work on new choreography with Tharp. In two seasons she had become another of Tharp's "finds" but after the movie Tharp wanted to work exclusively with ballet women. Melnick was called back for another season with Tharp, in 1993, but she piloted her own career back to downtown New York. She says the experience of creating new work with Tharp was amazing: "What I remember from the movie is being in the studio with her . . . and dancing behind her." Tharp still had the gift, even the appetite, for new dancers. She could walk into a studio and size them up immediately, then challenge them beyond their self-perceived limits. She kept herself in shape for dancing, because she believed her body still had unique information to transmit. She told an interviewer in 1993: "The only reason I keep dancing is because I still discover things that nobody else knows and understands about, and that I can only do them myself physically, through my own body. As long as that's the case, I'll keep working."

In 1992 Tharp began a half-year commercial project that netted a reported million dollars for herself and her costar, Mikhail Baryshnikov. With a small company (ballet dancers Stevens, Brown, Caddell, and Julie Michael; Jamie Bishton, Michael Whaites, Daniel Otevrel; and two showbiz dancers, Aaron Cash and Art Palmer) she went into rehearsal for a month at the Wexner Center prior to launching a three-month blitz tour of twenty-five cities. Booked by the prominent concert agency Columbia Artists, the tour bypassed New York. She didn't have much time to prepare, and unlike the first Wexner residency, the university didn't get a glimpse of what she was doing until *Cutting Up* was given in Mershon Auditorium at the end of November. A small tempest blew up between presenters over the fact that the University of Texas at Austin had bid to hold the official world premiere. At least two New York dailies sent their critics to Columbus a few days earlier. Although the Wexner carefully billed the show as a "first performance," Kisselgoff called it a premiere.

The ninety-minute show attracted capacity audiences at over-the-top ticket prices. At a time when other dance organizations were struggling and the Dance Boom had been declared a bust, the Twyla-Misha tour broke records. When Boston's Celebrity Series opened the box office two weeks before a weekend of performances at the 3,600-seat Wang Theater, it had the biggest sales day in its fifty-four-year history. In West Palm Beach, subscribers to the newly constructed Kravis Center bought up the whole house, and Tharp had to promise a return visit so that ordinary people could see the show. It wasn't easy for the hoi-polloi to get in. All across the country, tickets cost up to $150, not including the benefit receptions and dinners that many sponsors piggybacked onto the show's popularity.

The company traveled in a private jet with their own physical therapist, and the dancers were well paid. Although no one had any doubts about the box-office power of the two stars, the publicity was intense. A convergence of new hooks, partly fortuitous and partly calculated, began with Tharp's MacArthur and her *Dancing* segment on PBS. Prompted by the December release of her autobiography, writers combined their preview stories with book reviews. Baryshnikov gave no interviews, but Tharp made herself available, provocative as always. There was plenty to stir the public's curiosity. Both stars were pushing the age envelope, so how would Tharp (fifty-one) and Baryshnikov (forty-five) hold up in performance? More titillating, Tharp had described their long-ago liaison in the book, in dime-novel detail. Writers quoted the flaming parts extensively; one critic even referred readers to the spiciest page. By the time the show hit town, audiences were dying to see the stars together in person. Were they still an item? Would you be able to tell?

Two months before the tour opened, Tharp and Baryshnikov appeared together on PBS, in a short Annie Leibovitz film commissioned for the twentieth anniversary of *Great Performances*. Leibovitz had taken contrasting photographs of Tharp—one severe and one elfin—for an ABT fiftieth anniversary souvenir book in 1989, when Tharp was still listed as an artistic associate. Now the photographer was interested in the early motion-picture experiments of Eadweard Muybridge and others, and she enlisted Tharp and Baryshnikov to help her make *Zoetrope*. The six-and-a-half-minute film is a modern take on the zooscope, a machine that simulated motion by affixing a sequence of still pictures to the inside of a drum that revolved rapidly as the viewer looked through a peephole. Tharp and Baryshnikov worked on a circular stage with the movie camera in the center. They walk, jog, do simple phrases and duologs, and end up waltzing and laughing as the camera accelerates. Separately but appreciatively, they comment in voiceover on each other's working abilities. Tharp says she doesn't remember much about this film, except that it was used as promotional material for the tour. Bits of *Zoetrope's* movement also made their way into *Cutting Up*, as did material from the gutted movie musical.

Cutting Up was compared by more than one writer to a rock show and, like that sort of event, it drew attention almost exclusively to the stars. Critics focused on the middle section, a duet, and no one had much to say about the ensemble choreography. Even the dancers thought of themselves as a backup group. There were precedents for the enterprise in the dance field, Baryshnikov's several summer jaunts with ABT dancers, for instance. Rudolf Nureyev scooped up the Paul Taylor Company once, and another time the entire Joffrey Ballet, for his "Nureyev and Friends" tours. But these projects invariably used existing repertory: familiar low-production dances and brief star turns.

Tharp wasn't going to rely on repertory for this venture. She devised a program of favorite ideas newly choreographed and built around an overall concept. The three sections were made of short vignettes illustrating the wide range of materials that could go into making a dance. Each section drew on a different category of resources and included special numbers featuring the stars. *Schtick* was a sort of variety show, with music that might have accompanied toe and baton classes in a neighborhood dancing school. *Bare Bones* was a duet for the two stars, presumably created from scratch with only the considerable talents at their disposal. *Food* was a social-dance survey set in four famous American night spots of the twentieth century: "Palm Court 1917," "Coconut Grove 1942," "Rainbow Room 1953," and "Morton's LA 1992."

Tharp worked hard on her profit-makers, but she invested no more art in them than necessary. She thought the axiom "something for everybody" was a good thing, she told the *Boston Globe*'s Christine Temin. "I started thinking of the show as 50 great, enjoyable moments. There's nothing criminal in that. . . . Why antagonize an audience?" But her critics called *Cutting Up* Twyla-lite. *Dance View*'s editor, Alexandra Tomalonis, dismissed it as "a colossal ripoff," but had to admit the audience at Washington's Warner Theater didn't mind at all. "A vanity production for two aging dancers," began Kisselgoff's review. Some of the material did look recycled, and only the central duet seemed choreographically substantial, but the whole show was more thoughtful and generous than it seemed at first, star-bedazzled glance.

Along with the Victorian waltzing, imitation Fosse, and rock and roll of the first act, Tharp reprised her *Men's Piece* antics—collective lifts, slow duets, and marching drill. Baryshnikov partnered the four women in what might have been a sequel to *The Little Ballet*. Each of the restaurants in Act 3 became the pretext for a small if familiar dance portrait. In the "Palm Court," there were rags, tangos, polkas, and a rivalry on the dance floor that escalated into a silent-movie scuffle. For the '40s there were lindy hoppers and two zoot-suited singers. The "Rainbow Room" segment consisted of two solos. Tharp did her inimitable turns and high kicks and close-in undulations ("Someone to Watch over Me"). Baryshnikov danced his "One for My Baby" solo from the *Sinatra Suite*, the most recognizable item in the show, having been aired frequently on TV. She probably thought of this as the show's equivalent of *The Dying Swan*.

The evening wound up with a disco scene. During work on *I'll Do Anything*, director James Brooks had taken Tharp and Jamie Bishton, who was assisting her, on a research trip to Morton's restaurant, where they spent an evening observing the tribal behavior of the Hollywood social-climbing set. According to Bishton, there was to be a scene for Albert Brooks in the movie where, "as he was moving around through the restaurant, all this dancing was happening around him." This scene, minus Albert Brooks, turned up as the last number of *Cutting Up*.

"Bare Bones," the middle section, was a real suite of dances to the Baroque composer Giovanni Battista Pergolesi, with Tharp and Baryshnikov dancing together, then soloing. The whole thing was built on walking steps, backwards and forward, with interpolated chassés, bounces, shakes, and changes of speed and direction. She gave Baryshnikov two sequences of balletic movement that quoted gestures from his past famous roles: *Spectre de la Rose, Le Corsaire, Push Comes to Shove*. The solo suited him so well that he later acquired it, as *Pergolesi*, for his White Oak repertory.

Perhaps piqued by the purple passages in Tharp's book, critics wondered why the two never touched during the duet. Tharp at one point explained that due to Baryshnikov's past injuries, he couldn't lift her. "We dance duets in the sense of two people working in one piece." Anna Kisselgoff thought she was trying, ill-advisedly, to match her own style with the classical purity of her partner. They read, Kisselgoff thought, as "two guys doing pirouettes and other Tharp-treated ballet basics . . ." Tharp had made innumerable duets without physical contact, most recently for the Stompers of *In the Upper Room*. The whole of "Bare Bones" is a spectacular version of her longtime investigation into choreographic doubling. Side by side, the two dancers do the same things but in their own ways; she *wanted* the audience to see them as different.

Undeniably, the relationship between Tharp and Baryshnikov frosted over during the tour. They opened the show with a life-in-the-studio evocation, strolling onstage in sweats with water bottles, watching each other, trying steps and warm-ups accompanied by the song "I Get Along without You Very Well." "Possibly this means they hate each other," suggested Laura Shapiro. Before the tour ended, rumors circulated that they were no longer on speaking terms. When Baryshnikov arrived in Columbus shortly before the opening, he told Tharp that aside from the *Pergolesi*, he thought the show wasn't up to her standard of excellence. She didn't take kindly to his criticism. He must have been offended by Tharp's pulpy exposé of their 1975 seduction—he was just as protective of his private life as she—and he balked at promotional schemes that hinted at an ongoing liaison. Their affair was peripheral, Tharp insisted when critics inevitably asked about it, but she'd felt it necessary to include certain of her romantic adventures in the book because "People have to have the information to understand the [dance] work."

Tharp's mother died during the tour. She didn't leave to go to the funeral, but, according to Stacy Caddell, "She did a very beautiful, heart-wrenching solo that night."

The tour ended in Louisville in mid-February. After a break most of the dancers joined a newly constituted sixteen-member group for a two-week season at City Center (14–25 September 1993) and another period of touring. The company prepared the season at the University of the Arts in Philadelphia in July and the Wexner in August. The new show, billed as *Twyla Tharp and Dancers: Informal Talk and Performance*, was probably the last time Tharp convened a substantial chunk of her repertory—and in New York it was scantily produced. There were no sets or lighting effects, and the dancers wore practice clothes. Tickets were priced at a modest twenty dollars.

Tharp thought of the season as a thank offering, a form of payback to the city that had given her so much. It was essentially a beefed-up lecture-demonstration. She took the opportunity to explicate the construction of specific dances. Sara Rudner made a guest appearance, reprising their old interview ploy The Talky, where she danced while answering questions Tharp threw at her. Opening the program to Buddy Guy's recording of "Fever" with a solo Arlene Croce called "wide-ranging, multifaceted, typically ambiguous," Tharp explained how the frisson of love could generate art. On the first program there were complete performances of *Octet* and *Upper Room;* the second concentrated on Tharp's social-dance style, with *Nine Sinatra Songs*, *Sextet*, and excerpts from *Baker's Dozen*. Critics and audiences seemed to like seeing the mechanics of these pieces, and despite some grumbling about the bargain-basement aspects of the show, most people found it highly entertaining.

There were, however, some signs of apprehension about the direction Tharp's career was taking. Dale Harris, a staunch supporter, didn't like the audience-friendly setup of the season, which he found self-indulgent. "Why is Twyla Tharp not devoting her energies to choreography instead of squandering them on what is in effect a high-class chat show?" he asked in *The Wall Street Journal*. Arlene Croce, on the other hand, had been worried about Tharp's apparent attempts to circumvent creative burnout—the tour, the book, the movie. She voiced misgivings about the pointe work and partnering in *Sextet* and *Octet*, a recent trend that "make[s] me wish to God Tharp had never heard of either." But with *Demeter and Persephone*, Croce thought, Tharp had gotten back on track.

The centerpiece of the City Center season was a zany preview of *Demeter and Persephone*, the dance Tharp had just made for Martha Graham's company. Graham had singled out several younger choreographers she thought could carry on her company's mission after she passed on, and Tharp was the first to be given an assignment. She donated her services. She had studied with Graham in her early days in New York, and she professed her great respect for the modern dance master. Selecting one of the major Greek myths, Tharp found "a very female story," she told Janice Berman, "a myth about women and their various ages and times, about how we go away to learn certain things and then have to be reunited with ourselves. It's a myth about living, about women as godhead, about rejuvenation, a myth about proceeding in a way that women do." She told another interviewer at the time that she saw the myth in terms of Demeter's relationships, rather than an individual's drama as Graham might have done. The Demeter character, an older woman, sees the strands of her early life separate and then reunite in a different way. At fifty-two Tharp had given considerable thought to her own menopausal changes.

At City Center she glossed the story of the fertility goddess whose daughter, Persephone, was seduced and carried off to the Underworld by Hades. Distraught, Demeter bargained for a reprieve and secured Persephone's annual return to earth, a symbol of the coming of spring. Tharp set the dance as a Passion Play enacted by pilgrims on their way to carry out the Eleusinian rites—a framework used by Graham in her 1940 dance about the Christian rituals of the Southwest Indians, *El Penitente*. For City Center and a preview performance in Ohio, Tharp dispensed a hilarious narration full of double-entendres, while dancing most of the roles herself, opposite Jamie Bishton. She described Limbo as "an infinitely repeating loop of codependent family members." According to Tharp, Demeter, the world's first kvetch, incurred the displeasure of Zeus by forming the Eleusinian cult: "Nobody likes illegal franchises."

Anna Kisselgoff, one of Graham's most ardent supporters, detected a lack of the proper veneration in Tharp's "crib-sheet version." "A full performance by the Graham company, rather than these fragments, might produce fewer giggles," she wrote. This turned out to be an accurate prediction. The Graham company's performance succeeded too, when it premiered a few weeks later in the same theater, but despite some burlesque

passages, it was more festive than comic. The Graham company was beginning a difficult transition after the loss of its founder-choreographer, and
Tharp came up with a work that enlivened the group, at least temporarily.

Tharp had taken up the challenge conscientiously. By this time she had
evolved a process for making a coherent narrative structure in dance form.
After reading extensively around the myths of Demeter and the Eleusinian
Mysteries, she put together a throughline, puzzling her way through the
characters, the story, the dancing, the music, the cast, and the larger
mythical themes, to achieve a "lead sheet." Into this blueprint she wove
clusters of movement phrases that grew into scenes. Rather than impose
her own style on the dancers, she went back into the studio to recover
some of the Graham technique for herself. The dance turned out to be
more spacious and sculptural than anything Tharp had made for her own
dancers, and also faster and more rhythmically interesting than anything
in the Graham canon. She started choreographing the work to music by
John Adams and Terry Riley but she made an inspired switch to klezmer
music, as recorded by three popular bands. Pressed for the connections
between ancient Greek and contemporary Yiddish culture, she concocted
a few tenuous ones, but she told a questioner at the Columbus preview
that klezmer simply had more expressive range and would give the piece
life and passion.

Demeter was one of Tharp's most successful narrative dances, although it
was less a narrative than a series of dramatic sketches, beginning and ending
with a Tharpian farandole. It had its ambiguities, but the myth's preordained
plotline restrained her questing imagination and her tendency to fall into
farce whenever she confronted familial situations. She preserved the episodic
and archetypal feel of a Graham dance but gave the company a new lease on
movement. Declaring the dance a mutual success, Kisselgoff thought the
Graham dancers "brought out a dramatic projection through movement that
Ms Tharp never found anywhere else." Christine Dakin, whom Tharp had
cast as Demeter, confessed to Jennifer Dunning that "In the beginning I was
feeling very anxious and skeptical. Martha has been my guru for twenty
years. But Twyla won me over." According to Croce, Tharp did wonders for
the company: "It's an excellent opportunity for the dancers to come down
from their elevated perches in the Graham repertory and get happy, and the
opportunity is gratefully seized. . . . the success of the ballet doesn't derive
from Tharp meeting Graham; it derives from Tharp meeting klezmer."

A few years deeper into the process of self-invention, Tharp shamelessly told a lecture-demonstration audience that her past work didn't interest her. Erasing *Deuce Coupe II, III,* and *IV, The Catherine Wheel* 2 and 3, and more modest stagings of second thoughts, she stated that she hadn't revised a dance since her populist conversion of Willie Smith into *Eight Jelly Rolls.* In 1994, while in Ohio, she reconfigured *Brahms' Paganini* for another of her extraordinary male dancers. Jamie Bishton, whom Dale Harris called "as fine a male dancer as the choreographer has ever had in her troupe," had been with Tharp through all the transmutations of the past eight years, and he was at the peak of his form—technically splendid, tough but soft, with an unconcealed appetite for movement. Tharp gave him a composite tape of William Whitener, Richard Colton, and John Carrafa dancing the original twelve-minute solo, and Jennifer Way, slipping in and out during the Book II quartet section. When Bishton had learned all the variations and their differing interpretations, Tharp came in and worked on it with him, juxtaposing material from the original solo against the quartet. Bishton thus counterpointed the quartet in much the same way Jennifer Way had done in the original, but instead of merely hinting at the solo, he conveyed it all.

The original Book I of *Brahms' Paganini* is probably the most virtuosic solo dance Tharp has ever made, not only in terms of the movement but the expressive range it encompasses. Tharp and Bishton both think most of the Book I dance material was used in the integrated version. *Brahms' Paganini Book II* isn't as oddly shaped as the original. With a more unified and concise form, it's a powerful dance of contrasting elements: Bishton's confidence and virtuosic range against the almost demonic quartet that switches from intense social-dance partnering to intricate formality. The dance wasn't shown in New York, but it was done, as a new work, on the '93–'94 tours that followed City Center. Bishton treasures a memorable performance at a Paris Opera gala, when his parents flew over to see him with ten of their friends and were seated in the presidential box.

Somehow in between the movie, City Center, *Demeter,* and the tours, Tharp made a new work for Boston Ballet, *Waterbaby Bagatelles.* It premiered on 30 April 1994 at a gala performance celebrating the company's thirtieth anniversary, and wasn't scheduled again until the following spring. Despite its title, *Waterbaby Bagatelles* is neither a trifle nor an aquatic fancy. Once again boosting a good company into a higher sphere, Tharp made a large-scale work that began mysteriously and built, like *In the Upper Room,* to an irresistible climax. With a cast of twenty-seven dancers headed by principals Jennifer Gelfand and Patrick Armand, and with featured roles for several other dancers, *Waterbabies* has the properties of a formal ballet: classical movement arranged for groups and couples, who maintain constant relationships to one another even when they aren't deployed symmetrically.

The ballet has expected Tharpian quirks. During its twenty-eight minutes there are seven short musical selections, all from the twentieth century but perversely ranging from Webern to Bang-on-a-Can percussion to an Astor Piazzolla tango to "On the Dominant Divide" from John Adams's *Grand Pianola Music*. The vocabulary shifts from Tharp's expanded classicism, to floor-bound slides, splits, crouches, and sprints, to gestures and attitudes culled from martial arts, Tarzan movies, vaudeville, and social dancing. The movement is packed, pressured. Jennifer Tipton created a dramatic, almost lurid lighting effect with four sets of neon tubes that rose and fell to change the dimensions of the stage, alternately glowing and dimming in shades of blue and mauve. With rapidly changing textures and scale, Tharp illustrated how groups of women and men can function in a ballet, for display and seduction.

In one scene, four women reclined like mermaids or sirens, as a stream of goofy men seemed to be trying to impress them with alluring tricks belonging to both genders. The mermaids seemed frightened, but they captured most of the men, and then were carried off upside down. Except for this character episode, the ballet maintained a classical abstractness. The space darkened for a sensuous duet by Gelfand and Armand; later Gelfand led the women in an airborne rush of crossing and accumulating groups.

Overriding the stylistic contradictions of the ballet is Tharp's concern with gender roles. She makes a clear distinction between air work and floor work, but she resists the conventional equation female=air=sought-after/male=ground=pursuer. The "mermaid" section contrasts the floor-bound, coy women with butch showoffs. In the adagio duet, Gelfand manipulates Armand at moments instead of always passively following his lead. By the end of the piece, as the *Grand Pianola Music* builds bombastically to its climax, the men are actually throwing the women into the highest lifts and dragging them by the arms along the floor.

Early in 1994 Tharp was gripped by a new amorous frisson of her own. She met a prominent intellectual, Leon Wieseltier, and began a serious affair that lasted almost four years. Wieseltier, based in Washington as literary editor of *The New Republic*, was a journalist-maverick attracted to brainy pundits, popular culture, and celebrities. A 1999 profile in *The New York Times Magazine* called him "Part Maimonides, Part Oscar Wilde." Like Tharp, though more overtly, he leaned toward the conservative side of politics and ethics. He was trying to write a book on his relationship with his father, which, with Tharp's help, became the widely praised *Kaddish* (1998). In 1994 Tharp dreamed up a plan to spend the summer with him in Washington and do her own work at the same time. In September *Twyla Tharp in Washington—New Works* was shown informally for three weeks in the Kennedy Center's Terrace Theater as the in-process culmination of a ten-week workshop.

Tharp issued an unusual amount of preliminary information about this project, much of it oddly blurred and sentimental. She had found a way to make new work without fund-raising, and the scheme needed some justifying. First she talked Kennedy Center director of programming Sheldon Schwartz into giving her space, facilities, and administrative support in return for a public lecture-demonstration. Then, through American University's Naima Prevots and her own personal connections, she rounded up young dancers for an audition. The setup would be similar to Tharp's old workshop/apprentice system, only bigger and more public. According to *The Washington Post*, she chose fourteen out of the sixty hopefuls. The deal was they'd work gratis. They had to pay their own transportation, room, and board, and there was no guarantee there'd be a performance at the end. In an echo of the makeshift early days on the college touring circuit, Weiseltier and other D.C. contacts helped find housing and free meals for them. Later, Tharp told Charlie Rose on a national TV interview: "It makes the participation of the artists much closer to the community." Naima Prevots told her recruits to think of it as an exceptional learning opportunity.

Halfway into the workshop period, Tharp dismissed the heroic volunteers, saying that although the dancers were terrific, she couldn't get them into shape for a performance quickly enough. She then called in seven veterans she could count on to absorb the work and bond into an ensemble quickly. They too came onboard unsalaried, but they did get a percentage of the box office take. There were, naturally, hard feelings. According to Stacy Caddell, the dance world saw Tharp setting a bad precedent, especially when she called in the professional replacement group. But Tharp took the program to BAM a few months later, and there, Caddell says, "we were paid incredibly well, so it sort of balanced itself out."

Tharp shed a glow of idealism onto this escapade. To several interviewers she invoked bygone altruistic values. ". . . in the old days, dancers just went to work for the love of it," she told Alan Kriegsman, even though she'd campaigned for decades against that practice. Executing a neat public relations cartwheel, she explained to Jean Battey Lewis of *The Washington Times*: "We've become very confused about dollars, dollars and entertainers, dollars and athletes, and pretty soon everybody is kvetching, 'My honor is involved with my paycheck.' That's not true. The honor is involved with the work you do. . . ." She told interviewers how touched she was that the dancers had chosen to work with her, but this wasn't true for either group. She had gone after them, and the risk was all theirs.

Renamed *Red, White and Blues*, the program went to Brooklyn Academy after the first of the year. It was another version of the bare-bones lecture-demonstration format, with assorted untitled bits under the general theme of patriotism. The summer in Washington had started Tharp thinking about "what it means to be an American, both as a dancer and as a citizen." Still in an unusually mellow mood, she told Jennifer Dunning before the BAM season: "This whole thing is sort of about American belief and the fact that the old American dream can still come true." Wieseltier had helped her choose the music and aroused her interest in history and current affairs, earning a program credit as Musical Advisor and General Counsel. In both Washington and Brooklyn, the program proved entertaining and fabulously danced, but uneven. More than one critic dismissed the trivia and trusted that Tharp would develop the most promising bits into major works. Some observed that her own inimitable dancing was beginning to show its age.

The one substantial segment of the program was set to about half the vignettes in Bela Bartok's *Forty-four Duets for Two Violins*. The dance, provisionally called *The Exquisite Corpse*, became *Noir a.k.a. Bartok* in Tharp's official chronologies. A dance of death with comic overtones, it set five dancers in black practice clothes against Stacy Caddell, on pointe in a red unitard, described by Washington critic Jean Battey Lewis as "an avenging or challenging angel." Caddell thought of herself as Persephone, "who had just entered the Underworld and was given control over these five souls." Caddell strode and slid through the five civilians, commanding them to stop and start according to Bartok's short musical statements. In alternating slices of action they echoed her classical movements, froze, or bobbed up and down like puppets, and mimed a shadowy plot about partner switching reminiscent of *Short Stories*. The rivalry got ugly, fighting escalated into murder, and the whole incident went into reverse, then forward, again and again, until the shooting seemed to be on an endless loop. Finally Caddell put a stop to the charade by smiting them all down, then reviving them for a macabre farandole. At the end of the dance she mounted triumphantly on their shoulders.

Noir bears a glancing relationship to *Le Jeune Homme et la Mort* by Roland Petit. That 1946 ballet, originally starring the French dancer Jean Babilée and made into a beautiful 1968 film with Rudolf Nureyev, opened the movie *White Nights*. As the film's choreographer, Tharp had probably had a hand in staging it for Baryshnikov. An artist—frustrated, blocked, and dazzlingly depressed—awaits an enigmatic woman, who teases him and drives him to suicide, then leads him off over the Parisian rooftops. In *Noir* Stacy Caddell projected a mysterious allure very much like the seductress in the Nureyev film, Zizi Jeanmaire. Tharp included some props too, a chair, a magazine, a cigarette, tokens perhaps of the Roland Petit–Jean Cocteau scenario. She even created a poet surrogate in the role for John Selya, who separated himself from the civilian group at times to confront Caddell with virtuosic acrobatics and soaring leaps.

For some time Tharp had been attracted to themes of death and its predatory companion, aging. For her, death had to be resisted with physical force, with dancing. She had done this most dramatically in the golden transfiguration of *The Catherine Wheel*, and in her marathon comeback-signoff in *Fait Accompli*. Dance itself was an affirmation in the face of death (*Bum's Rush*), a power magical enough or even ugly enough (*Bad Smells*) to confront the ultimate, like an amulet, a protective charm. Even the compositional device of retrograde could defeat death, by rewinding events so that they could start again. Emerging once a year from the grip of Hades, the mythic Persephone represented a way of cheating death, or at least wrestling it to a standoff.

12

Near Heaven
1995–2005

In the spring of 1995 Tharp returned to American Ballet Theater. Kevin McKenzie had become artistic director, ending the chilly Jane Hermann era, and the budget deficit had been subdued in the intervening years. Although not listed on the company roster, Tharp was the only choreographer featured in the handsome 1995 souvenir program book. She wrote a gracious essay, riffing on the words *American, Ballet,* and *Theater,* and expressing her optimism about making a new start. She was welcomed back with great fanfare and a gala performance of three new works (1 May 1995). Tharp now offered the company an entirely different mix of choreographic flavors from the last eclectic all-new, all-Tharp evening in 1989. Instead of a cool balletic abstraction, a farce, and a minimusical (*Quartet, Bum's Rush,* and *Everlast*), she dipped into jazz, nostalgia, and metaphysics. To a commissioned score from trumpeter Wynton Marsalis she made *Jump Start,* a lively piece remarkable only for the way it turned ballet dancers into swingers who could handle the Lindy, waltz, mambo, and rags, blues, and bebop. *Americans We,* to nineteenth-century parlor songs and instrumental showpieces, resumed her reflections on American belief and American tragedy. Neither of these was scheduled to go into the repertory that season.

The centerpiece of the program, *How Near Heaven,* drew its title from Emily Dickinson and aspired to cosmic significance. Tharp told Anna

Kisselgoff in a Sunday preview piece that the ballet was about death and the transcendence of death. "The subject matter is subjectivity and objectivity and their unification, the ending of time. . . . That would be the poem if I set out to write one. I'm interested in a poetic handling of literary content, not in a literal plot." Set to Benjamin Britten's *Variations on a Theme of Frank Bridge*, *How Near Heaven* was a big classical work with the forces deployed unconventionally.

A pair of women (Susan Jaffe and Kathleen Moore in the first New York cast) danced as a team but were both partnered by two men (Gil Boggs and Guillaume Graffin). The corps of twelve was divided into four men and eight women, and there was an additional featured couple (Cynthia Harvey and Charles Askegard). Dressed in silken boudoir wear by Gianni Versace, all these units seemed to play different roles in a larger scheme that consolidated around the symbolic death of the two women, a brief exalted vision, and a posthumous celebration. Leon Wieseltier had led Tharp to the music. Britten's youthful tribute to his teacher provided considerable variety, from operatic parody to classical formality, but Tharp had never worked with a score of such intense colors and neoexpressionistic imagery. Arlene Croce thought "his taffeta strings and her macramé are from separate worlds."

Tharp's catalogue of musical resources was wide-ranging but not comprehensive. She had always skirted the great architectonics and orchestrated passions of the later classics. Her approach was to embrace a musical beat, a timbre, a phrase pattern, and to construct her own frame over it. Music could establish a tone, even an idea, but her dance had to be expressive primarily on her terms. She didn't enter the music by illustrating its drama, or append the dance to the score like another musical line as Balanchine often did. Despite her admiration for *Agon*, Stravinsky wasn't a composer she found congenial for her own classical efforts. His kind of intellectual game-playing would have competed with hers. She didn't internalize the ethnic promptings of folk-derived compositions like the Bartok two-violin impressions she'd used for *Noir*. Even her jazz dances don't really imitate the styles to which their music refers, despite the insertion of period dance steps. In the Britten, she didn't feel compelled to make a melodramatic solo when the music sang its parodistic "Aria Italiana," or launch a "Wiener Walzer," or follow any other colorful suggestion made by the composer, unless it suited her own scheme, as the "Funeral March" did.

Tharp's formalistic treatment made *How Near Heaven* look abstract against Britten's textured music. "My whole career has been about counterpoint," she told Kisselgoff. Allowing dissimilar themes to blend into a whole, counterpoint "gives real energy, and it is about optimism. . . . It's a philosophical tenet. It's also, in a way, a religious tenet." She described the HarveyAskegard couple as "intact," a reference perhaps to ideal love, but throughout the ballet she posed her large units against one another, the way she had contrasted Stacy Caddell's dominatrix with the group in *Noir a.k.a. Bartok.* Her dance counterpoint didn't always mesh with Britten's nine harmonious if dissonant variations, or even make its own convincing whole. Sometimes the groups would fall into a canon or a call-and-response pattern, but more often the soloists went their own way while the larger ensemble carried the musical momentum.

Halfway through, the ballet began to take on some drama. After the funeral section, the principal women were reunited in an unusually poignant and feminine duet. They suggested facets of one persona as they danced together, with the same movements individually shaded. Tharp had begun choreographing this duo for herself and Paloma Herrera, who danced in the ballet's first performances at the Kennedy Center with Kathleen Moore. When Susan Jaffe entered the work—she learned both parts—she thought one woman was an ingenue and one an earth mother type. For New York, Tharp assigned Jaffe the earthier role and shifted Moore into Herrera's younger persona.

It probably isn't farfetched to see this duo as a mother-daughter metaphor, given Tharp's recent immersion in the Demeter myth, and the death of her own mother shortly before that. At the end of the funeral scene, they're lifted high, horizontally, one above the other. Symbolically fused again into one body, they're carried off en cortège by the four men. This image is a more compassionate resolution of their differences than the forcible parting of *Demeter and Persephone,* who are carried off in the same positions but in opposite directions, after their temporary reunion. Tharp also told Anna Kisselgoff that she was attracted to Emily Dickinson's obsession with "the crossover point between mortality and immortality . . . because it has to do with the definition of physicality. You step across the line, and there is no longer physicality; that helps define, by its own absence, what is physical." In other words, she was translating her concerns with death and aging into the realm of thought.

How Near Heaven premiered in Washington before Tharp delivered her exegesis to Kisselgoff, and the critics there viewed it with equanimity. Tobi Tobias thought the pair of women were "guardian angels who shepherd its little society through some unnamed tribulation (war, with its handmaiden death, I assumed) to emerge serene, rather nearer to Heaven." Alan Kriegsman got the "impression of a community of dance angels in contrasting moods of joy and melancholy." In New York, despite—or because of—all Tharp's verbiage, the ballet eluded viewers on a conceptual level, and its choreographic contrasts read more like clashing idioms. Arlene Croce found it "almost totally opaque." She thought Tharp lacked the ballet dancer's built-in sense of visual coherence, which might have allowed the audience to make sense of her literary ideas. Tharp revised and tightened the work the following spring, but didn't completely extinguish what Deborah Jowitt called its "irritatingly mysterious eau de scenario."

Still under the brainy influence of Leon Wieseltier, Tharp next made an even more muddled and extravagant work for England's Royal Ballet. *Mr. Worldly Wise* premiered on 9 December 1995, a three-act spectacular with a pastiche of selections mostly drawn from the later, contemplative works of Gioachino Rossini. There were designs by David Roger and a large cast headed by RB principals Irek Mukhamedov, Darcey Bussell, and Tetsuya Kumakawa. A year after its debut, London critic Nicholas Dromgoole called it "perhaps the worst full-length ballet the Royal has ever danced," in a lengthy analysis of what he considered the sins of Anthony Dowell as RB artistic director.

The work brought out the best in the dancers, but looked frenetic. Even on paper it suffered from conceptual overload. Wieseltier's synopsis for the program book affected the archaic style of a *Pilgrim's Progress* fable, but the journey was almost untrackable on the stage. First among the ballet's many themes and scenarios there was the life of Rossini. Best known for his early theater music and operas, the composer went into a fallow period and emerged to create meditative and spiritual works. Thinking of this creative arc, which retraced her own perennial theme of salvation through art, Tharp conceived of the ballet's three acts as depicting excess, abstinence, and moderation. A musical celebrity, Rossini had inspired his own iconography, and some of the ballet's visual ideas came from amusing contemporary caricatures. Tharp was also trying to feature the RB dancers and to allegorize the company and its traditions.

The first act was a headlong divertissement of characters who might have inhabited historic operas and ballets—idealized ballerinas, demented nuns, dancing vegetables; references to the Royal's choreographic god, Frederick Ashton, and possibly to Léonide Massine's Rossini ballet *La Bou-*

tique Fantasque, with Balanchine hovering on the horizon. Mukhamedov's eponymous character was a dissolute genius with a wiser, more temperate assistant/alter ego, Master Bring-the-Bag. Nearly overwhelmed by the attractions of society, Mr. Worldly-Wise sees a vision, Mistress Truth-on-Toe, who shows him his ideal, a classical ballet in the mode of a Petipa/Ivanov second act. Reformed and purified, Mr. Worldly-Wise finds a way to balance his talents and sets off in pursuit of the ballerina. The assistant takes up his bag of tricks and prepares to become his successor.

The general scheme of *Mr. Worldly Wise* recalls that of *Push Comes to Shove*. Again Tharp was taking a fond look at the workings of a ballet company, in this case with a psychological spin: the creative artist getting in touch with his redemptive better self. But there was more clutter and slapstick than message apparent to the audience. In an appreciative essay, her old loyalist Allen Robertson deflected the naysayers and pointed out that Tharp had done "a rich, truly generous piece of dancemaking that showcases its performers as clever, sharp and dazzlingly alive. . . ." But despite its almost too-obvious icons, and the universally applauded performances by Mukhamedov, Bussell, Kumakawa, and the ensemble, the *Sunday Times*'s David Dougill spoke for the consensus in finding it "a perplexing disappointment [that] would be incomprehensible without the synopsis."

At this point Tharp was without a company. She had dissolved the *Red, White and Blues/Noir* group after BAM and spent the year freelancing at ABT, the Royal Ballet, and Hubbard Street. In the spring of 1996 ABT staged another all-Tharp gala, with revised versions of *Americans We* and *How Near Heaven*, and a new ballet, *The Elements*. For this big and compositionally dense work, set to a score by the eighteenth-century composer Jean-Fery Rebel, she revisited the order-from-chaos theme, with a few extra dance showpieces thrown in. Despite terrific performances by the dancers, and an admiring review from Deborah Jowitt, the piece wasn't generally well received. Writing in the *Daily News*, Terry Teachout was surprised to find it "solid, respectable, and, believe it or not, dull. . . . Tharp's homegrown approach to classical choreography has long since hardened into mannerism." Clive Barnes said *The Elements* and *How Near Heaven* exhibited "the same kind of pallid expertise."

By the time *The Elements* had its premiere (3 March 1996 in New York), she and Shelley Washington were scouting around the country for a new group. After callbacks in New York on 1 April 1996, she signed on a dozen young contemporary dancers. The enterprise called Tharp! was already booked for touring two years ahead. Tharp! was to be a commercial venture—various euphemisms were applied to it: for-profit, income-earning, self-sufficient. It was conceived by the producing company IPA and booked on the basis of Tharp's audience-friendly reputation. Tharp had, for the time being, slaked her interest in ballet dancers. Explaining her return to a producing mode she had disavowed so strenuously eight years before, she spoke of getting back to some basics of her own. She wanted to create a new technique, or at least a means of training that would prepare dancers for her work.

She had experienced "the dream potential of freelancing," she told Deborah Jowitt, and now knew its limits, chiefly that the dancers of any established company came with preexisting capabilities. She could choreograph quickly when necessary, but getting dancers to the point of feeling comfortable with her movement—and then making it their own—required more rehearsal time than a freelancer could demand. Her new group, relatively inexperienced, would discover its own fundamentals. The dancers would be able to "learn their lessons together and move in the same direction." She even taught class for a while at the outset of the new company.

The dancers understood the pragmatic nature of the enterprise. A generation into the era of "crossover" dance that Tharp had so brilliantly initiated, they recognized her as a master who could enhance their careers. "I've never been the kind of dancer that gets infatuated with a choreographer," says Gabrielle Malone, who had been trained at Miami's New World School of the Arts. "I was always kind of interested in doing lots of different things. And so, whatever opportunity is available to me at the time, and I feel like it will help me extend myself, then that's where it goes." Andrew Robinson had danced with London Contemporary Dance Company and other groups. He was drawn to the concentration of choreographic energy in New York, and when Shelley Washington encouraged him to audition, he got on the plane. He felt he would be breaking new ground with Tharp.

Over the next two years Tharp made two important dances for this group and four lesser items. None of them used pointe work and all of them disappeared immediately; the best elements dissolved into subsequent dances. Later, Malone and Robinson reflected that the group might have constituted a kind of laboratory for Tharp to work out her ideas. "I guess we were sort of transitional. But it never felt that way," he says. "In a way, for

Twyla everything is transitional," Malone adds. "Every group, every piece, every project. It's just one step to the next step. No grass grows under her feet."

Sweet Fields, for the first year's Tharp! package, embodied her back-to-basics hopes for the new company, and it activated the group as a community. Inspired by the Shakers, the dance was about working together to reach the fusion of art and spirituality that Tharp called truth. *Sweet Fields* was set to eleven hymns and praise songs from the Shaker and Sacred Harp (shape-note) traditions and the eighteenth-century American composer William Billings. These a cappella choral works with their ecstatic texts and open harmonies were related to Tharp's Quaker background, and the dance they prompted was perhaps her purest and most joyful. Choreographically unencumbered by literary allusions, allegorical characters, or even the complexities of counterpoint, *Sweet Fields* shows a community of men and women dancing out their spiritual faith. In clear lines and unambiguous groupings, solemn processions and playful rituals, they acknowledge the inevitability of an afterlife, a New Jerusalem of ease and delight.

As in other utopian dances (*Mud, Baker's Dozen, Bach Partita, How Near Heaven*), Tharp signaled her intentions with white costumes. Norma Kamali layered pants for the men, shorts and peekaboo midriff tops for the women, under open organza jackets and dusters. The effect was revealing and modest at the same time. Though disconcertingly chic, the costumes allowed the dance to bypass any period associations. Belief was not some anachronism, Tharp was saying; it belonged to our times.

Choreographers have been attracted to the Shakers, an American sect of celibate Christians, because dancing was part of their worship. Doris Humphrey's 1931 modern dance classic *Shakers* used some documentary gestures of shaking and ecstatic spinning, kept its men's and women's groups strictly separated in their own halves of the stage, and had a female leader, an Eldress, according to Shaker practice. Tharp may have consulted books on Shaker traditions, but what is striking about her dance is that it doesn't copy any actual Shaker moves or look like any modern dance interpretation of them. Both her movement and floor patterns express the spare functionality of the Shaker aesthetic through the contemporary physicality of her dancers.

Sweet Fields starts with an orderly series of entrances, first for a man followed by his four companions, then a woman and four others. These groups, with a sixth man added later, begin as separate units; they don't share the stage until the fifth song. Gradually a movement vocabulary is built up from the first man's linear phrase, a walking pattern that seems to diagram the space. His arms wheel through the vertical plane; he steps to the side and behind his body, outlining a square without changing front. The women expand on the men's wheeling gestures until they're swinging both arms in big overhead circles. They bend their whole upper bodies toward the ground, they shake their hands out from the wrists. They swing their legs through the step, until they're hopping, sliding to the side, and eventually stepping into full turns. They skip out in a line behind their leader.

A slow procession of men carries a comrade lying prone above their heads—another funeral formation. While the cortege moves across the stage, the "corpse" performs acts of levitation and other magical changes, trading roles with another man almost imperceptibly. The transportee is dropped nearly to the floor and rocked by the pallbearers, tossed in the air and rotated head to foot, and finally passed through their legs and lifted overhead again before he's carried off. This horizontal image becomes part of the vocabulary during the next section, when the men begin rolling on the floor. Interrupting the sections of perfectly balanced group work, one man appears alone, gazing and leaning into one direction, then another. He seems momentarily unsure and unable to go on. Then he makes a decision and strides off after his companions.

As the movement builds up and the traveling patterns grow more intricate, the dance keeps its sense of spatial clarity and industriousness. The movement has the feeling of carpentry or kitchen work—repetitive, vigorous, finicky, or sweeping. By the end of the dance, the lexicon has proliferated into jumps, lifts, and ecstatic turning. The community spans life and death, it can accommodate believers and doubters. In the last song, the men and women interweave and work in pairs, giving each other massages between the shoulder blades with chopping gestures. The men haul the women over their backs and the women shake out their legs in a controlled but joyous outburst. Groups of men rock the prone women near the ground and lift them in high vertical exclamations. Tharp had never made a dance more organically, or expressed her beliefs with less reserve. It earned universal praise from critics and was remembered as the standout work of the Tharp! company.

Sweet Fields and a second dance on the initial program were cocommissioned by the Kennedy Center and the University of California at Berkeley. For *Heroes* Tharp teamed up with Philip Glass again, and although the work was powerful, it didn't have the impact of the monumental *In the Upper Room*. Glass composed a "symphonic ballet," a set of variations on the Heroes Symphony of David Bowie and Brian Eno. Tharp told Thea Singer of *The Boston Globe* that *Heroes* was about the ability of leaders to stand their ground in the face of adversity: "The dance has a movement base that is very aggressive. It is relatively chaotic because that's the kind of world we're building."

Heroes could have been a direct antithesis to *Sweet Fields*. Tharp even used some of the same movement tropes. The gently rocking prone bodies of the women held by three-man teams at the end of *Sweet Fields* was transformed into an assault, as one woman threw herself horizontally at a wall of men who caught her unflinching, time after time. The dance was full of aggression, both the posturing macho kind and the sexually threatening kind. Tharp may have been digging into gender stereotypes and anti-types. The dance's title seemed to ask the audience to think about who are the heroes in our society and what is demanded of them. London critic Donald Hutera saw the "ferocious precision" and "kinetic desperation" of the dancing as a message of resistance, resilience, and even redemption. For all its harshness, Hutera said, *Heroes* had none of the brutality of "Euro-crash" dance—the hybrid styles that featured casual virtuosity and abusive partnering—then gaining popularity. Tobi Tobias found the meaning of *Heroes* "almost entirely obscure," but, along with everyone else, she applauded the dancing.

Tharp has made relatively few potboilers during her long and ambitious career (she would probably not admit to any) and even the slightest of her works have invoked accolades for the dancing. The Tharp! programs included two whiffs of old success stories—*66*, a pop evocation of middle-American romance, and *Roy's Joys*, a jazz piece to music of trumpeter Roy Eldridge—and a surprising new turn, *Yemayá*, which one of the dancers described as a "pseudo-Santeria meets Buena Vista Social Club piece."

Tharp would seem the least likely choreographer to be toying with Cuban drumming and trance possession, but there was some logic to this development, aside from her unending pursuit of new musical resources. Santeria religion, like that of the Shakers, led to ecstatic dancing, and Tharp had long been interested in goddess worship. She had made dream ballets before, to disclose an alternative lifestyle or time frame behind a more palpable stage reality. Yemayá, the sea queen in several religions of the African diaspora, was Tharp's metaphor for the ideal woman according to Gabrielle Malone, who danced the role. The plot shifted from a night club to an erotic fantasy, then back to reality. Tharp wanted to show the connection between spiritual and mundane life, but the dance proved more glossy than adventurous.

The company also learned *Baker's Dozen*, but the dance was sidelined without a performance in favor of getting the new material onto the stage. It's possible that, given more time, Tharp would have deepened and clarified the Tharp! repertory. Certainly *Heroes* had more potential. But IPA's heavy touring agenda turned out to be as unsuited to her creative process as the nonprofit setups of her earlier companies. In its two-year existence, Tharp! appeared in several American cities and made three overseas trips, to dance in Paris, Edinburgh, Australia, Singapore, Italy, and London. She was productive during this time, but her ideas needed a longer gestation period to ripen fully.

While the company was on the road, she gathered up other dancers. Tharp's patron Patsy Tarr has observed: "This is her great gift, that she can make dances. . . . And I think that it must be an enormous frustration to any artist to have a gift like that and not work." She'd formed a relationship with the Australian Ballet in 1997 when it revived *In the Upper Room*. Two of the company's staff, artistic director Ross Stretton and ballet master Danilo Radojevic, had worked admiringly with Tharp at American Ballet Theater. "All her works made me a better classical dancer," Radojevic told an Australian publication. As a favor to Stretton, she said, she agreed to make a ballet for the company. Six Australian dancers flew to New York in the summer of 1997 to work with her. After performances of *The Story Teller* in late 1997 and early 1998, the Australian critics were disappointed. "Much was expected" of the piece, wrote Patricia Laughlin in *Dance Australia*. Instead it turned out to be an enjoyable lightweight.

Tharp had also accepted some lecture-demonstration dates, and she invited one of her most congenial dancers from ABT, John Selya, to work with her. They made a duet to music by the eccentric street musician Moondog. Tharp still loved informal dialogues with the public, and for these outings she and Selya would perform the dance, then she'd talk about it and they'd do it again. He remembers *Moondog* as very naive, childlike, and he felt privileged to be dancing it with her. Later Andrew Robinson partnered her in it for a few showings.

For other public-outreach opportunities on the road, Tharp brought back *The One Hundreds* in an expansive new format, casting herself as the genial host of a '60s retrospective and audience-participation evening. Now she abandoned strict authenticity in the interest of entertainment and cut the initial phrases by half. Asking a contemporary audience to sit through the whole one hundred flat-out would be like offering them *Gone With the Wind*, Malone thought. She and Robinson would do the fifty phrases sitting in chairs—the better to allow the audience to dance along with them, Tharp explained. Then they'd stand and repeat them side by side as Tharp asked the audience to notice the differences between their performing, with an applause check at the end to pick the one it liked best. In at least one of these events, on 27 Feb. 1999, at Hunter College Auditorium in New York, Sara Rudner and Rose Marie Wright joined Tharp to dance for the last time as a trio. The eleven-second volunteers paid one hundred dollars to partici-pate, and the proceeds went to benefit Hunter College. Tharp was lectur-ing that year in Hunter's Dance Department on a Distinguished Visiting Professorship.

Around the middle of 1998 the Tharp! dancers' two-year contracts were coming to an end, just as they were beginning to look and feel like a com-pany. Shelley Washington left her job as ballet mistress and Tharp recalled Jamie Bishton to replace her. The giant pure-dance work to the Beethoven 33 Variations on a waltz of Anton Diabelli, Op. 120, turned out to be Tharp's last piece for this group. Excellent concert pianists were hired to play in each of the performance venues, and Geoffrey Beene recreated the tuxedo-front, backless unisex costumes of *Eight Jelly Rolls*. The dance was hardly a jazz baby, though. To Beethoven's wide-ranging extrapolations on what she called Diabelli's ditzy little tune, Tharp released an hour-long stream of invention. She joined the tour for *Diabelli*'s premiere in Palermo, Italy, in September 1998, but the dance was never performed in New York. She had run into trouble with her producers, IPA, and when the dancers re-turned from Europe she told them they wouldn't be continuing as a group.

Diabelli had been created under a three-way commission, from the Barbi-can Center in London, the Cité de la Musique in Paris, and the Hancher Auditorium at the University of Iowa. In order to satisfy performance com-mitments to these sponsors, Tharp put together another unit that included four from the dissolved Tharp! group (Malone, Robinson, Sandra Stanton, and Victor Quijada); two stellar ballet dancers from Denmark, Alexander Kølpin and Thomas Lund; two newcomers, Helen Saunders and Elizabeth Zengara; and stalwarts Jamie Bishton and Stacy Caddell. For London, Paris, and Iowa City, the work constituted the entire program. In Iowa the audi-ence was invited to a salsa party in the lobby afterward.

This project group disbanded as soon as *Diabelli* fulfilled its obligations. Lund, Caddell, Malone, and Robinson stayed with Tharp to make another Beethoven work. She had received the $100,000 Doris Duke Award from the American Dance Festival for new choreography. This time, instead of celebrating Beethoven the classicist, Tharp examined the composer's romantic side. The dance, to the Hammerklavier Sonata, was called *Grosse Sonate* for its premiere at the ADF in July of 1999. The dancers worked almost entirely in couples for the long, exhausting piece. Partnered by Lund, Caddell danced on pointe, and Malone, with Robinson, wore soft shoes. This suggested a familiar subject: the contrast between classical and contemporary dancing. But Tharp's movement was now such a stylistic mixture that the distinction didn't really apply. Caddell's pointe work was simply another ingredient in a technical panorama. Again, the work didn't get shown in New York, but Tharp expanded it into a sextet for a few more performances two years later.

These two encounters with the formidable Beethoven produced entirely different dances. *Diabelli* was like a classical ballet, with the ten dancers sorting out in seemingly infinite combinations and patterns, and moods shifting from formal to competitive to soulful. Tharp excelled at making her own theme-and-variations dances, and Beethoven's imaginative ruminations on his Diabelli motif supplied her with both psychic and dynamic energy. London critic Clement Crisp praised the piece warmly, comparing it to Jerome Robbins's *Dances at a Gathering*, "in which music and movement are no less good and responsive companions." But in its length as well as its formality, *Diabelli* could also be thought of as Tharp's *Goldberg Variations*, come to fruition a quarter century after her quixotic assertion in *The Bix Pieces*: "Today I thought of writing a dance to the *Goldberg Variations*, just because it's already been done." It had been done by Robbins in 1971.

The Hammerklavier presented a greater challenge, as one of the composer's last and most revolutionary excursions. His forty-three-minute sonata was as demanding structurally as it was virtuosic, filled with departures from traditional form, flamboyant pianism, and unexpected changes of key and tempo. Tharp's inventiveness never gave out, but the dance looks as if she simply jettisoned the density of Beethoven's work and went her own way. Balanchine saw music as the backbone of his work, she explained to critic Theodore Bale of *The Boston Herald*. "He gave a private place to music. I don't."

⊚⊛⊛⊚

Stacy Caddell had become one of Tharp's indispensable lieutenants by the end of the '90s. After the demise of the *Octet* project group in 1994, Caddell had turned her formidable technique to freelance ballet jobs. For four years she guest starred in classical showpieces and danced in the ballet at the Metropolitan Opera. When the American dancer Karole Armitage was looking for a Mozart ballet by Tharp for a company she was heading in Florence, Italy, Caddell convinced the choreographer to let her direct a production of *Ballare*. She went on to stage *Noir* in Geneva, and became a trusted regisseur as well as a studio dancer when Tharp was making new work. Caddell and her dance partner at that time, Alexander Kølpin, asked Tharp to stage *Sinatra Suite* for them. She offered them a choice: *Sinatra* or a new work. Without hesitation they chose the new work. They started with music by Donald "The Junkman" Knaack, and eventually, along with New York City Ballet dancers Kelly Cass and Tom Gold, they were making the duet material that ended up in the forty-two-minute ballet *Known by Heart*. Caddell and Kølpin danced the Junkman duet in Copenhagen, and Tharp later extracted it from the larger piece for a group of her own.

Known by Heart premiered during American Ballet Theater's fall 1998 season at City Center. Tharp returned to her practice of piecing together a score to match seemingly disparate dance styles, for a couple ballet about how classicism earns its longevity. Starting out with components that might have arrived from different aesthetic planets, she gradually folded material from one dance unit into the vocabulary of another until they became compatible if not totally integrated. In fact, Tharp was careful to show from the beginning that all three styles contained impurities and inconsistencies.

In the first cast Julie Kent and Angel Corella entered to a drumroll, announcing, Tharp has said, that "the court isn't far away from the military." The music, from Mozart and two anonymous composers, pointed out an often-overlooked folk-dance ingredient in classical music. Kent and Corella began with a well-bred classical pas de deux, then, as the sound of a rollicking village band was heard, their steps became broader, less proper. They finished with a coda of unison tropes typical of early nineteenth-century ballet—side-by-side romping, call-and-response patterns, and mirroring.

Susan Jaffe and Ethan Stiefel danced the Junkman duet, to Knaack's rhythms for cowbells, hubcaps, snare drums, rasps, and buzzers. They started out as a high-classical couple with some latent discord between them. Their fast balletic stunts and furious energies soon began to punch out into distortions and disconnections. Stiefel did a pugnacious, bouncing solo that delighted the audience. Jaffe stabbed the floor with her pointes and wrenched her balances into corkscrews. They traded karate kicks and hip bumps. They confronted each other with flat "Egyptian" poses, used by Jerome Robbins in his *Glass Pieces*. They acted out a skit in which they failed to meet at appointed times and fought when they did meet. Amid the punching, rolling skirmishes, she supported two of his expansive jumps, and at another moment he fell backwards into her arms, as if they were doing a fox-trot dip.

A third couple, Keith Roberts and Griff Braun, then took over, doing a cool Tharpian dance phrase in tandem. The music for the last half of the ballet was Steve Reich's twenty-two-minute *Six Pianos*, a dazzling work of evolved minimalism in which a single phrase is manipulated, modulated, overlapped, and gradually morphed to create a succession of driving rhythms. Braun and Roberts caught the spirit of this with repeating phrases, flattened-out dynamics, and phenomenal endurance. The movement itself, a set of unrelated, continuous actions, could have been a descendant of Tharp's most minimalistic piece, the *One Hundreds*, with the simple phrase exposition shaped into a choreographic scaffold that framed the whole ballet.

Starting out with walking, their weight sinking easily into the step, their arms swinging freely, Roberts and Braun pace together forward and backward into the space. Like vaudevillian comrades, comfortably shuffling through the time step, wrangling in knockabout sketches, jogging and shadowboxing, they travel through the space and around its perimeter. They vary the pace with finely coordinated rhythms, syncopations, suspensions, and naturalistic encounters, never losing their steady internal pulse. As the other couples pass in and out, doing their signature phrases, the twinned sidemen capture and incorporate motifs, competitions, seductions, and badinage while continuing to patrol the space.

With its fast, nonstop movement and entering and leaving couples, the dance begins to blur. At some point two more men appear and replace Braun and Roberts, like relay racers. After that, the couples begin to exchange partners as well as information, until two more couples appear, the doubles of Kent-Corella and Jaffe-Stiefel. This occurs very near the end, but the music gives no indication of subsiding. Without warning, it stops. In silence the lights go down as Roberts and Braun are doing their first phrase together downstage and their male alternates jog in place in the background. Tharp's message seemed to be that there would always be more dancers, and more dance possibilities.

Steve Reich, especially during the period of *Six Pianos*, was not a composer to everyone's taste. It took some attentive listening to discern the subtle shifts and variations going on inside his insistent repetition and unchanging pulse. It was the Reich, and the male marathoners, that implemented Tharp's theme of regeneration, but some observers found the music a turnoff. *Dance Magazine*'s reviewer, Harris Green, thought the ballet worked well in spite of the "grinding monotony" of the Reich section. Both Joan Acocella, who had succeeded Arlene Croce at *The New Yorker*, and Anna Kisselgoff focused on the dancers. Kisselgoff recognized the work as "one of Ms Tharp's true classical ballets" but she found the Reich "merely repetitive" and dismissed the whole second part as overextended. She found the ballet an example of Tharp's ability to "reveal the unsuspected about virtuoso classical dancers," and "above all, a fabulous showcase for Ethan Stiefel . . ." "A Hidden Brando" proclaimed the *Times* headline. Acocella thought *Known by Heart* "the best thing that A.B.T. has commissioned in years," because Tharp was one of the few choreographers who consistently gave dancers the challenges they needed to grow.

After *Known by Heart* Tharp made two more big ballets in quick succession. Her Beethoven investigations came to a climax at New York City Ballet with *The Beethoven Seventh*, premiered on George Balanchine's birthday in January of 2000. Two months later she finished a surpassing theme-and-variations ballet for a large cast of couples at ABT, the Brahms *Variations on a Theme by Haydn*.

Tharp gave a couple of explanations for taking on the well-known Beethoven symphony. She wanted to "make a case for Beethoven in the ballet world," where Balanchine's assertion that the composer was complete without dancing had invoked a fifty-year moratorium. Continuing her *Hammerklavier* train of thought, she'd started choreographing with the composer's complex late sonatas, but when the dancers balked, she'd switched to his more approachable music. She also feared the sound of their feet would drown out the piano. She had begun to identify with the successes and tragedies of Beethoven's life; his formal structuring she'd always understood. Listening to Alfred Brendel's recordings, she told an interviewer, she learned "that on the one hand there was this extreme intelligence, which we know about; on the other hand there was this really dumb sense of humor . . . quite crude and humanistic." Tharp said she wanted to counteract a certain "bleak and barren overreaction against romanticism," and the Seventh, with its range of emotions and rhythmic sophistication, represented "real romanticism" to her.

At a lecture-demonstration for New York City Ballet patrons shortly after the *Beethoven Seventh* premiere, Tharp was asked why it had taken fifteen years for her to return to the company. She gave a curiously poignant answer. After *Brahms/Handel*, she'd turned down invitations to choreograph so as not to use rehearsal time that Jerome Robbins might have needed. She called Peter Martins after Robbins died in the summer of 1998. She had also hesitated out of a kind of reverence about the company. "You don't come here to do a ballet," she said. "You come to address Balanchine." It had taken some time before she felt she'd earned the right to bring Beethoven to the NYCB dancers.

The Seventh Symphony had its own celebrated history. Richard Wagner had famously called it the Apotheosis of the Dance; Isadora Duncan had scandalously danced it as a solo; Léonide Massine had choreographed it as an allegory on the life and death of civilization. Tharp's more immediate forerunners for the ballet were Balanchine and Robbins. Though it was rare for her to take on a large symphonic structure, Balanchine had done so frequently. Like *Symphony in C* (Bizet) or *Four Temperaments* (Hindemith), *The Beethoven Seventh* was a showpiece for dancers and dancing of different qualities, each movement a self-contained essay, with the players and themes assembling for a grand, all-inclusive finale. Robbins's 1979 *Four Seasons*, set to a suite from Verdi's opera *Les Vêpres siciliennes*, had also switched tonalities from one section to the next, and, not so incidentally, included a Bacchanalian Autumn section that Robbins made for Baryshnikov, who was then having his sabbatical year at NYCB.

Tharp selected three outstanding male dancers from the company who represented a range of possibilities suited to the music. Peter Boal was the unimaginably pure classical dancer, whose continual striving for the ideal could "leaven our difficulties with lightness." Nikolaj Hübbe would illustrate the "perfect romantic world that is tragedy." Damian Woetzel was the agile, antic incarnation of the bacchanalian scherzo, a "spirit that looks to nature," said Tharp. Each man danced with a female partner (Jenifer Ringer, Wendy Whelan, and Miranda Weese). A corps of twelve dancers, mostly working in couples, backed up all three movements. Tharp gave small solo passages to the corps dancers. Tom Gold opened the ballet in a double-entendre acknowledging his participation in the preliminary stages of choreographing. As the curtain rose he emerged from a group posed in darkness, to personify

Beethoven's preamble. A concluding Allegro con Brio enlisted the whole cast, propelled by an "optimism to weld and bind all these forces together."

Longtime NYCB supporter Robert Gottlieb, writing for *The New York Observer* later on, thought the ballet was Tharp "at her bloated worst," but the dancers once again thrilled the critics. Nikolaj Hübbe, the tragic hero of the second movement, was singled out for what Anna Kisselgoff called his "weighted passion." Acocella was disappointed that the ballet wasn't more interesting, but she thought Tharp had drawn an exceptional performance from Wendy Whelan—as Hübbe's elusive muse, she became "not just human and serious but also sexy." Most of the critics hoped that Tharp's renewed association with New York City Ballet would prove more durable than her first. The company was in chronic need of choreographers who could supply the repertory without betraying its heritage. Tharp could invigorate dancers, and she'd even conquered the classical challenge. "She walked right in and felt at home," said Kisselgoff. But the ballet's derivative form seemed tamer than what critics expected of Tharp. Perhaps she was trying too hard to be respectful. Acocella thought being in the home of Balanchine gave her the jitters.

Two months after the premiere of *The Beethoven Seventh*, the *Brahms-Haydn* made its appearance during an ABT season at the Kennedy Center. Its first New York performance took place on 9 May 2000 at the company's sixtieth anniversary gala. If Tharp had any nervousness about entering Balanchine's temple of classicism, she now felt very confident. She was back at ABT, where she'd made over a dozen ballets and where she had a cadre of dancers who loved working with her. She was also back in the room with Brahms and another theme-and-variations project, the third such score of Brahms that she'd undertaken.

Tharp told an interviewer for *USA Today* she preferred the designation "neoromantic" to "neoclassic" for her work, although neoromantic was something she was still in the process of inventing. While preparing for the ballet she'd been reading Shakespeare's sonnets, but if *Brahms-Haydn* was neoromantic, there was little romance in it. She enlisted nearly half of Ballet Theater's principal dancers for a cast that consisted of three main couples, four demisoloist couples, and a corps of eight couples. It was a massive work, tightly structured and overflowing with movement. Although the scale of the ballet shifted to allow for solos and featured duets, her real innovation here was in plotting almost all the ensemble work for pairs of dancers. Partners not only executed a virtuosic array of lifts and traveling

footwork, they created group patterns in concert with other sets of partners. It wasn't easy to detect the ballet's inner workings. Tharp explained
the scheme to Deborah Jowitt as triple counterpoint, a "support system between the foreground, the middle ground and the background." Santo Loquasto's costumes, in subtle shades of some pale but indefinite color, didn't
help the audience to differentiate among the troops streaming through.

As a compositional spectacle, the work was unique and impressive.
Tharp felt she'd finally learned how to make a big ballet, and the press
agreed. Mindy Aloff thought *"The Beethoven Seventh* is a brave work; *The
Brahms-Haydn Variations* is a mastered one." Tharp spoke about the *Brahms* as
a kind of summation: "My career has been spent preparing me to be who I
am now. I think the *Brahms* obviously shows a certain control of form. Now
it's my responsibility to move forward. . . . Right now I am where I always
intended to be." The ballet surfaced only once more in ABT's repertory, a
year later, although Stacy Caddell soon taught it in Berlin. ABT found it
cumbersome—too big for the City Center stage where the company did its
fall seasons of contemporary work, and too much strain on the available
manpower—essentially it required thirty virtuoso dancers.

Mindy Aloff offered an admiring assessment of Tharp's classical achievement in a *New Republic* essay on the new Brahms and Beethoven ballets. Acknowledging Tharp's missteps, Aloff discounted them against the bigger
picture. It was evident that

> . . . she approaches ballet very seriously, and her flaws are more interesting
> than most of her colleagues' achievements. Her choreography is vital and
> musically intelligent, her vision of the stage as an arena of forces is huge, her
> highs are thrilling, and her ballets exhibit a fierce belief in classicism as a liv-
> ing potency, something that is relevant to the accelerated, almost manic dis-
> order of contemporary life. She is also a ballet democrat: her works on point
> consist of passionate assaults on symmetry and hierarchy; and in making
> those values into issues, Tharp acknowledges that they are central to the
> very identity of classical ballet.

By the time this tribute got into print, Tharp had made another hairpin
turn. In fact, she had gone back into the dance-company business. Claiming
she needed dancers of her own and overlooking the successful Tharp! com-

pany that she'd started and dismissed within the previous four years, she unveiled a new group, Twyla Tharp Dance, in the summer of 2000. "I need to be grounded again in my own company," she told Anna Kisselgoff. "These have been twelve years of exile." During this self-imposed exile, she hadn't exactly been on a desert island. She'd made over thirty dances, about half of them for her own groups.

For the new startup, although she didn't reveal it right away, she expected to have the kind of shelter she'd always wanted—a home base and an institutional partner with connections to big-money sources. In 1999 Harvey Lichtenstein had retired as director of Brooklyn Academy and moved over to a spinoff organization, the BAM Local Development Corporation. This office was ready to implement long-deferred plans for revitalizing BAM's downtown Brooklyn neighborhood. Lichtenstein had helped Mark Morris acquire a five-story loft building across the street from BAM which was in the final stages of a multimillion-dollar makeover—Morris's new school and studio space was set to open in the spring of 2001. The LDC now had a visionary plan, with significant government and business support, to transform the area into a "vibrant, new cultural district— complete with museums, theaters, artist and dance studios, retail stores, restaurants, a boutique hotel and housing." As Tharp was starting her new company, she called Lichtenstein to say she was looking for a space. He knew she would be an great asset to his plan. He found a church with some vacant space and convinced her to take a look at it.

On 17 January 2001, with the company back from its inaugural performances at the American Dance Festival and the Kennedy Center, BAM Local Development Corp. staged a major press event at the 139-year-old Lafayette Avenue Presbyterian Church to announce Tharp's imminent occupancy. The story was big news for the Fort Greene section of Brooklyn. The *Times* called the deal "a coup for efforts to create a cultural district in Brooklyn." The space, a former Sunday school, was a hall above the church sanctuary, where Tharp could hold rehearsals, classes, and informal performances. With help from the LDC she would renovate the space and open the doors in the spring. Despite some vocal community concerns about gentrification and the incursion of a high-profile, high-culture dance company into an African-American church, pastor David Dyson saw the proposed residency as "a blessing." The church had launched its own campaign to repair and restore the building, and LDC's contribution to the upgrade of the dance space would be "one more thing to help in our cause with funders."

Tharp would at last get her own home; she'd be able to start a school. Suspending her nearly pathological reluctance to talk about her future plans, she laid out a grandiose three-year agenda. The company would rehearse in the space, of course, with public classes arranged around their schedule and longer workshops taking place when they were on tour. Tharp wanted to revive about forty of her early works, all the way back to *Tank Dive*, and videotape them in the space. There would be informal showings of this repertory, with the space converted to hold an audience of 200 to 250, and then regular performances, starting with a duet program, at BAM and other theatrical venues. She would double the size of the company in the next year, then double it again. By 2003 it would be called the Brooklyn Ballet and it would produce not only Tharp's dances but revivals of modernist landmarks from the twentieth century, along the lines undertaken by Robert Joffrey. As for the school, there would be classes for everyone from adults and children to professional dancers, and open rehearsals for the community. And, with teachers like Sara Rudner and Stacy Caddell, she'd consolidate her "single unified technique." All this, she acknowledged, was "totally and completely dependent on building an administrative infrastructure."

Four months later the plan was dead. Tharp had looked at the $68,000 annual rent she'd be paying to LDC—essentially to amortize their outlay for the renovations—plus the cost of running the space, and she'd backed out. She told the *Times* that she was also concerned because the church board hadn't yet signed off on the deal—she wouldn't go where she wasn't wanted—although Reverend Dyson maintained he'd thought everything was moving toward completion. Tharp said she planned to look for another space. Her thirty-year-old son, Jesse Huot, was now managing her office, and she'd acquired a new booking agency to arrange engagements for the company, but up to the pullout she still hadn't begun to erect that all-important administrative structure to support the imposing new operation.

It was hard to fathom why she panicked. She'd backed away from a similar opportunity in 1982, when BAM offered to help install the company in the Strand Theater, but now she was well established at the top of the dance field. From her account of the financial responsibilities she'd be undertaking, the venture didn't seem overwhelming. She would have been earning income through the school and saving the cost of studio rentals. The touring side of the business would go on as before. There was still the inconvenient commute to Brooklyn, and the neighborhood hadn't improved greatly, although her arrival was meant to spearhead a renewal. And then, the modest circumstances, while satisfying the side of her that approved of shoestring art, might have seemed rather too modest in comparison with Mark Morris's spiffy and expansive new space up the block.

But the most serious stumbling block seems to have been the prospect of a long-term commitment. Her initial lease at the church was to be for five years, and the whole project was loaded with implications of permanence, for both school and company. In order to take this on, she would have to bring in a professional administrator and start fund-raising. Lichtenstein had been trying to convince her that she'd need to do this early in the process, but she saw it only as another drag on the payroll. The salary of an administrator, she indignantly told reporter Anne Midgette in a *Los Angeles Times* interview, could be "three times what a principal dancer is making." She preferred to work up to an infrastructure "organically." What Tharp really wanted, she told Laura Bleiberg of *The Orange County Register*, was to be treated like a professional ball club: "We need a nice new stadium and guaranteed salaries and whatever is required to travel to other cities and perform with pride."

The cancelation of the deal, after its glowing launch, was a huge disappointment to the LDC and the church officials, an embarrassment all around. Reverend Dyson was stunned. Tharp had been "lovely and gracious with us," and he'd been convinced the difficulties would be resolved. "I was deeply saddened," Lichtenstein told the *Times*. Perhaps the January announcement had been premature, but Lichtenstein was swept away by her enthusiasm; he thought she'd stick this time.

When the scheme collapsed, Tharp stopped talking about a repertory company and a school. She had the new Tharp Dance in gear, but contrary to her statements at its inception, she wasn't necessarily planning on settling down. In the summer of 2000, as the company was getting underway, she started planning a Broadway musical to the music of Billy Joel. She visualized her new dancers "in something big and ambitious. A two-hour dance extravaganza to all the hits of a major American pop idol. . . ." John Selya remembers that "Twyla said to us at the very first rehearsal, 'My ultimate goal for this group is to get them in a big commercial project', and of course I remembered it a year later when it became a reality." Almost immediately after abandoning Brooklyn, over the summer of 2001, she started workshopping the Billy Joel material.

The new Twyla Tharp Dance consisted entirely of ballet dancers. John Selya and Keith Roberts had already left American Ballet Theater by the

time she made the *Brahms-Haydn*. Both of them had been leading interpreters of her work since the *Everlast* and *Brief Fling* period. Selya had never
risen above corps de ballet status at ABT, and partly to assuage his frustration, he'd begun making dances there. He was thinking of giving up dancing to choreograph as a freelancer, and he'd taken a job with an Internet
company when Tharp invited him to join Tharp Dance. Roberts became an
ABT principal in 1997 but segued to Broadway as the Swan in the all-male
Swan Lake by English choreographer Matthew Bourne. After the limited run
of that ballet, Roberts returned briefly to ABT but left to dance in the show
Fosse. Ashley Tuttle, also an ABT principal since 1997, arranged to divide
her time between Tharp and the ballet company. Roberts enlisted former
Joffrey Ballet dancer Elizabeth Parkinson, who was appearing with him in
Fosse. The new company was completed with Benjamin Bowman from New
York City Ballet and Alexander Brady from Miami City Ballet. Two Paul
Taylor veterans, Andrew Asnes and Francie Huber, signed on initially but
soon dropped out.

For this unit of four men and two women, Tharp immediately made two
very good dances in contrasting modalities. The Apollonian *Mozart Clarinet
Quintet K.581*, set to one of the composer's most enchanting scores, was a
sunny, carefree work, so engaging that it was sometimes mistaken for a trifle. Tharp remarked after a performance in New York that she considered
the Quintet big music on a small scale—Beethoven's Seventh Symphony
was big on a big scale. *Surfer at the River Styx*, the most defiant battle between
dancing and death that Tharp had yet staged, overcame its muddled scenario with a revved-up orgy of dancing.

Mozart Clarinet Quintet began with a male trio, each of the players taking a
solo turn, and all of them showing off a well-behaved classicism—smooth
turns and softly curving, scooping arms. Selya and Tuttle were joined by
Roberts and Parkinson for the slow second movement. Their simultaneous
but different duets featured complicated lifts in which the men hardly ever
served as stationary porteurs but continued the momentum with traveling
or turning steps while they held the women in the air. The women weren't
on pointe, but that didn't make the piece any less a classical ballet.

Having presented the group in three possible configurations—male trio,
solos, and duets—Tharp introduced another trio possibility. Selya and Bowman partnered Tuttle in tricky two-man lifts and transfers, breaking into
their teamwork with periodic dueling. Roberts and Parkinson returned during Mozart's Ländler section for a goofy waltz that romped over the coy af-

fectations of the Romantic pas de deux. During the concluding theme and variations, the groups swirled in and out. In the last few bars Roberts carried Parkinson off, Tuttle fled, and Selya hoisted Bowman for a running exit. The whole dance explored the idea of groups and individuals blending, separating, answering, and complementing one another, a little like Mozart's instrumental game-playing. *Mozart Clarinet Quintet K.581* was initially performed as a program partner with *Surfer at the River Styx*, and critics were so overcome by the Dionysian *Surfer* that the Mozart didn't get much attention. In fact, it began to disappear after the first round of touring.

Surfer at the River Styx was another of Tharp's powerful examinations of death and transfiguration. Like *The Catherine Wheel* it went abruptly from darkness to light. The dancing itself, a passionate expenditure of disciplined energy, served as a metaphor and a medium for crossing over. Selya and Roberts danced related but individual characters, one rangy and restless, one intensely classical. Selya skimmed and slid close to the ground. He used a tightly wound power to lunge and catapult into barrel turns. Roberts did compact turns and huge jumps with an airy, relaxed upper body. Separately, they encountered two other pairs of dancers—a depersonalized chorus—sometimes leading them, sometimes becoming their victims. Donald Knaack's junk band supported the dances with African and Asian-derived rhythms.

The protagonists worked up to longer solo passages of nonstop turning—Roberts spinning with smoothly changing leg positions, Selya punching out karate kicks, pirouettes, break-dance windmills. A series of jetés en tournant brought them together for a mirroring duet, then a turn-taking challenge dance. They seemed to be approaching a merger when Selya was carried out by the chorus. A minute later Roberts, seemingly at the point of exhaustion, faltered away in the other direction. Then the frenzy was suddenly spent and the mood inverted. Selya reappeared, walking meditatively as the others enacted a cathartic vision of slow lifts and re-groupings, with Parkinson carried off in a split, into the light.

No one was in any doubt about the powerful performances, especially that of John Selya, but the *River Styx* baffled everyone who tried to understand it as a story or a character study. "Dithery and opaque," Joan Acocella called it. Tharp's dance was satisfyingly showy, but she was also going for depth, even secrets. She had aroused expectations by freely admitting the dance was suggested by *The Bacchae* of Euripides, a blood-and-thunder Greek drama about King Pentheus, who defied Bacchus/Dionysos by sneaking into the rites presided over by his mother and was punished, then for-given, by the Bacchantes. Tharp piled on more clues with the dance title, but neither the idea of surfing nor the fabled boundary between earth and the Underworld related immediately to the play. Tharp told interviewer Robert Johnson that the dance also included "an all-purpose Chaos and ex-plosion of the Earth," but that the ending signified "humility and compas-sion for human failings."

Critics went digging for connections. Some shared Anna Kisselgoff's view of the piece as "a sketchy allegory about a hero crossing over to the other side and toward redemption, complete with heavenly apotheosis." Others invoked the play's antagonists to explain the presence of two fea-tured dancers, but there was no agreement about which character either Selya or Roberts played, or whether they were exchanging roles or playing two sides of the same character. Selya says he and Roberts were contrasting characters but the specifics could be left ambiguous. The four other dancers may have stood for a Greek chorus; some writers thought they represented water.

Surfer reads as a series of discontinuous episodes and arias rather than a story. As usual, far too many themes were swirling around in Tharp's mind for easy assembly. She was working like a modern dance choreographer, layering several distantly related sources together so that the characters can represent more than one idea and don't have to act out a plot. Martha Gra-ham, in her Greek dramas, was a master at this kind of danced metaphor, and Tharp had diligently pursued Graham's example with *Demeter and Perse-phone*. *Surfer* also followed Graham's lead; its lesson about struggle and re-demption would "read" even if you didn't recognize its mythical underpinnings.

Tharp made one more piece for these dancers, a playful Americana piece called *Westerly Round*, with a featured role for Elizabeth Parkinson as a coun-try girl surrounded by three male admirers. The repertory now included the three recent pieces plus the Junkman duet from *Known by Heart*, the *Fugue*, and the *One Hundreds/Fifties*. From the time the BAM project was scuttled, in May of 2001, until the end of March 2002, the company played the Ah-manson Center in Los Angeles, Jacob's Pillow, several West Coast cities, the Holland Festival, and Lyon, France, followed by another two-month Amer-ican tour. Meanwhile Tharp was working on the Billy Joel material. She

held auditions for the show in November 2001, and by spring she had la-
dled the entire Tharp Dance company into *Movin' Out*.

The show began a summer of previews at the Shubert Theater in
Chicago, with a press opening midway, on 19 July. *Movin' Out* resisted the
categories. A story ballet with popular songs and a theme out of modern
American folklore, it had no dialogue and the dancers didn't sing. The
Chicago critics disliked it, but Tharp refused to surrender. For the next
three months she worked on tightening and clarifying the plot, a story line
she'd developed by stitching together about two dozen of the Piano Man's
songs. To add a conventional Broadway opening number, she retrieved some
choreography from her 1975 Chuck Berry dance *Ocean's Motion*. When
Movin' Out arrived in New York, it still didn't fit the mold, but the score and
the dancing covered its flaws.

Pitched to a Broadway demographic, a middle-aged, suburban audience
of Billy Joel fans who remembered the Vietnam War, *Movin' Out* was the
Broadway breakthrough Tharp had been seeking for years. In a sense, there
wasn't anything in it that she hadn't done before. She'd staged parades, calisthenics, combat, psychedelic fantasies, and joggers in the park. Kids in the
'60s were surfing and dancing and fooling around with cars in *Deuce Coupe*.
They went to Vietnam and some didn't come back in *Hair*. Misfits and outlaws endured their personal hell and were redeemed in *Noir a.k.a. Bartok,
Surfer at the River Styx,* and *I Remember Clifford,* the dance she made for Hubbard
Street Dance Chicago in 1995, about the life of jazz composer Clifford
Brown, who kicked his drug addiction after a religious conversion. *Movin'
Out* was Tharp's coming-of-age mantra all over again—adaptation to the
community, order out of chaos, the story of growing up and going home. Its
upward, upbeat trajectory from innocence to trials and trauma to celebration was perfect for the Broadway audience. She had crafted not only a
tremendous choreographic throughline, she accomplished it with pacing
and emotional variety, tapping into Billy Joel's anger, his doo-wop, his ten-
der ballads, and teenage testosterone.

In Tharp's scenario for *Movin' Out*, the Long Island teens are discovered
hanging out around a '65 Mustang convertible. Seized with patriotism, they
sign up for the army and leave their girlfriends behind. They slog through
basic training. Then they're in Vietnam and the show veers into darkness—
a killing in battle, a military funeral, and a descent into guilt, drugs, desperate sex, and psychological screwups. Years pass. They heal, as Tharp wants
the audience to do, after she's pricked its conscience. Tharp has said that

the show is a tribute to the veterans who deserved more honor than they got after the Vietnam War finally ended. She wanted the show to acknowledge that Vietnam was history, "that that rift in our culture was over." But as the country sank deeper into post-9/11 politics, the dancers began getting thank-you letters from veterans, while other members of the audience were moved by what they took as an antiwar message.

Tharp had at last welded together the polar opposites of popular culture and highbrow dancing, with a concept that burrowed deep into the American psyche. If there were clichés in the plot, said *The New York Times* theater critic Ben Brantley, Tharp had demonstrated why those clichés endured. She had created "a shimmering portrait of an American generation." Both theater and dance critics recognized the extraordinary performances of singer Michael Cavanaugh and the band, and of course the dancers. Once again Tharp had given them the chance to surpass themselves, physically and dramatically, by constructing their characters out of their own qualities. John Selya was Eddie, the antihero with mercurial power and adaptability. Keith Roberts, as his pal Tony, was fast and passionate. Elizabeth Parkinson was Brenda, the party girl with the extravagant legs. Ashley Tuttle and Benjamin Bowman were the nice kids who became casualties of war. The principals were backed up by an equally committed cast of alternates and a thirteen-member dance ensemble.

Once the show was a solid success, it was going to take significant maintenance. Dancers got injured and had to be replaced. Second-cast members and swings had to be rehearsed and spaced in. People left. There were more auditions. New hires had to learn their roles. And all eight shows a week had to be kept in polished condition. It took several coaches to manage this perpetual upkeep. Stacy Caddell was hired in December 2002 as dance supervisor, and Tharp checked on the production frequently when she was in town.

No sooner had the show gotten on its feet than Tharp hired another company of eight young dancers. They began touring in January of 2003 with the *River Styx/Westerly Round/Fugue/Junkman Duet* repertory plus a new story dance, *Even the King*, to Johann Strauss waltzes orchestrated by Arnold Schönberg. Soon it became apparent that Tharp was prepping the new Tharp Dance for the rigors of *Movin' Out*. *Surfer at the River Styx* fell into perspective as the forerunner of the show's demonic performing style. The little company cultivated an extroverted, Broadway attitude, even when delivering the structural rigors of *The Fugue*. After only a year Tharp disbanded Tharp Dance again and drafted four of the dancers for the show's first touring company. The tour opened in Detroit in January 2004, with bookings at least two years ahead.

Ever the entrepreneur, Tharp went along on the early stages of the tour, not only to supervise the show. She combined publicizing the tour with promoting a new book. *The Creative Habit*, published in September 2003 by Simon & Schuster, was based on her 1999 Hunter College lectures. Aimed at the general public as well as artists, it was a primer of how-to-do-it exercises, quizzes, anecdotes, and advice on how to maximize one's undeveloped talents and live a livelier life.

Movin' Out received ten Tony nominations, all under the Musical category except for Lighting Designer Donald Holder. Selya and Parkinson were nominated for Best Actor and Actress; Cavanaugh, Roberts, and Tuttle for featured roles. The show was nominated as Best Musical, and Tharp as Best Director as well as Best Choreographer. When the winners were named, on 8 June 2003, Billy Joel and Stuart Malina received the Tony for their orchestrations of Joel's songs. Tharp was named Best Choreographer, although she probably was hoping for more.

Hairspray won most of the honors that year, but *Movin' Out* occupied a featured spot on the televised award ceremonies. To open the show, Billy Joel and a concert grand piano were stationed in the middle of Times Square surrounded by a small crowd. After he sang "New York State of Mind," the cameras moved inside Radio City Music Hall, where Tharp had staged a four-minute opening dance for the combined casts of *Movin' Out*. Thirty minutes later, she strode down the aisle to accept her Tony, in a black, heavily brocaded sheath dress with spaghetti straps and an indefinable hemline. She began her curt speech with a story about auditioning for the Rockettes as a youngster, and how she didn't make it because she couldn't muster a cheery face. As she went on to thank her associates, she was almost smiling.

EPILOGUE

An Audience of One

The act of watching dancing, as critics pursue it, is a selective practice. With experience you acquire certain techniques for devising flimsy barricades against the loss of the elusive and the unpredictable. You begin to watch in certain ways, to sift out and discard information efficiently. Everyone's techniques are different; every performance demands slight adjustments. But you do develop working habits. Your first goal is to track what's happening. Then you hope to imprint, consciously or unconsciously, enough information to be able to give an evocative account of something, some version of a dance that will likely be long gone by the time anyone reads what you've written.

In this intensely inquisitive process, familiar things take on the status of tropes. The way a Paul Taylor dancer moves becomes pretty much a known quantity, with portents and resonances long established. A nineteenth-century ballet's plot demands little attention. When certain dancers enter the stage in a certain way, you almost know in advance what they'll do. All of these things may continue to give you pleasure, but it's not the pleasure of discovery. The number of striking images diminishes as the years go by. The sense of seeing something original—in large part a construction of the critic herself—occurs less frequently, and the deadening sense that you've seen this before recurs more often.

All of my years as a critic I've resisted this kind of perceptual burnout. But I think it's inevitable, and unless the critic can gain some new perspectives, what was once an enviable way to spend your life will become a routine. You can learn to overcome most of the handicaps to good criticism, but boredom is fatal. I've tried many strategies to refocus my relationship to dance performance, beginning with a broad definition of the field I'm trying to cover. Every writer knows the advantages of changing formats—sprinkling long articles in among short ones, writing things other than reviews and critical essays, immersing oneself in book-length projects. Then there's looking at dance on tape or film. There's traveling to see familiar repertory on unfamiliar companies, or to look at familiar companies in unfamiliar places.

It was in the course of one of these field trips—doing a story on Twyla Tharp's 1991 residency at the Wexner Center, Ohio State University—that I ran into dancer Jamie Bishton on the stairs at a postperformance party. Excited and happy, we chatted for a minute about Tharp's spectacular month-long encampment in Columbus. We talked about what a great opportunity it had been for Tharp to make new work and gather a new company together. Then I confessed that even more than the two performances, I'd been inspired by the day I spent watching Tharp choreograph a new dance for herself and six men. "That day you were there was the best of the whole time," he said. "We were having a ball, laughing and working hard. We were dong it for an audience of one. It was special."

The implications of this remark stayed with me for a long time. What was it in that very privileged, protected, and atypical situation that was so exhilarating, for both the dancers and their singular spectator? As a critic I'd sat in theaters much of my life, always feeling an obscure gratitude toward the dancers for what they gave me. I never imagined they got anything from me in return. Not right there, anyway. Criticism's payback usually comes later, in the form of bankable reviews. The Columbus rehearsal was another kind of exchange: an immediate, spontaneous trading of energies, a mutual recognition and participation in a creative process.

Watching Tharp choreograph in Ohio brought me back to the roots, the reason I became a dance critic. It didn't really teach me anything about her talent, of which I've been convinced for ages. It put me back in touch with fundamentals. Tharp's movement can be planned or spontaneous, personal, funny, hard as hell, precise enough to look thrown-away. She doesn't so much invent or create it, she prepares for it. Crusty, driven, demanding, and admiring, she hurls challenges at the dancers. Brave, virtuosic, and cheerful, they volley back what she gives them, and more. She watches them. They watch her. It's the most subtle form of competition and cooperation, a process so intuitive, so intimate that no one can say in the end whose dance it is, and none of the parties to that dance can be removed without endangering its identity. This process is the same for all theatrical dance making, all over the world, only most of it isn't quite so inspired or obsessed.

The dance that appears on the stage no longer embodies this process. It has become a distillation of the process, a new playing out of the process that the choreographer has edited. What was being explored is learned. What was a spontaneous interchange is now a set of practiced responses. An open-ended quest has become a structure. This is the work that the critic and the audience look at, hoping for revelation. But underneath it is that other, even more ephemeral and far less presentable scenario that is part of the dance's history, whether it takes place in the humble shelter of a loft or the staid splendor of an uptown theater. I think dancers treasure this nearly secret collaboration more than any other phase of performance life. They try to carry it into the performance itself, like a rabbit's foot, and they speak of its loss most often when they're trying to recover a dance that has been out of the repertory. But only in its loss is it usually acknowledged. When a critic can capture and communicate this spark which lights the tinder of choreographic intention, criticism unites most truly with the dance.

—Marcia B. Siegel
— reprinted from *Dance Ink*, summer 1992

NOTES

Much of the research for this book was conducted in the Twyla Tharp Archive at the Jerome Lawrence and Robert E. Lee Theatre Research Institute, The Ohio State University. Unpublished materials cited from that source are labeled with the abbreviation TTA. Other abbreviations used in the notes are as follows:

The 1995 interview of Sara Rudner by Rose Anne Thom was made for the Oral History Project of the Jerome Robbins Dance Division, New York Public Library for the Performing Arts at Lincoln Center. All quotes from that interview are used with permission of Rudner and Thom, and through the courtesy of the Dance Division.

PCTS—Twyla Tharp, *Push Comes to Shove*, 1992.
NYPL—Jerome Robbins Dance Division, New York Public Library for the Performing Arts at Lincoln Center.
NYT—*The New York Times*

1. Leotard Days 1965–1966
page

2. "sort of furry hootchy-kootchy": *PCTS*. 83.
4. "we had passed through the vale . . .": Ibid. 91.
5. "a trio in which visibility is determined . . .": Tharp Dance program book, 1981.
6. "I came out . . .": Tharp in conversation with author, April 15, 2000.

7. "The contemporary artist . . .": José Limón, "On Dance," *Seven Arts* #1, 1953.

7. "Dance form is logical . . .": Doris Humphrey, *The Art of Making Dances* (New York: Grove Press/ Evergreen, 1962), 31.

8. "If nothing else is clear . . .": Ronald Sukenick, *Down and In—Life in the Underground* (New York: Collier Books, 1987), 150.

9. "simple, undistinctive activities . . .": Yvonne Rainer, "Some retrospective notes on a dance for ten people and twelve mattresses . . .", *TDR*, vol. 10 no. 2, winter 1965. 170.

9. "how to move in the spaces . . .": Ibid., 178.

9. "NO to spectacle . . .": Ibid., 178.

10. They took their timing from Rudner . . . : Sara Rudner interview with Rose Anne Thom, Feb. 19, 1995. [Oral History Project, NYPL]

11. "she was kind of a formidable . . .": Margaret Jenkins interview with author, May 30, 2000.

11. "a silent ritual": Marcia Marks, *Dance*, January 1966, 58–59.

11. Jenkins remembers: Jenkins/MBS.

12. Huot remembers: Robert Huot interview with author, June 20, 2000.

12. "a man . . . indulged in some mock . . .": Clive Barnes, *NYT*, December 4, 1965.

12. "There certainly wasn't anything . . .": Jenkins/MBS.

12. "It was very dramatic stories . . .": Rudner/Thom, NYPL.

12. "Thank *God* I'm walking . . .": Rudner interviewed by author for *Making Dances*, Blackwood Productions, 1980.

13. "I've been trained . . .": Jenkins/MBS.

13. He thought it might be possible . . . : Huot/MBS.

2. Dance Activities 1967–1969

page

15. "2 Dance Companies . . .": *NYT*, February 15, 1967.

15. football signals: Huot/MBS, June 20, 2000.

15. "classical trio . . .": chronology in *Dance Magazine*, April 1973, unpaginated.

15. Rudner remembered . . . : Rudner/Thom, NYPL.

15. When one dancer was doing her solo . . . : Rudner e-mail to author, September 6, 2000.

15. "a melodramatic trio": chronology in *Dance Magazine*, April 1973.

15. "a total rage": Rudner/Thom, NYPL.

16. "when you took a step . . .": Ibid.

16. After an advance viewing . . . : Ibid.

16–17. "I must say . . .": "Eggs Don't Bounce," *Dance and Dancers*, May 1967.

17. Jenkins also felt . . . : Jenkins/MBS.

17–18. "I had given it up a few times . . .": Theresa Dickinson interview with author, May 16, 2000.

18. "Twyla's sitting there . . .": Ibid.

18–19. a thoughtful and admiring column . . . : "Prone Sprawl," *Village Voice*, February 15, 1968.

19. Johnston's interests . . . : Jill Johnston, Preface to *Marmalade Me* (Hanover, N.H.: Wesleyan University Press, 1998), xi–xv.

19. "three and a half minute spectacular": chronology in *Dance Magazine*, April 1973.

19. "highly controlled and choreographed . . .": Rudner/Thom, NYPL.

20. "light and absence of it . . .": Daniel Webster, *Philadelphia Inquirer*, January 14, 1969.

20. "a little chaos . . .": *PCTS*, 100–102.

20. "slip phrase": Rudner/Thom, NYPL.

22. "it was incredibly invigorating . . .": Jenkins/MBS.

22. "very attracted to Twyla's . . .": Dickinson/MBS.

22. Dickinson remembers . . . : Ibid.

23. tense, historic family portrait: The picture ran on October 20, 1968. Jack Mitchell recalled years later that "The shoot was brief, not especially convivial, and no one lingered after." (*Dance Magazine*, December 2000, 16.)

23. "There was a little bit of contempt . . .": Dickinson/MBS.

23. Anna Kisselgoff seemed caught . . . : *NYT*, February 4, 1969.

24. "dealt with movement . . .": Tharp interview with Deborah Jowitt, September 1975.

24. "centered balletic movements": *NYT*, February 4, 1969.

24. "It wasn't really close enough . . .": Lord/MBS, August 31, 2000.

24–25. "Quintet in three sections . . .": chronology in *Dance Magazine*, April 1973.

25. "very very dancey . . .": Tharp/Jowitt, September 1975.

25. "logical exercises": Gerald Mast, *A Short History of the Movies* (New York: MacMillan Publishing Company, 1986), 454.

25. "performed in three adjacent squares . . .": chronology in *Dance Magazine*, April 1973.

25. "arrangement of many situations . . .": choreographic notes, TTA.

25. Tharp arrived at rehearsals . . . : Rudner/Thom, NYPL.

25–26. Laudenslager was becoming . . . : Lord/MBS.

26. Wright found her way . . . : Rose Marie Wright/MBS, December 1, 1999.

26. "enigmatic but forceful": Daniel Webster, *Philadelphia Inquirer*, January 14, 1969.

26. "organized spontaneity": James Felton, *The Evening Bulletin*, January 14, 1969.

26–27. "Double quintet . . .": chronology in *Dance Magazine*, April 1973.

27. "Watching a piece . . .": "The Avant-Garde on Broadway," *Ballet Review*, Spring 1969, vol.2 no.3.

27. "We weren't thinking about getting paid . . .": R. M. Wright/MBS, December 1, 1999.

27. "extreme moment of Nirvana": Dickinson/MBS.

27. "We knew one another's abilities . . .": *PCTS*, 104–5.

27. "The things we worked on . . .": Rudner/Thom, NYPL.

3. The End of Amazonia 1969–1971

page

29. Reinhart felt a clean sweep . . .": Charles Reinhart interview with author, September 30, 2000.

29. Doris Humphrey Choreographic Fellowship. Ibid.

30. "we would find . . .": *PCTS*, 117.

31. "a dramatic situation": choreographic notes, TTA.

31. All six company dancers . . . : *PCTS*, 120–121.

32. Actually, Rudner was dancing . . . : Rudner conversation with author, November 6, 2000.

32. Tharp spent the rest of the evening . . . : *PCTS*, 122.

32–33. For example, her notes . . . : choreographic notes, TTA.

33. For Tharp, the axiomatic pedestrianism . . . : Tharp's notes for unpublished manuscript, Laura Shapiro and Twyla Tharp, note to p. 121, Item 24.

33. "a masterly coup . . .": *NYT*, July 21, 1969.

34. "a mounting density of movement . . .": Dickinson/MBS.

34. In September of 1969 he used it . . . : Shapiro, unpublished manuscript, 130.

35. *La Prose du Transsibérien* . . . : Roger Shattuck, *The Banquet Years* (New York: Vintage, 1968), 349.

35. Historian Stephen Kern . . . : Stephen Kern, *The Culture of Time and Space 1880–1918* (Cambridge: Harvard University Press, 1983), 72–74.

35. "the last of the great '60s art spectaculars": Calvin Tomkins, *Off the Wall* (New York: Penguin Books, 1983), 291.

35. (Tharp says . . .): *PCTS*, 125–126.

35. and the auditorium passages . . . : Lincoln Kaye, *Hartford Courant*, November 16, 1969.

36. "People are more accustomed . . .": Tharp interview with author, December 13, 2000.

36. "walking around the museum . . .": program for *Dancing in the Streets*, Hartford, November 11, 1969.

36. "quietly watching a monitor . . .": Ibid.

37. Rudner was hoping . . . : Rudner/Thom, NYPL.

37. "very dancey and steppy": R.M. Wright/MBS, December 27, 2000.

37. "a spectacular solo study . . .": *Dance Magazine*, March 1970, 90–92.

38. never intended to be finished: program for *Dancing in the Streets*, Hartford, November 11, 1969.

38. "we'd just walk by . . .": Tharp/MBS, December 27, 2000.

38. At the library . . . : Rudner conversation with author, January 11, 2001.

38. Tharp created a new solo . . . : R.M. Wright/MBS, December 27, 2000.

38. "aristocratic movement . . .": Don McDonagh, *The Rise and Fall and Rise of Modern Dance* (New York: Outerbridge & Dientsfrey, 1970), 116.

38. "chewed gum and did a sort of Swedish . . .": Lincoln Kaye, *Hartford Courant*, November 11, 1969.

38. "At the count of 42 . . .": Ibid.

38. The audience and the performers . . . : program for *Dancing in the Streets*.

38–39. finding herself dancing face-to-face with one of her teachers . . . : Rosalind Newman interview with author, March 7, 2000.

39. "She'd tell us . . .": R.M. Wright/MBS, December 1, 1999.

39. "Twyla didn't come up to you . . .": Rudner/Thom, NYPL.

39. "Twyla, when she *loves* you . . .": R.M. Wright/MBS, December 7, 1999.

39–40. "She really did care . . .": Newman/MBS.

40. "We shared adversities . . .": Tharp's notes for unpublished manuscript, Laura Shapiro and Twyla Tharp, note to p. 125, Item 26.

40. Tupling confirms this: Shapiro, unpublished manuscript, 124–125.

40. costumes borrowed from choreographer-designer James Waring: Tharp/MBS, December 13, 2000.

40. Bob Huot came up with the idea . . . : Huot/MBS, June 22, 2000.

41. "Twyla never figured out . . .": Newman/MBS.

41. "I know they can't see . . .": Marcia B. Siegel, "Two Museum Pieces," *At the Vanishing Point* (New York: Saturday Review Press, 1972), 272.

41. Anna Kisselgoff of the *Times* . . . : *NYT*, January 23, 1970.

41. "wearisome": *Dance Magazine*, March 1970, 90–92.

41. Roz Newman remembers . . . : Newman/MBS.

42. "I had every intention of quitting . . .": Tharp/MBS, December 13, 2000.

42. "political declamations . . .": Ibid.

43. Tharp's hometown . . . : Robert V. Hine, *California's Utopian Colonies* (Berkeley: University of California Press, 1983), 158.

43. "go back in and do better": Tharp's notes for unpublished manuscript, Laura Shapiro and Twyla Tharp, note to p. 131, Item 2.

43. "I made more dance . . .": *PCTS*, 132.

44. "We were like people who went out . . .": Shapiro, unpublished manuscript, 142.

44. "I thought it was fabulous . . .": Isabel Garcia-Lorca interview with author, January 18, 2001.

44. According to Wright . . . : R. M. Wright/MBS, December 1, 1999.

45. Tharp's notes for this . . . : choreographic notes, TTA.

45. According to Boston critic . . . : Jane Goldberg, *Boston Globe*, September 1, 1970.

45. Perhaps prompted by a dream . . . : "Margery Tupling had a dream in which we were working on a dance with one hundred parts." Tharp's notes for *Group Activities*, *Ballet Review*, vol.2 no.5, 1969, 20.

45–46. All 150 could be done . . . : choreographic notes, TTA.

46. "trying to get the world . . .": Tharp quoted in email, Allen Robertson to author, January 5, 2001.

46. Tharp compared it to a man's game: Shapiro, unpublished manuscript, 135–140.

46. deliberately acknowledging Bach: Tharp's notes for unpublished manuscript, Laura Shapiro and Twyla Tharp, note to p. 136, Item 6.

47. Tharp was furious . . . : Dana Reitz interview with author, August 17, 2000, and Kenneth Rinker interview with author, January 19, 2001.

47. Dana Reitz had just graduated . . . : Reitz/MBS.

48. Tharp thought this was a bad idea . . . : Brenda Way interview with author, January 9, 2001.

50. "a leg phrase . . .": R. M. Wright/MBS, March 2, 2001.

50. At Battery Park . . . : R. M. Wright/MBS, December 1, 1999.

50. "fairly elaborate improvisations . . .": "Twyla Tharp: Questions and Answers," *Ballet Review*, vol.4, no.1, 1971, 44.

50. Rudner and Wright thought the costumes . . . : R. M. Wright/MBS, December 1, 1999.

51. Paul Epstein, an attorney . . . : Paul Epstein conversation with author, February 8, 2005.

4. The Entertainer 1971–1973

page

52. "I realized early on . . .": Huot/MBS, June 20, 2000.

52. "I think I was probably . . .": Huot/MBS, June 22, 2000.

54. "this determined little figure . . .": Kosmas/MBS, January 29, 2001.

54–55. Dana Reitz, who was rehearsing . . . : Reitz/MBS, August 17, 2000.

55–56. Tharp explained that she had not intended . . . : choreographic notes, TTA.

56. "an excruciatingly specific time score . . .": Brenda Way/MBS, January 9, 2001

56. Tharp says she noted . . . : *PCTS*, 156.

57. 1974 broadcast of the dance: "Twyla Tharp and Eight Jelly Rolls," London Weekend Television, 1974. Derek Bailey, producer and director.

57. For Rudner's solo . . . : Rudner/Thom, NYPL.

58. "I hated that separation . . .": R. M. Wright/MBS, December 1, 1999.

59. one can't identify too closely . . . : Gerald Mast, *The Comic Mind—Comedy and The Movies* (Chicago: University of Chicago Press, 1979), 21.

59. The last Jelly Roll . . . : R. M. Wright/MBS, December 7, 1999.

60. lost interest in *The Fugue* . . . : Clive Barnes, *NYT*, September 19, 1971.

60. "two gawky, interminable essays . . .": Greer Johnson, *Cue*, September 22, 1971.

60. "Twyla Tharp's subject . . .": "Twyla Tharp's Red Hot Peppers," *Ballet Review*, winter 1971.

60. one of the hundred outstanding . . . : *The San Bernardino Sun*, June 22, 1971.

61. "You can't get to feeling safe . . .": Marcia B. Siegel, *The Boston Herald Traveler*, May 9, 1972.

61. "less bourgeois" venue . . . : Jean-Pierre Barbe, *l'Aurore*, November 4, 1971. [author's translation]

61. Tharp wanted to perform . . . : Tharp interview with Lise Brunel, *Chroniques de l'Art Vivant*, Paris, 1971.

61. Rudner only knew eighty . . . : Rudner conversation with author, February 17, 2001.

61. "We cried.": R. M. Wright/MBS, December 7, 1999.

62. nothing but pretension . . . : F. de S., *Le Figaro*, November 11, 1971. [author's translation]

62. "Poor Torelli!": Jean-Pierre Barbe, *l'Aurore*, November 4, 1971. [author's translation]

62. Claude Sarraute of *Le Monde* . . . : Sarraute, *Le Monde*, November 5, 1971.

62. John Percival came over . . . : Percival, *Dance and Dancers*, January 1972.

62. After the Festival . . . : Kosmas/MBS, January 29, 2001.

62. Tharp later acknowledged . . . : Tharp interview with Don McDonagh, May 30, 1973.

63. As recorded for television's *Camera Three* . . . : "The Bix Pieces," *Camera Three*, recorded May 18, 1973, Merrill Brockway, producer.

64. "Why They Were Made": all quotes from part two of *The Bix Pieces*, by Twyla Tharp.

65. Wright would start a phrase . . . : R. M. Wright/MBS, June 26, 2001.

67. "It's the amount of traffic . . .": William Whitener interview with author, October 15, 2001.

68. *The Raggedy Dances*: observations based on a tape made in performance at the College of St. Catherine in Minneapolis, November 1972.

68. "She dances for a long time . . .": Deborah Jowitt, "Enter the Dancers, Rippling Fastidiously," *Village Voice*, November 2, 1972.

68. "that it was somebody . . .": Garcia-Lorca/MBS, January 18, 2001.

69. Clive Barnes loved "The Bix Pieces": *NYT*, September 14, 1972.

69. "her work has a mixture . . .": Clive Barnes, *NYT*, November 5, 1972.

69. "Are modern dancers . . .": Ellen Jacobs, "Modern dance goes public," *Changes*, December/January 1973, 14.

69–70. Robert Joffrey attended the Delacorte . . . : Sasha Anawalt, *The Joffrey Ballet* (New York: Scribner, 1996), 278.

71. The rest of the songs . . . : *PCTS*, 180–181.

72. lack of condescension . . . : Greil Marcus, *Mystery Train* (New York: E.P. Dutton, 1976), 113.

72. "I was not a strong technical dancer . . .": Garcia-Lorca/MBS, January 18, 2001.

72. "I'm not a ballet dancer . . .": Rinker/MBS, January 19, 2001.

72. "I was just open . . .": Beatriz Rodriguez interview with author, July 20, 2001.

73. "Steps were being thrown out . . .": Richard Colton interview with author, June 26, 2001.

73. "I became Twyla's liaison . . .": R. M. Wright/MBS, December 7, 1999.

74. When money problems . . . : Tharp interview with DMcD, April 20, 1972.

74. "a 1950's ballet in sneakers . . .": Clive Barnes, *NYT*, March 18, 1973.

74. "choreographic squiggling": Clive Barnes, *NYT*, November 11, 1973.

74. When she heard about the mass exodus . . .": Rebecca Wright interview with author, July 19, 2001.

75. "out comes Beatriz Rodriguez . . .": Robb Baker, "Twyla Tharp's 'Deuce Coupe' or, How Alley Oop Came to Dance with the Joffrey," *Dance Magazine*, April 1973.

76. "If someone would run . . .": Colton/MBS, June 26, 2001.

76. "it felt like we were all dancing together . . .": Rinker/MBS, January 19, 2001.

76. "She was one of us . . .": Christine Uchida interview with author, April 12, 2002.

77. "An ongoing upstage mural . . .": *PCTS*, 181.

77. "I never lost sight . . .": *PCTS*, 177.

77. a cover story on graffiti: "The Graffiti 'Hit' Parade," *New York*, March 26, 1973.

78. "the marvelously zany . . .": Alan Rich, *New York*, March 26, 1973.

5. Local to Express 1973–1975

page

80. "I got on the Twyla Tharp train . . ." and subsequent quotes: Kenneth Rinker interview with author, January 19, 2001.

83. "Define classical": William Whitener interview with author, October 16, 2001.

85. "We knew exactly the direction . . .": Colton/MBS, June 26, 2001.

85. "the more feminine side . . .": Whitener/MBS, October 16, 2001.

86. Kisselgoff liked *As Time Goes By* . . . : Anna Kisselgoff, *NYT*, October 26, 1973.

86. his pleasure in it . . . : Clive Barnes, *NYT*, November 11, 1973.

86. "Miss Tharp creates for the moment . . .": Ibid.

87. "more to be censured . . .": Robert Commanday, *San Francisco Chronicle*, May 30, 1974.

87. "the Nijinska of our time.": Arlene Croce, "A Moment in Time," *The New Yorker*, November 19, 1973.

87. "a whole range of dynamics . . .": Deborah Jowitt, "Gimme a little time to play in," *Village Voice*, November 1, 1973.

87–88. She wrote rambling notes . . . : Tharp's choreographic notes, TTA.

88. "Staring success in the face . . .": Tharp interviewed by Mike Steele, *Minneapolis Tribune*, January 27, 1974.

88. "but that means traveling . . .": Tharp interview with Peter Williams, *Dance and Dancers*, May 1974.

88. In one of the three *Egg Stories* . . . : The first of the three *Egg Stories* filmed by WGBH was edited into a 1982 Tharp anthology video called the *Scrapbook*.

89. "Eggs Don't Bounce": John Percival, *Dance and Dancers*, May 1967.

89. "It involved a linear sequence . . .": Tom Rawe in email to the author, December 30, 2001.

89. She and Rinker performed . . . : R. M. Wright/MBS, December 1, 1999.

89. "taking dance into a larger context . . .": Mike Steele, *Minneapolis Tribune*, January 28, 1974.

89. introspection beneath the entertainment . . . : Peter Altman, *Minneapolis Star*, n.d.

90. "She wanted to find out . . .": Tom Rawe and Jennifer Way interview with the author, April 8, 2001.

91. "I think it was only then . . .": Ibid.

92. "When she was performing . . .": Rinker/MBS, January 19, 2001.

92. "It just makes sense . . .": Garcia-Lorca/MBS, January 18, 2001.

93. "I made it easy for her . . .": Ibid.

93. It was a risky venture . . . : Rinker/MBS, January 19, 2001.

93. two glowing reviews: Clement Crisp, "Twyla Tharp" and "The Raggedy Dances," *Financial Times*, May 1974, n.d.

93. "portentous meaning . . .": Peter Williams, "The Movable Tharp," *Dance and Dancers*, July 1974.

94. "one of my happiest evenings . . .": Mary Clarke, *Dancing Times*, May 1974.

94. "unqualified success . . .": Peter Rosenwald, *Dance News*, May 1974.

95. "With Twyla it was the intelligence . . .": Sara Rudner talking on documentary section of "Twyla Tharp and *Eight Jelly Rolls*," London Weekend Television, 1974.

95–96. Tharp came down with the flu . . . : R. M. Wright/MBS, March 2, 2001.

96. Along with *Eight Jelly Rolls* . . . : R. M. Wright/MBS, March 2, 2001, and Tharp's email to author, February 22, 2002.

97. For the finale . . . : R. M. Wright/MBS, March 2, 2001.

97. she admits to pursuing him . . . : *PCTS*, 167, 170, 186, 192.

99. She didn't have the patience . . .: William Kosmas interview with author, January 29, 2001.

99. She began a workshop . . . : Sharon Kinney interview with author, May 1, 2000.

99. "the most decisive young American . . .": *Vogue*, June 1975, 102–103.

99. "backed off . . .": Kosmas/MBS, January 29, 2001.

100. "I was out on a farm . . .": Tharp at lecture-demonstration, taped during Minneapolis-St. Paul residency, February 20, 1975.

100. "She processed information . . .": Rhoda Grauer interview with author, October 24, 2000.

100. She remembers making a deal . . . : Ibid.

101. This 1906 building . . . : *Minneapolis Star*, February 19, 1975 and Roy Close email to author, April 22, 2002.

101. Grauer saw Weil . . . : Grauer/MBS, October 24, 2000.

101. In addition to the open rehearsals . . . : press release, Walker Art Center, January 31, 1975.

101. They acquired a contingent . . . : Tom Rawe and Jennifer Way/MBS, April 8, 2001.

102. Tickets for the performances . . . : advertisement, *St. Paul Pioneer Press*, February 9, 1975.

102. "The result is like a spinning trip . . .": Allen Robertson, *Minnesota Daily*, February 28, 1975.

102. Tharp filtered the movement material . . . :" *PCTS*, 205–206.

102. she began making material . . ." : *PCTS*, 193.

102. "four desperate people . . .": *PCTS*, 194.

102. The title was a tribute . . . : Rawe and Way/MBS, April 8, 2001.

103. "really is a recapitulation . . .": R. M. Wright/MBS, June 26, 2001.

103. "The material was much more mushy . . .": Ibid.

103. the definitive Twyla Tharp style: Laura Shapiro, unpublished ms, 194.

104. a give-back piece: Rawe and Way/MBS, April 8, 2001.

104. chosen to initiate the PBS *Dance in America* series: "Sue's Leg: Remembering the '30s" first aired March 24, 1976.

104. "In my wildest imagination . . .": Rinker/MBS, January 19, 2001.

6. The Big Leagues 1975–1978

page

107. "sort of men and women on stage . . .": Mikhail Baryshnikov interview with author, July 25, 2002.

107. *The 49 Amici* . . . : *NYT*, July 13, 1975.

107. Tharp decided to dance . . . : *PCTS*, 206.

107. "how refined and delicate . . .": Baryshnikov/MBS, July 25, 2002.

107. "they were both obviously amazed . . .": Clive Barnes, *NYT*, January 11, 1976.

107. After Spoleto . . . : *PCTS*, 204.

107. "She was trying to explain to me . . .": Baryshnikov/MBS, July 25, 2002.

108. The first movement belonged to Baryshnikov . . . : These observations are based on the film *Baryshnikov by Tharp* (later called *Baryshnikov Dances Sinatra*), videotaped in 1984 and released by Kultur. I have also studied a performance taped at the Kennedy Center, April 10, 1977. The other principals in 1984 were Susan Jaffe, Elaine Kudo, Cheryl Yaeger, and Robert La Fosse. In my descriptions I have used the original cast to avoid confusion.

109–110. "She was trying to understand . . .": Baryshnikov/MBS, July 25, 2002.

110. "veneer of chaos": Laura Shapiro, *The Boston Globe*, February 1, 1976.

110. "alphabet dancing": Tharp interview with Jane Perlez, *New York Post*, January 1, 1976.

111. "We were a bit afraid . . .": Susan Jones interview with author, May 30, 2002.

113. Tharp had encouraged . . . : Tharp in studio runthrough, videotaped December 13, 1975.

113. Afterward, Gelsey Kirkland . . . : Charles France interview with author, August 1, 2002.

113. "simplistically Oedipal": John T. Elson, *Time*, January 19, 1976.

113. "It has charm, vivacity, humor . . .": Clive Barnes, *NYT*, January 11, 1976.

113. "a real work of art . . .": Arlene Croce, "More or Less Terrific," *The New Yorker*, January 26, 1976.

113. "slapstick . . .": Roger Copeland, *NYT*, February 1, 1976.

113. "rites of personality worship . . .": Dale Harris, *Atlantic Monthly*, August 1976.

114. "the hottest ticket . . .": George Gelles, *Washington Star*, February 8, 1976.

114. "a hit of such proportions . . .": Charles Payne, *American Ballet Theatre* (New York: Knopf, 1977), 251.

114. "adjusted his classic technique . . .": Ibid., 282.

114. Charles Payne relates in his company history . . . : Ibid., 243–239.

115. "lack of artistic encouragement": Dale Harris, *The Guardian*, January 20, 1976.

115. "I cannot think seriously . . .": Tharp to Alan Kriegsman, *The Washington Post*, March 28, 1976.

115. "You had to repeat it . . .": Martine Van Hamel interview with author, May 9, 2002.

115–116. "Balanchine's stage": Shapiro, unpublished ms, 244–248.

116. twenty-six photographs . . . : *Baryshnikov at Work—Mikhail Baryshnikov Discusses his Roles*, photography by Martha Swope, ed. Charles Engell France (New York: Knopf, 1976), 244–251.

116. Baryshnikov had to pull her on . . . : Baryshnikov/MBS, July 25, 2002.

116. "to experience Twyla . . .": *Baryshnikov at Work*, 245.

116. Tharp had miscalculated . . . : Ibid.

117. Tharp's real project . . . : Shapiro unpublished ms, 244–245.

117. a young television producer . . . : Don Mischer interview with author, September 18, 2002.

117. He remembers that he just couldn't . . . : Baryshnikov/MBS, July 25, 2002.

117. "I didn't make anything . . .": Tharp talking on *Making Television Dance: A Videotape by Twyla Tharp*, PBS, first aired October 4, 1977.

117. Six screens were to flank the stage . . . : Grauer/MBS, October 24, 2000.

118. "create dance with imagery . . .": Mischer/MBS, September 18, 2002.

118. Ken Rinker didn't like . . . : Rinker/MBS, January 19, 2001.

118. Rose Marie Wright was taking some time off . . . : Wright interviewed by Allen Robertson, *Minnesota Daily*, June 4, 1976.

118–119. Washington was a student . . . : Shelley Washington interview with author, May 14, 2002.

119. "All of a sudden . . .": Washington/MBS, October 28, 1991.

119. "Something about the way Twyla worked . . .": Washington/MBS, May 14, 2002.

119. Uchida, feeling stalled . . . : Christine Uchida interview with author, April 12, 2002.

119. "freezes with moves away": Mischer/MBS, September 18, 2002.

120. "skipping rope . . .": Grauer/MBS, October 24, 2000.

120. "Television can come closer . . .": Tharp talking on *Making Television Dance*.

122. Mischer notes how labor intensive . . . : Mischer/MBS, September 18, 2002.

123. she was a great fan of country music . . . : Tharp interview with author, February 24, 2003.

123. "makes an across-the-board difference . . .": Arlene Croce, "Tharp's Progress," *The New Yorker*, November 22, 1976.

123. the Joffrey Ballet was sliding . . . : Anawalt, *The Joffrey Ballet*, 314.

124. "I've always wanted to have . . .": Tharp interviewed by Amanda Smith, *womenSports*, March 1977, 22.

124. "dance, real dance, on ice . . .": Mary Grace Butler, letter to the author, May 23, 2000.

124. "I wasn't sure that I wanted to be involved . . .": Tharp/MBS, February 24, 2003.

124. Tom Rawe and Jennifer Way were able . . . : Rawe and Way/MBS, April 8, 2001.

125. The show's nearly nonexistent plot . . . : original script for *Hair*, Pocket Books, 1970.

125. Jack Kroll commented . . . : Jack Kroll, *Newsweek*, March 19, 1979.

125. "She made me realize . . .": Mischer/MBS, September 18, 2002.

125. "Milos didn't know anything about dance . . .": Rinker/MBS, January 19, 2001.

125–126. Forman managed to get the work suspended . . . : Milos Forman, *Turnaround: A Memoir* (New York: Villard Books, 1994), 241–242.

126. "a slight state of readiness": Rawe and Way/MBS, April 8, 2001.

126. On the day they finished . . . : Raymond Kurshals interview with author, February 20, 2003.

127. Tharp went on location . . . : *PCTS*, 217.

128. In an early version . . . : Tharp's choreographic notes, TTA.

129. Tharp was able to use . . . : Kurshals/MBS, February 20, 2003.

7. Hodge Podge Rummage 1975–1979

page

131. "the most inflated reputation . . .": Noel Gillespie, *Washington Times*, February 1976 (n.d.).

132. "one of the most disjointed . . .": Alan Kriegsman, *The Washington Post*, October 4, 1977.

132. "Wiggle, waggle . . .": *New York*, January 10, 1977, 54.

132. "discoveries and advances . . .": Tharp interviewed by John Rockwell, *NYT*, February 23, 1975.

132. Tom Rawe gave classes . . . : *NYT*, March 20, 1977.

133. withdrawal from dancing: Tharp interview, *The Minneapolis Star and Tribune*, 1977 (n.d.).

133. at least one newspaper preview . . . : *The Tenesseean*, October 13, 1977.

133. "Informed dance fans . . .": revised advertisement for performance of November 3, 1977.

134. "the best poems . . .": collage material, promotional flyer, Brooklyn Academy season, spring 1976.

134. One writer complained . . . : Julie Van Camp, *The HOYA*, September 30, 1977.

135. "it was such a treat . . .": Kurshals/MBS, September 2, 2003.

135. Anthony Ferro . . . : Anthony Ferro interview with author, October 8, 2003.

135. Technical problems arose . . . : Rudner/Thom, *NTPL*.

135. For the rehearsal directors . . . : Rawe and Way/MBS, April 8, 2001.

135. enjoyed seeing the alternate versions: Uchida/MBS, April 12, 2002.

135. the movement had been simple . . . : Rinker/MBS, January 19, 2001.

136. "glib and facile": Tharp interviewed by Amanda Smith, "Twyla Tharp: Dance Will Never Be the Same," *MS*, December 1976.

136. Tom Rawe and Jennifer Way discussed . . . : interview with Mike Steele, *Minneapolis Tribune*, May 30, 1977.

137. Rose Marie Wright remembers . . . : R. M. Wright/MBS, September 5, 2002.

137. "everything that I couldn't do . . .": Washington/MBS, October 28, 1991. Also discussed in Washington/MBS, May 14, 2002.

138. Washington gave a nod . . . : videotape of performance, Brooklyn Academy, March 26, 1976.

138. She felt miffed . . . : R. M. Wright/MBS, September 5, 2002.

138. After the Brooklyn performances . . . : Arlene Croce, "Twylathon," *The New Yorker*, April 12, 1976.

138. Wright injured her knee . . . : Rose Marie Wright interview with Allen Robertson, *Minnesota Daily*, June 4, 1976.

138. "As an audience piece . . .": "Twylathon," op. cit.

139. Before that show aired . . . : Tharp email to MBS, August 24, 2003.

139. participating luminaries . . . : The *Daily News*, May 8, 1977.

139. "Reviving those antics . . .": Arlene Croce, "Pure and Simple," *The New Yorker*, May 30, 1977.

140. Rudner realized how much . . . : Rudner/Thom, *NYPL*.

140. "when I first saw Ken dancing . . .": Rachel Lampert email to Kenneth Rinker, January 15, 2001.

140. "I don't think I'd ever seen . . .": Colton/MBS, June 26, 2001.

141. He felt his personal contribution . . . : Ibid.

141. Raymond Kurshals also entered the company . . . : Kurshals/MBS, February 20, 2003 and September 2, 2003.

141. Kurshals danced in the repertory . . . : David Vaughan, *Merce Cunningham—Fifty Years* (New York: Aperture Foundation, 1997), 296–297.

141. the Cage/Cunningham musical aesthetic . . . : Kurshals/MBS, February 20, 2003.

141. When Tom Rawe . . . : Kurshals/MBS, September 2, 2003.

143. an unpublished essay on *Mud* . . . : Allen Robertson, "Formalism as a State of Mind," unpublished.

143–144. Colton has commented . . . : "Making Musical Dance," *Ballet Review*, Winter 1986, 29.

144. "pensive yearnings . . .": Allen Robertson, "Formalism," op. cit.

144. "The Mozart still served . . .": "Making Musical Dance," op. cit.

145. all three performances were sold out . . . : *The Boston Globe*, September 30, 1977.

145. They got the ear . . . : Debra Cash, "The Selling of Twyla Tharp," *The Real Paper*, August 19, 1978.

145. "I had never experienced . . .": Judith Cohen interview with author, June 13, 2003.

145. "it gave real insight . . .": Ramelle Adams interview with author, June 18, 2003.

146. "learning the twenty-count base phrase . . .": Jeff Friedman interview with author, August 7, 2003.

146. turning the monitor toward a mirror . . . : Friedman/MBS, Ibid.

146. listened to the Bach B Minor Mass . . . : Colton/MBS, March 20, 2003.

146. "First and foremost . . .": Whitener/MBS, October 16, 2001.

147. Friedman had protected himself . . . : Friedman/MBS, August 7, 2003.

147. "ghosting affiliation": Katie Glasner interview with author, November 5, 2003.

148. "rebound" dances: *PCTS*, 247.

148. "she quite often needs . . .": Kimmary Williams interview with author, December 16, 2003.

148. "I had been exposed to waste . . .": Tharp commentary for *Confessions of a Cornermaker*, CBS Cable TV, first aired October 13, 1981.

149. The dancers were to enter . . . : Laura Shapiro, unpublished ms., 199.

149. "is trying to go on dancing . . .": Tharp interview with Robert J. Pierce, *Soho Weekly News*, February 1, 1979.

149. "Because of her own perceptions . . .": Santo Loquasto interview with author, November 14, 2002.

149. "this one extraordinary comic, free spirit . . .": Rudner/Thom, NYPL.

150. "She didn't really know . . .": Rudner phone conversation with author, January 3, 2004.

150. a game of jacks: *PCTS*, 246.

151. "theoretically the last passage . . .": Tharp interview with Robert J. Pierce, *Soho Weekly News*, op. cit.

8. Family Business 1979–1981

page

152. "a place where each dancer . . .": *PCTS*, 246.

152. "a society whose conventions are clear": Tharp commentary for *Confessions of a Cornermaker*.

152. Richard Colton remembers . . . : Colton/MBS, March 20, 2003.

152. "a series of small allegorical studies": Christine Temin, *The Boston Globe*, August 10, 1978.

152–153. The characters included . . . : Temin, Ibid., and Debra Cash, *The Real Paper*, August 19, 1978.

153. Tharp and the company had been listening . . . : Colton/MBS, March 20, 2003.

153. they did some of the new material . . . : *The Boston Globe*, August 3, 1978.

153. "a study in genteel cynicism": Tharp narrative for *Scrapbook Tape*, first aired on PBS, October 25, 1982.

153. "macabre figure of death . . .": Linda Small, *Other Stages*, March 8, 1979.

153. Morris auditioned more than once . . . : Joan Acocella, *Mark Morris* (New York: Farrar Straus Giroux, 1993), 45.

153. how to use big men: Colton/MBS, March 20, 2003.

154. "Three sections extracted . . .":program note, Brooklyn Academy, February 15–25, 1979.

154. the dancers had memorized . . . : Tom Rawe conversation with author, February 24, 2004.

155. Richard Colton thinks . . . : Colton/MBS, March 20, 2003.

155. Sunday overview of the season: Anna Kisselgoff, *NYT*, March 18, 1979.

155. Tharp's neutral stance . . . : Jack Anderson, *NYT*, February 15, 1979.

156. "obviously the great dance . . .": Nancy Goldner, *The Nation*, March 24, 1979.

156. "In connecting teen-agerism . . .": Nancy Goldner, *Christian Science Monitor*, February 21, 1979.

156. dramatize her own conflicts . . . : *PCTS*, 250.

156–157. Through mutual contacts . . . : *The Detroit News*, October 31, 1979 and Lewis Lloyd interview with author, April 27, 2000.

157. She had begun building . . . : Robert Coe, "Talking Legs," *Soho Weekly News*, March 19, 1980.

157. He told John Rockwell . . . : Thomas Babe interview with John Rockwell, *NYT*, March 23, 1980.

157. "it seemed to make growing up . . .": Robert Coe, op. cit.

158. "I could hear the intake . . .": Thomas Babe, program book for *When We Were Very Young*, 1981.

158. "a genuine, pleasure-seeking Broadway crowd . . .": Arlene Croce, "Murder, He Said, Said He," *The New Yorker*, April 21, 1980.

158. "I do want my work . . .": Tharp to Susan Reimer-Torn, *International Herald Tribune*, October 4–5, 1980.

159. "about the strenuousness . . .". Nancy Goldner, *Christian Science Monitor*, March 28, 1980

159. "Ironically, it is through cooperativeness . . .": Deborah Jowitt, *Village Voice*, April 7, 1980.

159. "I acknowledge the difficulty . . .": Tharp to Erica Abeel, *Cue*, February 15, 1980.

159. Tharp's foot was in a cast . . . : Colton/MBS, June 26, 2001.

159. Colton also taught . . . : Ibid.

160. "encompasses just about everything . . .": William Whitener to Josie Neal, *San Antonio Light*, February 26, 1984.

160. Deborah Jowitt contrasted . . ." *The Village Voice*, April 7, 1980.

160. "to breathe and behave": Colton/MBS, June 26, 2001.

161. "new ways to torture . . .": Tharp at preview showing, September 12, 1980, author's notes.

162. "formal movement problems . . .": Anna Kisselgoff, *NYT*, September 29, 1981.

162. she disdained being just one . . . : Steve Dennin interview with author, April 9, 2004.

162. "Brooklyn, like Berkeley . . .": Tharp to *San Francisco Chronicle*, March 5, 1981.

162. "We get the same fee . . .": Tharp to Marcia B. Siegel, "Twyla Tharp Goes Clean," *Soho Weekly News*, March 18, 1981.

162. the business became increasingly complicated: Dennin/MBS, April 9, 2004.

163. Forman called on her again: Forman, *Turnaround*, 257–279.

163. She delegated Shelley Freydont . . . : Shelley Freydont interview with author, January 12, 2004.

164. She started choreographing the scene . . . : Baryshnikov/MBS, July 25, 2002.

164. Merrill Brockway joined the venture . . . : *Dance Magazine*, August 1981.

164–165. He thinks he was offered the job . . . : Merrill Brockway interview with author, April 19, 2002.

165. Tharp got paid $50,000 . . . : *Wall Street Journal*, March 26, 1981.

165. full-page ad . . . : *Variety*, March 18, 1981.

165. But the new venture . . . : *Newsweek*, March 15, 1982.

165. within a year . . . : *Time*, September 27, 1982.

165. Five public television stations . . . : *NYT*, September 16, 1982.

165–166. According to Don Mischer . . . : Mischer/MBS, September 18, 2002.

166. In 1984 the whole American Ballet Theater cast . . . : Mischer/MBS, Ibid.

166. Arlene Croce didn't think . . . : Arlene Croce, "Murder, He Said, Said He," *The New Yorker*, April 21, 1980.

166. Thomas Babe was there too . . . : Thomas Babe, program book for *When We Were Very Young*, 1981.

166. No one remembers anything about it except . . . : Freydont/MBS, January 12, 2004.

166–167. Tharp tallied the number . . . *The Boston Globe*, June 26, 1980.

167. "Her voice was neutral . . .": *Boston Herald-American*, June 15, 1980.

167. From two retired earlier dances . . . : R. M. Wright/MBS, September 5, 2002.

167. she called the dancers . . . : *Dance Magazine*, July 1981.

167. The first Winter Garden season . . . : *PCTS*, 254.

168. "My company has never done . . .": Tharp to Robert Palmer, *NYT*, September 20, 1981.

168. she planned to dance this role . . . : *PCTS*, 264.

169–170. Byrne figured that . . . : David Byrne email to author, March 11, 2004.

170. one of 1981's ten best recordings . . . : *NYT*, December 30, 1981 and *Soho Weekly News*, December 30, 1981.

171. they quarreled bitterly . . . : Linda Shelton interview with author, June 3, 2004.

171. A complicated disposition . . . : David Byrne email, op. cit.

171. "message she has so purposefully muddled . . .": Anna Kisselgoff, *NYT*, September 23, 1981.

171. "lapses in seriousness . . .": Anna Kisselgoff, "Twyla Tharp's Growing Pains," *NYT*, October 4, 1981.

171. "a major event in our theatre . . .": Arlene Croce, "Oh, That Pineapple Rag!," *The New Yorker*, October 12, 1981.

171. Afterward Tharp claimed . . .": *PCTS*, 265.

172. she'd even invested . . . : Tharp/MBS, November 28, 1981.

172. the "Bumstead" narrative . . . : Anna Kisselgoff, *NYT*, September 23, 1981.

172. "sets forth the idea . . .": Janice Berman Alexander, *Newsday*, September 24, 1981.

172. "[It] begins as a grim epic . . .": Linda Winer, *New York Daily News*, September 25, 1981.

173. Tharp's story line . . . : Tharp's choreographic notes, TTA.

173. According to Tharp, Rudner's character . . . : Tharp/MBS, December 27, 1982.

173. She plotted every shot . . . : Grauer/MBS, October 24, 2000.

174. A month later she was vowing . . . : Tharp/MBS, November 28, 1981.

174. "It's quite clear . . .": *Wall Street Journal*, March 26, 1981.

175. Now, through a new BAM agency . . . : *NYT*, July 8, 1982 and *The Brooklyn Phoenix*, June 10, 1982.

9. Romance and the Opposite 1982–1983

page

177. the best *Deuce Coupe* . . . : *NYT*, August 27, 1981 and September 28, 1981.

177. "My priority has always got to be . . .": TT/MBS, November 28, 1981.

179. "world of vignettes . . .": Colton/MBS, March 20, 2003.

180. "clichéd youth culture . . .": Anna Kisselgoff, *NYT*, September 26, 1981.

180. "Its people are out of sync . . .": Tharp's narration, *Confessions of a Cornermaker*.

180. "verbs that we all know and recognize . . .": Tharp's introduction to video of *The Catherine Wheel*, first aired on the BBC, March 1, 1983 and on PBS *Dance in America*, March 28, 1983.

180. Before its stage premiere . . . : Tharp's own chronologies, in *Push Comes to Shove* and other internal documents, sometimes don't agree with premiere dates given in other sources. She often tried out works on tour, publicizing "premieres" in more than one city, then gave additional "premieres" when the company had its New York seasons.

181. Sometime after she had made the *Sinatra* . . . : PCTS, 274.

181. She worked out the early material . . . : Washington/MBS, May 14, 2002.

182. She remembers the *Sinatra* . . . : Amy Spencer interview with author, April 28, 2004.

183. She thought of it as a French nightclub dance . . . : Freydont/MBS, January 12, 2004.

183. Tharp said she'd been inspired . . . : PCTS, 271–272.

184. "the careful, faithful interdependency . . .": Burt Supree, *The Village Voice*, December 7, 1982.

184. "Older music has all its connotations . . .": Tharp to Robert Palmer, *NYT*, September 20, 1981.

185. The newly critical field of "dance theory" . . . : See Susan Leigh Foster's *Reading Dancing* (Berkeley: University of California Press, 1986), especially Chapter 4, for the initial salvo in what became a backlash against Tharp. Foster explains how she thought Tharp betrayed the postmodern agenda by making deliberately entertaining dances for the public.

185. "as the dance progresses . . .": Michael Fleming, *Fort Worth Star Telegram*, October 29, 1984.

185. "relaxation of concentration": Joan Acocella, *Dance Magazine*, November 1984.

186. "something like a panorama . . .": Arlene Croce, "Tharp's Sinatra," *The New Yorker*, February 13, 1984

186–187. The company rented itself out . . . : *Sun Reporter*, February 14, 1985.

187. "a beleaguered straight man . . .": Anna Kisselgoff, *NYT*, February 14, 1984.

187. "Suspicion, nothing better . . .": Laura Shapiro, *Seattle Weekly*, October 27, 1982.

187. "nature's darker forces": Tharp's narration, *Scrapbook Tape*.

187. thrift-shop underwear: Santo Loquasto/MBS, November 14, 2002.

187. she started thinking about ritual sacrifice . . . PCTS, 269–270.

187. Tharp says *Bad Smells* was conceived . . . : Tharp's narration, *Scrapbook Tape*.

188. "stark, austere minimalist . . .": Roger Copeland, "Why Women Dominate Modern Dance," *NYT*, April 18, 1982.

188. "a caprice for beautiful people": George Jackson, *The Washington Post*, April 17, 1982.

188. she was thinking about how rock concerts . . . : Tharp interview with Craig Bromberg, *Theatre Crafts*, January 1984.

188. how rock's intense noise levels could release . . . : TT/MBS, November 28, 1981.

188. "I always think of my own music . . .": Glenn Branca interview with John Rockwell, *NYT*, May 2, 1982.

189. *Bad Smells* also began as a film project . . . : Tom Rawe to Mike Steele, *Minneapolis Star and Tribune*, April 6, 1984.

189. "blossom and make abstract shapes . . .": Tharp with Craig Bromberg, *Theatre Crafts*, op. cit.

189. "dog carcasses and three-legged horses . . .": Claudia Dreifus, *Mademoiselle*, July 1982.

189. she wanted them to think of helicopter blades . . . : Richard Colton conversation with author, July 14, 2004.

190. Atlas's camera in *Locale* . . . : Richard Kostelanetz, "Twenty Years of Merce Cunningham's Dance," in *Merce Cunningham: Dancing in Space and Time*, ed. Richard Kostelanetz (New York: Da Capo Press, 1998), 19.

190. "On the stage . . .": Arlene Croce, "Tharp Against Tharp," *The New Yorker*, February 27, 1984.

190. "political, totalitarian, post-nuke resonance": Burt Supree, *The Village Voice*, December 7, 1982.

191. "clubs in which disco dancers . . .": Anna Kisselgoff, *NYT*, February 19, 1984.

191. "deliberately repulsive": Laura Shapiro, *Seattle Weekly*, October 27, 1982.

191. a balance between politesse and amorality . . . : Tharp interview with Janice Berman, *Newsday*, January 22, 1984.

191. "the physical, factual entity . . .": Ibid.

191. "concentration camps, life after death . . .": Tharp interview with Eric Taub, *Ballet News*, February 1984, 19.

191. "The last part of the piece . . .": *New York Beat*, January 1984.

192. wrapped them from head to foot . . . : Loquasto/MBS, November 14, 2002.

192. Mylar floor: Freydont/MBS, January 12, 2004.

192. Tom Rawe remembers . . . : Rawe and Way/MBS, April 8, 2001.

192–193. "What you were feeling . . .": Mary Ann Kellogg interview with author, January 8, 2004.

193. Remembering an effect . . . : Jennifer Tipton interview with author, May 22, 2002.

193. perhaps for practical reasons: Washington email to author, July 28, 2004.

194. "And so the end . . .": Anna Kisselgoff, *NYT*, February 19, 1984.

194. "The fiery Wagnerian beauty . . .": Arlene Croce, "Tharp Against Tharp," *The New Yorker*, February 27, 1984.

194. "a retrospective so energetic . . .": James Leverett, *American Theatre*, April 1984.

195. "The ballet is something we all depend on . . .": Tharp interview with Michael Robertson, *Dance Magazine*, March 1980.

195. "ballets being done . . .": Colton/MBS, April 29, 2004.

195. According to Shelley Freydont . . . : Freydont/MBS, January 12, 2004.

197. "a perfectly charming, diverting little piece . . .": Arlene Croce, "Tharp Against Tharp," *The New Yorker*, February 27, 1984.

197. Tharp had received one of four . . . : *Orlando Sentinel*, July 1, 1984.

198. she retrieved some of the material . . . : Tharp email to author, August 12, 2004.

198. Work on the movie . . . : *Gannett-Westchester Newspapers*, July 8, 1984.

198. previewed in June on a tour . . . : Shelton/MBS, June 3, 2004.

198. "the success of *Sorrow Floats*": Linda Belans, *Spectator* (Raleigh, N.C.), July 25, 1984.

198. Over the audience's loyal cheering . . . : Anne Levin, *The Oak Ridger*, July 13, 1984.

198. Tharp had persuaded . . . : Charles Reinhart interview with author, September 30, 2000.

199. Tharp started choreographing it . . . : Tharp/MBS, November 28, 1981.

199. "vulnerability and introspectiveness . . .": Dale Harris, *The Guardian*, June 10, 1983.

199. "nostalgia piece": Baryshnikov/MBS, July 25, 2002.

199. Tharp had been subtly revising . . . : Susan Jones/MBS, May 30, 2002.

199. "The changing imperatives . . .": Arlene Croce, "Baryshnikov Among Sylphs," *The New Yorker*, June 20, 1983.

199. "a succession of memorable dance images . . .": Dale Harris, *The Guardian*, June 10, 1983.

199. "ballet's collective consciousness": Laura Jacobs, *Boston Phoenix*, February 14, 1984.

10. Three-Way Stretch 1983–1990
page

200. "an incredible symbol . . .": Baryshnikov quoted in Bernard Taper (*Balanchine*, Berkeley: University of California Press, 1987), 354.

200. "he looked like someone . . .": Robert Garis, *Following Balanchine* (New Haven: Yale University Press, 1995), 233.

201. "Tharp's bid to become . . .": Christine Temin, *The Boston Globe*, February 3, 1984.

201. "filled the theater . . .": Jennifer Dunning, *NYT*, June 1, 1984.

201. "how desperately his company needs . . .": Dale Harris, *Wall Street Journal*, February 14, 1984.

201. He had always hoped . . . : Baryshnikov/MBS, July 25, 2002.

201. "sheer density of action . . .": Alan Kriegsman, *The Washington Post*, December 12, 1983.

202. "The object is to raise allegro dancing . . .". Mindy Aloff, *The Nation*, December 31, 1983–January 7, 1984.

202. "the role Gregory has waited . . .": Martha Duffy, *Time*, February 11, 1984.

202. "dance with new-found enthusiasm . . .": Dale Harris, *Wall Street Journal*, February 14, 1984.

202. Throughout the ballet's twenty-seven minutes . . . : Only a low-quality archival tape was available to study this ballet, now out of the repertory. The tape provides very little movement detail and scant information as to the identities of the dancers, but it does reveal Tharp's ingenious group patterns and musicality.

202. "an enormous, whirling, weightless ballet": Arlene Croce, "Guest in the House," *The New Yorker*, July 2, 1984.

203. They'd met in 1973 through Rhoda Grauer . . . : Grauer/MBS, October 24, 2000. Many sources follow the date given by Tharp in her autobiography, 1969, but this seems inaccurate.

203. Robbins had long wanted to collaborate: Deborah Jowitt, *Jerome Robbins—His Life, His Theater, His Dance* (New York: Simon & Schuster, 2004), 472.

203. they infiltrated each other's work . . . : *PCTS*, 294.

204. She hatched a scheme . . . : Tharp to Iris Fanger, *Boston Review*, June 1984.

204. Tharp sent Sara Rudner . . . : Rudner conversation with author, August 24, 2004.

205. "with despair of maintaining a company . . .": Tharp interview with Jennifer Dunning, *NYT*, June 9, 1985.

205. While Steve Dennin struggled . . . : Dennin/MBS, April 9, 2004.

205. "not merely compatible with but essential . . .": Tharp to Joseph Mazo, *Women's Wear*, July 13, 1984.

206. the Rosenfields approached Tharp: Account of the production largely drawn from Sharon Churcher, "Still Kicking—The amazing saga of *Singin' in the Rain*, the $5.7 million turkey that refuses to lie down," *New York Magazine*, October 14, 1985, 40–47.

206. "the lavish production numbers": *New York Post*, June 19, 1984.

206. "I would be able to park my company . . .": *PCTS*, 288.

206. "this is a time of transition . . .": Lewis Lloyd to Janice Ross, *The Oakland Tribune*, April 21, 1985.

206. No further touring . . . : *San Francisco Chronicle*, April 21, 1985.

206. "That worked just fine . . .": Shelton/MBS, June 3, 2004.

206. others had long sensed . . . : Colton/MBS, April 29, 2004.

206. excited about working in tap shoes . . . : Rawe and Washington to Nancy Goldner, *The Philadelphia Inquirer*, February 2, 1985.

206. Eleven company dancers . . . : *NYT*, June 9, 1985.

207. In one of the only sanguine statements . . . : Tharp to Sheryl Flatow, *Playbill*, June 1985.

207. the reason she left the original numbers alone . . . : *PCTS*, 288–289.

207. "look like they're trained dancers . . .": *Vogue*, June 1985, 243.

207. John Carrafa learned tap routines . . . : *The Boston Globe*, March 11, 1985.

208. Tharp was never officially replaced . . . : *The New York Post*, "Page Six," June 21, 1985.

209. "Miss Tharp and company have turned a celestial entertainment . . .": *NYT*, July 3, 1985.

209. *Daily News* headline: *Daily News*, July 3, 1985.

209. "Broadway needs the new blood . . .": Jack Kroll, *Newsweek*, July 15, 1985.

209. she describes herself as suffering . . . : *PCTS*, 297.

209. an effort to recoup the *Catherine Wheel* deficit: Shapiro unpublished ms, 292–293.

210. "an unheard of request . . .": "Footnotes," *Ballet News*, December 1985.

210. People told the story . . . : Doug Rosenberg conversation with author, January 11, 2004.

210. Tharp's tough business practices . . . : Shelton/MBS, June 3, 2004.

210. Twenty years later . . . : *Dance Magazine*, February 2005.

210. "I was just in joy . . .": Jamie Bishton interview with author, September 16, 2004.

210. The reconstituted company . . . : *Dance Magazine*, May 1986.

210. Amy Spencer and Richard Colton had left . . . : Spencer/MBS, April 24, 2004.

210. Mary Ann Kellogg had won . . . : Kellogg/MBS, January 8, 2004.

210. Raymond Kurshals also thought . . . : Kurshals/MBS, September 2, 2003.

210. William Whitener passed up the show . . . : Whitener conversation with author, March 4, 2005.

210. Katie Glasner thought she wouldn't fit . . . : Glasner/MBS, November 5, 2003.

211. "I like to develop movement . . .": Tom Rawe to Nancy Goldner, *Philadelphia Inquirer*, January 4, 1987.

211. "secular mass": Tharp's narrative for *Twyla Tharp—Oppositions* videotape, directed by Derek Bailey, *Dance in America*, 1996.

211. Jack Anderson supplied a New Testament reference . . . : *NYT*, February 5, 1987.

212. Sensing that Tharp would pull her back . . . : Uchida/MBS, April 12, 2002.

212. the Bomb Squad: Jennifer Gelfand interview with author, November 4, 2004.

212. "She *knew* she could make a piece . . .": Spencer/MBS, April 28, 2004.

213. "what one imagines pure oxygen . . .": Nancy Goldner, *The Philadelphia Inquirer*, January 8, 1987.

213. a crucial aesthetic question: Matthew Gurewitsch, *Ballet News*, October 1984, 18–22.

213–214. Croce rejected Lincoln Kirstein's theoretical closure . . . : Arlene Croce, "Postmodern Ballets," *The New Yorker*, February 23, 1987.

214. "Put the performers in pointe shoes . . .": Tobi Tobias, *New York Magazine*, February 23, 1987.

214. "ballet blanc": Tobi Tobias, *New York Magazine*, March 2, 1987.

214. Mindy Aloff assumed . . . : Mindy Aloff, *The Nation*, March 28, 1987.

214. "the most successful ever . . .": Anna Kisselgoff, *NYT*, March 8, 1987.

214. Croce saw the same opportunism . . . : Arlene Croce, *The New Yorker*, February 23, 1987.

214–215. Around the time of the BAM season . . . : Tharp to Janice Berman, *Newsday*, February 1, 1987.

215. "very little real imagination": Tharp to Holly Williams, *The Dallas Morning News*, September 23, 1987.

215. She even offered to move the company . . . : *Dallas Times Herald*, October 1, 1987.

215. "It's not an easy job . . .": Tharp to Lois Draegin, *Savvy*, February, 1987.

215. After the South American tour . . . : *NYM*, June 22, 1987.

215. She was determined . . . : *Albany Times Union*, August 9, 1987.

215. Jamie Bishton told a local paper . . . : *Albany Metroland*, August 20–26, 1987.

215. A special workshop . . . : Rawe and Way/MBS, April 8, 2001.

216. Preparations for the Australian tour . . . : The Australian press recounted most of this episode, which was corroborated and amplified by Linda Shelton. Shelton/MBS, June 3, 2004.

216. the dance material was ready: *NYT*, January 3, 1988.

216. Smeaton was experimenting . . . : Smeaton quoted in *West Australian*, November 18, 1987.

217. "an ideal introduction . . .": *The Australian*, February 3, 1988.

217. Washington did identify . . . : Washington to Sasha Anawalt, *The Los Angeles Herald Examiner*, April 17, 1988.

217. "vigorously gymnastic fun and games . . .": Neil Jillett, *The Age*, February 8, 1988.

217. Patsy Tarr remembers . . . : Patsy Tarr interview with author, September 16, 2004.

218. "temporarily disbanded": *Newsday*, June 24, 1988.

218. Tharp had revealed the dramatic move . . . : Washington/MBS, May 14, 2002.

218. "It was a harder moment": Colton/MBS, April 29, 2004.

218. Amy Spencer received a check . . . : Spencer/MBS, April 28, 2004.

218. Rawe and Way had been edging out . . . : Rawe and Way/MBS, April 8, 2001.

218. Bishton and Sanchez entered . . . : Bishton/MBS, September 16, 2004.

218. There were Negro and Spanish units . . . : Nancy Reynolds and Malcolm McCormick, *No Fixed Points* (New Haven: Yale University Press, 2003), 271–272.

218. Agnes de Mille brought in a package . . . : Carol Easton, *No Intermissions* (Boston: Little, Brown & Company, 1996), 406.

219. Bishton remembers the sojourn . . . : Bishton/MBS, September 16, 2004.

219. Baryshnikov gave her carte blanche: Baryshnikov/MBS, July 25, 2002.

219. Baryshnikov enlisted his patron . . . : *NYT*, June 22, 1989.

220. she'd audited screenwriting courses . . . : Tharp/MBS, October 17, 2004.

220. Tharp expected that *Everlast* . . . : *PCTS*, 328.

221. Arlene Croce analyzed the work . . . : Arlene Croce, "The Little American Girl," *The New Yorker*, June 12, 1989.

221. Jamie Bishton remembers working . . . : Bishton/MBS, September 16, 2004.

221. "all anger, fighting, being bamboozled . . .": Grauer/MBS, October 24, 2000.

221. "With death just around the corner . . .": Tharp in lecture-demonstration, Works and Process at Guggenheim Museum, reported by the *Westsider*, April 27–May 3, 1989.

221. Washington had developed extreme acting skills . . . : Washington/MBS, May 14, 2002.

221. Danny Sanchez did a break dance number . . . : *Chicago Sun Times*, February 20, 1989.

221. the Katzenjammer Kid . . . : Croce, "Little American Girl," op. cit.

222. Rumors surfaced . . . : *The New York Post*, June 22, 1989.

222. Baryshnikov announced his resignation . . . : *NYT*, June 22, 1989.

222. Tharp and fellow artistic associate Kenneth MacMillan . . . : *Los Angeles Times*, March 14, 1990. According to *The New York Times* (May 27, 1990), in July of 1989 ABT didn't renew the contracts of Tharp and MacMillan.

223. Not only did her ballets have cachet . . . : Tharp to Sasha Anawalt, *NYT*, May 27, 1990.

223. "these modern people . . .": Bishton/MBS, September 16, 2004.

224. "It was a success . . .": *PCTS*, 331.

224. "an exhilarating statement . . .": Arlene Croce, "Classical Values," *The New Yorker*, July 2, 1990.

224. "The audience's applause . . .": Deborah Jowitt, *The Village Voice*, May 22, 1990.

224. "as if she would rather appeal . . .": Arlene Croce, "Classical Values," op. cit.

224. Tharp's ballets could cost the company $100,000 . . . : Jane Hermann to *NYT*, June 16, 1991.

II. The Anti-company 1990–1995

page

225. an autobiographical book . . . : This account draws on three conversations between author and Laura Shapiro, September 26, October 14, and November 27, 2004, and an interview between Tharp and Elizabeth Zimmer, August 9, 1992.

226. "it uncannily captures . . .": *The New York Times Book Review*, December 13, 1992.

227. he attended the performance . . . : *NYT*, February 6, 1987.

227. During a hiatus . . . : Shelton/MBS, June 3, 2004.

227. "a young man from the lower ranks . . .": Dale Harris, *Wall Street Journal*, January 31, 1989.

227. suddenly refused to participate . . . : *Pour la danse*, March 1989.

227. Tharp said she had to rebuild . . . : *PCTS*, 323–326.

227. "Her phrases twist, hiccup and backtrack . . .": Barbara Newman, *Sunday Telegraph*, March 26, 1989.

227. "serious and fine work . . .": Anna Kisselgoff, *NYT*, March 8, 1989.

228. "rhythmically slow-clapping . . .": Allen Robertson, *Los Angeles Times/Calendar*, March 5, 1989.

228. Through Linda Shelton's contacts . . . : Shelton/MBS, June 3, 2004.

228. The deal started . . . : *Chicago Tribune*, July 8, 1990.

228. Hubbard Street's artistic director . . . : Conte to Janice Berman, *Newsday*, August 23, 1990.

228. she realized she couldn't continue . . . : Washington/MBS, May 14, 2002.

229. "She kind of just guided me . . .": Ibid.

229. Finally she agreed . . . : Tharp/MBS, October 17, 2004.

229. According to legend . . . : Doug Rosenberg conversation with author, January 11, 2004.

229. Reinhart says Tharp's eccentricities · Reinhart/MBS, September 30, 2000.

229. "a living artist . . .": Wexner Center Foundation press release.

230. Kevin O'Day, feeling restless . . . : Bishton/MBS, September 16, 2004.

230. She toyed with several titles . . . : author's notes, September 13, 1991.

231. Jamie Bishton learned the first fifty . . . : Vera Blaine interview with author, October 6, 1991.

231. she likened the gift . . . : tape of press conference at Ohio State, September 12, 1991.

231. rehearsal and performance videotapes . . . : Although Tharp noted at the time that she had received a National Endowment for the Arts grant to transfer the videos, most of them remained in New York more than a decade after her gift to OSU.

231. a work in progress, and also as a "World Premiere" . . . : program at Mershon Auditorium, October 4 and 5, 1991.

232. Bishton remembers one sequence . . . : Bishton/MBS, September 16, 2004.

232. "which is what tore men and women apart . . .": Tharp's narrative for *Men's Piece* in performance.

232. Tharp was a little late . . . : Tullia Limarzi, *Staten Island Advance*, January 31. 1992.

234. Nancy Goldner thought the false endings . . . : Nancy Goldner, *Philadelphia Inquirer*, January 30, 1992.

234. "An egregiously empty . . .": Jennifer Dunning, *NYT*, February 3, 1992.

234. "an inspired piece of work . . .": Anna Kisselgoff, *NYT*, February 1, 1992.

234. before Tharp settled on the music . . . : Susan Jaffe interview with author, January 21, 2004.

234. "a suite of bubble-rock/Latin numbers . . .": Alastair Macaulay, *The New Yorker*, February 12, 1992.

235. "she takes them further . . .": Joseph Mazo, *The Record*, February 3, 1992.

235. For the last four performances . . . : *New York Post*, February 6, 1992.

235. "Premieres that Restored Faith . . .": Anna Kisselgoff, *NYT*, December 27, 1992.

235. "Dancers, no matter how virtuosic . . .": Linda Winer, *Newsday*, February 7, 1992.

236. Arlene Croce compared . . . : Arlene Croce, "Someone's in the Kitchen with Demeter," *The New Yorker*, October 25, 1993.

237. Jodi Melnick remembers scenes . . .". Jodi Melnick interview with author, November 9, 2004

237. Kinney admired the way Tharp could hold her own . . . : Sharon Kinney interview with author, May 1, 2000.

237. another of Tharp's "finds": Allen Robertson, *Dance Theatre Journal*, summer 1992, 34.

237. Melnick was called back for another season . . . : Melnick/MBS, November 9, 2004.

237–238. "The only reason I keep dancing . . .": Tharp/MBS, October 8, 1993.

238. netted a reported million dollars . . . : Laura Shapiro, *Newsweek*, December 14, 1992.

238. a small tempest . . . : Barbara Zuck, *Dance Magazine*, March 1993, 36, and Chuck Helm of Wexner Center in conversation with the author, November 16, 2004.

238. Kisselgoff called it a premiere: *NYT*, December 2, 1992.

238. the biggest sales day . . . Christine Temin, *The Boston Globe*, January 24, 1993.

238. In West Palm Beach . . . : Elizabeth Zimmer, *Dance View*, summer 1993, 15.

239. a short Annie Leibovitz film . . . : *Los Angeles Times*, September 17, 1992.

239. it was used as promotional material . . . : Tharp/MBS, October 17, 2004.

239. Bits of *Zoetrope*'s movement . . . : Stacy Caddell interview with author, October 17, 2004.

239. Even the dancers . . . : Caddell/MBS, Ibid.

240. "I started thinking of the show . . .": Tharp to Christine Temin, *The Boston Globe*, January 24, 1993.

240. "a colossal ripoff": Alexandra Tomalonis, *Dance View*, autumn 1993, 32.

240. "A vanity production . . .": Anna Kisselgoff, *NYT*, December 2, 1992.

241. "as he was moving around . . .": Bishton/MBS, December 13, 2004.

241. "We dance duets . . .": Tharp interviewed by *Toledo Blade*, November 22, 1992.

241. "Possibly this means . . .": Laura Shapiro, *Newsweek*, December 14, 1992.

241. When Baryshnikov arrived in Columbus . . . : Baryshnikov/MBS, July 25, 2002.

241. he balked at promotional schemes . . . : Bishton/MBS, December 13, 2004.

241. "People have to have the information . . .": Tharp to Barbara Zuck, *Dance Magazine*, March 1993.

242. "She did a very beautiful . . .": Caddell/MBS, October 17, 2004.

242. Tharp thought of the season . . . : TT/MBS, October 8, 1993.

242. "wide-ranging, multifaceted . . .": Arlene Croce, "Someone's in the Kitchen with Demeter," *The New Yorker*, October 25, 1993.

242. Tharp explained how the frisson . . . : Tharp in lecture-demonstration videotaped at Mershon Auditorium, August 27, 1993.

242. "Why is Twyla Tharp not devoting her energies . . .": Dale Harris, *Wall Street Journal*, September 27, 1993.

242–243. Arlene Croce, on the other hand . . . : Croce, "Someone's in the Kitchen with Demeter," op. cit.

243. She donated her services: Robert Johnson, *Dance Magazine*, October 1993.

243. "a very female story": Tharp to Janice Berman, *Newsday*, September 14, 1993.

243. she saw the myth in terms of Demeter's relationships . . . : TT/MBS, October 8, 1993.

243. "A full performance by the Graham company . . .": Anna Kisselgoff, *NYT*, September 16, 1993.

244. she had evolved a process . . . : TT/MBS, October 8, 1993.

244. klezmer simply had more expressive range . . . : Tharp in lecture-demonstration videotaped at Mershon Auditorium, August 27, 1993.

244. "brought out a dramatic projection . . .": Anna Kisselgoff, *NYT*, October 31, 1993.

244. "In the beginning I was feeling very anxious . . .": Christine Dakin to Jennifer Dunning, *NYT*, October 3, 1993.

244. "It's an excellent opportunity . . .": Croce, "Someone's in the Kitchen with Demeter," op. cit.

245. her past work didn't interest her: Tharp in lecture-demonstration videotaped at the New York State Theater, January 24, 2000.

245. "as fine a male dancer . . .": Dale Harris, *Wall Street Journal*, September 27, 1993.

245. Tharp gave him a composite tape . . . : Bishton/MBS, December 13, 2004.

245. Bishton treasures a memorable performance . . . : Bishton/MBS, Ibid.

247. A 1999 profile . . . : Sam Tanenhaus, "Wayward Intellectual," *The New York Times Magazine*, January 24, 1999, 20–23.

247. First she talked Kennedy Center director of programming . . . : Tharp to Charlie Rose, transcript of broadcast, January 13, 1995.

247. through American University's Naima Prevots and her own personal connections: Naima Prevots interview with author, April 9, 2001, and Jennifer Gelfand interview with author, November 4, 2004.

247. she chose fourteen . . . : *The Washington Post*, September 14, 1994.

247. "It makes the participation . . .": Tharp on Charlie Rose transcript, op. cit.

247. they did get a percentage . . . : George Jackson, *Dance Magazine*, December 1994.

247. "we were paid incredibly well . . .": Caddell/MBS, October 17, 2004.

248. "in the old days . . .": Tharp to Alan Kriegsman, *The Washington Post*, September 14, 1994.

248. "We've become very confused . . .": Tharp to Jean Battey Lewis, *The Washington Times*, September 11, 1994.

248. how touched she was: Tharp on Charlie Rose transcript, op. cit.

248. "what it means to be an American": Tharp to Jack Anderson, *NYT*, September 26, 1994.

248. "This whole thing . . .": Tharp to Jennifer Dunning, *NYT*, January 12, 1995.

248. her own inimitable dancing . . . : Janice Berman, *New York Newsday*, January 18, 1995.

248. "an avenging or challenging angel": Jean Battey Lewis, *The Washington Times*, September 15, 1994.

248. "who had just entered the Underworld . . .": Caddell/MBS, October 17, 2004.

12. Near Heaven 1995–2005

page

251. "The subject matter is subjectivity and objectivity . . .": Tharp to Anna Kisselgoff, *NYT*, April 30, 1995.

251. "his taffeta strings . . .": Arlene Croce, "Choreographers We," *The New Yorker*, May 22, 1995.

252. Tharp had begun choreographing this duo . . . : Janice Berman, *Newsday*, January 16, 1995.

252. When Susan Jaffe entered the work . . . : Jaffe/MBS, January 21, 2004.

252. "the crossover point . . .": Tharp to Anna Kisselgoff, *NYT*, April 30, 1995.

252–253. Tobi Tobias thought the pair of women: Tobi Tobias, *New York Magazine*, March 27, 1995.

253. "impression of a community . . .": Alan Kriegsman, *The Washington Post*, March 7, 1995.

253. "almost totally opaque": Arlene Croce, "Choreographers We," op. cit.

253. "irritatingly mysterious eau de scenario": Deborah Jowitt, *The Village Voice*, May 21, 1996.

253. "perhaps the worst . . .": Nicholas Dromgoole, *London Telegraph*, January 26, 1997.

253. Tharp conceived of the ballet's three acts . . . : Tharp interview with Allen Robertson, 1995, n.d.

253. Tharp was also trying . . . : I have never seen this dance live. The only videotape available to me lacked a soundtrack, so I am unable to discuss the way Tharp used Rossini's music.

254. "a rich, truly generous piece . . .": Allen Robertson, *Dance Now*, spring 1996.

254. "a perplexing disappointment . . .": David Dougill, *Sunday Times*, December 17, 1995.

254. an admiring review . . . : Deborah Jowitt, "In Her Elements," *The Village Voice*, May 21, 1996.

254. "solid, respectable, and, believe it or not . . .": Terry Teachout, *Daily News*, May 6, 1996.

254. "the same kind of pallid expertise": Clive Barnes, *New York Post*, May 6, 1996.

255. "the dream potential": Tharp to Deborah Jowitt, *The Village Voice*, September 30, 1997.

255. She even taught class . . . : Andrew Robinson, joint interview, Robinson and Malone, with author, January 18, 2005.

255. "I've never been the kind of dancer . . .": Robinson and Malone/MBS, January 18, 2005.

258. "a symphonic ballet": program information, I.P.A. press packet.

258. "The dance has a movement base . . .": Tharp to Thea Singer, *The Boston Globe*, March 22, 1998.

258. "ferocious precision": Donald Hutera, *Dance Now*, Winter 1996.

258. "almost entirely obscure": Tobi Tobias, *New York Magazine*, November 18, 1996.

258. "pseudo-Santeria meets Buena Vista . . .": Malone in Robinson and Malone/MBS, January 18, 2005.

259. the dance was sidelined . . . : Robinson and Malone/MBS, Ibid.

259. "This is her great gift . . .": Patsy Tarr/MBS, September 16, 2004.

259. "All her works . . .": Danilo Radojevic to *Weekend Australian*, January 10–11, 1998.

259. "Much was expected": Patricia Laughlin, *Dance Australia*, February/March 1998, 59.

259. They made a duet . . . : John Selya interview with author, January 21, 2005.

259. Later Andrew Robinson partnered her . . . : Robinson and Malone/MBS, January 18, 2005.

260. Asking a contemporary audience . . . : Gabrielle Malone in Robinson and Malone/MBS, Ibid.

260. Distinguished Visiting Professorship: *NYT*, March 2, 1999.

260. Tharp recalled Jamie Bishton . . . : Bishton/MBS, December 13, 2004.

260. Diabelli's ditzy little tune: *Des Moines Register*, September 1999.

261. Clement Crisp praised the piece: *Financial Times*, June 22, 1999.

261. "Today I thought of writing . . .": Tharp script for *The Bix Pieces*.

261. "He gave a private place . . .": Tharp to Theodore Bale, *Boston Herald*, June 22, 2001.

262. Caddell convinced the choreographer . . . : Caddell/MBS, October 17, 2004.

262. "the court isn't far away . . .": Tharp teaching class at Hunter College, November 5, 1998, author's notes.

264. "grinding monotony": Harris Green, *Dance Magazine*, January 2000, 72.

264. Acocella and Kisselgoff: *The New Yorker*, December 7, 1998 and *NYT*, November 4, 1998.

264. she'd switched to his more approachable music: Tharp during Q & A at videotaped lecture-demonstration, New York State Theater, January 24, 2000.

264. She also feared . . . : Twyla Tharp, *The Creative Habit* (New York: Simon & Schuster, 2003), 130.

264. Listening to Alfred Brendel's recordings . . . : Tharp to Astrida Weeks, *Madison*, June 1999, 57.

265. She gave a curiously poignant answer: Tharp during Q & A at videotaped lecture-demonstration, New York State Theater, January 24, 2000.

265. It had taken some time . . . : Tharp/MBS, November 10, 1999.

265. Tharp selected three . . . : Tharp at videotaped lecture-demonstration, New York State Theater, January 24, 2000.

266. "optimism to weld and bind . . .": Ibid.

266. "at her bloated worst": Robert Gottlieb, *New York Observer*, March 12, 2001.

266. "weighted passion": Anna Kisselgoff, *NYT*, January 25, 2000.

266. Acocella was disappointed . . . : Joan Acocella, *The New Yorker*, February 7, 2000.

266. she preferred the designation "neoromantic": Tharp to Cathy Lynn Grossman, *USA Today*, May 9, 2000.

267. "a support system between the foreground . . .": Tharp to Deborah Jowitt, *The Village Voice*, February 20, 2001.

267. Mindy Aloff thought . . . : Mindy Aloff, "Spitballs at Euclid," *The New Republic*, June 18, 2001.

267. "My career has been spent preparing me . . .": Tharp to Cathy Lynn Grossman, *USA Today*, op. cit.

267. "she approaches ballet very seriously . . .": Mindy Aloff, "Spitballs at Euclid," op. cit.

268. "I need to be grounded again . . .": Tharp to Anna Kisselgoff, *NYT*, July 6, 2000.

268. "vibrant, new cultural district . . .": BAM Local Development Corporation press release, January 2001.

268. As Tharp was starting her new company . . . : Tharp and Harvey Lichtenstein conversation in *NYT*, February 2001.

268. He knew she would be an asset . . . : Harvey Lichtenstein interview with author, January 17, 2001.

268. "a coup for efforts . . .": *NYT*, January 17, 2001.

268. some vocal community concerns . . . : Amy Eddings, "No Longer Slumming: A Cultural District for Downtown Brooklyn," transcript of radio piece, WNYC, air date, January 18, 2001.

268. "one more thing to help": *NYT*, January 17, 2001.

269. she laid out a grandiose three-year agenda: Tharp and Harvey Lichtenstein conversation in *NYT*, February 2001.

269. amortize their outlay . . . : Harvey Lichtenstein conversation with author, February 22, 2005.

269. the plan was dead: *NYT*. May 9, 2001.

270. Lichtenstein had been trying to convince her: Lichtenstein/MBS, February 22, 2005.

270. "three times what a principal dancer is making": Tharp to Anne Midgette, *Los Angeles Times*, June 17, 2001.

270. "We need a nice new stadium . . .": Tharp to Laura Bleiberg, *Orange County Register*, June 19, 2001.

270. Reverend Dyson was stunned. *NYT*, May 9, 2001

270. "something big and ambitious": *The Creative Habit*, 83–84.

270. "Twyla said to us . . .": Selya/MBS, January 21, 2005.

271. Selya had never risen above corps de ballet . . . : Selya/MBS, Ibid.

271. she considered the Quintet big music . . . : Tharp in postperformance Q & A, Joyce Theater, February 21, 2001.

272. "Dithery and opaque": Joan Acocella, *The New Yorker*, March 12, 2001.

273. "an all-purpose Chaos . . .": Tharp to Robert Johnson, *Newark Star-Ledger*, February 16, 2001.

273. "a sketchy allegory . . .": Anna Kisselgoff, *NYT*, February 22, 2001.

273. Selya says he and Roberts . . . : Selya/MBS, January 21, 2005.

274. she retrieved some choreography . . . : *The Creative Habit*, 225.

274. Tharp's coming-of-age mantra . . . : TT/MBS, February 11, 2004.

274–275 . Tharp has said the show is a tribute . . . : TT/MBS, Ibid.

275. She wanted the show to acknowledge . . . : *Providence Journal*, February 22, 2004.

275. "a shimmering portrait . . .": Ben Brantley, *NYT*, October 25, 2002.

276. ten Tony nominations: *NYT*, May 13, 2003.

A NOTE ON SOURCES

I started watching and writing about Tharp dance in about 1968. With the exception of a handful of works that were not performed in New York or in touring cities accessible to me, I have seen all of her dances live at least once. Tharp was impatient with maintaining her works after they had reached what she considered their optimum form, but this determined resistance to repertory meant that a very limited sample of her phenomenal output lasted on the stage long enough to gain a wide audience. All dance is inherently vulnerable to disappearance, but history demands more. Any artwork must be able to transcend the impressions it made on first viewing in order to gain the deep appreciation that can only come with familiarity and context.

Fortunately, Tharp was ahead of the dance field in recognizing the importance of videotape and film very early in her career, and some records exist of almost everything she ever choreographed. For purposes of this book I have made every effort to revisit and study the repertory, either live or by means of videotaped records. These records vary greatly in quality, from fixed single-camera studio documentation to archival recordings of stage performances to professional television translations made for both commercial and experimental purposes. I have gleaned whatever information I could from this material, and in my viewing of it I've attempted to compensate for distortions, camera adaptations, and technical glitches. Despite their shortcomings, and in lieu of a live repertory, these videos have been essential to the writing of this book. I am grateful to Twyla Tharp and the presenting companies for having the foresight to see that they were made, and for making them available to me.

In 1991 Tharp donated her archives to The Ohio State University, where they have been scrupulously preserved and protected by curator Nena Couch and the staff of the Jerome Lawrence and Robert E. Lee Theater Research Institute. Although the public and scholars may view press clippings and design materials in this collection, Tharp hasn't permitted total access to it. I have examined it as thoroughly as her restrictions will allow. To compensate for the areas of information that were not open to me—correspondence, business records, and all "choreographic notes" except a few early ones—I have interviewed more than sixty dancers, managers, and associates during the six years of researching and writing this book. In addition, I have had access to published and unpublished materials provided by other professional dance writers. I hope that I have represented these respondents and their subject fairly.

Tharp often tried out new work on the road, announcing "world premieres" of dances in one or more locations before she considered them finished. Premiere dates as given here sometimes differ from those in Tharp's own chronologies. In the text, I have tried to indicate the circumstances of first performances discussed.

Tharp usually did not double-cast when choreographing but, especially in big ballet companies and her own touring ensembles, anything that went into repertory had more than one cast. When I've listed one set of dancers, I refer to the original cast, or to the cast on a videotape available for study.

I have adopted the practice of quoting from my interviews in the present tense, even though most of the interviews were conducted over a five-year period, in order to differentiate them from material published or recorded concurrently with the dance work. I hope that those who spoke to me can still be represented in the same terms.

The photograph of *Jam* is reprinted courtesy of the Jerome Robbins Dance Division, New York Public Library for the Performing Arts at Lincoln Center.

The photographs of *Re-Moves, Disperse, Dancing in the Streets, Deuce Coupe, Sue's Leg, Country Dances,* Carrafa and Uchida in *The Catherine Wheel, Bad Smells,* and *Fait Accompli* are used with permission from the Twyla Tharp Archive, Jerome Lawrence and Robert E. Lee Theatre Research Institute, The Ohio State University.

SELECTED BIBLIOGRAPHY

Acocella, Joan. "Twyla Tharp's Bottom Line." *The New Yorker*. Nov. 30, 1992. 166–74.

Babe, Thomas. "Twyla Tharp Dance." Program book, Twyla Tharp Dance Foundation, 1981.

Baker, Rob. "Dancing Head, Talking Feet." Interview with Twyla Tharp and David Byrne. *Soho Weekly News*. October 13, 1981. 13–15.

Brubach, Holly. "Counter to the World at Large." An interview with Twyla Tharp. *American Arts*. May 1981. 16–19.

Churcher, Sharon. "Still Kicking—The amazing saga of 'Singin' in the Rain,' the $5.7 Million turkey that refuses to lie down." *New York* magazine. Oct. 14, 1985. 39–47.

Colton, Richard et al. "Making Musical Dance." Interview-discussion, Kate Johnson, Robert Irving, Karole Armitage & Colton with John Mueller and Don McDonagh. For the Dance Critics Association and *Ballet Review*. *Ballet Review*, winter 1986. 23–44.

Draegin, Lois. "The World According to Tharp." *Savvy*. Feb. 1987. 30 ff.

Forman, Milos and Jan Novak, *Turnaround—a Memoir*. New York: Villard Books, 1994.

Friedman, Jeffrey Phillip. *Embodied Narrative: A Laban Movement Analysis of Dance Oral History Toward Ontological Awareness*. Ph.D. dissertation, University of California Riverside, 2003.

SELECTED BIBLIOGRAPHY

Guillermoprieto, Alma. "Dancing in the City." *The New Yorker*. Feb. 10, 2003. 70–79.

Johnston, Jill. *Marmalade Me* [1971], with new preface and essays by Deborah Jowitt and Sally Banes. Middletown, CT: Wesleyan University Press, 1998.

Kendall, Elizabeth. "Twyla Tharp—An unorthodox choreographer with a mind of her own." *Horizon*. April 1980. 26–33.

Kisselgoff, Anna. "Twyla Tharp and Ballet—An Uneasy Match." *The New York Times*. March 8, 1987.

———. "Twyla Tharp's Metaphysical Muse." *The New York Times*. April 30, 1995.

Kostelanetz, Richard, ed. *Merce Cunningham: Dancing in Space and Time*. [1992] New York: Da Capo Press, 1998.

Jowitt, Deborah. *Jerome Robbins: His Life, His Theater, His Dance*. New York: Simon & Schuster, 2004.

Mazo, Joseph H. "Twyla Tharp—Advance from the 1960s" in *Prime Movers—The Makers of Modern Dance in America*. New York: William Morrow & Company, 1977. 271–98.

McDonagh, Don. "Twyla Tharp / Controlled Living Space" in *The Rise and Fall and Rise of Modern Dance*. New York: Outerbridge & Dienstfrey, 1970. 105–118.

Secrest, Meryle. *Stephen Sondheim—A Life*. New York: Delta/Random House, 1998.

Shapiro, Laura, "Ain't Misbehavin': Two Decades of Twyla." *On the Edge: Challenges to American Dance*. Proceedings of the 1989 Dance Critics Association Conference. 67–73.

Siegel, Marcia B. *The Shapes of Change—Images of American Dance* (1979). Berkeley: University of California Press, 1985.

Smith, Cecil and Glenn Litton. *Musical Comedy in America*. New York: Routledge/Theatre Arts Books, 1991.

Supree, Burt. "Absolutely Twyla." *Los Angeles Times Calendar*. March 3, 1989.

Taplin, Diana Theodores. *Criticism and Choreography*. M.A. thesis. York University, Toronto. December 1978.

Tharp, Twyla. *Push Comes to Shove—An Autobiography*. New York: Bantam Books, 1992.

———. with Mark Reiter. *The Creative Habit—Learn it and use it for life*. New York: Simon & Schuster, 2003.

Throughout her long career, Tharp has been written about extensively by American and international critics. Her work seems to inspire exceptionally thoughtful writing as well as heartfelt response. In addition to works cited in the Notes, the following is a selective list of articles with informative and insightful commentary on particular dances or periods.

Company and Choreographic Style:

Albert, Steven. "Utopia Lost—and Found? A Look at Tharp's Way." *Ballet Review*. spring 1986. 17–35.

Aloff, Mindy. "Twyla Tharp Dance." (*Nine Sinatra Songs, Ballare, In the Upper Room*). *The Nation*. March 28, 1987.

———. "Spitballs at Euclid" (*The Beethoven Seventh, Brahms-Haydn*). *The New Republic*. June 18, 2001.

Brubach, Holly. "Twyla Tharp's Return." (*Ballare, In the Upper Room*). *The Atlantic*. March 1987.

Croce, Arlene. "Choreographers We." (*How Near Heaven, Americans We, Jump Start*). *The New Yorker*. May 22, 1995.

Gurewitsch, Matthew. "Kinetic Force." *Ballet News*. October 1984. 18–23.

Jacobs, Laura. "Role Model." (*Men's Piece, Octet*). *New Dance Review*. January-March 1992. 3–6.

Shapiro, Laura. "The art of Twyla Tharp." (*Nine Sinatra Songs, Bad Smells, Short Stories*). *Seattle Weekly*. October 27, 1982.

Nine Sinatra Songs:

Croce, Arlene. "Tharp's Sinatra." *Writing in the Dark, Dancing in* The New Yorker. New York: Farrar, Straus and Giroux, 2000. 463–66.

Short Stories:

Goldner, Nancy. "Twyla got her gun." *Soho Weekly News*. October 13, 1981. 47–48.

Fait Accompli:

Leverett, James. "The (Im)Pure Theatre of Twyla Tharp." *American Theatre*. April 1984. 22–23.

Push Comes to Shove (book):

Reiter, Susan. "Twyla's Way." *Dance View*. Winter 1993. 9–14.

Demeter and Persephone:

Croce, Arlene. "Someone's in the Kitchen with Demeter." *The New Yorker*. Oct. 25, 1993. 111–16.

I have not quoted from my own publications about Tharp because I wanted to look at the work with fresh eyes for this book. Several reviews and essays have been reprinted in my collections *At the Vanishing Point* (1972), *Watching the Dance Go By* (1977), and *The Tail of the Dragon* (1991). Additional pieces that may be of interest are listed below.

Features:

"The World According to Tharp" [original title: "The Saint of Cybernetics"]. (*The Catherine Wheel* on PBS). *The Dial.* March 1983.

"Home on the Residency." (Tharp at the Wexner Center, Ohio State University). *Dance Ink.* spring 1992.

Essays:

"Success Without Labels." (*Nine Sinatra Songs, Bad Smells* in San Francisco). *Hudson Review.* spring 1983.

"Couples." (*Nine Sinatra Songs, Fait Accompli*). *Hudson Review.* summer 1994.

"Tharporama." (*Bach Partita, Brahms/Handel, Sorrow Floats*). *Hudson Review.* winter 1984–85.

"Strangers in the Palace." (Tharp and company in ABT). *Hudson Review.* autumn, 1989.

"Both Doors Open." (City Center season). *Hudson Review.* summer 1992.

"Twyla's Tour." (*Cutting Up* in Boston). *Ballet Review.* spring 1993.

"Ancestral Passages." (*Demeter and Persephone*). *Hudson Review.* spring 1994.

Reviews:

"Happily On and On." (*Happily Ever After*). *Soho Weekly News.* Nov. 11, 1976.

"'In the Upper Room': Carefully crafted, constantly interesting." *Christian Science Monitor.* Feb. 10, 1987.

"Twyla Tharp hitting 'Ecstatic Highs.'" (ABT in San Francisco—*In the Upper Room, Quartet, Everlast*). *Christian Science Monitor.* Mar. 17, 1989.

"Too Brief a Fling." (*Brief Fling* at ABT gala). *Christian Science Monitor.* May 30, 1990

"Annals of mischief." (Tharp! in Boston—*Fugue, Heroes, Sweet Fields*). *Boston Phoenix.* Apr. 3, 1998.

"Tharpbeats." (*Known by Heart*). *Boston Phoenix.* Nov. 13, 1998.

"Tharp revels." (*Beethoven Seventh*). *Boston Phoenix.* Jan. 28, 2000.

"How choreography lives." (*Variations on a Theme by Haydn*). *Boston Phoenix*. May 19, 2000.

"Past and future." (*Mozart Clarinet Quintet K. 581, Surfer at the River Styx*). *Boston Phoenix*. Mar. 2, 2001.

"Cracking the code." (*Movin' Out*). *Boston Phoenix*. Nov. 1, 2002.

ACKNOWLEDGMENTS

This book is not an "authorized" work. It is my own attempt to understand the immense talent of Twyla Tharp, which has always seemed bigger than anything that could be encompassed within the regular practice of criticism. To take an overview of an artist I've been watching and commenting on for the length of both our careers, I needed the help of many people, Twyla Tharp above all. The book could not have been written without her cooperation. She generously made herself available to me for interviews, responded to my quizzes and requests, and facilitated my access to primary source materials. She did this even though it was understood that she would not see or approve my manuscript before publication. I am grateful as well to Jesse Huot and Ginger Montel of Tharp Productions for answering my questions and for dubbing and sending a constant stream of videotapes.

Tharp Dance is more than a catalogue of vanished choreographic works. A continually evolving cast of extraordinary dancers and collaborators took up Tharp's challenge and carried the idea of dance into unknown territory. More than sixty individuals agreed to talk to me about their work with Tharp, and then submitted to my follow-up questions and bewildered phone calls. Getting together with old and new acquaintances to recall cherished dance experiences was a source of great pleasure to me during the course of this long, many-sided dialogue. The generosity of these respondents has added a dimension to my research that I hadn't anticipated at the start.

Rose Marie Wright dug into her phenomenal memory eight times for my tape recorder, and submitted to innumerable phone calls. Sara Rudner shared her wise and searching thoughts over the years. Shelley Washington, William Whitener, and Richard Colton supplied invaluable information and insight about the company and the work. I interviewed Twyla Tharp five times during the writing of this book.

The other friends and strangers who offered their thoughts and memories to me were: Ramelle Adams, Mikhail Baryshnikov, Jamie Bishton, Vera Blaine, Merrill Brockway, David Byrne, Stacy Caddell, Joseph Carman, Judy Cohen, Steve Dennin, Theresa Dickinson, Jeffrey Edwards, Anthony Ferro, Charles France, Shelley Freydont, Jeff Friedman, Isabel Garcia-Lorca, Jennifer Gelfand, Katie Glasner, Rhoda Grauer, Robert Huot, Susan Jaffe, Margaret Jenkins, Susan Jones, Paula Josa-Jones, Marty Kapell, Mary Ann Kellogg, Sharon Kinney, William Peter Kosmas, Elaine Kudo, Raymond Kurshals, Harvey Lichtenstein, Lewis Lloyd, Santo Loquasto, Carolyn Lord, Gabrielle Malone and Andrew Robinson, Jodi Melnick, Don Mischer, Rosalind Newman, Roddy O'Connor, Naima Prevots, Tom Rawe and Jennifer Way, Charles Reinhart, Dana Reitz, Kenneth Rinker, Beatriz Rodriguez, John Selya, Linda Shelton, Amy Spencer, Patsy Tarr, Jennifer Tipton, Christine Uchida, Martine Van Hamel, Brenda Way, Kimmary Williams, and Rebecca Wright.

The Reverend Peter Laarman, Betsy Fisher, Diane Jacobowitz, Jane Goldberg, Shelley Masar, Emma Lou Thomas, and Douglas Rosenberg talked to me informally and responded to questions.

I spent many hours examining material in the Jerome Lawrence and Robert E. Lee Theater Research Institute at The Ohio State University, Alan Woods, director, with the unfailing help of Nena Couch, curator of the Twyla Tharp Archive, and the efficient services of Val Pennington, Beth Kattleman, and the staff. In New York, at the Jerome Robbins Dance Division of the New York Public Library at Lincoln Center, Madeleine Nichols, director, I had essential help from Monica Moseley, Pat Rader, Susan Kraft, Phil Karg, and the staff of librarians and pages as I made my way through databases and archival resources.

Other individuals I turned to for information and assistance included: Charles Sens, Rosemary Hanes, and Vickie Wulff Risner at the Library of Congress; Susan Hood, Elizabeth Hoke and Eugene Gaddis at the Wadsworth Atheneum; Jennifer Williams at KUSC Los Angeles; Ben Mayer at WGBH Boston; Florence Palomo at Condé Nast Publications; Matt Hoffman of HMS Video; Christina Sterner of Baryshnikov Productions; Kelly Ryan at American Ballet Theater; Rob Daniels at New York City Ballet; Gail Kalver at Hubbard Street Dance Chicago; Cynthia Rostiac at the Stevens Estate and Conference Center at Osgood Hill; archivists Deborah Elfenbein and Greta Reisel at the American Dance Festival; and Laura Raucher at the Martha Graham Center. Charles Atlas, Steve Sheppard, Mary Waters, and Constance Old led me along the trails to sources of information.

Many dance writers responded to my call for published and unpublished documentation of their encounters with Tharp. I'm deeply grateful to longtime Tharp admirers and collaborators Laura Shapiro and Allen Robertson for their loving support. Sara Rudner and her interviewer, Rose Anne Thom, allowed me complete access to the 1995 interviews made for the Oral History Project of the Jerome Robbins Dance Division at the New York Public Library. Besides works published and collected in various archives, contributions were supplied by Joan Acocella, Sally Banes, Carl Blumenthal, Mary Grace Butler, Roy Close, Amy Eddings, Robert Greskovic, Ellen Jacobs, Elizabeth Kendall, Rachel Lampert, Katy Matheson, Selma Odom, Barbara Palfy, Susan Reiter, Elinor Rogosin, Susanna Sloat, Amanda Smith, Tobi Tobias, and Astrida Woods.

Gathering the photographs for this book afforded me the chance to revisit the dances in another way. I want to thank the photographers who made these evocative images, especially those who opened their files to me so that I could make selections. Robert Barry, Tom Brazil, Tom Caravaglia, James Elliott, Paul B. Goode, Lois Greenfield, Herb Migdoll, Tom Rawe, Tony Russell, Marty Sohl, Martha Swope, Nathaniel Tileston, Jack Vartoogian, Max Waldman, and Monroe Warshaw collectively created an extraordinary visual record. I wish I could have included more of it in these pages.

For help in the acquisition of photographs I'm also grateful to Carol Greunke of the Max Waldman Archive, Sandra Powell of London Weekend Television/Granada Films, Trudi Kammerling at REX Features, and Stephen K. Sachs at the New York Public Library.

All my visits to Ohio State were enriched by classes, performances, and collegial conversations with Dance department faculty members Candace Feck, Karen Eliot, Sheila Marion, Michael Kelly Bruce, Melanie Bales, Vera Blaine, Scott Marsh, and Dean of the College of Arts Karen Bell.

Patsy Tarr's devotion to Twyla Tharp extended to this project, much to my benefit, and I'm tremendously grateful for her encouragement, and for several research grants she provided to me through the 2wice Arts Foundation.

For their help, support, and ever-willing ears, for overnight beds and recuperative dinners, I could not have survived without my friends Deborah Jowitt and Murray Ralph, Gay Morris and Gordon Gamsu, Elizabeth Zimmer, John and Judy Mueller, and my Rockport dance companion, Jeanne Hays Beaman.

I'm grateful to my literary agent, Joe Spieler, for believing in this book before it was a book. I want to thank Katherine Tiernan and the editors and production staff at St. Martin's Press for ensuring that the book would be fastidious and beautiful. As the manuscript made its slow progress, my editor, Michael Flamini, was confident it would finally be accomplished. He has supported and encouraged me throughout the process, never losing his enthusiasm or his conviction that Tharp should be written about, and that I could do it.

INDEX

THE LIBRARY
LEWIS - CLARK STATE COLLEGE